# Contents

**Velázquez, Museo del Prado (p99)**

......................................

(above) **Plaza Mayor (p52)**

......................................

(right) **Monastery and palace of San Lorenzo de El Escorial (p159)**

......................................

**Parque del Oeste & Northern Madrid**
p146

**Salamanca**
p118

**Malasaña & Conde Duque**
p128

**Chueca**
p137

**Plaza Mayor & Royal Madrid**
p50

**Sol, Santa Ana & Huertas**
p83

**El Retiro & the Art Museums**
p97

**La Latina & Lavapiés**
p69

# Welcome to Madrid

*No city on earth is more alive than Madrid, a beguiling place whose sheer energy carries a simple message: this city really knows how to live.*

## Beautiful Architecture

Madrid may lack the cachet of Paris, the history of Rome, or Barcelona's reputation for Modernista masterpieces. And no, there is no equivalent of the Eiffel Tower, Colosseum or La Sagrada Família that you can point to and say 'this is Madrid'. But Madrid has a lot of envy-inducing features of its own. Spain's broad sweep of architectural history provides a glorious backdrop to city life, from medieval mansions and royal palaces to the unimagined angles of Spanish contemporary architecture, from the sober brickwork and slate spires of Madrid baroque to the extravagant confections of the belle époque. Put simply, this is one beautiful city.

## An Artistic City

Few cities boast an artistic pedigree quite as pure as Madrid's: many art lovers return here again and again. For centuries, Spanish royals showered praise and riches upon the finest artists of the day, from homegrown talents such as Goya and Velázquez to Flemish and Italian greats. Masterpieces by these and other Spanish painters such as Picasso, Dalí and Miró now adorn the walls of the city's world-class galleries. Three in particular are giants – the Museo del Prado, Centro de Arte Reina Sofía and Museo Thyssen-Bornemisza – but in Madrid these are merely good places to start.

## Killing the Night

Madrid nights are the stuff of legend, and the perfect complement to the more sedate charms of fine arts and fine dining. The city may have more bars than any other city on earth – a collection of storied cocktail bars and nightclubs that combine a hint of glamour with non-stop *marcha* (action). But that only goes some way to explaining the appeal of after-dark Madrid. Step out into the night-time streets of many *barrios* and you'll find yourself swept along on a tide of people, accompanied by a happy crowd intent on dancing until dawn.

## A Culinary Capital

Rising above the humble claims of its local cuisine, Madrid has evolved into one of the richest culinary capitals of Europe. The city has wholeheartedly embraced all the creativity and innovation of Spain's gastronomic revolution. But this acceptance of the new is wedded to a passion for the enduring traditions of Spanish cooking, for the conviviality of the eating experience and for showcasing the infinite variety of food from every Spanish region. From tapas in sleek temples to all that's new to sit-down meals beneath centuries-old vaulted ceilings, eating in Madrid is a genuine pleasure.

## Why I Love Madrid

By Anthony Ham, Writer

More than a decade after I fell for Madrid and decided to call it home, the life that courses relentlessly through the streets here still excites me. Here is a place where the passions of Europe's most passionate country are the fabric of daily life, a city with music in its soul and an unshakeable spring in its step. But Madrid is also one of the most open cities on earth and it doesn't matter where you're from for the oft-heard phrase to ring true: 'If you're in Madrid, you're from Madrid'.

**For more about our writer, see p256**

Above: The Edificio Metrópolis (p86) marks the southern end of Gran Vía (p130)

# Madrid's
# Top 10

## Museo del Prado *(p99)*

**1** Spain's premier collection of Spanish and European art belongs among the elite of world art museums. Goya and Velázquez are the stars of the show in the beautiful Museo del Prado, which occupies pride of place along the city's grand boulevard, Paseo del Prado. But the Prado's catalogue has such astonishing depth and breadth, from the other Spanish masters to the outstanding Flemish collection, from Rubens and Rembrandt to Botticelli and Bosch, that you'll require more than one visit to take it all in.

◉ *El Retiro & the Art Museums*

## Plaza Mayor *(p52)*

**2** Madrid is distinguished by some extraordinary plazas, but Plaza Mayor is easily the king. The plaza's constituent elements are easy to list and combine beauty and buzz, scale and detail: uneven cobblestones, perfectly proportioned porticoes, slate spires and facades in deep ochre offset by marvellous frescoes of mythic figures and wrought-iron balconies. This stately square is the heartbeat of a city, the scene of so many grand events in Madrid's historical story and where the modern city most agreeably throngs with life.

STATUE OF KING FELIPE III

◉ *Plaza Mayor & Royal Madrid*

**3**

**4**

### Tapas in La Latina (p75)

**3** One of the most important gastronomic streets in Spain, La Latina's Calle de la Cava Baja is lined with tapas bars. Some have elevated these tiny morsels into art forms, others serve up specialities in traditional clay pots. Such is Madrid's love affair with tapas and the culture of enjoying them that even this long and graceful thoroughfare cannot contain the neighbourhood's tapas offerings. Nearby you'll find Madrid's best *tortilla de patatas* (potato and onion omelette; pictured top left), a dish beloved by the king.

✘ *La Latina & Lavapiés*

### Parque del Buen Retiro (p110)

**4** The alter ego to Madrid's tableau of sound and movement, Parque del Buen Retiro is one of our favourite corners of the city. Beautiful by any standards, with eye-catching architectural monuments and abundant statues among the trees, El Retiro is where *madrileños* (people from Madrid) come to stroll or laze on the lawns in great numbers on weekends. As such it's one of the most accessible slices of local culture, at once filled with life and an escape from Madrid's frenetic pace.

◉ *El Retiro & the Art Museums*

### Centro de Arte Reina Sofía (p108)

**5** In a city where world-class art galleries are everywhere, it takes something special for one painting to tower above the rest. But such is the strange and disturbing splendour of Picasso's *Guernica* that its claim to being Madrid's most extraordinary artwork is unrivalled. After decades of wandering the globe, it looks very much at home in the Centro de Arte Reina Sofía, alongside works by Salvador Dalí and Joan Miró. Put it all together and you've some of the finest art of the 20th century.

◉ *El Retiro & the Art Museums*

## Museo Thyssen-Bornemisza
*(p104)*

**6** Of all Madrid's major art galleries, it is the Museo Thyssen-Bornemisza that most often appeals to the uninitiated. Here, beneath one roof, are works from seemingly every European painter of distinction, from 13th-century religious art to zany 21st-century creations. There may just be one painting, or a handful of paintings from each artist, but the museum's broad-brush-strokes approach makes a visit here akin to a journey through all that has been refined and masterful during centuries of European art. CARRAVAGIO'S *SAINT CATHERINE OF ALEXANDRIA*

⊙ *El Retiro & the Art Museums*

## Palacio Real *(p53)*

**7** Built on the site where Madrid was born in the 9th century, Madrid's Palacio Real is one of the city's most significant (and most beautiful) buildings. Watching over a pretty square and shadowed by gorgeous ornamental gardens, the palace is a stately affair, combining grandeur, all the symbolism of an imperial past and unusual accessibility in the city's heart. The interior is as lavish and extravagant as you'd expect, a reminder of the glory days when Spanish royalty ruled the world.

⊙ *Plaza Mayor & Royal Madrid*

**6**

**8**

### Plaza de Santa Ana & Night-time Huertas *(p87)*

**8** Nights around the Plaza de Santa Ana (pictured left) and neighbouring *barrio* of Huertas are long, loud and filled with variety. The plaza is both epicentre and starting point of so many epic Madrid nights, with outdoor tables a fabulous vantage point from which to take the pulse of the night and plan your journey through it. Within a short radius of the square, live music venues, old-style sherry bars and sleek rooftop lounge bars for sybarites will get your night going, with legendary Madrid nightclubs nearby.

🍷 *Sol, Santa Ana & Huertas*

## Malasaña & Chueca Nightlife

*(p133; p142)*

**9** The legend of Madrid's hedonistic nights was born in the narrow, inner-city streets of Malasaña and Chueca. In gritty and grungy Malasaña, hard-living rock venues share punters with elegant 19th-century literary cafes. Next door in Chueca, a cool and predominantly gay clientele fills cocktail bars and nightclubs (pictured right) to capacity most nights. More than anywhere in the city, this is where locals come for a night out, and the diversity of what's on offer here is representative of a city whose contradictory impulses are legion.

🍷*Malasaña & Conde Duque; Chueca*

## Ermita de San Antonio de la Florida *(p148)*

**10** One of Madrid's best-kept secrets, the Ermita de San Antonio de la Florida is nonetheless one of the city's most significant artistic landmarks. Here in a small and otherwise nondescript hermitage in 1798, Goya, one of the city's most favoured adopted sons, painted a series of frescoes under royal orders; these extraordinary paintings remain exactly where he first painted them. Breathtaking in their vivid portrayal of Madrid life and the Miracle of St Anthony, they're definitely worth the trip across town to get here.

👁*Parque del Oeste & Northern Madrid*

# What's New

### Gran Vía Closure

Lined with some of Madrid's grandest facades, this imposing boulevard through the heart of the city was closed to all but public transport in 2018, making it that much easier to enjoy. (p130)

### Paseo del Prado on Sunday

The city authorities are determined to make central Madrid more pedestrian-friendly. On Sunday from 9am to 2pm (or 4pm), the eastern side of the Paseo del Prado closes and families and cyclists take over.

### New Tarjeta Multi

The new, rechargeable Tarjeta Multi makes Madrid's public transport system easier to use than ever.

### Craft Beer

You can still walk into any Madrid bar and order *una cerveza* (a beer) and the bartender will serve you a Mahou. But craft beers are making inroads, at places like Fábrica Maravillas (p134), La Tape (p133) or Irreale (p133).

### New Flamenco Venues

For years Madrid's flamenco scene, while high quality, had been a little expensive and one-dimensional. The arrival of Teatro Flamenco Madrid (p135) and Café Ziryab (p80) have started the change.

### Calle Pez

Calle Pez has been Malasaña's coolest street for a while now, but it just keeps getting better, with fabulous bars, a boutique hotel, a theatre, a flamenco venue and great places to eat.

### Vermouth in Chamberí

Chamberí is one of Madrid's most *castizo* (traditional) *barrios* (districts) and there are few more Madrid pastimes quite as traditional as going for a vermouth. La Vaquería Montañesa (p155) and La Violeta (p155) bring class to the experience.

### Museo Municipal de Arte Contemporáneo

The reopening of this contemporary art museum has added yet another art gallery to Madrid's portfolio. It has some of Spain's big names from the 20th century. (p130)

### Atlético de Madrid's New Home

It was quite traumatic for many fans of Atléti to leave their beloved Estadio de Vicente Calderón, but they have warmed quickly to their state-of-the-art new home, the Wanda Metropolitano (www.atleticodemadrid.com).

### Asian Food

Asian cuisine used to be restricted to cheap Chinese and pricey Japanese restaurants, but it's getting easier to find sushi and outstanding, affordable options are many, including Tuk Tuk Asian Street Food (p141) and Vietnam (p89).

### Cycle Friendly

Cyclists still take their lives in their hands on major Madrid thoroughfares, but bicycle lanes are appearing across the city. The city's not quite there yet as a cycle-friendly place, but it's finally on its way.

For more recommendations and reviews, see **lonelyplanet.com/madrid**

# Need to Know

**For more information, see Survival Guide (p203)**

## Currency
Euro (€)

## Language
Spanish (Castellano)

## Visas
Generally not required for stays of up to 90 days (not at all for members of EU or Schengen countries). Some nationalities need a Schengen visa.

## Money
ATMs are widely available. Credit cards are accepted in most hotels, restaurants and shops.

## Mobile Phones
Local SIM cards are widely available and can be used in European and Australian mobile phones. Other phones may need to be set to roaming.

## Time
Western European (GMT/UTC plus one hour during winter, plus two hours during daylight-saving period)

## Tourist Information
**Centro de Turismo de Madrid** (www.esmadrid.com; Plaza Mayor 27; ⊙9.30am-8.30pm; Ⓜ Sol) Main tourist office; other branches and information points are located around the city.

## Daily Costs

### Budget: less than €100
➡ Dorm bed: €15–25;

➡ *Hostal* (budget hotel) double: €50–70

➡ Three-course *menú del día* (daily set menu) lunches: €10–15

➡ Sightseeing during free admission times

### Midrange: €100–200
➡ Double room in midrange hotel: €71–150

➡ Lunch and/or dinner in decent restaurants: €20–50 per person per meal

➡ Museum entry: €10–15

### Top end: more than €200
➡ Double room in top-end hotel: from €150

➡ Fine dining for lunch and dinner: from €50 per person per meal

➡ Cocktails: €8–15

## Advance Planning
**Three months before** Book dinner at DiverXo (p154), Santceloni (p155), La Terraza del Casino (p91) or Zalacaín (p154).

**One month before** Book your accommodation, especially at the top end of the market.

**One week before** Book online entry to the Museo del Prado (p99) and tickets to a Real Madrid game (p155).

## Useful Websites
**EsMadrid.com** (www.esmadrid.com) The tourist office website.

**LeCool** (http://madrid.lecool.com) Alternative, offbeat and avant-garde.

**Lonely Planet** (www.lonelyplanet.com/spain/madrid) An overview of Madrid with hundreds of useful links.

**Turismo Madrid** (www.turismomadrid.es) Regional Comunidad de Madrid tourist office site.

**Madrid Diferente** (www.madriddiferente.com) Offbeat guide to the city's attractions.

## WHEN TO GO

Spring and autumn are the best times to visit. Summer can be fiercely hot, although it's a dry heat, while winter can be bitterly cold and snow is possible though rare.

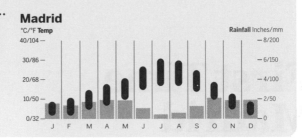

### Arriving in Madrid

**Aeropuerto de Barajas (Adolfo Suárez Madrid-Barajas Airport)** Metro (6.05am to 1.30am), bus (€5) and minibus (both 24 hours) to central Madrid; taxis €30.

**Estación de Atocha (Atocha Train Station)** Metro and bus to central Madrid (6.05am to 1.30am); taxi from €8.

**Estación de Chamartín (Chamartín Train Station)** Metro and bus to central Madrid (6.05am to 1.30am); taxi around €13.

**Estación Sur de Autobuses (Bus Station)** Metro and bus to central Madrid (6.05am to 1.30am); taxi from around €13.

For much more on **arrival** see p204

### Getting Around

Ten-trip Metrobús tickets cost €12.20, charged to your Tarjeta Multi, are valid for journeys on Madrid's metro and bus network. Tickets can be bought from most newspaper kiosks and *estancos* (tobacconists), as well as in staffed booths and ticket machines in metro stations.

➡ **Metro** The quickest and easiest way to get around. Runs 6.05am to 1.30am.

➡ **Bus** Extensive network but careful planning is needed to make the most of over 200 routes. Runs 6.30am to 11.30pm.

➡ **Taxi** Cheap fares by European standards; plentiful.

➡ **Walking** Compact city centre makes walking a good option, but it's hillier than it first appears.

For much more on **getting around** see p206

### Sleeping

Madrid has high-quality accommodation at prices that haven't been seen in the centre of other European capitals in decades. Five-star temples to good taste and a handful of buzzing hostels bookend a fabulous collection of midrange hotels; most of the midrangers are creative originals, blending high levels of comfort with an often-quirky sense of style.

#### Useful Websites

**Centro de Turismo de Madrid** (www.esmadrid.com) Good for an overview of the accommodation scene.

**Spain Select** (www. spain-select.com) Dozens of apartments across Madrid for short or long stays.

**Atrapalo** (www.atrapalo.com) Spanish-language booking service for flights and hotels.

**Lonely Planet** (www.lonely planet.com/spain/madrid/hotels) Reviews and online booking.

For much more on **sleeping** see p169

# First Time Madrid

**For more information, see Survival Guide (p203)**

## Checklist

➡ Make sure your passport is valid for at least six months past your arrival date

➡ Inform your debit-/credit-card company of your intention to travel

➡ Arrange appropriate travel insurance

➡ Plan your route into the city on the metro

➡ Ask your mobile-phone provider about roaming charges (if any)

➡ Check the calendar to work out which festivals to visit or avoid

## What to Pack

➡ Good walking shoes – Madrid is best appreciated on foot

➡ A small day pack

➡ Two-pin continental Europe electrical adaptors

➡ Sunscreen in summer, warm clothes in winter

➡ Ear plugs to keep out Madrid's night-time noise

➡ Spanish phrasebook – not everyone speaks English

## Top Tips for Your Trip

➡ Plan to spend at least part of every day sipping wine in one of Madrid's plazas and watching the world go by.

➡ Madrid is a compact city when compared with other European capitals. Although most of it can be easily explored on foot, if time is tight don't hesitate to make use of the metro as cross-city trips are rarely more than four or five stops.

➡ To avoid going hungry, adjust your body clock on arrival. In no time, you'll be eating lunch at 2.30pm and dinner at 9pm.

➡ A few words of Spanish can go a long way. English is widely (but not universally) spoken.

➡ Spain is a food-obsessed country and you'll miss half the fun if you don't linger over your meals. Always ask for the local speciality.

## What to Wear

Like most Western European cities, Madrid is a fashion-conscious place. Smart casual is considered the bare minimum any time you step outside. For men, that means jeans and T-shirt at least, for women a little more. As a guide, you'd probably dress up more here than you would in London, but it's not quite Paris or Rome. If you're going out for a meal or to a nightclub, the same rules apply – smart casual is the norm – although it depends on the place. In Malasaña you're more likely to see people dressing down.

## Be Forewarned

Madrid is generally safe, but as in any large European city, keep an eye on your belongings and exercise common sense.

➡ El Rastro, around the Museo del Prado and the metro are favourite pickpocketing haunts, as are any areas where tourists congregate in large numbers.

➡ Avoid park areas (such as the Parque del Buen Retiro) after dark.

➡ Keep a close eye on your taxi's meter and try to keep track of the route to make sure you're not being taken for a ride.

## Money

ATMs are widely available. Credit cards are accepted in most hotels, restaurants and shops.

**For more information, see p210.**

## Taxes & Refunds

➡ In Spain, value-added tax (VAT) is known as IVA (ee-ba; *impuesto sobre el valor añadido*).

➡ Hotel rooms and restaurant meals attract an additional 10% (usually included in the quoted price but always ask); most other items have 21% added.

➡ Visitors are entitled to a refund of the 21% IVA on purchases costing more than €90.16 from any shop, if they are taking them out of the EU within three months. Ask the shop for a cash-back (or similar) refund form showing the price and IVA paid for each item, and identifying the vendor and purchaser.

➡ Present your IVA refund form to the customs booth for refunds at the airport, port or border when you leave the EU.

## Tipping

Tipping is not common in Madrid.

**Taxis** Locals usually round up fares to the nearest euro.

**Restaurants** Locals leave a few coins; in better restaurants, 5% is considered ample.

## Language

English is generally widely spoken (although sometimes not very well), but Spaniards seem happy to give it a try. Many restaurants have English-language menus. It always helps to learn a few basic phrases (see also the Language chapter, p214).

 **What time does it open/close?**
¿A qué hora abren/cierran? a ke o·ra ab·ren/thye·ran

The Spanish tend to observe the siesta (midday break), so opening times may surprise you.

 **Are these complimentary?**
¿Son gratis? son gra·tees

Tapas (bar snacks) are available pretty much around the clock at Spanish bars. You'll find they're free in some places.

 **When is admission free?**
¿Cuándo es la entrada gratuita?
kwan·do es la en·tra·da gra·twee·ta

Many museums and galleries in Spain have admission-free times, so check before buying tickets.

 **Where can we go (salsa) dancing?**
¿Dónde podemos ir a bailar (salsa)?
don·de po·de·mos eer a bai·lar (sal·sa)

Flamenco may be the authentic viewing experience in Spain, but to actively enjoy the music you'll want to do some dancing.

 **How do you say this in (Catalan/Galician/Basque)?**
¿Cómo se dice ésto en (catalán/gallego/euskera)?
ko·mo se dee·the es·to en (ka·ta·lan/ga·lye·go/e·oos·ke·ra)

Spain has four official languages, and people in these regions will appreciate it if you try to use their local language.

## Etiquette

**Greetings** Greetings should precede even the most casual encounter – *hola, buenos días* is the perfect way to start.

**Bars** Don't be surprised to see people throwing their serviettes and olive stones on the floor – don't be the first to do it, but you might as well join in because a waiter will come around from time to time to sweep them all up.

**Metro** Stand on the right on escalators in metro stations.

**Churches** Unless you're there for religious reasons, avoid visiting churches (or taking photos) during Mass.

**Bargaining** Haggling is OK at El Rastro, but not the done thing elsewhere.

# Top Itineraries

## Day One

### Plaza Mayor & Royal Madrid (p50)

 So many Madrid days begin in the **Plaza Mayor** or nearby with a breakfast of *chocolate con churros* (chocolate with deep-fried doughnuts) at **Chocolatería de San Ginés**. Drop by the **Plaza de la Villa** and **Plaza de Oriente**, then stop for a coffee or wine at **Cafe de Oriente** and visit the **Palacio Real**.

>  **Lunch** Mercado de San Miguel (p58) is one of Madrid's most innovative gastronomic spaces.

### El Retiro & the Art Museums (p97)

Spend as much of the afternoon as you can at the **Museo del Prado**. When this priceless collection of Spanish and European masterpieces gets too much, visit the **Iglesia de San Jerónimo El Real** and **Caixa Forum**.

> **Dinner** Restaurante Sobrino de Botín (p62) is the world's oldest restaurant.

### Plaza Mayor & Royal Madrid (p50)

To kick off the night, take in a flamenco show at **Teatro Flamenco Madrid**, followed by a leisurely drink at **Café del Real** or **Anticafé**. If you're up for a long night, **Teatro Joy Eslava** is an icon of the Madrid night.

## Day Two

### El Retiro & the Art Museums (p97)

 Get to the **Centro de Arte Reina Sofía** early to beat the crowds, then climb up through sedate streets to spend a couple of hours soaking up the calm of the **Parque del Buen Retiro**. Wander down to admire the **Plaza de la Cibeles**.

> **Lunch** Estado Puro (p114) is one of Madrid's most creative tapas bars.

### Parque del Oeste & Northern Madrid (p146)

Catch the metro across town to admire the Goya frescoes in the **Ermita de San Antonio de la Florida**. Afterwards **Templo de Debod** and **Parque del Oeste** are fine places for a stroll.

>  **Dinner** Casa Alberto (p89) is one of Madrid's most storied *tabernas* (taverns).

### Sol, Santa Ana & Huertas (p83)

Begin the night at **Plaza de Santa Ana** for a drink or three at an outdoor table if the weather's fine. After another tipple at **La Venencia**, check out if there's live jazz on offer at wonderful **Café Central**. Have an after-show drink at **El Imperfecto**. The night is still young – **Costello Café & Niteclub** is good if you're in the mood to dance, **La Terraza del Urban** if you're in need of more sybaritic pleasures.

MAYLAT/SHUTTERSTOCK ©

Plaza Mayor (p52)

# Day Three

## El Retiro & the Art Museums (p97)

 Begin the morning at the third of Madrid's world-class art galleries, the **Museo Thyssen-Bornemisza**. It's such a rich collection that you could easily spend the whole morning here. If you've time to spare, consider dipping back into the Prado or Reina Sofía.

 **Lunch** Platea (p124) is one of Madrid's most exciting culinary experiences.

## Salamanca (p118)

Head out east to take a tour of the **Plaza de Toros** bullring, before dipping into the **Museo Lázaro Galdiano**. Spend the rest of the afternoon shopping along Calle de Serrano, Calle de José Ortega y Gasset and surrounding streets.

**Dinner** Txirimiri (p75) has a lovely selection of tapas in La Latina.

## La Latina & Lavapiés (p69)

As dusk approaches, make for La Latina and spend as long as you can picking your way among the tapas bars of **Calle de la Cava Baja** – even if you're not hungry, stop by for a beer or wine to soak up the atmosphere. A wine at **Taberna El Tempranillo** and a mojito out on Plaza de la Paja at **Delic** should set you up for the night ahead.

# Day Four

## Sol, Santa Ana & Huertas (p83)

 Start the day with some souvenir shopping at **Casa de Diego**. If you really love your art, **Real Academia de Bellas Artes de San Fernando** will nicely round out your experience of Madrid's exceptional art scene.

 **Lunch** Choose between Albur (p131) and La Musa (p132) along Calle de Manuela Malasaña.

## Malasaña & Conde Duque (p128)

You've been around almost long enough to be a local and it's therefore worth exploring the laneways of Malasaña between Calle Pez, Plaza del Dos de Mayo and the Glorieta de Bilbao. Stop off at **Lolina Vintage Café** along Calle del Espíritu Santo, **Café Manuela** on Calle de San Vincente Ferrer, as well as the **Museo de Historia**.

**Dinner** La Tasquita de Enfrente (p132) is loved by celebrities and foodies.

## Chueca (p137)

Get to know multifaceted Chueca from the dignified calm and boutiques of **Calle de Almirante**, pass by **Plaza de Chueca** to watch the *barrio* (district) come to life, then get seriously into the cocktail bars along Calle de la Reina, followed by the legendary **Museo Chicote**. **El Junco Jazz Club** will leave you with great memories of the city.

# If You Like...

## Art Galleries

**Museo del Prado** One of the world's best, with Goya, Velázquez and more. (p99)

**Centro de Arte Reina Sofía** Picasso, Dalí, Miró and other 20th-century masters. (p108)

**Museo Thyssen-Bornemisza** Astonishing private collection with centuries of European masters. (p104)

**Real Academia de Bellas Artes de San Fernando** Underrated bastion of Spain's fine artistic tradition. (p85)

**Ermita de San Antonio de la Florida** Goya's frescoes in their original setting. (p148)

**Museo Sorolla** Spanish master painter's works in a lovely Chamberí mansion. (p149)

## Bastions of Culinary Tradition

**Restaurante Sobrino de Botín** The world's oldest restaurant and brimful of local specialities. (p62)

**Lhardy** Much-celebrated Madrid table with impeccable quality and service. (p91)

ITZAVU/SHUTTERSTOCK ©

Statue of Bartolomé Esteban Murillo next to the Museo del Prado (p99)

**Posada de la Villa** Ancient Madrid inn with reliable cooking and repeat clientele. (p79)

**Taberna La Bola** Traditional bar-restaurant focused on Madrid specialities. (p60)

**Casa Lucio** Celebrity clientele and assured cooking of Spanish staples. (p79)

**Casa Alberto** Historic Huertas *taberna* where the tapas are all about tradition. (p89)

**Zalacaín** Grand old *señor* of Madrid restaurants, with an extraordinary wine list. (p154)

**Casa Revuelta** Essence of the Madrid tapas experience. (p58)

## City Squares

**Plaza Mayor** A perfectly proportioned centrepiece of Madrid life. (p52)

**Plaza de Oriente** The heart of Royal Madrid, with a royal palace, an opera house, statues and gardens. (p55)

**Plaza de la Villa** Surrounded by impressive examples of Madrid's architectural centuries. (p55)

**Plaza de Santa Ana** Pretty architecture and a city intent on having a good time. (p87)

**Plaza de la Paja** On the site of the city's medieval market, it now resembles a ramshackle village square. (p72)

## Innovative Cooking

**DiverXo** Culinary experimentation with surprising twists in service. (p154)

**Estado Puro** Tapas from the lab of some of Spain's most innovative chefs. (p114)

**Viridiana** Breaking the rules long before it became fashionable to do so. (p114)

**La Terraza del Casino** Glorious setting and state-of-the-art nouvelle cuisine. (p91)

**Astrolabius** Old recipes with a modern twist in an informal setting. (p123)

## Green Spaces

**Parque del Buen Retiro** Madrid's finest city park and scene of so much that's good about Madrid life. (p110)

**Parque del Oeste** Sloping stand of greenery northwest of the city centre with fine views and scarcely a tourist in sight. (p151)

**Real Jardín Botánico** An intimate oasis of exotic plants right alongside one of Madrid's busiest boulevards. (p113)

**Casa de Campo** Vast expanse of parkland west of downtown Madrid with the city's zoo, an amusement park, and a cable car to get there. (p150)

**For more top Madrid spots, see the following:**
➜ Eating (p31)
➜ Drinking & Nightlife (p36)
➜ Entertainment (p39)
➜ Shopping (p44)

**PLAN YOUR TRIP** IF YOU LIKE...

**Madrid Río** Kilometres of developed parkland alongside Madrid's long-forgotten river. (p76)

**Campo del Moro** Gorgeous monumental gardens in the Palacio Real shadow. (p55)

## Nightlife

**Teatro Joy Eslava** Consistently good times every night of the week, every day of the year. (p62)

**Teatro Kapital** Multistorey club with a cross-section of Madrid's dancing public. (p115)

**Why Not?** Where Chueca gets up close and personal in a quirky, intimate space. (p143)

**Ya'sta** Get all hot and sweaty at Madrid's best throwback to the heady, rock-fuelled 1980s. (p135)

**Museo Chicote** One of Europe's most storied cocktail bars, with smooth music and even smoother mojitos. (p142)

**1862 Dry Bar** Cocktails at their most creative to kick-start a love affair with Malasaña. (p133)

# Month By Month

## TOP EVENTS

**Fiestas de San Isidro Labrador,** May

**Suma Flamenca,** June

**Festimad,** May

**Día del Orgullo de Gays, Lesbianas Y Transexuales,** June

**Jazz Madrid,** November

## January

Not much happens in Madrid until after 6 January, although the Christmas to New Year period can be high season for some hotels. Temperatures can be bitterly cold, but wonderfully clear, crisp days are also common.

### 🎊 Año Nuevo

Many *madrileños* gather in Puerta del Sol on Noche Vieja (New Year's Eve) to wait for the 12 *campanadas* (bell chimes), whereupon they try to stuff 12 grapes (one for each chime) into their mouths to mark Año Nuevo (New Year).

### 🎊 Reyes

On Día de los Reyes Magos (Three Kings' Day), three wise men lead the sweet-distributing frenzy of Cabalgata de Reyes. Horse-drawn carriages and floats make their way from the Parque del Buen Retiro to Plaza Mayor at 6pm on 5 January.

## February

Usually the coldest month in Madrid, February always has a chill in the air. In warmer years, late February can be surprisingly mild, heralding the early onset of spring.

### 🎊 Carnaval

Carnaval spells several days of fancy-dress parades and merrymaking in many *barrios* (districts) across the Comunidad de Madrid, usually ending on the Tuesday, 47 days before Easter Sunday. Competitions for the best costume take place in the Círculo de Bellas Artes.

### 🍴 Gastro Festival Madrid

All the Spanish chefs who have made it big come to Madrid for this gastronomy summit (www.gastrofestival madrid.com), with work-shops and events where masters of the Spanish kitchen show off their latest creations. Over 400 bars and restaurants participate with special menus, tapas routes and competitions.

## March

Freezing temperatures possible, but early spring sunshine prompts restaurants to set up their outdoor tables. *Madrileños* often evacuate the city for Semana Santa (Holy Week), but it can still be high season for some hotels.

### ☆ La Noche de los Teatros

On the Night of the Theatres (www.lanoche delosteatros.com), Madrid's streets become the stage for all manner of performances, with a focus on comedy and children's plays. It usually takes place on the last Saturday of March, and lasts from 5pm to midnight.

### 🎊 Jueves Santo

On Jueves Santo (Holy Thursday), local *cofradías* (lay fraternities) organise colourful yet solemn religious processions. The main procession concludes by crossing Plaza Mayor to the Basílica de Nuestra Señora del Buen Consejo. Iglesia de San Pedro El Viejo is another important focal point.

### ★★ Viernes Santo

Viernes Santo (Good Friday) and Easter in general are celebrated with greater enthusiasm in some of the surrounding towns. Chinchón, Ávila and Toledo in particular are known for their lavish Easter processions.

# April

**Mid-spring can be a delightful time to visit Madrid, when weather extremes are rare. Most *madrileños* emerge from hibernation to take over the streets and squares.**

# May

**May is arguably Madrid's biggest month for festivals, and with the weather warming up, it's one of our favourite times to be in the city.**

### ☆ Festimad

Festimad (www.festimad. es) is the biggest of Spain's year-round circuit of major music festivals. Bands from all over the country and beyond converge on Móstoles or Leganés (on the MetroSur train network), for two days of indie-music indulgence; The Jesus and Mary Chain headlined in 2017.

### ☆ Festival Flamenco

Five days of fine flamenco music in one of the city's theatres (www.deflamenco. com). Big names in recent years have included Enrique Morente, Carmen Linares and Diego El Cigala. Dates are movable.

### ★★ Fiesta de la Comunidad de Madrid

On 2 May 1808 Napoleon's troops put down an uprising in Madrid, and commemoration of the day has become an opportunity for much festivity. The day is celebrated with particular energy in the bars of Malasaña, especially around the Plaza Dos de Mayo.

### ★★ Fiestas De San Isidro Labrador

The Fiestas de San Isidro Labrador (www.esmadrid. com), the city's big holiday on 15 May, marks the feast day of its patron saint, San Isidro. Crowds gather in central Madrid to watch the colourful procession, which kicks off a week of cultural events across the city.

# June

**A select group of festivals usher in the Spanish summer. The city has a real spring in its step with warm weather and summer holidays just around the corner.**

### ★★ Día Del Orgullo De Gays, Lesbianas Y Transexuales

The city's Gay and Lesbian Pride Festival and Parade (p209) takes place on the last Saturday of the month. The extravagant

floats begin on Plaza de la Independencia, passing along Gran Vía to Plaza de España. At all other times, Chueca is the place to be.

### ☆ Suma Flamenca

A soul-filled flamenco festival (www.madrid.org/ sumaflamenca) that draws some of the biggest names in the genre to Teatros del Canal and some of the better-known *tablaos* (flamenco venues), such as Casa Patas, Villa Rosa and Corral de la Morería.

# July

**Madrid can really cook in July and the city's pace slows in response. Those not at the beach are preparing to head there in August. Hotel prices often drop when things are quiet.**

### ☆ Veranos de la Villa

Half of Madrid evacuates to the beach in July, but those who remain are rewarded with concerts, opera, dance, theatre and exhibitions as part of Summers in the City (www. veranosdelavilla.com). Many take place at outdoor venues. The program starts in July and runs to the end of August.

# August

**Temperatures soar and the city can be eerily quiet as locals flock to the coast or mountains. Many restaurants and other businesses close and some museums open reduced hours.**

## 🎆 Neighbourhood Summer Festivals

Small-time but fun, the neighbourhood summer festivals (held during the period from mid-August to September), such as San Cayetano in Lavapiés, and San Lorenzo and La Paloma in La Latina, are great for cheap entertainment.

# September

**The worst of the summer heat should have passed and most locals are back from their summer holidays, but the weather's still warm enough to enjoy being outdoors. A couple of artistic highlights to watch for...**

## ☆ DCode

Held in September at Madrid's Complutense University, this terrific music festival (www.dcode fest.com) gets better with each passing year. Franz Ferdinand, Liam Gallagher, Amaral and Kings of Convenience are recent headline acts on a program that includes local and international groups.

## ◉ Madrid Gallery Weekend

In mid- to late September, more than 50 private art galleries inaugurate their exhibitions at the same time, with day and night events to accompany this explosion of artistic creativity, known as Arte Madrid – Apertura (p139).

# October

**Autumn in Madrid can be lovely, with clear days and autumnal colours in the parks. The first winter chill can also make an appearance so bring warm clothes just in case.**

## ☆ Fiesta de Otoño a Primavera

The Autumn Festival in Spring (www.madrid.org/ fo) involves a busy calendar of musical and theatrical activity. The name derives from the fact that it was once a spring festival, but has dropped down the calendar.

# November

**November is when Madrid's winter chill usually starts to bite. The city's jazz festival and a dance festival headline an otherwise quiet month.**

## ☆ Jazz Madrid

Madrid's annual jazz festival (p40) draws a prestigious cast of performers from across the globe and is an increasingly important stop on the European jazz circuit. Venues vary, from the city's intimate jazz clubs to grander theatrical stages across town.

## ☆ Madrid en Danza

The best-known names of Spanish dance, including flamenco performers, are joined by international acts in Madrid for almost three weeks of concerts (www. madrid.org/madriden danza) at stages around the city.

# December

**The run-up to Christmas sees the city full of festive spirit – crowds throng the city centre in astonishing numbers, many of them en route to Plaza Mayor's Christmas market. There are high-season prices in many hotels.**

## 🎆 Navidad

The main family meal for Navidad (Christmas) is served on Nochebuena (Christmas Eve). Elaborate nativity scenes are set up in churches around the city and an exhibition is held in Plaza Mayor (otherwise taken over by a somewhat tacky, but wildly popular, Christmas market).

# Travel with Children

*Madrid has plenty of child-friendly (and even a handful of excellent child-specific) sights and activities. The city centre is relatively compact and easy to get around on foot, which is just as well because the metro can be a bit of an obstacle course for those with prams.*

Peacock wandering the paths in Parque del Buen Retiro (p110)

## Child-Friendly Attractions

### Art Galleries

Most major art galleries have children's activities (usually in Spanish), and most of the museum bookshops also sell guides to the museums designed specifically for kids.

### Museo de Cera

This wax museum (p139) has enough footballers, actresses and international celebrities to get the kids excited. It's a reliable rainy-day option.

### Museo de Ferrocarril

Madrid's Railway Museum, the **Museo del Ferrocarril** (☑ 902 228 822; www.museodel ferrocarril.org; Paseo de las Delicias 61; adult/ child Mon-Fri €6/4, admission Sat & Sun €3; ☺10am-3pm Jun-Sep, 9.30am-3pm Tue-Fri, 10am-7pm Sat & Sun Oct-May; Ⓜ Delicias), has around 30 pieces of rolling stock lined up along the platforms, as well as dioramas of train stations, model trains, and tracks in the shop on the way out.

### Casa Museo de Ratón Perez

The Spanish version of the tooth fairy is a cute little mouse called 'El Ratón Perez', and this small museum (p86) close to Sol takes you into a recreation of his home. Entry is by guided tour and the commentary is only in Spanish.

### Estadio Santiago Bernabéu

Go to a game, visit the glittering trophy room or take the tour out onto the pitch at the home of Real Madrid (p150).

## Parks & Playgrounds

### Parque del Buen Retiro

Kids generally love the Parque del Buen Retiro (p110) as much as adults. There's ample lawn space in which they can run free, plus numerous playgrounds dotted around the park. Most get a kick out of the peacocks in the Jardines del Arquitecto Herrero Palacios. Renting a **row boat** (per 45min weekdays/ weekends €6/8; ☺10am-8.30pm Apr-Sep, to 5.45pm Oct-Mar; Ⓜ Retiro) is also a great way to pass the time, while there are occasionally puppet shows at various points around the park on weekends.

## Playgrounds

Beyond the Parque del Buen Retiro, play areas for children are fairly thinly spread in central Madrid and most get pretty busy on weekends and after school. Most (but not all) squares or plazas have at least a small playground.

# Primarily for Kids

### Zoo Aquarium de Madrid

Madrid's zoo (p151), out west of the city centre in the Casa de Campo, is a fine way to spend a day with your kids. Weekends can be busy, so try and visit during the week, although check the opening hours and program online before setting out.

### Parque de Atracciones

Rides for all ages are what this old-style amusement park (p151), also out west in the Casa de Campo, are all about. Long queues form on weekends, both at the rides and to get in, so either get here early or come another day if you can.

### Warner Brothers Movie World

This movie **theme park** (☑902 024 100; www.parquewarner.com; San Martín de la Vega; adult/child €40/30; ☺hours vary), 25km south of central Madrid, has much to catch the attention. The park is divided into themes (Cartoon World, the Old West, Hollywood Boulevard, Super Heroes and Warner Brothers Movie World Studios). Opening times are complex and tickets are cheaper if purchased online.

### Cable Car

The gentle Teleférico cable-car ride (p150) is a worthwhile activity for its own sake, but it can also be a useful way to get out to the Casa de Campo; there's a good playground just below the Casa de Campo station.

# Shopping

### Models

Model trains, plains and automobiles (for collectors and for kids) from Bazar Matey (p157) are brilliant little tokens to take home. MacChinine (p145) specialises in Matchbox cars and other perfectly proportioned miniatures.

### Flamenco

For dancing shoes and genuine polka-dot flamenco dresses, stop by Maty (p66).

### Books

In a quiet street in Chamberí, El Dragón Lector (p157) is one of Madrid's best bookshops for kids.

### Board Games

Over in Salamanca, Cuarto de Juegos (p127) has all manner of games with not a single battery needed.

# Like a Local

*In Madrid local knowledge is the difference between falling in love with the city and just passing through. Immerse yourself in Malasaña and Chamberí, and in the local passion for tapas, chocolate con churros (Spanish doughnuts with chocolate) and alfresco living. Knowing where to go on Sunday will transform your weekend.*

resco drinking in La Latina (p79)

VICTOR TORRES/SHUTTERSTOCK ©

## A Madrid Sunday

*Madrileños* love their Sundays, and although there are numerous variations on the theme, they usually go something like this.

### El Rastro

The day begins in the morning (early or otherwise) at the flea market of El Rastro (p72).

### La Hora del Vermut

Having shopped for bargains or simply reasserted one's right to partake of this age-old tradition, *madrileños* then fan out into the bars of La Latina (p79). It is customary at 1pm to order a vermouth (many of the bars have it on tap) to accompany the inevitable rounds of tapas, either as a precursor to lunch or as the main meal itself.

### Parque del Buen Retiro

Later, many gather in the Parque del Buen Retiro (p110) to do everything from reading the Sunday papers, taking a boat ride on the lake or falling asleep (or all of the above), to having a picnic or waiting for the drums to start.

## Chamberí

Of all the *barrios* (districts) that encircle Madrid's city centre, Chamberí is the one where it's easiest to access life as locals live it away from tourist crowds.

### Plaza de Olavide

Plaza de Olavide (p149) is the hub of Chamberí life. Here, old men and women pass the day on park benches, small children tumble out into the plaza's playgrounds and queues form at the outdoor tables of the bars that encircle the plaza. Inside Bar Méntrida at No 3 you'll find a stirring photographic record of the plaza's history.

### Calle de Fuencarral

Sunday morning (from 8am to around 2pm) is a great time to be here when they close Calle de Fuencarral (between the metro stations of Bilbao and Quevedo) to cars and the whole neighbourhood comes out for a stroll.

## Old Neighbourhood Shops

There are some ageless old shops in the streets of Chamberí, including Papelería Salazar (p156), one of Madrid's oldest stationery shops; Relojería Santolaya (p157), watch repairer to royalty; and Calzados Cantero (p157), an old-world shoe shop.

# Chocolate con Churros

### Chocolatería de San Ginés

In most places around the world, chocolate and deep-fried doughnuts would be a dessert. In Madrid this ultimate form of street food is many things, but it's most often breakfast, a hangover cure and/or an early-hours cure for the munchies. Chocolatería de San Ginés (p62) is the most famous venue for this tradition.

### El Brillante

El Brillante (p114) sometimes has queues forming when it opens. It's utterly unpretentious and filled with local colour.

### Chocolatería Valor

Chocolatería Valor (p63) keeps much more reasonable hours than many other *churrerías,* but they've more selection too, with some really fancy choices to mix things up a little.

# Ir de Tapear (Go out for Tapas)

### Calle de la Cava Baja

One of Spain's most celebrated eating streets, with tapas bars lining the street all along its length.

### Plaza de la Paja & Around

Plaza de la Paja has plenty of choice, but not far away try some of Madrid's best *tortilla de patatas* at Juana La Loca (p76) or Txirimiri (p75).

### Mercado de San Miguel

Truly one of Spain's best tapas experiences, this converted market (p58) is at its best outside meal times when it's not so busy.

### Plaza de Santa Ana

To drink or eat? Why choose? Grab a table and do both for as long as you have to spare at one of Madrid's most irresistible squares.

### Estado Puro

Down on the Paseo del Prado, designer tapas keep pulling in the crowds at Estado Puro (p114).

# Malasaña Cafes

Back in the early 20th century, Malasaña was an important centre for Madrid's intellectual and cultural life, its cafes providing a meeting place for the great minds of the day. A handful of these cafes remain.

### Café Comercial

One of Madrid's most storied cafes (p133), recently reborn, inhabits Malasaña's northern fringe, close to where it spills over into Chamberí. Expect marble-top tables, fluted columns and old-style service.

### Café-Restaurante El Espejo

This marvellous old cafe (p142) keeps going strong, remaining an important meeting place for the great, the good and the creative of Madrid.

### Plaza Dos de Mayo & Around

There are so many cafes in the vicinity, it's difficult to know where to start. Perhaps with Café de Mahón (p134), **Café Ajenjo** (☑91 447 70 76; www.facebook.com/cafeajenjo; Calle de la Galería de Robles 4; ⊗3.30pm-2am Mon-Fri, to 2.30am Fri & Sat; Ⓜ Bilbao), **Café de Ruiz** (☑91 446 12 32; www.cafederuiz.com; Calle de Ruiz 11; ⊗3.30pm-2am Mon-Thu, to 2.30am Fri & Sat, to 11.30pm Sun; Ⓜ Bilbao) or Café Manuela (p135).

# For Free

*Madrid can be expensive, but with careful planning, the combination of free attractions and specific times when major sights offer free entry enables you to see the best the city has to offer without burning a large hole in your pocket.*

LUCVI/SHUTTERSTOCK ©

Iglesia de San Ginés (p56)

## Always Free

Most of Madrid's world-class attractions have admission fees, and these have, for the most part, been rising steadily in price over recent years. Even so, a significant number of attractions – from parks and churches to museums and art galleries – remain free, regardless of when you decide to visit.

**Parque del Buen Retiro** (p110) One of Europe's loveliest city parks.

**El Rastro** (p72) Outstanding Sunday morning flea market.

**Ermita de San Antonio de la Florida** (p148) Goya frescoes right where he painted them.

**Museo de Historia** (p130) Wonderful journey through Madrid's history.

**Museo de San Isidro** (p72) Go looking for Madrid's patron saint.

**Iglesia de San Jerónimo El Real** (p113) Church of choice for Spanish royalty.

**Iglesia de San Ginés** (p56) Medieval church with an El Greco painting.

**Campo del Moro** (p55) Expansive gardens below the royal palace.

**Templo de Debod** (p152) Madrid's very own Egyptian temple.

**Catedral de Nuestra Señora de la Almudena** (p57) Madrid's cavernous cathedral.

**Casa de Lope de Vega** (p87) One-time home of Spain's favourite playwright.

**Museo al Aire Libre** (p122) Open-air sculptures by Spain's finest.

**Biblioteca Nacional & Museo del Libro** (p123) Grand architecture and book museum.

**Sociedad General de Autores y Editores** (p139) Madrid's answer to Gaudí.

**Estación de Chamberí** (p149) The metro as it once was.

## Free for EU Citizens & Residents

Palaces, convents and other buildings overseen by Spain's heritage authorities have free entry at limited times of the week, but only for EU citizens and permanent residents.

KIEV.VICTOR/SHUTTERSTOCK ©

Convento de las Descalzas Reales (p56)

**Palacio Real** (p53) Free for EU citizens and residents for last two hours Monday to Thursday.

**Convento de las Descalzas Reales** (p56) Free for EU citizens and residents Wednesday and Thursday afternoons.

**Convento de la Encarnación** (p56) Free for EU citizens and residents Wednesday and Thursday afternoons.

## Sometimes Free

Most of Madrid's attractions have times during the week when they offer free admission – sometimes a whole day, sometimes a few hours every day. Madrid's big three art galleries – the Prado, the Thyssen and the Reina Sofía – all have free-entry periods, though inevitably you'll have plenty of company at these times.

**Museo del Prado** (p99) Free 6pm to 8pm Monday to Saturday and 5pm to 7pm Sunday.

**Museo Thyssen-Bornemisza** (p104) Free Monday.

**Centro de Arte Reina Sofía** (p108) Free 1.30pm to 7pm Sunday and 7pm to 9pm Monday and Wednesday to Saturday.

**Real Academia de Bellas Artes de San Fernando** (p85) Free Wednesday.

**Museo Sorolla** (p149) Free Sunday and 2pm to 8pm Saturday.

**Museo de Cerralbo** (p151) Free Sunday, 2pm to 3pm Saturday and 5pm to 8pm Thursday.

**Museo de América** (p151) Free Sunday.

**Museo del Romanticismo** (p139) Free 2.30pm to 8.30pm Saturday.

*Paella de marisco* (seafood paella)

 # Eating

*Madrid has transformed itself into one of Europe's culinary capitals, not least because the city has long been a magnet for people (and cuisines) from all over Spain. Travel from one Spanish village to the next and you'll quickly learn that each has its own speciality; travel to Madrid and you'll find them all.*

## NEED TO KNOW

### Opening Hours

Lunch takes place between 1pm and 4pm and dinner from 8.30pm to midnight or later.

### Price Ranges

The following price ranges refer to a main course:

€ less than €12

€€ €12–€20

€€€ more than €20

### Tipping

A service charge is usually added to most bills in Madrid, so any further tipping is a matter of personal choice. Spaniards often leave no more than €1 per person or nothing more than small change. If you're particularly happy, 5% on top would be fine.

### Reservations

Reservations for restaurants (not tapas bars) are strongly recommended on Friday and Saturday nights when many restaurants may have two sittings – one around 9pm, the second around 11pm. Reserving for lunch on Saturday or Sunday is also a good idea.

### Restaurant Guide

If you read Spanish, watch out for the annual (and indispensable) *Guía Metrópoli – Comer y Beber en Madrid*. It's available from news kiosks for €13 and has reviews of over 1800 Madrid restaurants and bars by the food critics of *ABC* newspaper.

## The Culture of Eating

Aside from the myriad tastes on offer, it's the buzz that accompanies eating in Madrid that defines the city as a memorable gastronomic experience. Here, eating is not a functional pastime to be squeezed in between other more important tasks; instead, it is one of life's great pleasures, a social event always taken seriously enough to allocate hours for the purpose and to be savoured like all good things in life. Treat it in the same way and you're halfway to understanding why *madrileños* are so passionate about their food.

*Cocido a la madrileña* (meat, chickpea and broth stew)

## Local Specialities

On the bleak *meseta* (plateau) of inland Spain, food in medieval Madrid was a necessity, good food a luxury, and the dishes that developed were functional and well suited to a climate dominated by interminable, bitterly cold winters. The city's traditional local cuisine is still dominated by these influences to a certain extent. At the same time, Madrid has wholeheartedly embraced dishes from across the country. The city has a thriving tapas culture and has become one of the biggest seafood-consuming cities in the world. It's an excellent place to understand just why Spanish cuisine has taken the world by storm.

### SOUPS & STEWS

When the weather turns chilly, in Madrid that traditionally means *sopa de ajo* (garlic soup) and *legumbres* (legumes) such as *garbanzos* (chickpeas), *judías* (beans) and *lentejas* (lentils). Hearty stews are the order of the day and there are none more hearty than *cocido a la madrileña;* it's a kind of hotpot or stew that starts with a noodle broth and is followed by or combined with carrots, chickpeas, chicken, *morcilla* (blood sausage), beef, lard and possibly other sausage meats – there are as many ways of eating *cocido* as there are *madrileños*. *Repollo* (cabbage) usually makes an appearance.

*Madrileños* love *cocido*. They dream of it while they're away from home and they wonder why it hasn't caught on elsewhere. There was even a hit song written about it in the 1950s. However, we'll put this as

## MENÚ DEL DÍA

One great way to cap prices at lunchtime on weekdays is to order the *menú del día*, a full three-course set menu, water, bread and wine. These meals are priced from around €12, although €15 and up is increasingly the norm. You'll be given a menu with a choice of five or six starters, the same number of mains and a handful of desserts – you choose one from each category; it's possible to order two starters, but not two mains.

gently as we can: you have to be a *madrileño* to understand what all the fuss is about because it may be filling but it's not Spain's most exciting dish.

### ROASTED MEATS

Madrid shares with much of the Spanish interior a love of roasted meats. More specifically, *asado de cordero lechal* (spring lamb roasted in a wood-fired oven) is a winter obsession in Madrid just as it is on much of the surrounding *meseta* of central Spain. Usually served with roasted potatoes (it's customary to also order a green salad to accompany the lamb and lighten things up a little), it's a mainstay in many of Madrid's more traditional restaurants. Less celebrated (it's all relative) is *cochinillo asado* (roast suckling pig) from the Segovia region northwest of Madrid.

### SEAFOOD

Every day tonnes of fish and other seafood are trucked in from Mediterranean and Atlantic ports to satisfy the *madrileño* taste for the sea to the extent that, remarkably for a city so far inland, Madrid is home to the world's second-largest fish market (after Tokyo). There's nothing you can't get here if you know where to look. From Galicia in Spain's Atlantic northwest comes *pulpo gallego* (boiled octopus cooked with oil, paprika and garlic) as well as all manner of weird-and-wonderful shellfish. From Asturias, Cantabria and the Basque Country come a passion for delicious *anchoas* (anchovies) and *bacalao* (cod), while Mediterranean Spain has mastered the art of seafood-laden rice dishes, which *madrileños* have embraced as their own. The lightly fried fish of Andalucía rounds out an extraordinary banquet of seafood choice.

### JAMÓN

An essential presence on many a Madrid table, and available from just about any city bar or restaurant, is the cured ham known as *jamón*, from the high plateau. *Jamón* from Extremadura or Salamanca is widely considered to be the finest.

Spanish *jamón* is, unlike Italian prosciutto, a bold, deep red and well marbled with buttery fat. At its best, it smells like meat, the forest and the field. Like wines and olive oil, Spanish *jamón* is subject to a strict series of classifications. *Jamón serrano* refers to *jamón* made from white-coated pigs introduced to Spain in the 1950s. Once salted and semidried by the cold, dry winds of the Spanish sierra, most now go through a similar process of curing and drying in a climate-controlled shed for around a year. *Jamón serrano* accounts for approximately 90% of cured ham in Spain.

*Jamón ibérico* – more expensive and generally regarded as the elite of Spanish hams – comes from a black-coated pig indigenous to the Iberian Peninsula and a descendant of the wild boar. Gastronomically, its star appeal is its ability to infiltrate fat into the muscle tissue, thus producing an especially well-marbled meat. If the pig

Churros (Spanish doughnuts)

MARGARET STEPHEN/LONELY PLANET ©

gains at least 50% of its body weight during the acorn-eating season, it can be classified as *jamón ibérico de bellota,* the most sought-after designation for *jamón.*

### OTHER SPECIALITIES

The line between Spain-wide specialities and those from Madrid is often blurred but most *madrileños* aren't too fussed about whether the first *tortilla de patatas* (potato and onion omelette) was cooked in Madrid or elsewhere – all that matters is that it has become one of the best-loved dishes in the city. The same could also be said for *croquetas* (croquettes) and *patatas con huevos fritos* (baked potatoes with eggs, also known as *huevos rotos*).

## Tapas

Nowhere is the national pastime of *ir de tapear* (going out to eat tapas) so deeply ingrained in local culture as it is in Madrid, where tapas are as much a social event as they are a much-loved culinary form. Anything can be a tapa, from a handful of olives or a slice of *jamón* on bread to a *tortilla de patatas* served in liquefied form. That's because tapas are the canvas upon which Spanish chefs paint the story of a nation's obsession with food, the means by which

they show their fidelity to traditional Spanish tastes even as they gently nudge their compatriots in never-before-imagined directions. By making the most of very little, tapas serve as a link to the impoverished Spain of centuries past. By re-imagining even the most sacred Spanish staples, tapas are the culinary trademark of a confident country rushing headlong into the future. The La Latina *barrio* has Madrid's richest portfolio of tapas bars.

## Vegetarians & Vegans

Pure vegetarianism remains something of an alien concept in most Spanish kitchens; cooked vegetable dishes, for example, often contain ham. That said, Madrid has a growing cast of vegetarian restaurants. Even in those restaurants that serve meat or fish dishes, salads are a Spanish staple and, in some places, can be a meal in themselves. You'll also come across the odd vegetarian paella, as well as dishes such as *verduras a la plancha* (grilled vegetables), *garbanzos con espinacas* (chickpeas and spinach), *patatas bravas* (potato chunks bathed in spicy tomato sauce) and the *tortilla de patatas.* The prevalence of legumes ensures that *lentejas* and *judías* are also easy to track down, while *pan* (bread), *quesos* (cheeses), *alcachofas* (artichokes) and *aceitunas* (olives) are always easy to find. If vegetarianism is rare among Spaniards, vegans will feel as if they've come from another planet. However, some of the established vegetarian restaurants may have certain vegan dishes.

### Eating by Neighbourhood

**Plaza Mayor & Royal Madrid** (p58) Reasonable collection of restaurants and tapas bars.

**La Latina & Lavapiés** (p75) Madrid's undisputed home of tapas.

**Sol, Santa Ana & Huertas** (p88) Plenty of restaurants from Spain's regions.

**El Retiro & the Art Museums** (p114) A handful of stand-out options between the galleries.

**Salamanca** (p123) Terrific tapas and some refined sit-down restaurants.

**Malasaña & Chueca** (p130; p139) Arguably Madrid's widest choice of restaurants.

**Parque del Oeste & Northern Madrid** (p152) Thinly spread but plenty of good places to eat.

BRIAN KINNEY/SHUTTERSTOCK ©

Mercado de San Miguel (p58)

## Lonely Planet's Top Choices

**Restaurante Sobrino De Botín** (p62) The world's oldest restaurant and a bastion of tradition.

**DiverXo** (p154) Three Michelin stars and cutting-edge cooking at its most confronting.

**Estado Puro** (p114) Tapas that push the boundaries of nouvelle Spanish cuisine.

**Bazaar** (p139) Classy cooking in the heart of Chueca.

**Mercado de San Miguel** (p58) Arguably Madrid's most varied gastronomic space.

## Best By Budget

### €

**Bazaar** (p139) Style, substance and celebrities at budget prices.

**Casa Revuelta** (p58) Classic bar bonhomie and great food.

**Casa Julio** (p131) Madrid's best croquettes.

**La Gloria de Montera** (p88) Outstanding food and atmosphere.

### €€

**Mercado de San Miguel** (p58) Madrid's most diverse eating experience.

**Taberna Matritum** (p76) Tapas, tradition and innovation in La Latina.

**Casa Alberto** (p89) Celebrated old *taberna* (tavern) with tapas and sit-down meals.

**La Carmencita** (p140) Madrid classic in the heart of Chueca.

**Frida** (p141) Lovely setting and fresh tastes in a quiet Chueca setting.

### €€€

**DiverXo** (p154) Experimental cooking in all its glory.

**Santceloni** (p155) Enduring success story of innovative cooking.

**La Terraza del Casino** (p91) Brilliant cooking in brilliant surrounds.

**Palacio de Cibeles** (p115) Castilla-La Mancha meets Madrid with great views.

## Best Chocolate con Churros

**Chocolatería de San Ginés** (p62) Epicentre of the *churros* tradition.

**Chocolatería Valor** (p63) Unimaginable things they do with chocolate.

**El Brillante** (p114) Simplicity itself in the wee small hours.

## Best by Cuisine

### Best Cocido a la Madrileña

**Taberna La Bola** (p60) Faultless *cocido* in a fine *taberna* setting.

**Malacatín** (p77) *Cocido* whichever way you like it.

**Lhardy** (p91) Over 150 years of *cocido* excellence.

**Casa Paco** (p61) Storied old *taberna* with a fine *cocido* pedigree.

**Restaurante Los Galayos** (p61) Arguably the best restaurant on the Plaza Mayor.

### Best Croquetas

**Casa Julio** (p131) Madrid's best – just ask U2.

**Bar Melo's** (p75) Large and late-night comfort food.

**La Gastrocroquetería de Chema** (p132) New wave croquettes in wonderful variety.

**Pez Tortilla** (p130) Malasaña bar with terrific choice.

**Casa Labra** (p88) *Bacalao* (cod) croquettes at their best.

### Best Rice Paella

**Costa Blanca Arrocería** (p154) Mediterranean rice and atmosphere.

**El Pato Mudo** (p59) Delicious rice dishes in all their wonderful variety.

**La Paella Real** (p61) Assured rice cooking opposite the Teatro Real.

**Albur** (p131) Casual setting, classy rice dishes.

## Best Roast Lamb or Suckling Pig

**Restaurante Sobrino de Botín** (p62) Fantastic all-round dining experience.

**Posada de la Villa** (p79) Lovely setting for this feast of roasted meat.

**El Pedrusco de Aldealcorvo** (p154) Cochinillo direct from its Segovian heartland.

**Casa Ciriaco** (p61) Roasted meats a speciality for more than a century.

## Best Tortilla de Patatas

**Juana La Loca** (p76) Our vote for Madrid's best tortilla.

**Txirimiri** (p75) Just around the corner and not far behind.

**Estado Puro** (p114) Served in a glass in liquefied form.

**Bodega de la Ardosa** (p131) No-frills potato omelettes at their best.

**José Luis** (p124) Consistently ranked among Madrid's best.

## Best for Vegetarians & Vegans

**El Estragón** (p78) Reliable mainstay in La Latina

**Viva Burger** (p78) Veggie burgers like no others.

**Restaurante Integral Artemisa** (p91) Varied menu not far from Sol.

# Drinking & Nightlife

*Nights in the Spanish capital are the stuff of legend. They're invariably long and loud most nights of the week, rising to a deafening crescendo as the weekend nears. And what Ernest Hemingway wrote of the city in the 1930s remains true to this day: 'Nobody goes to bed in Madrid until they have killed the night.'*

## Killing the Night

Madrid has more bars than any other city in the world – six, in fact, for every 100 inhabitants, and wherever you are in town, there'll be a bar close by. But bars are only half the story. On any night in Madrid, first drinks, tapas and wines then segue easily into cocktail bars and the nightclubs that have brought such renown to Madrid as the unrivalled scene of all-night fiestas.

## Cafes

Madrid's thriving cafe culture dates back to the early and mid-20th century, when old-style coffee houses formed the centrepiece of the country's intellectual life. Although many such cafes were torn down in the rush to modernise, many that recall those times remain, with period architecture and an agreeably formal atmosphere; their clientele long ago broadened to encompass the entire cross-section of modern Madrid society. Added into the mix are some terrific and usually more casual modern cafes, although here, too, the principle remains the same: they're at once social and cultural meeting places and places to escape from the often frenetic pace of city life.

## Cocktail Bars

The mojito (a rum-based drink with sugar, fresh mint, crushed ice and lemon) may have its origins in Cuba, but it has arguably become Madrid's favourite adopted child. As a consequence, the reputation of the city's cocktail bars can rise and fall according to the quality of its mojitos, and those that have lasted the distance have usually done so on the back of a mighty fine mojito. Other cocktails of breathtaking variety are also possible in the city's cocktail bars that range from slick and trendy temples to all that's new to storied bastions of tradition where bow-tied waiters and cocktail makers are as celebrated as the *famosos* (celebrities) who have visited through the decades.

## Nightclubs

People here live fully for the moment. Today's encounter can be tomorrow's distant memory, perhaps in part because Madrid's nightclubs

---

### THE SECRET LANGUAGE OF BEER

In the majority of bars you won't have much choice when it comes to beer, but thankfully Madrid's flagship beer, Mahou, goes down well and comes as both draught and bottled. Cruzcampo is a lighter beer. Otherwise, two Catalan companies, Damm and San Miguel, each produce about 15% of all Spain's beer. The most common order is a *caña*, a small glass of *cerveza de barril* (draught beer). A larger beer (about 300ml), more common in the hipper bars and clubs, usually comes in a *tubo* (a long, straight glass). The equivalent of a pint is a *pinta*, while a *jarra* refers to a jug of beer.

## GETTING HOME

Madrid's extensive metro system can get you most places, but it grinds to a halt between 2am and 6.05am. If you're trying to get back to your hotel at these hours, there are two main options (apart from walking). The first is a taxi – although these hours attract a higher flag fall and per-kilometre rate than during daylight hours, it should rarely cost you more than €10 to get back to your hotel. The other option is the night buses known as *búhos* (owls), with more than two-dozen routes fanning out across the city from Plaza de la Cibeles.

(also known as *discotecas*) rival any in the world. The best places are usually the megaclubs, with designer decor, designer people and sometimes enough space for numerous dance floors, each with their own musical style to suit your mood. Themed nights are all the rage, so it's always worth checking in advance to see what flavour of the night takes your fancy.

Admission prices vary widely, depending on the time of night you enter, the way you're dressed and the number of people inside. The standard entry fee is €12, which usually includes the first drink, although megaclubs and swankier places charge a few euros more.

## Drinking & Nightlife by Neighbourhood

**Plaza Mayor & Royal Madrid** (p62) Plenty of nightclubs in the city centre.

**La Latina & Lavapiés** (p79) Terrific for wine bars and fortifying tapas.

**Sol, Santa Ana & Huertas** (p92) The epicentre of Madrid's night-time action.

**El Retiro & the Art Museums** (p115) A daytime *barrio* with little happening after dark.

## NEED TO KNOW

### Opening Hours

➡ Local watering holes that serve as centres of community life usually open throughout the day from breakfast to last drinks.

➡ Trendier bars often get going around 8pm and stay open until 1am or 2am during the week, 3am on weekends.

➡ Nightclubs don't usually open until midnight or 1am and stay open until 5am or 6am. Some open all week, others from Thursday to Saturday.

### Top Tips

➡ If you plan to stay out the whole night, sleeping the siesta the afternoon before could be the key to your staying power.

➡ Another essential element to surviving the long Madrid night is to never drink on an empty stomach – fill up on tapas or a late dinner wherever possible.

➡ Most *madrileños* take a localised approach to a night out – once they've begun to drink and settle into the night, they tend to move from one place to the next within the same *barrio*.

➡ Even those nightclubs that let you in for free will play catch up with hefty prices for drinks, so don't plan your night around looking for the cheapest entry cost.

**Salamanca** (p125) A small collection of nightclubs.

**Malasaña & Chueca** All-night neighbourhoods with terrific cocktail bars (Chueca; p142) and fabulous cafes (Malasaña; p133).

**Parque del Oeste & Northern Madrid** (p155) Some nightlife focal points but thinly spread.

## Lonely Planet's Top Choices

**La Venencia** (p92) Timeless Huertas sherry bar that hasn't changed in decades.

**Museo Chicote** (p142) One of Europe's most celebrated cocktail bars.

**Teatro Joy Eslava** (p62) The pick of Madrid's city-centre nightclubs.

**Chocolatería de San Ginés** (p62) A Madrid institution whatever the hour.

**1862 Dry Bar** (p133) Our favourite Madrid cocktail bar.

## Best Cocktail Bars

**Museo Chicote** (p142) Madrid's top pick for decades.

**Del Diego** (p143) Some of the city's best cocktails.

**Bar Cock** (p143) Cocktails, *famosos* and bow-tied waiters.

**1862 Dry Bar** (p133) An extensive and innovative cocktail list.

**José Alfredo** (p135) Long-standing cocktail bar off Gran Vía.

**Salmón Gurú** (p92) A cocktail guru at the top of his game.

## Best Craft Beer

**Fábrica Maravillas** (p134) Malasaña Ale in the heart of the *barrio*.

**Irreale** (p133) Ten on tap and dozens by the bottle.

**La Tape** (p133) A veteran on the scene with local and international choices.

## Best Gay & Lesbian

**Café Acuarela** (p144) Mellow bar-cafe for any hour.

**Why Not?** (p143) Hetero-friendly but gay at heart.

**Club 54 Studio** (p143) New York–style gay club.

## Best Grand Old Cafes

**Café-Restaurante El Espejo** (p142) A storied echo of another age.

**Gran Café de Gijón** (p142) Gilded cafe down on Paseo de los Recoletos.

**Cafe Comercial** (p133) A Madrid classic reborn as it always was.

**Café del Círculo de Bellas Artes** (p93) Bow-tied waiters and stunning decor.

**Café Manuela** (p135) Magical air with board games.

**Cafe de Oriente** (p63) Germanic charm with fine views.

## Best Mojitos

**Café Belén** (p142) Long-standing favourite in Chueca.

**Delic** (p79) Some of Madrid's best on Plaza de la Paja.

**Taberna Chica** (p80) Exceptional mojitos in La Latina.

**Museo Chicote** (p142) Mojitos as Hermingway used to like them.

**El Eucalipto** (p80) Cuban vibe and Cuban know-how.

**Dos Gardenias** (p94) Secret recipe in this Huertas nook.

## Best Nightclubs

**Teatro Kapital** (p115) Ibiza megaclub meets Madrid.

**Teatro Joy Eslava** (p62) Madrid's most diverse nightclub, every night.

**Ya'sta** (p135) Enduring icon of the Madrid night.

**Sala Morocco** (p63) Consistently full Malasaña club.

**Why Not?** (p143) Smaller than most but a good time guaranteed.

## Best Vermouth

**La Vaquería Montañesa** (p155) Chamberí outpost of Madrid's passion for a great vermouth.

**La Violeta** (p155) Vermouth on tap and in great variety.

**Casa Alberto** (p89) The essence of Madrid's love affair with *vermut*.

Flamenco dancer

 # Entertainment

*Madrid has a happening live-music scene that owes a lot to the city's role as the cultural capital of the Spanish-speaking world. There's flamenco, world-class jazz and a host of performers you may never have heard of but who may just be Spain's next big thing. For a dose of high culture, there's opera and zarzuela (satirical musical comedy).*

## NEED TO KNOW

### Opening Hours

Theatre box offices are generally open from about 10am until 1pm and again from 5pm until the start of the evening's show.

### Reservations

→ Tickets for live music should always be made in advance.

→ Theatre tickets can generally be bought at the box office on the day of the performance, but for new or weekend shows book ahead.

→ Tickets for Real Madrid football matches can be bought online. They also usually go on sale the Monday before a game at Gate 42 of the stadium on Calle de Conche de Espina.

→ Tickets for most jazz clubs go on sale an hour or two before the scheduled performance start.

### What's On

**EsMadrid Magazine** (www.esmadrid. com) Monthly tourist-office listings.

**Guía del Ocio** (www.guiadelocio.com) Weekly magazine available for €1 at news kiosks.

**In Madrid** (www.in-madrid.com) Free monthly English-language publication.

**Metropoli** (www.elmundo.es/metropoli) *El Mundo* newspaper's Friday supplement magazine.

**La Noche en Vivo** (www.lanocheenvivo. com) Live music listings.

## Flamenco

Madrid has numerous venues with nightly live performances, but seeing flamenco in Madrid can be expensive: at the *tablaos* (restaurants where flamenco is performed) expect to pay at least €35 just to see the show. The admission price usually includes your first drink, but you pay extra for meals (up to €50 per person) that, put simply, are rarely worth the money. For that reason, we suggest you eat elsewhere and go only for the show (after having bought tickets in advance), on the understanding that you won't have a front-row seat.

## Jazz

Madrid was one of Europe's jazz capitals in the 1920s. It's taken a while, but it's once again among Europe's elite for live jazz. There's only a small number of places devoted exclusively to jazz, but the quality is world-class and the range of styles includes the kind of classic jazz designed to keep the purist happy as well as Latin, nu jazz and countless variations on the theme. Beyond the signature jazz venues, numerous multigenre live music stages broaden out the experience, often with a weekly jazz jam session. November's **Jazz Madrid** (www. festivaldejazzmadrid.com; ⊙Nov) is a great time for jazz enthusiasts to be in town.

## Other Live Music

Madrid made its name as a live music city back in the 1980s, when drugs and rock music fuelled the decade-long fiesta known as *la movida madrileña* (the Madrid scene). At the height of *la movida,* an estimated 300 rock bands were performing in the bars of Malasaña alone. While rock remains a Madrid mainstay and the doors of a handful of classic venues remain open, the live music scene now encompasses every genre imaginable. Many venues double as clubs where DJs follow the live acts, making it possible to start off the night with a great concert and stay on to party until late.

## Classical Music & Opera

Madrid loves to party, but scratch beneath the surface and you'll find a thriving city of high culture, with venues dedicated to year-round opera and classical music. Orchestras from all over Europe perform regularly here, but Madrid's own **Orquesta Sinfónica** (www.osm.es) also performs (or accompanies) in the Teatro Real (p56) or Auditorio Nacional de Música (p156). The **Banda Sinfónica Municipal de Madrid** (www.munimadrid.es/bandasinfonica) plays at the Teatro Monumental (p95).

## La Zarzuela

What began in the late 17th century as a way to amuse King Felipe IV and his court has become Spain's own unique theatre style. With a light-hearted combination of music and dance, and a focus on everyday people's problems, *zarzuelas* quickly became popular in Madrid, which remains the genre's capital. Although you're likely to

Above: Teatro Real (p56)

Right: Real Madrid footballer, Isco

## BOOKING CONCERT & THEATRE TICKETS

Outlets selling tickets online for concerts, theatre and other live performances include the following:

**El Corte Inglés** (www.elcorteingles. es) Click on 'Todos Los Departamentos', then 'Entradas'.

**Entradas.com** (www.entradas.com)

**Fnac** (www.fnac.es) Click on 'Entradas'; mostly modern, big-name music groups.

**Servicaixa** (www.servicaixa.com) You can also get tickets in Servicaixa ATMs.

**Ticketmaster** (www.ticketmaster.es)

have trouble following the storyline (*zarzuelas* are notoriously full of local references and jokes), seeing a *zarzuela* gives an entertaining look into local culture. The best place to catch a show is the Teatro de la Zarzuela (p94). For more information about *zarzuela,* including current performance reviews, visit www.zarzuela.net.

### Dance

Spain's lively **Compañía Nacional de Danza** (http://cndanza.mcu.es) performs worldwide and has won accolades for its marvellous technicality and original choreography. Madrid is also home to the **Ballet Nacional de España** (☑91 517 99 99; www.balletnacional. mcu.es), a classical company known for its unique mix of ballet and traditional Spanish styles, including flamenco and *zarzuela.* When in town, both companies perform at venues that include the Teatro Real (p56) or Teatro de la Zarzuela.

### Film

Plenty of cinemas offer *versión original* (VO; original version) films, which are shown in the original language with Spanish subtitles; otherwise foreign-language films are dubbed in mainstream cinemas. The highest concentrations of Spanish-language cinemas are on Gran Vía and Calle de Fuencarral, between the Glorieta de Bilbao and Glorieta de Quevedo.

### Spectator Sports

The Estadio Santiago Bernabéu (p150) is one of the world's great football arenas; watching a game here alongside 80,000 passionate Madridistas (Real Madrid supporters) will send chills down your spine.

If you're lucky enough to be in town when Real Madrid wins a major trophy, head to Plaza de la Cibeles (p112) and wait for the all-night party to begin.

Madrid's other team, **Atlético de Madrid** (www.clubatleticodemadrid.com) has a cult following, attracts passionate support and fans of the *rojiblancos* (red-and-whites) declare theirs to be the real Madrid team.

### Bullfighting

Love it or loathe it, bullfighting is a national institution. In the afternoons there are generally six bulls and three star *toreros* dressed in the dazzling *traje de luces* (suit of lights). Madrid's main bullfighting season begins during the Fiesta de San Isidro, with daily *corridas* (bullfights) from mid-May onwards.

Some regions of Spain, notably Catalonia, have banned bullfighting, and the election of the left-wing Ahora Madrid municipal government in 2015 changed the status quo in the capital. One of the party's policy platforms was to remove all municipal funding for the industry, and Manuela Carmena, the new mayor, ensured that the box reserved for the mayor and her representatives was empty, for the first time in decades, during the Fiesta de San Isidro bullfights in 2015. It remains to be seen what impact this change in policy will have on a spectacle that many animal lovers feel is immoral, and which is vehemently opposed by numerous animal-welfare organisations, among them the World Society for the **Protection of Animals** (www.world animalprotection.org.uk) and the **League Against Cruel Sports** (www.league.org.uk).

## Entertainment by Neighbourhood

**Plaza Mayor & Royal Madrid** (p65) Plenty of cinemas, theatres and live music venues.

**La Latina & Lavapiés** (p80) A small handful of flamenco and live music venues.

**Sol, Santa Ana & Huertas** (p94) One of the best *barrios* for jazz, flamenco, theatre and live music.

**El Retiro & the Art Museums** (p112) Football celebrations but not much else.

**Salamanca** (p125) Upmarket nightclubs scattered thinly.

**Malasaña & Chueca** (p135; p144) Quirky theatres and grungy live music stages.

**Parque del Oeste & Northern Madrid** (p155) A heady mix of football and classical music.

## Lonely Planet's Top Choices

**Café Central** (p94) One of the best jazz clubs on earth.

**Sala El Sol** (p94) Mythic Madrid stage for rock and other live acts.

**Villa Rosa** (p94) Top-notch flamenco behind an extravagantly tiled facade.

**Estadio Santiago Bernabéu** (p150) Legendary home stadium of Real Madrid.

**Teatro de la Zarzuela** (p94) Home theatre for Spain's home-grown operatic theatre.

## Best Classical Music Opera

**Teatro Real** (p56) Madrid's premier stage for opera, ballet and classical concerts.

**Auditorio Nacional de Música** (p156) The home stage for the capital's very own symphony orchestra.

**Fundación Juan March** (p125) Intimate venue with solo and chamber recitals.

**Teatro Monumental** (p95) Top-notch auditorium for all things classical.

**Teatro de la Zarzuela** (p94) Catch Spain's very own operatic form.

## Best Flamenco Beyond the Tablaos

**Teatro Flamenco Madrid** (p135) Excellent venue with reasonable prices.

**Café Ziryab** (p80) Neighbourhood flamenco with fine atmosphere.

**BarCo** (p135) Live flamenco every Sunday.

**Sala Clamores** (p156) Diverse club with regular flamenco.

**Sala Juglar** (p81) A live-at-8pm flamenco show.

## Best Flamenco Venues

**Corral de la Morería** (p80) Prestigious downtown Madrid venue.

**Villa Rosa** (p94) Iconic flamenco stage on Plaza de Santa Ana.

**Café de Chinitas** (p65) World-famous flamenco venue.

**Teatro Flamenco Madrid** (p135) Top-notch flamenco in a theatre setting.

**Café Ziryab** (p80) A chance to hear more improvised flamenco.

**Casa Patas** (p80) Serious flamenco performers.

## Best Jazz Clubs

**Café Central** (p94) Spain's best jazz venue.

**El Junco Jazz Club** (p144) Live jazz and all-night DJs.

**El Despertar** (p81) Intimate venue with impeccable jazz cred.

**Bogui Jazz** (p144) Live jazz Thursday to Saturday.

**Jazz Bar** (p93) Non-stop jazz on the sound system.

**Sala Clamores** (p156) Jazz club at heart but with so much more.

## Best Live Music Venues

**Moby Dick** (p156) Concerts by almost-superstars.

**Café La Palma** (p136) Fabulous venue with a number of stages.

**Sala Clamores** (p156) Nightly concerts across all genres.

**Costello Café & Niteclub** (p94) New York meets Madrid in cool fashion.

**Thundercat** (p144) Classic rock in all its glory.

## Best Theatres

**Teatro Español** (p95) Gorgeous theatre for Spanish plays on Plaza de Santa Ana.

**Teatros del Canal** (p156) Diverse modern stage with fine theatre and concerts.

**Teatro Pavón** (p81) One of the best places in Spain to see classical theatre.

**Teatro Valle-Inclán** (p81) Stunning theatre complex for Spanish plays.

# Shopping

*Our favourite aspect of shopping in Madrid is the city's small boutiques and quirky shops. Often run by the same families for generations, they counter the over-commercialisation of mass-produced Spanish culture with everything from fashions to old-style ceramics to rope-soled espadrilles or gourmet Spanish food and wine.*

## Fashion

The world's most prestigious catwalks are clamouring for Spanish designers and with good reason. Spain's fashion industry, with Madrid as its capital, has a pedigree of bold colours and eye-catching designs born in the creative outpouring of *la movida madrileña* (the Madrid scene) in the 1980s. As such, even a cursory glance in the shop windows of Salamanca, Malasaña and Chueca in particular can be a revelation, confirming that there's so much more to *la moda española* (Spanish fashion) than Zara and Mango.

## Souvenirs & Handicrafts

You could buy your friends back home a vividly coloured flamenco dress of the kind that hangs from the doorway of many a downtown Madrid souvenir shop. Then again, you could instead opt for a touch more class and take home an artfully designed papier-mâché figurine, a carefully crafted ceramic bowl made by the family potters of central Spain, or an intricately designed Spanish fan. And then there are guitars favoured by everyone from The Beatles to flamenco greats, and dresses from the shops where the flamenco greats get their gear...

## Gourmet Foods

Nowhere is Spanish cuisine more accessible than in the city's purveyors of Spanish foods. At these places – some traditional, some representative of the revolution sweeping Spanish cooking – you can point to your favourite *jamón* (ham) or tub of olives and in no time they'll be packaged up and ready for that Retiro picnic or flight back home. Some are small specialist stores where the packaging is often as exquisite as the tastes on offer. Elsewhere, Madrid's markets have also been transformed into vibrant spaces where you can eat as well as shop.

## Shopping in Madrid by Neighbourhood

**Plaza Mayor & Royal Madrid** (p65) A little bit of everything.

**La Latina & Lavapiés** (p82) Offbeat boutiques and a fabulous Sunday flea market.

**Sol, Santa Ana & Huertas** (p95) Some of Madrid's best souvenirs.

**El Retiro & the Art Museums** (p115) Museum giftshops and bookshops are the main drawcard.

**Salamanca** (p125) The home of Spanish fashion.

**Malasaña & Chueca** (p136; 144) Retro fashions in Malasaña alongside more upmarket style in Chueca.

**Parque del Oeste & Northern Madrid** (p156) Outposts of tradition aimed at a local market.

## Lonely Planet's Top Choices

**El Rastro** (p82) Europe's largest flea market and Madrid's favourite Sunday pastime.

**El Arco Artesanía** (p66) Modern souvenirs with an art gallery aesthetic.

**Helena Rohner** (p82) Designer jewellery from catwalk to casual.

**Agatha Ruiz de la Prada** (p125) Candy bright colours from a household name in Madrid fashion.

**Antigua Casa Talavera** (p65) Handpainted ceramics from small family kilns.

## Best Flea Markets

**El Rastro** (p82) Possibly Europe's best flea market.

**Art Market** (p68) Local art and prints of the greats.

**Cuesta de Claudio Moyano Bookstalls** (p115) Madrid's answer to the bookstalls on Paris' Left Bank.

**Mercadillo Marqués de Viana** (p157) A calmer version of El Rastro in northern Madrid.

**Mercado de Monedas y Sellos** (p68) Old coins and stamps.

## Best Gourmet Food & Wine

**Mantequería Bravo** (p126) Madrid's best deli for traditional Spanish foods.

**Bombonerías Santa** (p126) Individually wrapped Spanish sweets.

**Gourmet Experience** (p67) One-stop shop for Spanish wines, cheeses etc.

**Licores Cabello** (p95) Madrid's most atmospheric wine merchant.

**Oriol Balaguer** (p126) Designer chocolates from one of Spain's master chefs.

## Best Souvenirs & Handicrafts

**El Arco Artesanía** (p66) Designer flair brought to Spanish themes.

**Maty** (p66) Authentic flamenco clothes and shoes.

**Antigua Casa Talavera** (p65) Old-world, hand-crafted ceramics.

**Botería Julio Rodríguez** (p82) The real deal when it comes to Spanish wineskins.

**El Flamenco Vive** (p67) Flamenco music and other memorabilia.

**Casa de Diego** (p95) Ornate Spanish fans and umbrellas.

## Best Spanish Fashion

**Camper** (p127) Comfortable, casual footwear for the fashion conscious.

**Agatha Ruiz de la Prada** (p125) Fun, colourful fashions from a Madrid veteran.

**Loewe** (p144) The Louis Vuitton of Spanish fashion.

**Manolo Blahnik** (p126) World-famous women's shoes.

**Lurdes Bergada** (p145) Natural fibres, warm colours and cutting-edge cuts.

# Explore Madrid

## MADRID'S TOP SIGHTS

# Neighbourhoods at a Glance

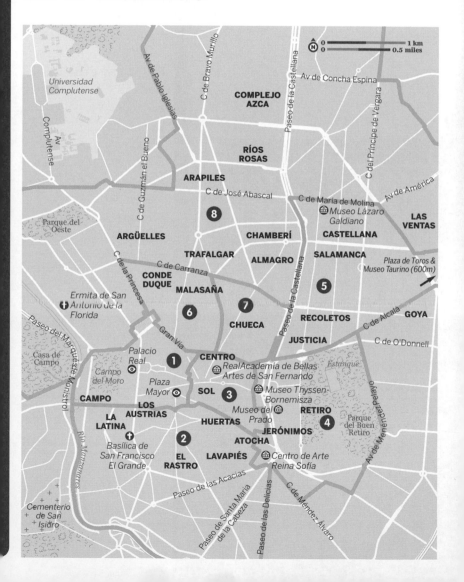

## ❶ Plaza Mayor & Royal Madrid (p50)

The bustling, compact and medieval heart of the city is where Madrid's story began and where the city became the seat of royal power. It's also where the splendour of imperial Spain was at its most ostentatious –imagine palaces, ancient churches, elegant squares and imposing convents. It's an architectural high point of the city, with plenty of fine eating and shopping options.

## ❷ La Latina & Lavapiés (p69)

La Latina combines Madrid's best selection of tapas bars, fine little boutiques and a medieval streetscape studded with elegant churches; graceful Calle de la Cava Baja could be our favourite street for tapas in town. Down the hill, Lavapiés is one of the city's oldest *barrios* (districts) and the heart of multicultural Madrid. Spanning the two neighbourhoods is the Sunday flea market of El Rastro.

## ❸ Sol, Santa Ana & Huertas (p82)

These tightly packed streets are best known for nightlife that doesn't seem to abate once the sun goes down, but there's also the beguiling Plaza de Santa Ana, a stirring literary heritage in the Barrio de las Letras and, at the Sol end of things, Madrid's beating heart, you'll find the sum total of all Madrid's personalities, with fabulous shopping, eating and entertainment options.

## ❹ El Retiro & the Art Museums (p97)

From Plaza de la Cibeles in the north, the buildings arrayed along Paseo del Prado read like a roll-call of Madrid's most popular attractions. Temples to high culture include the Museo del Prado, Museo Thyssen-Bornemisza and Centro de Arte Reina Sofía, which rank among the world's most prestigious art galleries. Up the hill to the east, the marvellous Parque del Buen Retiro helps to make this one of the most attractive areas of Madrid in which to spend your time.

## ❺ Salamanca (p118)

The *barrio* of Salamanca is Madrid's most exclusive quarter. Like nowhere else in the capital, this is where stately mansions set back from the street share *barrio* space with designer boutiques from the big local and international fashionistas. Salamanca's sprinkling of fine restaurants, designer tapas bars and niche museums are also very much at home here.

## ❻ Malasaña & Conde Duque (p128)

The two inner-city *barrios* of Malasaña and Conde Duque are more about experiences of life as lived by *madrileños* (people from Madrid) than ticking off a list of wonderful, if more static, attractions. Malasaña is the city's retro heartbeat, a land of rock bars and vintage-clothing stores with a fine square at its centre. Conde Duque is more refined, even as it buys into Malasaña's energetic spirit.

## ❼ Chueca (p137)

Chueca is where Madrid gets up close and personal. The tangle of tightly packed streets contain some of Madrid's best shopping, fine eating options and classy little corners that come from being the centre of the city's gay community. It's a great place to get to know the city and its beguiling mix of hedonism and style.

## ❽ Parque del Oeste & Northern Madrid (p146)

Madrid's north contains some of the city's most attractive *barrios,* including Chamberí, which is a wonderful escape from the downtown and offers unique insights into how locals enjoy their city. Estadio Santiago Bernabéu is a major highlight for sports fans, Parque del Oeste is a gorgeous expanse of green, while a series of fascinating sights – from Goya frescoes to an Egyptian temple – add considerable appeal.

# Plaza Mayor & Royal Madrid

## Neighbourhood Top Five

**1 Plaza Mayor** (p52) Immersing yourself in the street life that courses across the cobblestones or taking up residence at an outdoor table surrounding this most elegant of city squares.

**2 Palacio Real** (p53) Soaking up the grandeur of Madrid's seat of royal power, and one of its most imposing architectural landmarks.

**3 Plaza de la Villa** (p55) Spending time in one of the city's most architecturally pleasing corners, with baroque Madrid architecture.

**4 Chocolatería de San Ginés** (p62) Stopping by for Madrid's best *chocolate con churros* (Spanish doughnuts

with chocolate) at any hour of the day or night.

**5 Mercado de San Miguel** (p58) Learning why locals are obsessed with food, and experiencing the irresistible buzz that goes with going out for tapas in the capital.

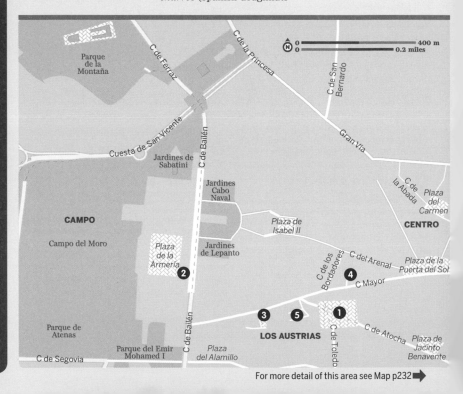

For more detail of this area see Map p232 ➡

# Explore: Plaza Mayor & Royal Madrid

Plaza Mayor is the hub of Madrid's most medieval quarter, an area known as Madrid de los Austrias, in reference to the Habsburg dynasty, which ruled Spain from 1517 to 1700. The plaza is a place both to admire and to get your bearings, the place where so many explorations of the neighbourhood (and wider city) begin. That's because it is at once the hub of neighbourhood life and the topographical high point of the *barrio* (district).

Build your day exploring this neighbourhood around this and other squares, which are lovely and quiet in the morning, and lively and pretty in the soft light of late afternoon. Running close to its northern edge, Calle Mayor connects Plaza Mayor with the rest of the neighbourhood, running down the hill past the wonderful Mercado de San Miguel to Plaza de la Villa with tangled lanes of medieval origin twisting away on either side. Away to the north are Plaza de Oriente, the royal palace and the cathedral.

Although it's no hard-and-fast rule, the shops, restaurants, bars and nightclubs tend to be concentrated at the eastern end of the neighbourhood, close to Plaza Mayor, while the architectural highlights are more evenly spread.

## Local Life

→ **Hang-out** The broad appeal of the neighbourhood is summed up by two of its favourite gathering places for locals: the stunningly converted Mercado de San Miguel (p58) and the timeless Chocolatería de San Ginés (p62).

→ **Meeting points** The equestrian statue of Felipe III in the centre of Plaza Mayor was moved here in 1848 and has ever since been a favoured meeting point for locals who arrange to meet 'under the balls of the horse'.

→ **Shopping** Ignore the tacky souvenir shops that overflow from shopfronts across the centre: small artisan shops abound throughout the neighbourhood and are well worth tracking down.

→ **Nightclubs** Watch out for themed nights that might make Monday a better night to dance than the weekend.

## Getting There & Away

→ **Metro** A short step from Plaza Mayor, Sol metro station is one of the most useful in Madrid, with lines 1, 2 and 3 all passing through. Ópera (lines 2 and 5) is another useful neighbourhood station – line 2 can carry you to the Paseo del Prado (leaving a short walk to the galleries), Parque del Buen Retiro or Salamanca in no time.

## Lonely Planet's Top Tip

Treat Plaza Mayor as a place to soak up the atmosphere, and order a coffee or wine to justify your presence at one of the outdoor tables. Come in the morning when the pressure to order something more substantial is minimal. For a meal you're better off heading to the Mercado de San Miguel (p58).

### ✖ Best Places to Eat

→ Mercado de San Miguel (p58)
→ Restaurante Sobrino de Botín (p62)
→ Taberna La Bola (p60)
→ Casa Revuelta (p58)
→ Casa Paco (p61)
→ Gourmet Experience (p59)

For reviews, see p58.

### 🍷 Best Places to Drink

→ Chocolatería de San Ginés (p62)
→ The Sherry Corner (p62)
→ Teatro Joy Eslava (p62)
→ Café del Real (p63)
→ Cafe de Oriente (p63)
→ Anticafé (p63)

For reviews, see p62.

### 🛍 Best Places to Shop

→ Antigua Casa Talavera (p65)
→ El Arco Artesanía (p66)
→ Maty (p66)
→ Convento del Corpus Cristi (p67)
→ Casa Hernanz (p66)
→ El Flamenco Vive (p67)

For reviews, see p65.

## TOP SIGHT
## PLAZA MAYOR

It's easy to fall in love with Madrid in the Plaza Mayor. This is the monumental heart of the city and the grand stage for so many of its most important historical events. Here, Madrid's relentless energy courses across its cobblestones beneath ochre-hued apartments, wrought-iron balconies, frescoes and stately spires.

**DON'T MISS**
......................................
➡ Spires & Slate Roofs
➡ Real Casa de la Panadería
➡ Markets

**PRACTICALITIES**
......................................
➡ Map p232, G6
➡ Ⓜ Sol

### A Grand History

Ah, the history the plaza has seen! Inaugurated in 1619, its first public ceremony was suitably auspicious – the beatification of San Isidro Labrador (St Isidro the Farm Labourer), Madrid's patron saint. Thereafter, it was as if all that was controversial about Spain took place in this square.

Bullfights, often in celebration of royal weddings or births, with royalty watching on from the balconies and up to 50,000 people crammed into the plaza, were a recurring theme until 1878. Far more notorious were the *autos-da-fé* (the ritual condemnations of heretics during the Spanish Inquisition), followed by executions – burnings at the stake and deaths by garrotte on the north side of the square, hangings to the south.

### A Less-Grand History

Not all the plaza's activities were grand events and, just as it is now surrounded by shops, it was once filled with food vendors. In 1673, King Carlos II issued an edict allowing the vendors to raise tarpaulins above their stalls to protect their wares and themselves from the refuse and raw sewage that people habitually tossed out of the windows above! Well into the 20th century, trams ran through Plaza Mayor.

### Real Casa de la Panadería

The exquisite frescoes of the 17th-century **Real Casa de la Panadería** (Royal Bakery; Map p232; Plaza Mayor 27) rank among Madrid's more eye-catching sights. The present frescoes date to just 1992 and are the work of artist Carlos Franco, who chose images from the signs of the zodiac and gods (eg Cybele) to provide a stunning backdrop for the plaza. The frescoes were inaugurated to coincide with Madrid's 1992 spell as European Capital of Culture. The building now houses the city's main tourist office.

### Spires & Slate Roofs

The plaza was designed in the 17th century by Juan Gómez de Mora who, following the dominant style of the day, adopted a Herrerian style (named after Spanish Renaissance architect Juan de Herrera). The slate spires and roofs are the most obvious expression of this pleasing and distinctively Madrid style, and their sombre hues are nicely offset by the warm colours of the uniformly ochre apartments and their 237 wrought-iron balconies.

ANIBAL TREJO/SHUTTERSTOCK ©

# TOP SIGHT
## PALACIO REAL

You can almost imagine how the eyes of Felipe V, the first of the Bourbon kings, lit up when the *alcázar* (Muslim-era fortress) burned down in 1734 on Madrid's most exclusive patch of real estate. His plan? Build a palace that would dwarf all its European counterparts. The resulting 2800-room royal palace never attained such a scale, but it's still an Italianate baroque architectural landmark of arresting beauty.

## Comedor de Gala

In the midst of such extravagance, the spacious Comedor de Gala (Gala Dining Room) is where grand ceremonial occasions were once (and are still occasionally) held. The stately air is enhanced by the extravagant chandeliers, hoary old artworks on the walls and lavishly adorned archway.

## Farmacia Real

At the southern end of the Plaza de la Armería courtyard, the Farmacia Real contains a formidable collection of medicine jars and stills for mixing royal concoctions; the royals were either paranoid or decidedly sickly. At the time of research, there was talk of moving the pharmacy to new premises; we hope it's only talk.

## Gasparini & Porcelana

Close to the Throne Room, the Salón de Gasparini (Gasparini Room) has an exquisite stucco ceiling and walls resplendent with embroidered silks. The aesthetic may be different in the Sala de Porcelana (Porcelain Room), but the aura of extravagance continues with myriad pieces from the one-time Retiro porcelain factory screwed into the walls.

### DON'T MISS

→ Farmacia Real
→ Plaza de la Armería
→ Salón del Trono
→ Gasparini & Porcelana
→ Comedor de Gala
→ Jardines de Sabatini

### PRACTICALITIES

→ Map p232, D5
→ ☎91 454 88 00
→ www.patrimonio nacional.es
→ Calle de Bailén
→ adult/concession €11/6, guide/audioguide €4/3, EU citizens free last 2hr Mon-Thu
→ ⊙10am-8pm Apr-Sep, to 6pm Oct-Mar
→ Ⓜ Ópera

## PALACE VIEWS

Some of the best views of the Palacio Real are through the trees from the northern end of the Plaza de Oriente, but less well known are the superlative views from the western side, the lush ornamental gardens of Campo del Moro.

## PART-TIME PALACE

The Palacio Real is occasionally closed for state ceremonies and official receptions (the only way you'll know is if you turn up and it's closed), but the present king is rarely in residence – he and his family live in the smaller, less ostentatious Palacio de la Zarzuela just outside Madrid.

## History's Tale

A little understanding of the Palacio Real's genesis and subsequent development will enhance your appreciation of what you see. The Italian architect Filippo Juvara (1678–1736), who had made his name building the Basílica di Superga and the Palazzo di Stupinigi in Turin, was called in to try and fulfil Felipe V's dream, but, like Felipe, he died without bringing the project to fruition. Upon Juvara's death, another Italian, Giovanni Battista Sacchetti, took over, finishing the job in 1764.

## Jardines de Sabatini

The French-inspired **Jardines de Sabatini** (Map p232; ⊙9am-10pm May-Sep, to 9pm Oct-Apr; M Ópera; FREE) lie along the northern flank of the Palacio Real. They were laid out in the 1930s to replace the royal stables that once stood on the site. These quite formal gardens with fountains and small labyrinths offer a fine alternative view of the palace's northern facade.

## Plaza de la Armería

The Plaza de la Armería (Plaza de Armas; Plaza of the Armoury) courtyard puts the sheer scale of the palace into perspective, and it's from here that Madrid's cathedral (Catedral de Nuestra Señora de la Almudena) takes on its most pleasing aspect. The colourful changing of the guard in full parade dress takes place at noon on the first Wednesday of every month (except August and September) between the palace and the cathedral, with a less extravagant changing of the guard inside the palace compound at the Puerta del Príncipe every Wednesday from 11am to 2pm.

The plaza also provides access to the **Armería Real** (Royal Armoury; Map p232; www.patrimonionacional. es; Plaza de la Armería, Palacio Real; admission incl with Palacio Real entry; ⊙10am-8pm Apr-Sep, to 6pm Oct-Mar), a hoard of weapons and striking suits of armour, mostly dating from the 16th and 17th centuries.

## Salón del Trono

From the northern end of the Plaza de la Armería, the main stairway, a grand statement of imperial power, leads to the royal apartments and eventually to the Salón del Trono (Throne Room). The room is nauseatingly lavish with its crimson-velvet wall coverings complemented by a ceiling painted by the dramatic Venetian baroque master, Tiepolo, who was a favourite of Carlos III.

# ◉ SIGHTS

As you'd expect from the former centrepiece of old Madrid, there are numerous highlights in this corner of the city: the royal palace, ornamental gardens (Jardines de Sabatini and the Campo del Moro), lavish convents, and storied plazas (Plaza Mayor, Plaza de la Villa, even Plaza de la Puerta del Sol) where the architecture is as beguiling as the street life that animates it. And in the absence of a cathedral worthy of the name, it's the smaller churches, including two of Madrid's oldest, that provide the focal point for those seeking the city's religious past.

**PLAZA MAYOR**                                    SQUARE
See p52.

**PALACIO REAL**                                    PALACE
See p53.

**PLAZA DE LA VILLA**                              SQUARE
Map p232 (MÓpera) The intimate Plaza de la Villa is one of Madrid's prettiest. Enclosed on three sides by wonderfully preserved examples of 17th-century *barroco madrileño* (Madrid-style baroque architecture – a pleasing amalgam of brick, exposed stone and wrought iron), it was the permanent seat of Madrid's city government from the Middle Ages until recent years, when Madrid's city council relocated to the grand Palacio de Cibeles on Plaza de la Cibeles (p112).

On the western side of the square is the 17th-century **former town hall**, in Habsburg-style baroque with Herrerian slate-tile spires. On the opposite side of the square is the Gothic **Casa de los Lujanes**, whose brickwork tower is said to have been 'home' to the imprisoned French monarch François I after his capture in the Battle of Pavia (1525). Legend has it that as the star prisoner was paraded down Calle Mayor, locals are said to have been more impressed by the splendidly attired Frenchman than they were by his more drab captor, the Spanish Habsburg emperor Carlos I, much to the chagrin of the latter. The plateresque (15th- and 16th-century Spanish baroque) **Casa de Cisneros**, built in 1537 with later Renaissance alterations, also catches the eye.

**PLAZA DE ORIENTE**                               SQUARE
Map p232 (MÓpera) A royal palace that once had aspirations to be the Spanish Versailles. Sophisticated cafes watched over by apartments that cost the equivalent of a royal salary. The Teatro Real (p65), Madrid's opera house and one of Spain's temples to high culture. Some of the finest sunset views in Madrid... Welcome to Plaza de Oriente, a living, breathing monument to imperial Madrid.

At the centre of the plaza, which the palace overlooks, is an equestrian **statue of Felipe IV**. Designed by Velázquez, it's the perfect place to take it all in, with marvellous views wherever you look. If you're wondering how a heavy bronze statue of a rider and his horse rearing up can actually maintain that stance, the answer is simple: the hind legs are solid, while the front ones are hollow. That idea was Galileo Galilei's. Nearby are some 20 marble statues, mostly of ancient monarchs. Local legend has it that these ageing royals get down off their pedestals at night to stretch their legs when no-one's looking.

The adjacent **Jardines Cabo Naval** are a great place to watch the sunset.

**PALACIO GAVIRIA**                               MUSEUM
Map p232 (☑902 044226; Calle del Arenal 9; adult/child €12/free; ☺10am-8pm Sun-Thu, to 9pm Fri & Sat; MSol) Until recently this 19th-century Italianate palace was a nightclub. It has since been artfully converted to a dynamic artistic space, with major temporary art exhibitions that have included an Escher retrospective and the works of Alphonse Mucha. Coupled with high-quality exhibitions is a soaring Renaissance palace with extraordinary ceiling frescoes. Put all of this together and you've one of the more exciting additions to Madrid's artistic portfolio.

**CAMPO DEL MORO**                               GARDENS
Map p232 (☑91 454 88 00; Paseo de la Virgen del Puerto; ☺10am-6pm Apr-Sep, to 6pm Oct-Mar; MPríncipe Pío) FREE These gardens beneath the Palacio Real were designed to mimic the gardens surrounding the palace at Versailles; nowhere is this more in evidence than along the east–west **Pradera**, a lush lawn with the Palacio Real as its backdrop. The gardens' centrepiece, which stands halfway along the Pradera, is the elegant **Fuente de las Conchas** (Fountain of the

Shells), designed by Ventura Rodríguez, the Goya of Madrid's 18th-century architecture scene. The only entrance is from Paseo de la Virgen del Puerto.

From the park you can also gain an appreciation of Madrid in its earliest days – it was from here, in what would become known as Campo del Moro (Moor's Field), that an Almoravid army laid siege to the city in 1110. The troops occupied all but the fortress (where the Palacio Real now stands), but the Christian garrison held on until the Almoravid fury abated and their forces retired south.

The 20 hectares of gardens that now adorn the site were first laid in the 18th century, with major overhauls in 1844 and 1890.

### TEATRO REAL                    NOTABLE BUILDING
Map p232 (☑91 516 06 96; www.teatro-real.com; Plaza de Oriente; guided tour €8-30, audioguide €7; ◷guided visits 10.30am-1pm, self-guided visits 9.30am-3.30pm, last entry 2.30pm; MÓpera) Backing onto Plaza de Oriente, Madrid's signature opera house took on its present neoclassical form in 1997 and, viewed from Plaza de Isabel II, it's a fine addition to the central Madrid cityscape; in Plaza de Oriente, however, it's somewhat overshadowed by the splendour of its surrounds. The 1997 renovations combined the latest in theatre and acoustic technology with a remake of the most splendid of its 19th-century decor.

### CONVENTO DE LAS DESCALZAS REALES                    CONVENT
Map p232 (Convent of the Barefoot Royals; www.patrimonionacional.es; Plaza de las Descalzas 3; €6, incl Convento de la Encarnación €8; ◷10am-2pm & 4-6.30pm Tue-Sat, 10am-3pm Sun; MÓpera, Sol) The grim plateresque walls of the Convento de las Descalzas Reales offer no hint that behind the facade lies a sumptuous stronghold of the faith. The compulsory guided tour (in Spanish) leads you up a gaudily frescoed Renaissance stairway to the upper level of the cloister. The vault was painted by Claudio Coello, one of the most important artists of the Madrid School of the 17th century and whose works adorn San Lorenzo de El Escorial.

You then pass several of the convent's 33 chapels – a maximum of 33 Franciscan nuns is allowed to live here (perhaps because Christ is said to have been 33 when he died) as part of a closed order. These nuns follow in the tradition of the Descalzas Reales (Barefooted Royals), a group of illustrious

women who cloistered themselves when the convent was founded in the 16th century.

The first of these chapels contains a remarkable carved figure of a dead, reclining Christ, which is paraded in a Good Friday procession each year. At the end of the passage is the antechoir, then the choir stalls themselves. Buried here is Doña Juana, Carlos I's widowed daughter who, in a typical piece of 16th-century collusion between royalty and the Catholic Church, commandeered the palace and had it converted into a convent. A *Virgen la Dolorosa* by Pedro de la Mena is seated in one of the 33 oak stalls.

In the former sleeping quarters of the nuns are some extraordinary tapestries. Woven in the 17th century in Brussels, they include four based on drawings by Rubens. To produce works of this quality, four or five artisans could take up to a year to weave just 1 sq metre.

### IGLESIA DE SAN GINÉS                    CHURCH
Map p232 (Calle del Arenal 13; ◷8.45am-1pm & 6-9pm Mon-Sat, 9.45am-2pm & 6-9pm Sun; MSol, Ópera) FREE Due north of Plaza Mayor, San Ginés is one of Madrid's oldest churches: it has been here in one form or another since at least the 14th century. What you see today was built in 1645 but largely reconstructed after a fire in 1824. The church houses some fine paintings, including El Greco's *Expulsion of the Moneychangers from the Temple* (1614), which is beautifully displayed; the glass is just 6mm from the canvas to avoid reflections.

The church has stood at the centre of Madrid life for centuries. It is speculated that, prior to the arrival of the Christians in 1085, a Mozarabic community (Christians in Muslim territory) lived around the stream that later became Calle del Arenal and that their parish church stood on this site. Spain's premier playwright Lope de Vega was married here and novelist Francisco de Quevedo was baptised in its font.

### CONVENTO DE LA ENCARNACIÓN                    CONVENT
Map p232 (www.patrimonionacional.es; Plaza de la Encarnación 1; €6, incl Convento de las Descalzas Reales €8; ◷10am-2pm & 4-6.30pm Tue-Sat, 10am-3pm Sun; MÓpera) Founded by Empress Margarita de Austria, this 17th-century mansion built in the Madrid baroque style is still inhabited by nuns of the Augustine order. The large art collection dates mostly from the 17th century, and among the many

gold and silver reliquaries is one that contains the blood of San Pantaleón, which purportedly liquefies each year on 27 July. The convent sits on a pretty plaza close to the Palacio Real.

## PALACIO DEL DUQUE
## DE UCEDA                                ARCHITECTURE

Map p232 (Calle Mayor 79; ⓜÓpera) Just down the hill from Plaza de la Villa is the 18th-century baroque remake of the Palacio del Duque de Uceda. Now used as a military headquarters (the Capitanía General), it is a classic of the Madrid baroque architectural style and was designed by Juan Gómez de Mora in 1608. It's closed to the public.

## CONVENTO DEL
## CORPUS CRISTI                                CONVENT

Map p232 (Las Carboneras; ☑91 548 37 01; Plaza del Conde de Miranda; ⊙9.30am-1pm & 4-6.30pm; ⓜÓpera) FREE Architecturally nondescript but culturally curious, this church hides behind sober brickwork on the western end of a quiet square. A closed order of nuns occupies the convent building; when Mass is held, the nuns gather in a separate area at the rear of the church. They maintain a centuries-old tradition of making sweet biscuits that can be purchased from the entrance just off the square on Calle del Codo (p67).

## CATEDRAL DE NUESTRA
## SEÑORA DE LA ALMUDENA          CATHEDRAL

Map p232 (☑91 542 22 00; www.catedraldela almudena.es; Calle de Bailén; cathedral & crypt by donation, museum adult/child €6/4; ⊙9am-8.30pm Mon-Sat, museum 10am-2.30pm Mon-Sat; ⓜÓpera) Paris has Notre Dame and Rome has St Peter's Basilica. In fact, almost every European city of stature has its signature cathedral, a standout monument to a glorious Christian past. Not Madrid. Although the exterior of the Catedral de Nuestra Señora de la Almudena sits in harmony with the adjacent Palacio Real, Madrid's cathedral is cavernous and largely charmless within; its colourful, modern ceilings do little to make up for the lack of old-world gravitas that so distinguishes great cathedrals.

Carlos I first proposed building a cathedral here back in 1518, but construction didn't actually begin until 1879. It was finally finished in 1992 and its pristine, bright-white neo-Gothic interior holds no pride of place in the affections of *madrileños* (people from Madrid).

It's possible to climb to the cathedral's summit, which has fine views. En route you climb up through the cathedral's museum; follow the signs to the **Museo de la Catedral y Cúpula** (www.museocatedral.archimadrid.es), opposite Palacio Real.

Just around the corner in Calle Mayor, the low-lying **ruins of Santa María de la Almudena** are all that remain of Madrid's first church, which was built on the site of Mayrit's Great Mosque when the Christians arrived in the 11th century.

And just down the hill beneath the cathedral's southern wall on Calle Mayor is the neo-Romanesque **crypt**, with more than 400 columns, 20 chapels and fine stained-glass windows.

## MURALLA ÁRABE                              LANDMARK

Map p232 (Cuesta de la Vega; ⓜÓpera) Behind Catedral de Nuestra Señora de la Almudena's apse and down Cuesta de la Vega is a short stretch of the original 'Arab Wall', the city wall built by Madrid's early-medieval Muslim rulers. Some of it dates as far back as the 9th century, when the initial Muslim fort was raised. Other sections date from the 12th and 13th centuries, by which time the city had been taken by the Christians.

## PLAZA DE RAMALES                             SQUARE

Map p232 (ⓜÓpera) This pleasant little triangle of open space is not without historical intrigue. Joseph Bonaparte ordered the destruction of the Iglesia de San Juanito to open up a pocket of fresh air in the then-crowded streets. It is believed Velázquez was buried in the church; a small monument announces this as the last resting place of the master painter who died on 6 August 1660.

## IGLESIA DE SAN NICOLÁS
## DE LOS SERVITAS                              CHURCH

Map p232 (☑91 559 40 64; Plaza de San Nicolás 6; ⊙8am-1.30pm & 5.30-8.30pm Mon, 8-9.30am & 6.30-8.30pm Tue-Sat, 9.30am-2pm & 6.30-9pm Sun & holidays; ⓜÓpera) Tucked away up the hill from Calle Mayor, this intimate little church is Madrid's oldest surviving building of worship; it may have been built on the site of Muslim Mayrit's second mosque. The most striking feature is the restored 12th-century Mudéjar (a Moorish architectural style) bell tower; much of the remainder dates in part from the 15th century. The vaulting is late Gothic while the fine timber ceiling, which survived a 1936 fire, dates from about the same period.

## PLAZA DE ESPAÑA SQUARE

Map p232 (MPlaza de España) It's hard to know what to make of this curiously unprepossessing square. The square's centrepiece is a 1927 statue of Cervantes with, at the writer's feet, a bronze statue of his immortal characters Don Quijote and Sancho Panza. The 1953 **Edificio de España** (Spain Building) on the northeast side clearly sprang from the totalitarian recesses of Franco's imagination such is its resemblance to austere Soviet monumentalism. To the north stands the 35-storey **Torre de Madrid** (Madrid Tower).

There are plans afoot to beautify and otherwise overhaul the square in 2018 – don't be surprised if you find the errant knight facing a different direction next time you're here.

## BASÍLICA DE SAN MIGUEL CHURCH

Map p232 (☑91 548 40 11; www.bsmiguel.es; Calle de San Justo 4; ☺10am-1pm & 6-9pm Mon-Fri Jul–mid-Sep, 9.45am-1.15pm & 5.30-9.15pm Mon-Fri mid-May–Jun; MLa Latina, Sol) FREE Hidden away off Calle de Segovia, this basilica is something of a surprise. Its convex, late-baroque facade sits in harmony with the surrounding buildings of old Madrid. Among its fine features are statues representing the four virtues, and the reliefs of Justo and Pastor, the saints to whom the church was originally dedicated. The rococo and Italianate interior, completed by Italian architects in 1745, is another world altogether with gilded flourishes and dark, sombre domes.

## PALACIO DE SANTA CRUZ HISTORIC BUILDING

Map p232 (Plaza de la Provincia; MSol) Just off the southeastern corner of Plaza Mayor and dominating Plaza de Santa Cruz is this baroque edifice, which houses the **Ministerio de Asuntos Exteriores** (Ministry of Foreign Affairs) and hence can only be admired from the outside. A landmark with its grey slate spires, it was built in 1643 and initially served as the court prison.

## ✗ EATING

**Steer clear of the tourist traps, especially those that surround Plaza Mayor, and you'll eat well in these parts. Old taverns serving traditional local food abound, as do a catch-all of vegetarian, Mexican, Japanese and even a stunning** food court with a view. There's also the fabulous **Mercado de San Miguel and the world's oldest restaurant.**

## ★MERCADO DE SAN MIGUEL TAPAS €

Map p232 (☑91 542 49 36; www.mercadodesanmiguel.es; Plaza de San Miguel; tapas from €1.50; ☺10am-midnight Sun-Wed, to 2am Thu-Sat; MSol) This is one of Madrid's oldest and most beautiful markets, within early-20th-century glass walls and an inviting space strewn with tables. You can order tapas and sometimes more substantial plates at most of the counter-bars, and everything here (from caviar to chocolate) is as tempting as the market is alive. Put simply, it's one of our favourite experiences in Madrid.

All the stalls are outstanding, but you could begin with the fine fishy *pintxos* (Basque tapas) atop mini toasts at **La Casa de Bacalao** (Stalls 16–17), follow it up with some *jamón* or other cured meats at **Carrasco Guijuelo** (Stall 18), cheeses at Stalls 20–21, all manner of pickled goodies at Stall 22, or the gourmet tapas of **Lhardy** (Stalls 61–62). There are also plenty of places to buy wine, Asturian cider and the like; at Stall 24, The Sherry Corner (p62) has sherry tastings with tapas.

## ★CASA REVUELTA TAPAS €

Map p232 (☑91 366 33 32; Calle de Latoneros 3; tapas from €3; ☺10.30am-4pm & 7-11pm Tue-Sat, 10.30am-4pm Sun, closed Aug; MSol, La Latina) Casa Revuelta puts out some of Madrid's finest tapas of *bacalao* (cod) bar none – unlike elsewhere, *tajadas de bacalao* don't have bones in them and slide down the throat with the greatest of ease. Early on a Sunday afternoon, as the Rastro crowd gathers here, it's filled to the rafters. Other specialities include *torreznos* (bacon bits), *callos* (tripe), and *albóndigas* (meatballs).

## TAQUERÍA MI CIUDAD MEXICAN €

Map p232 (☑91 559 87 11; www.taqueriamiciudad.com; Calle de las Hileras 5; tacos €1.50; ☺1.30-4.30pm & 8pm-1.30am; MÓpera) This family-run Mexican bar has something of a cult following, serving up bite-sized tacos (the *cochinita pibil* is our favourite) washed down by fabulous margaritas (including those flavoured with tamarind). It's wildly popular on weekend nights. If you get the munchies between meals, try their tiny sister outlet around the corner.

## TAQUERÍA MI CIUDAD                MEXICAN €
Map p232 (☑608 621 096; www.taqueriami
ciudad.com; Calle de las Fuentes 11; tacos €1.50;
⊗11am-1.30am; ⓂÓpera) An outlet of the
hugely popular Taquería Mi Ciudad around
the corner. This place stays open later and
doesn't close in the afternoon.

## HORNO DE SANTIGUESA            BAKERY €
Map p232 (☑91 559 62 14; Calle Mayor 73; pastries
from €2.50; ⊗8am-9pm Mon-Fri, to 9.30pm Sat,
9am-9pm Sun; ⓂÓpera) Everything's a speciality at this wonderful old *pastelería,* from
cakes and pastries to bite-sized sweets and
Christmas *turrón* (a nougat-like sweet).

## MUSEO DEL PAN
## GALLEGO                     GALICIAN, BAKERY €
Map p232 (☑91 542 51 60; www.museodelpangall
ego.com; Plaza Herradores 9; salty pastries from
€13/kilo; ⊗8.30am-3pm Mon, 8.30am-3pm &
5-9pm Tue-Fri, 8.30am-3.30pm & 5-9pm Sat,
8.30am-3pm Sun; ⓂÓpera) Part bakery, part
temple to a handful of Galician staples, this
simple bakery with a wood-fired oven is
one of Madrid's oldest, dating back to the
18th century. It's an institution for its mix
of salty and sweet – *empanadas* (pastries)
filled with tuna/cod and even baby clams or
octopus, and *tarta de Santiago* (sweet Galician almond cake).

## LA CAMPANA                       SPANISH €
Map p232 (☑91 364 29 84; Calle de Botoneras
6; bocadillos from €2.90; ⊗9am-11pm Sun-Thu,
to midnight Fri & Sat; ⓂSol) This basic bar is
hugely popular for its *bocadillos de calamares* (filled rolls stuffed with deep-fried
calamari) – Madrid fast food at its greasy,
filling best.

## LA IDEAL                         SPANISH €
(☑91 365 72 78; Calle de Botoneras 4; bocadillos
from €2.90; ⊗9am-11pm Sun-Thu, to midnight Fri
& Sat; ⓂSol) Spanish bars don't come any
more basic than this, but it's the purveyor
of that enduring and wildly popular Madrid
tradition – the *bocadillo de calamares.* If
it's closed, which is rare, plenty of bars elsewhere around the plaza offer the same deal.

## MUSEO DEL JAMÓN                  SPANISH €
Map p232 (☑91 531 45 50; www.museodeljamon.
com; Calle Mayor 7; raciones from €3; ⊗8am-
midnight; ⓂSol) Famous for having appeared
in Pedro Almodóvar's 1997 film *Carne
Trémula* (Live Flesh), and equally beloved
by first-time visitors to Spain for the sight

### ⓘ MERCADO DE SAN MIGUEL
The Mercado de San Miguel has become almost too popular for its own
good and, as a consequence, lunchtime and evenings can be uncomfort-
ably crowded. Although it's always
busy and snaffling a table or a bar stool
is invariably a game of chance, we
recommend coming for an early lunch
(from around 12.30pm), or a late lunch
or early dinner from 5pm to 7pm when
there's usually far more room to move.

of hundreds of hams hanging from the ceiling, Museo del Jamón is definitely a local
landmark. Prices for a *ración/bocadillo*
(large tapas serving/filled roll) start at €3/2
and can go much higher depending on the
quality of the *jamón.*

## CERVECERÍA 100 MONTADITOS      SPANISH €
Map p232 (www.spain.100montaditos.com; Calle
Mayor 22; montaditos €1-3; ⊗noon-midnight;
ⓂSol) This bar with outlets all across the
city serves up no fewer than 100 different varieties of mini-*bocadillos* that span
the full range of Spanish staples, such as
chorizo, *jamón,* tortilla, a variety of cheeses
and seafood, in more combinations than
you could imagine. You order at the counter
and your name is called in no time.

## ★GOURMET EXPERIENCE          FOOD HALL €€
Map p232 (www.elcorteingles.es; 9th fl, Plaza del
Callao 2; mains €8-20; ⊗10am-10pm; ⓂCallao)
Ride the elevator up to the 9th floor of the
El Corte Inglés department store for one of
downtown Madrid's best eating experiences.
The food is excellent, with everything from
top-notch tapas or sushi to gourmet hamburgers, and the views fabulous, especially
those that look over Plaza del Callao and
down Gran Vía.

## EL PATO MUDO                    SPANISH €€
Map p232 (☑91 559 48 40; elpatomudo@hotmail.
es; Calle Costanilla de los Ángeles 8; mains €13-
24; ⊗1-4pm & 8-11.30pm Wed-Sun; ⓂÓpera) El
Pato Mudo isn't the most famous paella restaurant in Madrid, but it's known to locals
for its variety of outstanding rice dishes at
reasonable prices. Specialities include black
rice with squid ink, soupy rice, authentic
*paella valenciana* and shellfish paella.
Served directly from the pan for two or more
people, they go well with the local wines.

### TABERNA DEL ALABARDERO
SPANISH €€

Map p232 (☑91 547 25 77; www.grupolezama.es; Calle de Felipe V 6; bar raciones €6-26, restaurant mains €20-28; ⊙noon-1am; ⓂÓpera) This fine old Madrid *taberna* (tavern) is famous for its croquettes, fine *jamón, montaditos de jamón* (small rolls of cured ham) and *montaditos de bonito* (small rolls of cured tuna) in the bar, while out the back the more classic cuisine includes *rabo de toro estofado* (bull's tail, served with honey, cinnamon, mashed potato and pastry with herbs).

Madrid's notoriously fussy diners generally accept that the prices here are worth it. The sister restaurant around the corner in Plaza de Oriente, La Mar del Alabardero, is renowned for its high-quality seafood and rice dishes.

### TABERNA LA BOLA
SPANISH €€

Map p232 (☑91 547 69 30; www.labola.es; Calle de la Bola 5; mains €8-25; ⊙1.30-4.30pm & 8.30-11pm Mon-Sat, 1.30-4.30pm Sun, closed Aug; ⓂSanto Domingo) Going strong since 1870 and run by the sixth generation of the Verdasco family, Taberna La Bola is a much-loved bastion of traditional Madrid cuisine. If you're going to try *cocido a la madrileña* (meat-and-chickpea stew; €21) while in Madrid, this is a good place to do so. It's busy and noisy and very Madrid.

### LA CRUZADA
SPANISH €€

Map p232 (☑658 320 577; www.tabernalacruzada. es; Calle de la Amnistía 8; mains €11-20; ⊙noon-5pm Sun-Tue, to midnight Wed-Sat; ⓂÓpera) Claiming to be the oldest *taberna* in Madrid (there's been a tavern here since 1827), and with a cup on display that was used by Alfonso XII when he popped by for drink, this place is all about tradition. High-quality tapas revolve around Spanish staples, while it also does a fine *cocido a la madrileña*. Champagne is its drink of choice.

### SUBLIME TOKYO
JAPANESE €€

Map p232 (☑91 137 63 63; www.facebook.com/sublimetokyoes; Cuesta de Santo Domingo 24; mains €7-18; ⊙1.30-4.30pm Tue-Sun & 8pm-midnight Tue-Thu, 8.30pm-12.30am Fri & Sat, 8-11pm Sun; ⓂSanto Domingo) In Japan, Sublime Tokyo is a chain with nearly 300 locations, but this cosy restaurant is its first overseas eatery. Specialising in authentic Tokyo cuisine such as *okonomiyaki* – a type of omelette made with cabbage, eggs and pork or shellfish – it's not your typical sushi restaurant.

### CASA JACINTO
SPANISH €€

Map p232 (☑91 542 67 25; www.restaurantecasajacinto.com; Calle del Reloj 20; mains €12-19; ⊙1-4.30pm & 8.30pm-midnight Tue-Sat, 1-4.30pm Sun; ⓂPlaza de España) A favourite of local politicians due to its location just outside the Senate building, Casa Jacinto is famous for its meat, fish of the day and wide selection of wines. You can try the *setas con almejas* (succulent mushrooms with clams) or stop by on weekends for *cocido a la madrileña,* a traditional thick chickpea stew with meat and vegetables.

---

### BETWEEN MEALS & SPANISH FAST FOOD

If you're still adjusting to Spanish restaurant hours and need a meal in between, there are a number of options in the centre.

When it comes to local fast food, one of the lesser-known culinary specialities of Madrid is a *bocadillo de calamares* (a small baguette-style roll filled to bursting with deep-fried calamari). You'll find them in many bars in the streets surrounding Plaza Mayor and neighbouring bars along Calle de Botoneras off Plaza Mayor's southeastern corner. At around €2.70, it's the perfect street snack.

**Mercado de San Miguel** (p58) All-day tapas

**Taquería Mi Ciudad** (p59) Budget tacos

**La Campana** (p59) *Bocadillos de calamares*

**La Ideal** (p59) *Bocadillos de calamares*

**Viandas de Salamanca** (Map p238; ☑91 521 27 74; www.viandasdesalamanca.es; Calle del Carmen 27; bocadillos €4; ⊙10.30am-10.30pm Sun-Thu, to 11pm Fri & Sat; ⓂCallao, Sol) *Jamón* rolls

**Cervecería 100 Montaditos** (p59) Tiny *bocadillos*

## EL ANCIANO REY DE LOS VINOS
SPANISH €€

Map p232 (☎91 559 53 32; www.elancianoreyde
losvinos.es; Calle de Bailén 19; mains €9-20;
⊗8.30am-midnight Wed-Mon; Ⓜ Sol) With
outdoor seating that gives you an unbeat-
able view of the cathedral, this bar has
been serving its unique house wine since it
opened in 1909. Food specialities include *cazuela del anciano* (shellfish stew featuring
octopus and prawns) and *regalitos de toro*
(crispy puff pastry stuffed with oxtail and
red peppers).

## CASA PACO
SPANISH €€

Map p232 (☎91 366 31 66; www.casapaco1933.
es; Plaza de Puerta Cerrada 11; mains €12-20; ⊗1-
4pm & 8pm-midnight Tue-Sat, 1-4pm Sun; Ⓜ La
Latina, Sol) The gaily painted exterior of this
old Madrid tavern, which opened in 1933,
is hard to miss and the food is even harder
to resist, especially in winter when the local Madrid specialities – *callos, cocido* and
succulent steaks – come into their own. The
bar area, its walls lined with celebrity visitors past and present, is also a good place
for tapas or a wine.

## LA PAELLA REAL
SPANISH €€

Map p232 (☎91 542 09 42; www.lapaellareal.es;
Calle de Arrieta 2; mains €15-32, 3-course set menu
€30; ⊗1-4pm & 7.30-10pm Mon-Sat, 1-4pm Sun;
Ⓜ Ópera) Finding a good paella in Madrid
can be surprisingly difficult, but it's almost
guaranteed at this august place opposite
the Teatro Real. *Paella de marisco* (seafood
paella), *paella de bogavante* (lobster paella)
and *arroz negro* (black rice cooked in squid
ink) are the house specialities, but there are
plenty of rice dishes to choose from. You'll
need a minimum of two for an order.

## RESTAURANTE LOS GALAYOS
SPANISH €€

Map p232 (☎91 366 30 28; www.losgalayos.
net; Calle de Botoneros 5; mains €13-25; ⊗1pm-
12.30am; Ⓜ Sol) Most of the restaurants surrounding Plaza Mayor are tourist traps,
but Los Galayos, a few steps off the plaza's
southeastern corner and open for a mere
120 years, is an exception. Renowned for
its *cocido* (€18.75; lunch only, in the cooler
months), it's a good place to sample traditional local cooking from around Spain.

There are two *terrazas* (open-air areas
for restaurants and bars), a quieter one on
Calle de Botoneras, the other on Plaza May-
or. Inside check out the wooden bar, which
was handcrafted in the 17th century.

## CASA CIRIACO
SPANISH €€

Map p232 (☎91 548 06 20; Calle Mayor 84; mains
€14-25, set menus €15-30; ⊗1-4pm & 8pm-
midnight Thu-Tue, closed Aug; ⊛ℳ; Ⓜ Ópera)
One of the *grande dames* of the Madrid
restaurant scene, Casa Ciriaco has wit-
nessed attempted assassinations (of King
Alfonso XIII in 1906) and was immortalised by the Spanish writer Valle-Inclán
who set part of his novel *Luces de Bohe-
mia* here. Its legend made, it now puts all
its energies into fine *madrileño* cooking.
Offerings range from seafood and robust
meat dishes such as roast suckling pig to
*cocido a la madrileña*.

## ALGARABÍA
SPANISH €€

Map p232 (☎91 542 41 31; www.restaurante
algarabia.com; Calle de la Unión 8; mains €11-18, set
menu €18-36; ⊗2-4pm & 9.30-11.30pm Mon-Fri,
9.30-11.30pm Sat, closed Aug; ⊛; Ⓜ Ópera) You
know the wines of La Rioja, but the food of
this northern Spanish region is also filled
with flavour. The La Rioja cuisine here is all
about home cooking, and choosing the *menú
de degustación* is a great way to get an overview of the regional specialities. The *croquetas* (croquettes) have a loyal following.

## YERBABUENA
VEGETARIAN €€

Map p232 (☎91 548 08 11; www.yerbabuena.
ws; Calle de los Bordadores 3; mains €10-13.50;
⊗1-4.30pm & 8pm-midnight; ⊘; Ⓜ Sol, Ópera)
Cheerful bright colours, a full range of vegetarian staples (soya-bean burgers, biologi-
cal rice and homemade yoghurt) and plenty
of creatively conceived salads add up to one
of central Madrid's best restaurants for vegetarians and vegans.

## EL BISTRO DE LA CENTRAL
BISTRO €€

Map p232 (☎91 790 99 30; www.lacentral.com;
Postigo de San Martín 8; mains €11-16; ⊗9am-
midnight Mon-Wed, to 1am Thu & Fri, 9.30am-1am
Sat, 9.30am-midnight Sun; Ⓜ Callao) Housed on
the ground floor of one of Madrid's coolest
bookstores, this highly recommended cafe-
bistro serves up an excellent three-course
lunch menu (€14) from Monday to Friday.
The desserts (which include Ferrero Rocher
brownies) are very hard to resist. It was
closed for renovations when we last visited.

## CASA MARÍA
SPANISH €€

Map p232 (☎91 559 10 07; www.casamariaplaza
mayor.com; Plaza Mayor 23; tapas from €2.90,
4/6 tapas from €12/19, mains €9-19; ⊗noon-
11pm; Ⓜ Sol) A rare exception to the generally

pricey and mediocre options that surround Plaza Mayor, Casa María combines professional service and a menu that effortlessly spans the modern and traditional. There's something for most tastes, with carefully chosen tapas, lunchtime stews (such as *cocido a la madrileña* for €19.90) and dishes such as sticky rice with lobster.

### LA MAR DEL ALABARDERO SEAFOOD €€

Map p232 (📞91 541 33 33; Plaza de Oriente 6; mains €14-26; ⊗1.30-4pm & 8.30-11pm; MÓpera) La Mar del Alabardero is renowned for its high-quality seafood and rice dishes. Try the *chipirones en su tinta* (squid in their own ink) or one of the seafood-rich rice dishes.

### ★RESTAURANTE SOBRINO DE BOTÍN CASTILIAN €€€

Map p232 (📞91 366 42 17; www.botin.es; Calle de los Cuchilleros 17; mains €18-27; ⊗1-4pm & 8pm-midnight; MLa Latina, Sol) It's not every day that you can eat in the oldest restaurant in the world (as recognised by the *Guinness Book of Records* – established in 1725). The secret of its staying power is fine *cochinillo asado* (roast suckling pig) and *cordero asado* (roast lamb) cooked in wood-fired ovens. Eating in the vaulted cellar is a treat.

Yes, it's filled with tourists. And yes, staff are keen to keep things ticking over and there's little chance to linger. But the novelty value is high and the food excellent.

The restaurant has also appeared in many novels about Madrid, most notably Ernest Hemingway's *The Sun Also Rises* and Frederick Forsyth's *Icon* and *The Cobra*. Much of this history is told in 'The Botín Experience' tours run by Insider's Madrid (p207), which include a six-course lunch or dinner.

### RESTAURANTE SANDÓ CONTEMPORARY SPANISH €€€

Map p232 (📞91 547 99 11; www.restaurantesando.es; Calle de Isabel la Católica 2; mains €16-28; menú de degustación €49; ⊗1-4pm & 8-11pm Tue-Sat; MSanto Domingo) Juan Mari Arzak, one of Spain's most famous chefs, has finally set up shop in Madrid just off Plaza de Santo Domingo. Bringing Basque innovation to bear upon local tradition, its cooking is assured with dishes like tuna chunks with ginger and hibiscus. If you can't decide, try the *menú de degustación* or head around the corner to the tapas bar.

## 🍷 DRINKING & NIGHTLIFE

**Plaza Mayor and Royal Madrid have a little bit of everything for you to make the most of the nightlife. Cafes, both cool and traditional, not to mention places to indulge your chocolate fantasies, are everywhere. Nightclubs are similarly plentiful, while corner bars fill in the gaps in between. In short, you're never far from a cool place to drink.**

### ★THE SHERRY CORNER WINE BAR

Map p232 (📞68 1007700; www.sherry-corner.com; Stall 24, Mercado de San Miguel, Plaza de San Miguel; ⊗10am-9pm; MSol) The Sherry Corner, inside the Mercado de San Miguel, has found an excellent way to give a crash course in sherry. For €30, you get six small glasses of top-quality sherry to taste, each of which is matched to a different tapa. Guiding you through the process is an audioguide available in eight languages.

### ★TEATRO JOY ESLAVA CLUB

Map p232 (Joy Madrid; 📞91 366 37 33; www.joy-eslava.com; Calle del Arenal 11; admission €12-15; ⊗11.30pm-6am; MSol) The only things guaranteed at this grand old Madrid dance club (housed in a 19th-century theatre) are a crowd and the fact that it'll be open (it claims to have operated every single day since 1981). The music and the crowd are a mixed bag, but queues are long and invariably include locals and tourists, and the occasional *famoso* (celebrity).

Every night's a little different but the weekend is all about the best that Madrid has to offer. There's even the sometime no-alcohol, no-smoking 'Joy Light' on Saturday evenings (5.30pm to 10pm) for teens aged between 14 and 17. Throw in live acts and cabaret-style performances on stage and it's a point of reference for Madrid's professional party crowd.

### ★CHOCOLATERÍA DE SAN GINÉS CAFE

Map p232 (📞91 365 65 46; www.chocolateriasangines.com; Pasadizo de San Ginés 5; ⊗24hr; MSol) One of the grand icons of the Madrid night, this *chocolate con churros* cafe sees a sprinkling of tourists throughout the day, but locals pack it out in their search for sustenance on their way home from a nightclub somewhere close to dawn. Only in Madrid...

## COFFEE & KICKS
COFFEE

Map p232 (🔊66 308 90 30; Calle de las Navas de Tolosa 6; ⏰9.30am-1.30pm & 3.30-7.30pm Mon-Fri, 10am-2pm & 4-8pm Sat & Sun; 📶; MCallao) Coffee & Kicks is the place for aficionados. You can get your flat white on or try one of the pastries while perching on a stool and flipping through a fashion magazine, or hook up to the wi-fi and stay awhile. The decor and furniture is minimal, with well-worn tile floors and long wooden bars instead of tables.

## BODEGAS RICLA
BAR

Map p232 (🔊91 365 20 69; Calle Cuchilleros 6; ⏰1-4pm & 7pm-midnight Wed-Sat & Mon, 1-4pm Sun; MTirso de Molina) Bodegas Ricla is so tiny you might be rubbing haunches with other customers as you sip your wine. For more than 100 years, it's been serving tasty authentic tapas and local vintages: red, white and pink wines, *cavas* and vermouth. Inside, little has changed in decades, with old-style terracotta barrels and pictures of bullfighters lining the walls.

## ANTICAFÉ
CAFE

Map p232 (www.anticafe.es; Calle de la Unión 2; ⏰5pm-2am Tue-Sun; MÓpera) Bohemian kitsch at its best is the prevailing theme here and it runs right through the decor and regular cultural events (poetry readings and concerts). As such, it won't be to everyone's taste, but we think it adds some much-needed variety to the downtown drinking scene.

Coffees, milkshakes and juices are as popular as the alcohol, although that predilection wears off as the night progresses and the cocktails take over.

Just don't mention our name. A rather unfortunate translation a few years back led them to think we don't like them. We do, we really do.

## CAFE DE ORIENTE
CAFE

Map p232 (🔊91 541 39 74; Plaza de Oriente 2; ⏰8.30am-1.30am Mon-Thu, 9am-2.30am Fri & Sat, 9am-1.30am Sun; MÓpera) The outdoor tables of this distinguished old cafe are among the most sought-after in central Madrid, providing as they do a front-row seat for the beautiful Plaza de Oriente, with the Palacio Real as a backdrop. The building itself was once part of a long-gone, 17th-century convent and the interior feels a little like a set out of Mitteleuropa.

It's the perfect spot for a coffee when the weather's fine.

## EL CAFÉ DE LA OPERA
CAFE

Map p232 (🔊91 542 63 82; www.elcafedelaopera.com; Calle de Arrieta 6; ⏰8am-midnight; 📶; MÓpera) Opposite the Teatro Real, this classic before-performance cafe has one unusual requirement for some of its would-be waiters – they have to be able to sing opera. They break into song from around 9.30pm on Friday and Saturday evenings, when you'll have to fork out a minimum €45 for a meal – not bad value if you don't have tickets for the show across the road.

## CHOCOLATERÍA VALOR
CAFE

Map p232 (🔊915 22 92 88; www.chocolateriasvalor.es; Postigo de San Martín; ⏰8am-10.30pm Mon-Thu, to 1am Fri, 9am-1am Sat, 9am-10.30pm Sun; MCallao) It may be Madrid tradition to indulge in *chocolate con churros* around sunrise on your way home from a nightclub, but for those who prefer a more reasonable hour, this is one of the best *chocolaterías* in town. Our favourite chocolate variety among many has to be *cuatro sentidos de chocolate* (four senses of chocolate; €7.95).

## CAFÉ DEL REAL
BAR

Map p232 (🔊91 547 21 24; Plaza de Isabel II 2; ⏰8am-1am Mon-Thu, to 2.30am Fri, 9am-2.30am Sat, 10am-11.30pm Sun; MÓpera) A cafe and cocktail bar in equal parts, this intimate little place serves up creative coffees and a few cocktails (the mojitos are excellent) to the soundtrack of chill-out music. The best seats are upstairs, where the low ceilings, wooden beams and leather chairs make for a great place to pass an afternoon with friends.

## SALA MOROCCO
CLUB

Map p246 (🔊91 531 51 67; http://salamorocco.com; Calle del Marqués de Leganés 7; €10; ⏰midnight-6am Fri & Sat; MSanto Domingo, Noviciado) Owned by the zany Alaska, the standout musical personality of *la movida madrileña* (the Madrid scene), Morocco has decor that's so kitsch it's cool, and a mix of musical styles that never strays too far from 1980s Spanish and international tunes, with electronica another recurring theme. The bouncers have been known to show a bit of attitude.

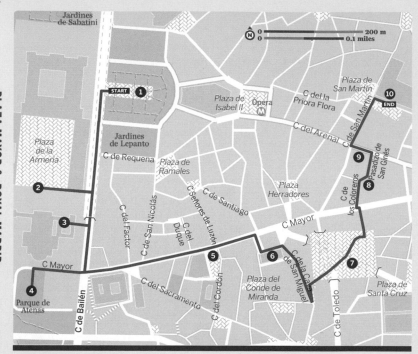

# Walking Tour
## Old Madrid

**START** PLAZA DE ORIENTE
**END** CONVENTO DE LAS DESCALZAS REALES
**LENGTH** 2KM; TWO HOURS

This walk takes you past the iconic architecture of imperial Madrid and into the heart of the modern city.

Begin in **1 Plaza de Oriente** (p55), a splendid arc of greenery and graceful architecture that could be Madrid's most agreeable plaza. You'll find yourself surrounded by gardens, the Palacio Real and the Teatro Real, peopled by an ever-changing cast of *madrileños* at play. Overlooking the plaza, **2 Palacio Real** (p53) was Spain's seat of royal power for centuries. Almost next door is **3 Catedral de Nuestra Señora de la Almudena** (p57); it may lack the solemnity of other Spanish cathedrals, but it's a beautiful part of the skyline.

From the cathedral, drop down to the **4 Muralla Árabe** (p57), a short stretch of the original 'Arab Wall', then climb gently up Calle Mayor, pausing to admire the last remaining ruins of Madrid's first cathedral, Santa María de la Almudena, then on to **5 Plaza de la Villa** (p55), a cosy square surrounded on three sides by some of the best examples of Madrid baroque architecture. A little further up the hill and just off Calle Mayor, **6 Mercado de San Miguel** (p58), one of Madrid's oldest markets, has become one of the coolest places to eat and mingle with locals in downtown Madrid.

Head down the hill along Cava de San Miguel, then climb up through the Arco de Cuchilleros to **7 Plaza Mayor** (p52), one of Spain's grandest and most beautiful plazas. Down a narrow lane north of the plaza, **8 Chocolatería de San Ginés** (p62) is justifiably famous for its *chocolate con churros*, the ideal Madrid indulgence at any hour of the day. Almost next door, there's the pleasing brick-and-stone **9 Iglesia de San Ginés** (p56), one of the longest-standing relics of Christian Madrid.

A short climb to the north, the **10 Convento de las Descalzas Reales** (p56) is an austere convent with an extraordinarily rich interior. In the heart of downtown Madrid, it's a great place to finish up.

# ⭐ ENTERTAINMENT

### LAS TABLAS                                    FLAMENCO
Map p232 (📞91 542 05 20; www.lastablasmadrid.com; Plaza de España 9; admission incl drink from €29; ⊙shows 8pm & 10pm; Ⓜ️Plaza de España) Las Tablas has a reputation for quality flamenco and reasonable prices; it's among the best choices in town. Most nights you'll see a classic flamenco show, with plenty of throaty singing and soul-baring dancing. Antonia Moya and Marisol Navarro, leading lights in the flamenco world, are regular performers here.

### LA COQUETTE BLUES                       LIVE MUSIC
Map p232 (📞91 530 80 95; Calle de las Hileras 14; ⊙8pm-3am Tue-Thu, to 3.30am Fri & Sat, 7pm-3am Sun; Ⓜ️Ópera) Madrid's best blues bar has been around since the 1980s and its 8pm Sunday jam session is legendary. Live acts perform Tuesday to Thursday at 10.30pm and the atmosphere is very cool at any time.

### TORRES BERMEJAS                           FLAMENCO
Map p232 (📞91 532 33 22; www.torresbermejas.com; Calle de los Mesoneros Romanos 11; admission incl drink from €35; ⊙shows 7pm & 9pm; Ⓜ️Callao) For decades this was the Madrid stage for flamenco legend Camarón de la Isla, and after a drop in quality for a few years, it's once again a good place to see flamenco. The atmosphere is aided by the extravagantly tiled interior.

### CAFÉ BERLIN                                       JAZZ
Map p232 (📞91 559 74 29; www.berlincafe.es; Costanilla de los Ángeles 20; €5-20; ⊙9pm-3am Tue-Thu, to 5am Fri & Sat; Ⓜ️Santo Domingo) El Berlín has been something of a Madrid jazz stalwart since the 1950s, although a makeover has brought flamenco (Wednesday is a flamenco jam session), R&B, soul, funk and fusion into the mix. Headline acts play at 11pm, although check the website as some can begin as early as 9pm.

### LAS CARBONERAS                            FLAMENCO
Map p232 (📞91 542 86 77; www.tablaolascarboneras.com; Plaza del Conde de Miranda 1; show incl drink/meal €35/70; ⊙shows 8.30pm & 10.30pm Mon-Thu, 8.30pm & 11pm Fri & Sat; Ⓜ️Ópera, Sol, La Latina) Like most of the *tablaos* (flamenco venues) around town, this place sees far more tourists than locals, but the quality is nonetheless excellent. It's not the place for gritty, soul-moving spontaneity, but it's still an excellent introduction

and one of the few places that flamenco aficionados seem to have no complaints about.

### CAFÉ DE CHINITAS                          FLAMENCO
Map p232 (📞91 547 15 02; www.chinitas.com; Calle de Torija 7; admission incl drink/meal €36/55; ⊙shows 8.15pm & 10.30pm Mon-Sat; Ⓜ️Santo Domingo) One of the most distinguished *tablaos* in Madrid, drawing in everyone from the Spanish royal family to Bill Clinton, Café de Chinitas has an elegant setting and top-notch performers. It may attract loads of tourists, but its authentic flamenco also gives it top marks. Reservations are highly recommended.

### TEATRO REAL                                     OPERA
(📞902 244848; www.teatro-real.com; Plaza de Oriente; Ⓜ️Ópera) After spending over €100 million on a long rebuilding project, the Teatro Real is as technologically advanced as any venue in Europe, and is the city's grandest stage for elaborate operas, ballets and classical music. The cheapest seats are so far away you'll need a telescope, although the sound quality is consistent throughout.

### CINESA CAPITOL                                CINEMA
Map p232 (📞902 333231; www.cinesa.es/Cines/Capitol; Gran Vía 41; Ⓜ️Callao) One of the stalwarts of the Madrid cinema scene where you can expect Hollywood more than art house.

# 🛍️ SHOPPING

**The shopping around Plaza Mayor and Royal Madrid is generally excellent. It's at its best in the small traditional shops that haven't changed in a century, but there are also fabulous food stores, fine bookshops, respected repositories of flamenco finery and music, small weekly flea markets and large department stores. You can even buy freshly baked goodies from the local nuns.**

### ⭐ANTIGUA CASA TALAVERA            CERAMICS
Map p232 (📞91 547 34 17; www.antiguacasatalavera.com; Calle de Isabel la Católica 2; ⊙10am-1.30pm & 5-8pm Mon-Fri, 10am-1.30pm Sat; Ⓜ️Santo Domingo) The extraordinary tiled facade of this wonderful old shop conceals an Aladdin's cave of ceramics from all over Spain. This is not the mass-produced stuff aimed at a tourist market, but instead comes from the small family potters of Andalucía and Toledo, ranging from the decorative

(tiles) to the useful (plates, jugs and other kitchen items). The elderly couple who run the place are delightful.

## ★EL ARCO ARTESANÍA ARTS & CRAFTS

Map p232 (☑91 365 26 80; www.artesaniaelarco. com; Plaza Mayor 9; ☺11am-10pm; ⓂSol, La Latina) This original shop in the southwestern corner of Plaza Mayor sells an outstanding array of homemade designer souvenirs, from stone, ceramic and glass work to jewellery and home fittings. The papier-mâché figures are gorgeous, but there's so much else here to turn your head. It sometimes closes earlier in the depths of winter.

## MATY FLAMENCO

Map p232 (☑91 531 32 91; www.maty.es; Calle del Maestro Victoria 2; ☺10am-1.45pm & 4.30-8pm Mon-Fri, 10am-2pm & 4.30-8pm Sat, 11am-2.30pm & 4.30-8pm 1st Sun of month; ⓂSol) Wandering around central Madrid, it's easy to imagine that flamenco outfits have been reduced to imitation dresses sold as souvenirs to tourists. That's why places like Maty matter. Here you'll find dresses, shoes and all the accessories that go with the genre, with sizes for children and adults. These are the real deal, with prices to match, but they make brilliant gifts.

## CASA HERNANZ SHOES

Map p232 (☑91 366 54 50; www.alpargateriaher nanz.com; Calle de Toledo 18; ☺9am-1.30pm & 4.30-8pm Mon-Fri, 10am-2pm Sat; ⓂLa Latina, Sol) Comfy, rope-soled *alpargatas* (espadrilles), Spain's traditional summer footwear, are worn by everyone from the king of Spain down. You can buy your own pair at this humble workshop, which has been hand-making the shoes for five generations; you can even get them made to order. Prices range from €6 to €40 and queues form whenever the weather starts to warm up.

## ATLÉTICO DE MADRID STORE SPORTS & OUTDOORS

Map p232 (☑902 260403; www.en.atletico demadrid.com/shop; Gran Vía 47; ☺10am-9.30pm Mon-Thu, to 10pm Fri & Sat, 11am-9pm Sun; ⓂSanto Domingo) Atlético de Madrid has something of a cult following in the city and has enjoyed considerable footballing success in recent years. Its downtown store has all the club's merchandise. In theory you can also buy tickets to games here, but most matches are sold out before you'll get a chance.

## DESPERATE LITERATURE BOOKS

Map p232 (☑91 188 80 89; www.desperateliter ature.com; Calle de Campomanes 13; ☺10.30am-2.30pm & 5-10.30pm Sun-Fri, 10.30am-10.30pm Sat; ⓂSanto Domingo) One of Madrid's best international bookshops, Desperate Literature sells mostly English books, with some in Spanish, French and other languages. Fiction is their main focus, but you'll find plenty of other sections to turn your head, including a children's corner.

## ASÍ TOYS

Map p232 (☑91 521 97 55; www.tiendas-asi.com; Calle del Arenal 20; ☺10am-8.30pm Mon-Sat, noon-3.30pm & 4.30-8pm Sun; ⓂÓpera) Beautifully crafted baby dolls make a lovely gift or souvenir of your little one's visit to the city. These are the real deal, not mass-produced, and there are some fine baby's outfits to go with them.

## LA MADRILEÑA FOOD

Map p232 (☑91 522 34 36; www.fiambresla madrilena.com; Calle del Arenal 18; ☺9.30am-2pm & 5.30-8.30pm Mon-Fri, 10am-2pm Sat; ⓂSol) La Madrileña has been serving its customers ham, cured meats and sausages since 1909. Its white sausages are perfect for the griddle, or you can try the *sobrasada* – a pâté made from ground pork and paprika. It's delectable spread on a piece of baguette. Other specialities are the *conservas* – high-quality, artisan fish, legumes and vegetables in tins or jars.

## TALLER PUNTERA FASHION & ACCESSORIES

Map p232 (☑91 364 29 26; www.puntera.com; Plaza Conde de Barajas 4; ☺10am-2.30pm & 4-8.30pm Mon-Sat; ⓂTirso de Molina) If you're looking for high-quality gifts to take back home, Taller Puntera has leather goods of all kinds. From notebooks to briefcases, backpacks and wallets, there's something for every taste and budget. The leather is cured with an environmentally-friendly vegetable tanning process, and all products are handmade in Spain – many of them in the shop itself.

## SOMBRERERÍA MEDRANO FASHION & ACCESSORIES

Map p232 (☑91 366 42 34; www.sombrereria medrano.com; Calle Imperial 12; ☺10am-2.30pm & 4.30-8pm Mon-Fri, 10am-2pm Sat; ⓂSol) They've been making hats at this place since 1832, and while concessions have been made to modern fashions, the look here is reassuringly a classic one. It's a marvellous old shop-workshop where the quality is unimpeachable. It does hats and gloves for men, women and children.

### ARTELEMA
ARTS, SOUVENIRS

Map p232 (☑91 559 78 17; www.artelema.com; Calle Mayor 74; ☺10.30am-2pm & 5-8pm Mon-Fri, 10.30am-2pm Sat; ⓂÓpera) High-quality prints and old photos of Madrid dominate this quiet store just down the hill from Plaza de la Villa. Old Madrid maps, bronze sculptures, etchings, pens and other classy gifts and wall hangings are also for sale.

### CODO 3
JEWELLERY

Map p232 (☑91 548 09 48; www.codo3.com; Calle del Codo 3; ☺11am-2pm & 5-8pm Tue-Sun; ⓂÓpera) Classy designer jewellery hand-crafted in Barcelona from silver, pewter and other natural products are a real find down this quiet pedestrian lane off the back of Plaza de la Villa. Necklaces, bracelets, rings and earrings range from the understated to those calculated to make a bold statement.

### GOURMET EXPERIENCE
FOOD & DRINKS

(☑91 379 80 00; www.elcorteingles.es; 9th fl, Plaza del Callao 9; ☺10am-10pm Mon-Sat; ⓂCallao) On a winning perch high above Plaza del Callao and with stunning views down Gran Vía, this food court (p59) has a fabulous store for foodies looking for Spanish products, including cheeses, wines, cured meats and Spanish craft beers.

### EL JARDÍN DEL CONVENTO
FOOD

Map p232 (☑91 541 22 99; www.eljardindelconvento.net; Calle del Cordón 1; ☺11am-2.30pm & 5.30-8.30pm Tue-Sun; ⓂÓpera) In a quiet lane just south of Plaza de la Villa, this appealing little shop sells homemade sweets baked by nuns in abbeys, convents and monasteries all across Spain.

### CONVENTO DEL CORPUS CRISTI
FOOD & DRINKS

Map p232 (Las Carboneras; ☑91 548 37 01; Plaza del Conde de Miranda; ☺9.30am-1pm & 4.30-6.30pm; ⓂÓpera) The cloistered nuns at this convent also happen to be fine pastry chefs. You make your request through a door, then a grille on Calle del Codo, and the products (sweet biscuits) are delivered through a little revolving door that allows the nuns to remain unseen by the outside world.

### LA LIBRERÍA
BOOKS

Map p232 (☑91 454 00 18; Calle Mayor 80; ☺10am-2pm & 5-8pm Mon-Fri, 11am-2pm Sat; ⓂÓpera, Sol) This bookshop may be small, but it's the place to find books (mostly in Spanish) covering everything to do with Madrid, from coffee-table books to histories of every *barrio* in the capital.

### EL FLAMENCO VIVE
FLAMENCO

Map p232 (☑91 547 39 17; www.elflamencovive.es; Calle Conde de Lemos 7; ☺10am-2pm & 5-8.30pm Mon-Fri, 10am-2pm Sat; ⓂÓpera) This temple to flamenco has it all, from guitars and songbooks to well-priced CDs, polka-dotted dancing costumes, shoes, colourful plastic jewellery and literature about flamenco. It's the sort of place that will appeal as much to curious first-timers as to serious students of the art. It also organises classes in flamenco guitar.

### THE CURIOSITY SHOP
GIFTS & SOUVENIRS

Map p232 (☑91 365 84 22; www.facebook.com/curiosity.madrid; Calle de los Latoneros 1; ☺10.30am-2pm & 5-9pm Mon-Fri, 10.30am-2pm Sat, noon-3pm Sun) We've been walking past this shop for years and every time we do we stop for a look. There's so much here to turn the head – it's a bit of an Aladdin's cave of knick-knacks, with faux antiques and a whole range of lovely little pieces that defy description.

### LIBRERÍA DE SAN GINÉS
BOOKS

Map p232 (☑91 366 46 86; Pasadizo de San Ginés 2; ☺10am-8.30pm; ⓂSol) With its wooden shutters and old-style clutter, this second-hand bookshop is an utterly charming little corner of old Madrid. Most books are in Spanish but there are a few English titles and bibliophiles will love the atmosphere as much as what's for sale.

### LA CHINATA
FOOD

Map p232 (☑91 152 20 08; www.lachinata.es; Calle Mayor 44; ☺10am-9pm Mon-Sat, noon-3.30pm & 4.30-8pm Sun; ⓂSol, Ópera) Olive oil is the centrepiece of this gourmet *'oleoteca'* just across from the Plaza Mayor. You can buy bottles of the stuff, as well as olive-oil-based cosmetics and carefully selected gourmet food products.

### LA CENTRAL DE CALLAO
BOOKS, SOUVENIRS

(☑91 790 99 30; www.lacentral.com; Postigo de San Martín 8; ☺10am-9.30pm Mon-Thu, to 10pm

Fri & Sat, 11am-9pm Sun; MCallao) Inhabiting an old palace, La Central is a fabulous multistorey bookstore, cafe and purveyor of better-than-average Madrid souvenirs.

### FRANSEN ET LAFITE · HOMEWARES, FLOWERS
Map p232 (☑91 142 85 25; www.fransenetlafite.com; Calle del Espejo 5; ☺10am-8pm Tue-Sat; MÓpera) A stunning collection of flowers from all over Europe is the main business here, but that's not why we include it. Spread over three floors and with a tranquil outdoor patio, this charming space also has carefully selected homewares, antiques, candles and all manner of decorative pieces.

### LA GRAMOLA · MUSIC
Map p232 (☑91 559 25 12; Postigo de San Martín 4; ☺10am-2pm & 5-9pm Mon-Sat; MCallao) In this era of music downloads, stores like La Gramola are cause for nostalgia and strangely reassuring. Don't come looking for something in particular, but do come to spend a blissful hour thumbing your way through CDs and vinyl just like in the old days.

### CHOCOLALABELGA · FOOD
Map p232 (☑91 843 77 57; Calle de Bonetillo 1; ☺10am-2.30pm & 5-8.30pm Tue-Sun; MÓpera) Madrid's love affair with chocolate keeps rolling on. The chocolates from the Belgian homeland of chocolatier Paul-Hector Bossier are, as you would expect, sinfully delicious, with plenty of modern flavours blended in.

### SALVADOR BACHILLER · FASHION & ACCESSORIES
Map p232 (☑91 559 83 21; www.salvadorbachiller.com; Gran Vía 65; ☺10am-9.30pm Mon-Sat, 11am-9pm Sun; MPlaza de España, Santo Domingo) The stylish high-quality leather bags, wallets, suitcases and other accessories of Salvador Bachiller are a staple of Spanish shopping aficionados. This is leather with a typically Spanish twist – the colours are dazzling in bright pinks, yellows and greens. Sound garish? You'll change your mind once you step inside. It also has a **discount outlet** (Map p250; ☑91 523 30 37; Calle de Gravina 11; ☺10.30am-9.30pm Mon-Thu, to 11pm Fri & Sat, noon-9pm Sun; MChueca) in Chueca.

### FNAC · DEPARTMENT STORE
Map p232 (☑91 595 61 00; www.fnac.es; Calle de Preciados 28; ☺10am-9.30pm Mon-Sat, 11.30am-9.30pm Sun; MCallao) This four-storey megastore has a terrific range of CDs, DVDs, video games, electronic equipment and books (including English- and other foreign-language titles); there's a large children's section on the 4th floor.

### MERCADO DE MONEDAS Y SELLOS · MARKET
Map p232 (Plaza Mayor; ☺9am-2pm Sun; MSol) A market selling old coins, stamps and a few antiques under the archways in the Plaza Mayor.

### ART MARKET · MARKET
Map p232 (Plaza del Conde de Barajas; ☺10am-2pm Sun; MSol) Sells local art and prints of the greats.

## 🏃 SPORTS & ACTIVITIES

### ALAMBIQUE · COOKING
Map p232 (☑91 547 42 20; www.alambique.com; Plaza de la Encarnación 2; per person from €45; MÓpera, Santo Domingo) Most classes here last from 2½ to 3½ hours and cover a range of cuisines. Most are conducted in Spanish, but some are in English and French.

### BIKE SPAIN · CYCLING
Map p232 (☑91 559 06 53; www.bikespain.info; Calle del Codo; bike rental half-/full day from €12/18, tours from €30; ☺10am-2pm & 4-7pm Mon-Fri Mar-Oct, 10am-2pm & 3-6pm Mon-Fri Nov-Feb; MÓpera) Bicycle hire plus English-language guided city tours by bicycle, by day or (Friday) night, as well as longer expeditions.

### VISITAS GUIADAS OFICIALES · TOURS
(Official Guided Tours; ☑902 221424; www.esmadrid.com/programa-visitas-guiadas-oficiales; Plaza Mayor 27; ☺4pm Thu & Fri, noon Sat & Sun; MSol) FREE The official guided tours of the city are worth considering, although they're much reduced from what they once were. Two routes (those on Thursday and Friday) are based on Madrid's main monuments, but the two we like are the 'Madrid of Cervantes' (Saturday) and 'Women in the History of Madrid' (Sunday). Tours last for two hours and are in Spanish only.

### URBAN MOVIL · TOURS
Map p232 (☑637 263886, 91 017 98 56; www.urbanmovil.com; Plaza de San Miguel 2; 1/2hr Segway tours €29/53; ☺10am-8pm; MÓpera) Segway tours around Madrid. Prices include 10 minutes of training before you set out. It also organises bike tours and rental.

# La Latina & Lavapiés

## Neighbourhood Top Five

**1 Calle de la Cava Baja** (p75) Moving from bar to bar ordering wine and tapas along one of the world's great culinary streets.

**2 Basílica de San Francisco El Grande** (p71) Looking for Goya under the fourth-largest church dome in the world.

**3 El Rastro** (p72) Joining the local crowds on Sunday mornings for one of Europe's busiest flea markets and a Madrid institution.

**4 Plaza de la Paja** (p72) Getting to the heart of medieval Madrid in the delightfully sloping gateway to Madrid's Moorish Quarter, La Morería.

**5 Corral de la Morería** (p80) Letting flamenco fill your soul with a live performance at one of the city's most prestigious flamenco stages.

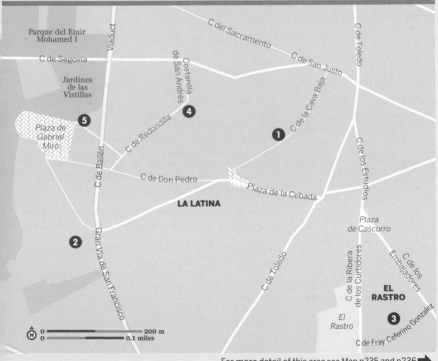

For more detail of this area see Map p235 and p236 ➡

## Lonely Planet's Top Tip

If you can't stomach an entire meal of *cocido* (meat-and-chickpea stew), or if you just want to see what all the fuss is about, head to Malacatín (p77) where the *degustación de cocido* (taste of *cocido*; €5) at the bar is a great way to try Madrid's favourite dish without going all the way – although locals might say it's a bit like smoking without inhaling.

###  Best Places to Eat

➡ Casa Lucio (p79)

➡ Taberna Matritum (p76)

➡ Txirimiri (p75)

➡ Juana La Loca (p76)

➡ Almendro 13 (p75)

➡ Posada de la Villa (p79)

For reviews, see p75.➡

### 🍷 Best Places to Drink

➡ Delic (p79)

➡ Taberna El Tempranillo (p79)

➡ Café del Nuncio (p80)

➡ El Eucalipto (p80)

➡ El Viajero (p80)

For reviews, see p79.➡

### ⊙ Best Churches

➡ Basílica de San Francisco El Grande (p71)

➡ Iglesia de San Andrés (p74)

➡ Basílica de Nuestra Señora del Buen Consejo (p73)

➡ Capilla del Obispo (p73)

For reviews, see p71.➡

# Explore: La Latina & Lavapiés

La Latina's proximity to Plaza Mayor and the downtown area make it an easy area to dip into. Need a break nursing a mojito on a warm afternoon? Head for Plaza de la Paja and linger for as much time as you can spare. Eager to understand the buzz surrounding tapas and the local passion for going on a tapas crawl? Most evenings of the week are busy along Calle de la Cava Baja, but early Sunday lunchtime when the El Rastro crowds pour into La Latina is when you'll most appreciate being here.

With few sights to speak of, Lavapiés is a good place for an afternoon stroll or an evening spent catching the sights and sounds of Madrid's most multicultural corner. Access to Lavapiés is either a steep downhill walk from La Latina or an easy stroll along Calle de Argumosa from near the lower end of Paseo del Prado.

Belonging to and connecting both neighbourhoods is El Rastro, which centres on Calle de la Ribera de los Curtidores. Quiet and really rather pretty for six days of the week, it gets overwhelmed on Sundays when market stalls spill out onto the surrounding streets. To make the most of your El Rastro experience, arrive here early to avoid the crowds, or stay long enough to join the post-market dispersal into La Latina's tapas bars.

# Local Life

➡ **Hang-out** On Sunday afternoons after El Rastro's clamour has faded and the tapas crowds are thinning, head for Plaza de la Puerta de Moros for an infectious street party.

➡ **Mojitos** Many people in Madrid reckon the mojitos at Delic (p79) are the city's best. The others might just vote for Taberna Chica (p80), just around the corner. But we also love El Eucalipto (p80). Why not try all three?

➡ **Local tradition** In Madrid 1pm Sunday is *la hora del vermut* (vermouth hour), when friends and families head out for a quick aperitif before Sunday lunch. Calle de la Cava Baja is the epicentre of this long-standing, civilised tradition.

# Getting There & Away

➡ **Metro** Unless you're walking from Plaza Mayor (an easy, agreeable stroll), La Latina metro station (line 5) is the best metro station both for the tapas bars of La Latina and El Rastro; Tirso de Molina station (line 1) is also OK. If you're only visiting Lavapiés or don't mind a steep uphill climb to La Latina, Lavapiés station (line 3) is your best bet.

## TOP SIGHT
# BASÍLICA DE SAN FRANCISCO EL GRANDE

The Basílica de San Francisco El Grande is a leading candidate for the title of Madrid's favourite church. Its imposing scale, artworks by master painters and the presence of St Francis de Assisi in the story of the church's origins add both a whiff of legend and an unmistakable sense of gravitas.

### Goya
Of all the basilica's chapels, most people rush to the Capilla de San Bernardino, where the central fresco was painted by Goya in the early stages of his career. It lacks the sophistication of his later work, but is notable, unusually, for the fact that Goya has painted himself into the scene.

### Museum Artworks
A series of corridors behind the high altar (accessible only as part of the guided visit) is lined with works of art from the 17th to 19th centuries; highlights include a painting by Francisco de Zurbarán, and another by Francisco Pacheco, the father-in-law and teacher of Velázquez. In the sacristy, watch out for the fine Renaissance *sillería* (the sculpted walnut seats where the church's superiors would meet).

### St Francis & Sabatini
Legend has it that St Francis of Assisi built a chapel on this site in 1217. The current version was designed by Francesco Sabatini in the 18th century. He also designed the Puerta de Alcalá and finished off the Palacio Real, and his unusual floor plan has a circular nave surrounded by chapels.

### The Dome
You could easily spend an hour admiring the basilica's frescoed dome (pictured above), whose eight main panels, completed in the 18th century, are devoted to the Virgin Mary. This is the largest-diameter dome in Spain and the fourth largest in the world.

### DON'T MISS
➜ The dome
➜ St Francis & Sabatini
➜ Goya

### PRACTICALITIES
➜ Map p236, A4
➜ Plaza de San Francisco 1
➜ adult/concession €5/3
➜ ⊘mass 8-10.30am Mon-Sat, museum 10.30am-12.30pm & 4-6pm Tue-Sun Sep-Jun, 10.30am-12.30pm & 5-7pm Tue-Sun Jul & Aug
➜ Ⓜ La Latina, Puerta de Toledo

# ◉ SIGHTS

Although there are exceptions, these two *barrios* (districts) are more about experiences than traditional sights. That said, a handful of fine churches rise above La Latina, Plaza de la Paja is one of Madrid's loveliest squares, and the tangled streets of La Morería are a return to the city's distant past. And then, of course, there's El Rastro, Madrid's flea market par excellence, and the gateway to some of Madrid's most enjoyable traditions.

## BASÍLICA DE SAN FRANCISCO EL GRANDE CHURCH
See p71.

## ★EL RASTRO MARKET
Map p235 (Calle de la Ribera de los Curtidores; ⊗8am-3pm Sun; MLa Latina) A Sunday morning at El Rastro flea market is a Madrid institution. You could easily spend an entire morning inching your way down the hill and the maze of streets. Cheap clothes, luggage, old flamenco records, even older photos of Madrid, faux designer purses, grungy T-shirts, household goods and electronics are the main fare. For every 10 pieces of junk, there's a real gem (a lost masterpiece, an Underwood typewriter) waiting to be found.

The crowded Sunday flea market was, back in the 17th and 18th centuries, largely a meat market (*rastro* means 'stain', in reference to the trail of blood left behind by animals dragged down the hill). The road leading through the market, Calle de la Ribera de los Curtidores, translates as 'Tanners' Alley' and further evokes this sense of a slaughterhouse past. On Sunday mornings this is the place to be, with all of Madrid (in all its diversity) here in search of a bargain.

A word of warning: pickpockets love El Rastro as much as everyone else, so keep a tight hold on your belongings.

## PLAZA DE LA PAJA SQUARE
Map p236 (Straw Square; MLa Latina) Around the back of the Iglesia de San Andrés, the delightful Plaza de la Paja slopes down into the tangle of lanes that once made up Madrid's Muslim quarter. In the 12th and 13th centuries, the city's main market occupied the square. At the top of the square is the Capilla del Obispo, while down the bottom (north side) is the walled 18th-century Jardín del Príncipe Anglona, a peaceful garden.

## MATADERO MADRID ARTS CENTRE
(☑91 252 52 53; www.mataderomadrid.com; Paseo de la Chopera 14; MLegazpi) FREE This contemporary arts centre is a stunning multipurpose space south of the centre. Occupying the converted buildings of the old Arganzuela livestock market and slaughterhouse, Matadero Madrid covers 148,300 sq metres and hosts cutting-edge drama, musical and dance performances and exhibitions on architecture, fashion, literature and cinema. It's a dynamic space and its proximity to the landscaped riverbank makes for a nontouristy alternative to sightseeing in Madrid, not to mention a brilliant opportunity to see the latest avant-garde theatre or exhibitions.

## LA MORERÍA HISTORIC SITE
Map p236 (MLa Latina) The area stretching northwest from Iglesia de San Andrés to the viaduct was the heart of the *morería* (Moorish Quarter). Strain the imagination a little and the maze of winding and hilly lanes even now retains a whiff of the North African medina. This is where the Muslim population of Mayrit was concentrated in the wake of the 11th-century Christian takeover of the town.

## MUSEO DE SAN ISIDRO MUSEUM
Map p236 (Museo de los Orígenes; ☑91 366 74 15; www.madrid.es; Plaza de San Andrés 2; ⊗10am-7pm Tue-Sun mid-Jun–mid-Sep, 9.30am-8pm Tue-Sun rest of year; MLa Latina) FREE This engaging museum occupies the spot where San Isidro Labrador, patron saint of Madrid, ended his days in around 1172. A particular highlight is the large model based on Pedro Teixeira's famous 1656 map of Madrid. Of great historical interest (though not much to look at) is the 'miraculous well', where the saint called forth water to slake his master's thirst. In another miracle, the son of the saint's master fell into a well, whereupon Isidro prayed until the water rose and lifted his master's son to safety.

The museum is housed in a largely new building with a 16th-century Renaissance courtyard and a 17th-century chapel. Apart from the focus on San Isidro, the collection has archaeological finds from the Roman period, including a 4th-century mosaic found on the site of a Roman villa in the *barrio* of Carabanchel, maps, scale models, paintings and photos of Madrid down through the ages.

## BASÍLICA DE NUESTRA SEÑORA DEL BUEN CONSEJO
CHURCH

Map p236 (Catedral de San Isidro; ☑91 369 20 37; Calle de Toledo 37; ☺7.30am-1pm & 6-9pm; ⓜTirso de Molina, La Latina) Towering above the northern end of bustling Calle de Toledo, and visible through the arches from Plaza Mayor, this imposing church long served as the city's de facto cathedral until the Catedral de Nuestra Señora de la Almudena (p57) was completed in 1992. Still known to locals as the Catedral de San Isidro, the austere baroque basilica was founded in the 17th century as the headquarters for the Jesuits.

The basilica is today home to the remains of San Isidro (in the third chapel on your left after you walk in). His body, apparently remarkably well preserved, is only removed from here on rare occasions, such as in 1896 and 1947 when he was paraded about town in the hope he would bring rain (he did, at least in 1947).

Official opening hours aren't always to be relied upon.

## CAPILLA DEL OBISPO
CHURCH

Map p236 (☑91 559 28 74; reservascapilladelobispo@archimadrid.es; Plaza de la Paja; €2; ☺6-8.30pm Mon & Wed, noon-1.30pm & 6-8.30pm Tue & Thu, noon-1.30pm & 6-9.30pm Fri, noon-1.30pm & 8-10pm Sat, noon-2pm & 6.45-8.30pm Sun; ⓜLa Latina) The Capilla del Obispo is a hugely important site on the historical map of Madrid. It was here that San Isidro Labrador was first buried. When the saint's body was discovered there in the late 13th century, two centuries after his death, decomposition had not yet set in. Thus it was that King Alfonso

XI ordered the construction in San Andrés of an ark to hold his remains and a chapel in which to venerate his memory.

In 1669, 47 years after the saint was canonised, the last of many chapels was built on the site and that's what you see today. Don't go looking for the saint's remains though – San Isidro made his last move to the Basílica de Nuestra Señora del Buen Consejo in the 18th century. From Tuesday to Friday at 12.30pm, stop by for the sung service 'Oficio del Mediodía'.

Visits are by 40-minute guided tour only, and advance reservations must be made at the Museo de la Catedral y Cúpola in the Catedral de Nuestra Señora de la Almudena. Most weeks they happen at 10am, 10.45am and 11.30am on Tuesday, and 4pm and 4.45pm Thursday.

## VIADUCT & CALLE DE SEGOVIA
HISTORIC SITE

Map p236 (ⓜÓpera) High above Calle de Segovia, Madrid's viaduct, which connects La Morería with the cathedral and royal palace, was built in the 19th century and replaced by a newer version in 1942; the plastic barriers were erected in the late 1990s to prevent suicide jumps. Before the viaduct was built, anyone wanting to cross from one side of the road or river to the other was obliged to make their way down to Calle de Segovia and back up the other side.

If you feel like re-enacting the journey, head down to Calle de Segovia and cross to the southern side. Just east of the viaduct, on a characterless apartment block wall (No 21), is a **coat of arms**, one of the city's oldest.

LA LATINA & LAVAPIÉS SIGHTS

---

### DISAPPEARED LA LATINA LANDMARKS

The narrow streets of **Calle de la Cava Alta** and **Calle de la Cava Baja** delineate where the second line of medieval Christian city walls ran from the 13th century onwards. They continued north along what is now **Calle de los Cuchilleros** (Knifemakers St) and along **Calle de la Cava de San Miguel**, and were superseded by the third circuit of walls, which was raised in the 15th century. The *cavas* (caves or cellars) were initially ditches dug in front of the walls, later used as refuse dumps and finally given over to housing when the walls no longer served any defensive purpose.

Just west of La Latina metro station, the busy and bar-strewn corner of Madrid marked by the ill-defined **Plaza de la Cebada** (Barley Square) occupies an important historical space. In the wake of the Christian conquest, the square was, for a time, the site of a Muslim cemetery, and the nearby **Plaza de la Puerta de Moros** (Moors' Gate) underscores that this area was long home to the city's Muslim population. Plaza de la Cebada later became a popular spot for public executions – until well into the 19th century, the condemned would be paraded along Calle de Toledo, before turning into the square and mounting the gallows. Later the plaza was the site of one of the largest markets in Madrid.

## MADRID'S OLDEST STREET

There are numerous candidates for the title of Madrid's oldest street. Calle del Arenal stakes a strong claim, although the date when it ceased to be a small river and became a street remains unresolved by historical records. According to the historian Rafael Fraguas, the oldest street in Madrid is Calle de Grafal, which dates back to 1190 when it was called Calle del Santo Grial. But not that you'd notice: in the midst of La Latina's medieval streets, Calle de Grafal is not the *barrio's* prettiest thoroughfare, with largely modern brick apartment blocks. It runs southwest off Plaza de Segovia Nueva between Calle de Toledo and Calle de la Cava Baja.

The site once belonged to Madrid's Ayuntamiento (Town Hall).

A punt would ferry people across what was then a trickling tributary of the Río Manzanares. You could follow that former trickle's path west, down to the banks of the Manzanares and a nine-arched bridge, the **Puente de Segovia**, which Juan de Herrera built in 1584.

### INSTITUTO DE
### SAN ISIDRO    HISTORIC BUILDING

Map p236 (☑91 365 12 71; Calle de Toledo 39; ⓂTirso de Molina, La Latina) Next door to the Basílica de Nuestra Señora del Buen Consejo (p73), the Instituto de San Isidro once went by the name of Colegio Imperial and, from the 16th century on, was where many of the country's leading figures were schooled by the Jesuits.

### JARDÍN DEL PRÍNCIPE ANGLONA    GARDENS

Map p236 (Plaza de la Paja; ⊙10am-10pm Apr-Oct, to 6.30pm Nov-Mar; ⓂLa Latina) Down the bottom (at the northern side) of the Plaza de la Paja is the walled 18th-century Jardín del Príncipe Anglona. It's a peaceful garden.

### IGLESIA DE SAN ANDRÉS    CHURCH

Map p236 (Plaza de San Andrés 1; ⊙9am-1pm & 6-8pm Mon-Sat, 10am-1pm Sun; ⓂLa Latina) This proud church is more imposing than beautiful. Stern, dark columns with gold-leaf capitals against the rear wall lead your eyes up into the dome – all rose, yellow and green, and rich with sculpted floral fantasies and cherubs poking out of every nook and cranny. What you see today is the result of restoration work completed after the church was gutted during the civil war.

### PLAZA DE LAVAPIÉS    SQUARE

Map p235 (ⓂLavapiés) The triangular Plaza de Lavapiés is one of the few open spaces in Lavapiés and is a magnet for all that's good (a thriving cultural life) and bad (drugs and a high police presence) about the *barrio*. It's been cleaned up a little in recent years and the Teatro Valle-Inclán (p81), on the southern edge of the plaza, is a striking addition to the eclectic Lavapiés streetscape.

To find out what makes this *barrio* tick, drop in to the Asociación de Vecinos La Corrala, the local neighbours' association just up the hill from the plaza, where staff are happy to highlight Lavapiés' attractions without dismissing its problems.

### JARDINES DE LAS VISTILLAS    GARDENS

Map p236 (ⓂÓpera) West across Calle de Bailén from La Morería are the *terrazas* (open-air cafes) of Jardines de Las Vistillas, which offer one of the best vantage points in Madrid for a drink, with views towards the Sierra de Guadarrama. During the civil war, Las Vistillas was heavily bombarded by nationalist troops from the Casa de Campo, and they in turn were shelled from a republican bunker here.

### IGLESIA DE SAN PEDRO EL VIEJO    CHURCH

Map p236 (☑91 365 12 84; Costanilla de San Pedro; ⊙9am-12.30pm & 5-8pm Mon-Thu & Sat, 7am-9pm Fri, 9am-12.30pm Sun; ⓂLa Latina) This fine old church is one of the few remaining windows on post-Muslim Madrid, most notably its clearly Mudéjar (a Moorish architectural style) brick bell tower, which dates from the 14th century. The church is generally closed to the public, but it's arguably more impressive from the outside; the Renaissance doorway has stood since 1525. If you can peek inside, the nave dates from the 15th century, although the interior largely owes its appearance to 17th-century renovations.

The church is the focus of important Good Friday celebrations. Along with the Iglesia de San Nicolás de los Servitas (p57), it is one of very few sites where traces of Mudéjar Madrid remain in situ. Otherwise, you need to visit Toledo, 70km south of Madrid, to visualise what Madrid once was like.

## LA CORRALA
HISTORIC BUILDING

Map p235 (cnr Calles de Mesón de Paredes & del Tribulete; MLavapiés) One building that catches the community spirit of the lively *barrio* of Lavapiés is La Corrala, an example of an intriguing traditional (if much tidied up) tenement block, with long communal balconies built around a central courtyard. Working-class Madrid was once strewn with buildings like this and very few survive. Almost opposite are the ruins of an old church.

## LA CASA ENCENDIDA
CULTURAL CENTRE

(☑902 430322; www.lacasaencendida.es; Ronda de Valencia 2; ⊘10am-10pm Tue-Sun; MEmbajadores) FREE This cultural centre is utterly unpredictable, if only because of the quantity and scope of its activities – everything from exhibitions to cinema sessions and workshops. The focus is often on international artists or environmental themes, but if it has an overarching theme, it's the alternative slant it takes on the world.

## ✖ EATING

La Latina is Madrid's best *barrio* for tapas, complemented by a fine selection of sit-down restaurants. If you're planning only one tapas crawl while in town, do it here in Calle de la Cava Baja and the surrounding streets. Lavapiés is more eclectic and multicultural and, generally speaking, the further down the hill you go, the better it gets, especially along Calle de Argumosa.

## ★ TXIRIMIRI
TAPAS €

Map p236 (☑91 364 11 96; www.txirimiri.es; Calle del Humilladero 6; tapas from €3; ⊘noon-4.30pm & 8.30pm-midnight; MLa Latina) This *pintxos* (Basque tapas) bar is a great little discovery just down from the main La Latina tapas circuit. Wonderful wines, gorgeous *pinchos* (the *tortilla de patatas* – potato and onion omelette – is superb) and fine risottos add up to a pretty special combination.

## BAR MELO'S
TAPAS €

Map p235 (☑91 527 50 54; www.facebook.com/barmeloslavapies; Calle del Ave María 44; mains from €7.50; ⊘2.30pm-1.30am Tue-Sat, closed Aug; MLavapiés) There's no tradition of kebab shops for midnight attacks of the munchies, but there's always Bar Melo's. One of those Spanish bars that you'd normally walk past without a second glance, Bar Melo's is famous across the city for its *zapatillas* – great, spanking *bocadillos* (filled rolls) of *lacón* (cured shoulder of pork) and cheese.

They're big, they're greasy and they're damn good. The place is packed on Friday and Saturday nights when a *zapatilla* is the perfect accompaniment to a night of drinking. The *croquetas* (croquettes) are also famously good, not to mention epic in scale.

## TABERNA TXAKOLINA
TAPAS €

Map p236 (☑91 366 48 77; www.tabernatxacoli.com; Calle de la Cava Baja 26; tapas from €4; ⊘8pm-midnight Tue, 1-4pm & 8pm-midnight Wed-Sat, 1-4pm Sun; MLa Latina) Taberna Txakolina calls its *pintxos* 'high cuisine in miniature'. If ordering tapas makes you nervous, it couldn't be easier here – they're lined up on the bar, Basque style, in all their glory, and you can simply point. Whatever you order, wash it down with a *txacoli*, a sharp Basque white.

## ALMENDRO 13
TAPAS €

Map p236 (☑91 365 42 52; www.almendro13.com; Calle del Almendro 13; mains €7-15; ⊘1-4pm & 7.30pm-midnight Sun-Thu, 1-5pm & 8pm-1am Fri & Sat; MLa Latina) Almendro 13 is a charming *taberna* (tavern) where you come for traditional Spanish tapas with an emphasis on quality rather than frilly elaborations. Cured meats, cheeses, omelettes and variations on these themes dominate the menu.

It serves both *raciones* (full-plate) and half-sized plates – a full *ración* of the famously good *huevos rotos* ('broken eggs') served with *jamón* (ham) and thin potato slices is a meal in itself. The only problem is that the wait for a table requires the patience of a saint, so order a wine or *manzanilla* (dry sherry) and soak up the buzz.

## BAR SANTURCE
SPANISH €

Map p235 (☑646 238303; www.barsanturce.com; Plaza General Vara del Rey 14; bocadillos/raciones from €2.50/4.50; ⊘noon-4pm Tue & Wed, noon-4pm & 7.30-10.30pm Thu-Sat, 9am-4pm Sun; MLa Latina) This basic bar is famous for its *sardinas a la plancha* (sardines cooked on the grill) and *pimientos de padrón* (fiery green peppers). It's wildly popular on Sundays during El Rastro market when it can be difficult to even get near the bar. The *media ración* (half serve) of six sardines for €2.50 is Madrid's best bargain.

**WORTH A DETOUR**

## MADRID RÍO

For decades, nay centuries, Madrid's Río Manzanares (Manzanares River) was a laughing stock. In the 17th century, renowned Madrid playwright Lope de Vega described the beautiful Puente de Segovia over the river to be a little too grand for the 'apprentice river'. He suggested the city buy a bigger river or sell the bridge. Thus it remained until the 21st century, when Madrid's town hall decided to bring the river up to scratch.

Planned before the economic crisis swung a wrecking ball through the city's long list of planned infrastructure projects, the Madrid Río development saw the M-30 motorway driven underground and vast areas – up to 500,000 sq metres by some estimates – of abandoned riverside land turned into parkland that one former mayor described as 'a giant green carpet'. A summer beach à la Paris, bike paths, outdoor cafes and children's playgrounds are all part of the mix in this attractive 10km-long stretch of parkland. It has also made more accessible a number of appealing sights.

The two easiest ways to access Madrid Río are to walk down the hill from La Latina to the western end of Calle de Segovia or follow the signs from Matadero Madrid.

### JULIAN BECERRO
FAST FOOD €

Map p236 (☑91 366 15 24; www.julianbecerro.com; Calle de la Cava Baja 41; ⊙10am-10pm; Ⓜ La Latina) This purveyor of some of the finest *embutidos* (cured meats) is perfectly at home on this, one of Madrid's most important culinary streets. The *jamón* comes from the renowned Salamanca region of Castilla y León, with cheeses and other products from around Spain.

### CERVECERÍA 100 MONTADITOS
SPANISH €

Map p236 (www.spain.100montaditos.com; Calle del Nuncio; montaditos €1-3.50; ⊙noon-midnight; Ⓜ La Latina) This bar with outlets all across the city serves up no fewer than 100 different varieties of mini-*bocadillos* (*montaditos,* or small filled rolls) that span the full range of Spanish staples, such as chorizo, *jamón,* tortilla, a variety of cheeses and seafood, in more combinations than you could imagine. Order at the counter and your name will be called in no time.

### ★TABERNA MATRITUM
MODERN SPANISH €€

Map p236 (☑91 365 82 37; www.tabernamatritum.es; Calle de la Cava Alta 17; mains €13-19.50; ⊙1.30-4pm & 8.30pm-midnight Wed-Sun, 8.30pm-midnight Mon & Tue; Ⓜ La Latina) This little gem is reason enough to detour from the more popular Calle de la Cava Baja next door. The seasonal menu encompasses terrific tapas, salads and generally creative cooking – try the Catalan sausage and prawn pie or the winter *calçots* (large spring onions), also from Catalonia. The wine list runs into the hundreds.

### ★JUANA LA LOCA
TAPAS €€

Map p236 (☑91 366 55 00; www.juanalalocamadrid.com; Plaza de la Puerta de Moros 4; tapas from €4, mains €10-24; ⊙1.30-5.30pm Tue-Sun, 7pm-midnight Sat-Wed, to 1am Thu-Fri; Ⓜ La Latina) Juana La Loca does a range of creative tapas with tempting options lined up along the bar, and more on the menu that they prepare to order. But we love it above all for its brilliant *tortilla de patatas,* which is distinguished from others of its kind by the caramelised onions – simply wonderful.

### LA BOBIA
ASTURIAN €€

Map p236 (☑91 737 60 30; www.facebook.com/labobiamadrid; Calle de San Millán 3; tapas from €3, mains €9-18; ⊙1-11pm Sun-Thu, to midnight Fri & Sat; Ⓜ La Latina) An icon of 1980s Madrid, La Bobia has been updated for the 21st century, but is still the authentic Asturian cider house that lies at the secret of its longevity. Pungent blue cheeses, fine *croquetas, fabada asturiana* (an Asturian stew) and high-quality steaks dominate an extensive menu, but when it comes to drinks, it's cider straight from the barrel.

### ALMACÉN DE VINOS
TAPAS €€

(Casa Gerardo; ☑91 221 96 60; Calle de la Calatrava 21; tapas/raciones from €3/8.50; ⊙1-4pm & 8.30pm-midnight Sun-Thu, 1-5pm & 8.30pm-12.30am Fri & Sat; Ⓜ La Latina) It doesn't come much more traditional in La Latina than this tiled space with a marble bar and *tostas* (toasts; with *bacalao,* for example), *raciones* (such as *jamón ibérico* with wild mushrooms) and vermouth on tap. When busy, it has that unmistakeable buzz of a place beloved by locals whose attitude seems to be, 'Why change something this good?'.

### LA CALETA
ANDALUCIAN €€

Map p235 (☑645 388077; www.lacaletagaditana.es; Calle de los Tres Peces 21; mains €8-20; ☺1.30-4.45pm & 8.30pm-midnight Wed-Sat, 1.30-4.45pm Sun; Ⓜ Antón Martín) Around halfway down the Lavapiés hill, La Caleta is Andalucian down to its white-walled, flower-strewn dining area. The food is all about Cádiz, where *pescaito frito* (fried fish) is an obsession. As is the case in the south, the fish and seafood is lightly fried in the lightest of batter – it's never overdone and never oily.

### CASA CURRO
ANDALUCIAN €€

Map p236 (☑91 364 22 59; www.tabernacasacurro.com; Calle de la Cava Baja 23; raciones €6-14; ☺7pm-1.30am Tue, noon-4.30pm & 7pm-1.30am Wed & Thu, noon-1.30am Fri-Sun; Ⓜ La Latina) This fine Andalucian bar serves tasty salted prawns from Huelva and all manner of other dishes from Spain's south – the emphasis is on seafood, but there are a few token meat dishes as well. The look is modern and they have a passion for good food without too many elaborations.

### LA ANTOÑITA
MODERN SPANISH €€

Map p236 (☑91 119 14 24; www.posadadeldragon.com; Calle de la Cava Baja 14; raciones from €6.90, mains €13-17; ☺1.30pm-12.30am; Ⓜ La Latina) The restaurant of the stunning Posada del Dragón (p174) retains some features of the original inn, including exposed wooden beams and heavy stonework. There are tapas at the bar and a range of creative dishes ('fun market cooking' such as *secreto ibérico con guacamole* – pork fillet with guacamole – or the tiger-mussel croquettes) in the rear sit-down restaurant.

### ENOTABERNA DEL LEÓN DE ORO
SPANISH €€

Map p236 (☑91 119 14 94; www.posadadeleondeoro.com; Calle de la Cava Baja 12; tapas from €6, mains €13-23; ☺1-4pm & 8pm-midnight; Ⓜ La Latina) The stunning restoration work that brought to life the Posada del León de Oro (p174) also bequeathed to La Latina a fine bar-restaurant. The emphasis is on matching carefully chosen wines with creative dishes (such as baby squid with potato emulsion and rocket pesto) in a casual atmosphere. There are also plenty of gins to choose from. It's a winning combination.

### LA MUSA LATINA
MODERN SPANISH €€

Map p236 (☑91 354 02 55; www.grupolamusa.com/restaurante-lamusalatina; Costanilla de San Andrés 1; tapas €3-7, mains €11-17; ☺10am-1am Mon-Wed, to 1.30am Thu, to 2am Fri & Sat, to 1am Sun; Ⓜ La Latina) Laid-back La Musa Latina has an ever-popular dining area and food that's designed to bring a smile to your face. The outdoor tables are lovely when the weather is warm, while the downstairs bar in the former wine cellar, complete with table tennis and table football, is also charming. Like its sister restaurant in Malasaña, it serves creative tapas, including international adaptations.

### SANLÚCAR
ANDALUCIAN €€

Map p236 (☑91 354 00 52; www.latabernasanlucar.com; Calle de San Isidro Labrador 14; mains €12-19; ☺1-5pm & 8.30pm-midnight Tue-Sat, 1-5pm Sun; Ⓜ La Latina) The seafood-dominated cooking of the Andalucian province of Cádiz is what this place is all about, with every imaginable sea creature (usually lightly fried) sharing the menu with gazpacho served in a tall drinking glass. It's quiet at lunchtime (except on Sunday) but it can be hard to find a place in the evenings.

### MALACATÍN
SPANISH €€

Map p235 (☑91 365 52 41; www.malacatin.com; Calle de Ruda 5; mains €11-15; ☺11am-5.30pm Mon-Wed & Sat, 11am-5.30pm & 8.15-11pm Thu & Fri, closed Aug; Ⓜ La Latina) If you want to see *madrileños* (residents of Madrid) enjoying their favourite local food, this is one of the best places to do so. The clamour of conversation bounces off the tiled walls of the cramped dining area adorned with bullfighting memorabilia. The speciality is as much *cocido* (meat-and-chickpea stew) as you can eat (€21).

The *degustación de cocido* (taste of *cocido;* €5.50) at the bar is a great way to try Madrid's favourite dish.

### LA CHATA
TAPAS €€

Map p236 (☑91 366 14 58; www.lachatacavabaja.com; Calle de la Cava Baja 24; mains €9-23, tapas from €3.70, set menu €18; ☺1-4pm & 8.30pm-midnight Thu-Mon, 8.30pm-midnight Tue & Wed; Ⓜ La Latina) Behind the lavishly tiled facade, La Chata looks for all the world like a neglected outpost of the past. The decor may be run-down and the bullfighting memorabilia not to everyone's taste, but this is an essential stop on a tapas tour of La Latina.

## BETWEEN MEALS & SPANISH FAST FOOD
.................................................

If you just can't wait until lunch and/ or dinnertime ticks around, there are a number of options scattered around La Latina in particular.

**La Antoñita** (p77) Creative tapas

**La Buga del Lobo** (p78) Traditional tapas

**La Musa Latina** (p77) Fun tapas

**El Estragón** (p78) All-day vegetarian

**Cervecería 100 Montaditos** (p76) Mini-rolls

Don't come here without ordering a *cazuela* (stew cooked and served in a ceramic pot, including wild mushrooms with clams).

### CASA LUCAS                                    TAPAS €€
Map p236 (📞91 365 08 04; www.casalucas.es; Calle de la Cava Baja 30; tapas/raciones from €5/12; ⏰1-3.30pm & 8pm-midnight Thu-Tue, 1-3.30pm Wed; MLa Latina) Receiving plaudits from food critics and ordinary punters alike, Casa Lucas takes a sideways glance at traditional Spanish tapas and heads off in new directions (the grilled tenderloin of pork on candied onion is an example). There are a range of hot and cold tapas and larger *raciones* on the menu.

### LA BUGA DEL LOBO                          SPANISH €€
Map p235 (📞91 528 88 38; www.facebook.com/ labugadellobo; Calle de Argumosa 11; mains €12-20; ⏰11am-2am Wed-Mon; MLavapiés) La Buga del Lobo has been one of the 'in' places in cool and gritty Lavapiés for years now and it's still hard to get a table. The atmosphere is bohemian and inclusive, with funky, swirling murals, contemporary art exhibitions and jazz or lounge music. The food's traditional with a few creative detours.

### OLIVEROS                                      SPANISH €€
Map p236 (📞91 354 62 52; Calle de San Milán 4; mains €12-19; ⏰1-4pm & 8.30pm-midnight Tue-Sat, noon-6pm Sun mid-Sep–mid-Aug; MLa Latina) This famous old *taberna* (tavern) has been in the Oliveros family since 1921 and nothing seems to have changed much since it opened. It's a tiny, warm, bottle-lined den that doesn't disappoint with its *solomillo ibérico al Cabrales* (sirloin with blue cheese) and local dishes of *cocido a la madrileña* (meat-and-chickpea stew).

### EL ESTRAGÓN                            VEGETARIAN €€
Map p236 (📞91 365 89 82; www.elestragon vegetariano.com; Plaza de la Paja 10; mains €8-15; ⏰1pm-1am; 🍴; MLa Latina) A delightful spot for crêpes, veggie burgers and other vegetarian specialities, El Estragón is undoubtedly one of Madrid's best vegetarian restaurants, although attentive vegans won't appreciate the use of butter. Apart from that, we're yet to hear a bad word about it.

### NAÏA BISTRO                                  FUSION €€
Map p236 (📞91 366 27 83; www.naiabistro.com; Plaza de la Paja 3; mains €12-22; ⏰1.30-4.30pm & 8.30-11.30pm Tue-Sun; MLa Latina) Naïa has a real buzz about it, with modern Spanish cuisine, a chill-out lounge downstairs and outdoor tables on lovely Plaza de la Paja. The emphasis throughout is on natural ingredients, healthy food and exciting tastes.

### TABERNA DE ANTONIO SÁNCHEZ                                    TAPAS €€
Map p235 (📞91 539 78 26; Calle de Mesón des Paredes 13; tapas from €4.50; ⏰noon-4pm & 8pm-midnight Mon-Sat, noon-4.30pm Sun; 🔊; MTirso de Molina) Behind one of the best-preserved old *taberna* facades in Madrid hides this gem of a traditional tapas bar famous for its Madrid specialities – *tortilla de san isidro*, *callos* (tripe), *morcilla* (blood sausage), *huevos estrellados* (fried eggs) and a host of other excellent local favourites.

### LAMIAK                                        TAPAS €€
Map p236 (📞91 365 52 12; Calle de la Cava Baja 42; raciones €5-14; ⏰1-4pm & 8pm-midnight Tue-Sat, 1-4pm Sun; MLa Latina) Another casual La Latina tapas bar, Lamiak is filled to the rafters on Sunday and busy at other times, thanks to its contemporary exhibitions, laid-back atmosphere, good wines and tapas dishes.

### VIVA BURGER                            VEGETARIAN €€
Map p236 (📞91 366 33 49; www.vivaburger.es; Costanilla de San Andrés 16; mains €11-14; ⏰noon-midnight Sun-Thu, to 2am Fri & Sat; 🍴; MLa Latina) Viva Burger does veggie burgers of the highest order – the patties are made from soya beans, nuts and fruit, and come with all manner of options, from blue cheese and mushrooms to seaweed, ginger, asparagus and red onions. It also does wraps. Its terrace spills over onto Plaza de la Paja.

★**CASA LUCIO** SPANISH €€€

Map p236 (☑91 365 32 52, 91 365 82 17; www.casalucio.es; Calle de la Cava Baja 35; mains €18-29; ⊘1-4pm & 8.30pm-midnight, closed Aug; MLa Latina) Casa Lucio is a Madrid classic and has been wowing *madrileños* with his light touch, quality ingredients and homestyle local cooking since 1974, such as eggs (a Lucio speciality) and roasted meats in abundance. There's also *rabo de toro* (bull's tail) during the Fiestas de San Isidro Labrador and plenty of *rioja* (red wine) to wash away the mere thought of it.

The lunchtime *guisos del día* (stews of the day), including *cocido* on Wednesday, are also popular. Casa Lucio draws an august, well-dressed crowd, which has included the former king of Spain, former US president Bill Clinton and Penélope Cruz.

**POSADA DE LA VILLA** SPANISH €€€

Map p236 (☑91 366 18 80; www.posadadelavilla.com; Calle de la Cava Baja 9; mains €21-32.50; ⊘1-4pm & 8pm-midnight Mon-Sat, 1-4pm Sun, closed Aug; MLa Latina) This wonderfully restored 17th-century *posada* (inn) is something of a local landmark. The atmosphere is formal, the decoration sombre and traditional (heavy timber and brickwork), and the cuisine decidedly local – roast meats, *cocido* (which usually needs to be pre-ordered), *callos* (tripe) and *sopa de ajo* (garlic soup).

**RESTAURANTE JULIÁN**
**DE TOLOSA** SPANISH €€€

Map p236 (☑91 365 82 10; www.casajuliandetolosa.com; Calle de la Cava Baja 18; mains €26-34; ⊘1.30-4pm & 9pm-midnight Mon-Sat, 1.30-4pm Sun; MLa Latina) Navarran cuisine is treated with respect at this classy place that's popular with celebrities and well regarded by food critics. There are only four main dishes to choose from – two fish and two meat – and they haven't changed in years, but there's still a contemporary feel. Why change the *chuletón* (T-bone steak) when it's already close to perfection?

# 🍷⊥ DRINKING & NIGHTLIFE

**La Latina and Lavapiés have numerous memorable cafes and bars, although few stay open until dawn. Most nights (and Sunday afternoons), crowds hop from bar to bar across La Latina. Most of the action takes place along Calle de la** Cava Baja, the western end of Calle del Almendro and Plaza de la Paja. Many of these places are better known for their tapas, but they're equally great for a drink. Lavapiés is a completely different kettle of fish, with an alternative, often bohemian crowd and quirky bars brimful of personality. Not everyone loves Lavapiés, but we do.

★**TABERNA EL TEMPRANILLO** WINE BAR

Map p236 (☑91 364 15 32; Calle de la Cava Baja 38; ⊘1-4pm Mon, 1-4pm & 8pm-midnight Tue-Sun; MLa Latina) You could come here for the tapas, but we recommend Taberna El Tempranillo primarily for its wines, of which it has a selection that puts numerous Spanish bars to shame. It's not a late-night place, but it's always packed in the early evening and on Sunday after El Rastro.

★**DELIC** BAR

Map p236 (☑91 364 54 50; www.delic.es; Costanilla de San Andrés 14; ⊘11am-2am Sun & Tue-Thu, to 2.30am Fri & Sat; MLa Latina) We could go on for hours about this long-standing cafe-bar, but we'll reduce it to its most basic elements: nursing an exceptionally good mojito or three on a warm summer's evening at Delic's outdoor tables on one of Madrid's prettiest plazas is one of life's great pleasures. Bliss.

Due to local licensing restrictions, the outdoor tables close two hours before closing time, whereafter the intimate interior is almost as good.

**BOCONÓ SPECIALTY COFFEE** CAFE

Map p236 (☑91 040 20 19; www.bocono.es; Calle de los Embajadores 3; coffee €1.60-3; ⊘8.30am-8.30pm Mon-Thu, to 9pm Fri & Sat, 9.30am-8.30pm Sun; 🛜; MLa Latina) Close attention to every detail makes Boconó unique – coffee is roasted on-site and fanatics have a choice of styles: espresso, AeroPress and Chemex, among others. Coffee is weighed before brewing and water is dosed out by the millilitre. The decor is minimal, with reclaimed wood and rough brick, the wi-fi is fast and the service is friendly.

**EL EUCALIPTO** COCKTAIL BAR

Map p235 (☑91 527 27 63; www.facebook.com/eeucalipto; Calle de Argumosa 4; ⊘5pm-2am Sun-Thu, to 3am Fri & Sat; MLavapiés) This fine little bar is devoted to all things Cuban – from the music to the clientele and the Caribbean cocktails (including nonalcoholic), it's a sexy, laid-back place. Not surprisingly, the mojitos are a cut above average, but the juices and daiquiris also have a loyal following.

### TABERNA CHICA
BAR

Map p236 (☑683 269114; Costanilla de San Pedro 7; ⊙8pm-2am Mon-Thu, 5pm-2am Fri, 1pm-2am Sat & Sun; ⓂLa Latina) Most of those who come to this narrow little bar are after one of two things: the famous Santa Teresa rum that comes served in an extra-large mug, or some of the finest mojitos and caipirinhas in Madrid. The music is chill-out with a nod to lounge, which makes it an ideal pit stop if you're hoping for conversation.

### EL VIAJERO
BAR

Map p236 (☑91 366 90 64; www.elviajeromadrid. com; Plaza de la Cebada 11; ⊙5pm-2am Tue-Fri, noon-2.30am Sat, noon-midnight Sun; ⓂLa Latina) The undoubted highlight of this landmark of La Latina nights is the rooftop *terraza,* which boasts fine views down onto the thronging streets. When the weather's warm, it's nigh on impossible to get a table. Our secret? It often closes the *terraza* around 8pm to spruce it up a little; be ready to pounce when it reopens and thereafter guard your table with your life.

### EL BONANNO
WINE BAR

Map p236 (☑91 366 68 86; www.elbonanno.com; Plaza del Humilladero 4; ⊙noon-2am; ⓂLa Latina) If much of Madrid's nightlife starts too late for your liking, Bonanno could be for you. It made its name as a cocktail bar, but many people also come here for the great wines. It's usually full of young professionals from early evening onwards. Be prepared to snuggle up close to those around you if you want a spot at the bar.

### NUEVO CAFÉ DE BARBIERI
CAFE

Map p235 (☑91 527 36 58; www.facebook.com/cafebarbieri; Calle del Ave María 45; ⊙8am-1am Mon-Thu, to 2am Fri, 9am-2am Sat, 9am-1am Sun; ⓂLavapiés) This *barrio* classic is Lavapiés' grandest old cafe, the sort of place for quiet conversation amid the columns and marble-topped tables right on Plaza de Lavapiés. It does everything from coffee and cakes to cocktails. It's always been an intellectual hub of *barrio* life and it gets busy with a younger crowd on weekend nights.

### CAFÉ DEL NUNCIO
BAR

Map p236 (☑91 366 08 53; www.cafedelnuncio. es; Calle de Segovia 9; ⊙11am-1am; ⓂLa Latina)

Café del Nuncio straggles down a laneway to Calle de Segovia. You can drink on one of several cosy levels inside or, better still in summer, enjoy the outdoor seating that one local reviewer likened to a slice of Rome. By day it's an old-world cafe with great coffee, but by night it's one of the best no-frills bars in the *barrio.*

### LA INQUILINA
BAR

Map p235 (☑91 055 81 76; www.lainquilina.es; Calle del Ave María 39; ⊙7pm-2am Tue-Thu, to 3am Fri, 1pm-2.30am Sat & Sun; ⓂLavapiés) One of our favourite *barrio* bars, La Inquilina has a cool-and-casual feel and deep roots in the Lavapiés soil. Contemporary artworks by budding local artists adorn the walls and you can either gather around the bar or take a table out the back. It's a small slice of sophistication in a *barrio* not known for such characteristics.

# ☆ ENTERTAINMENT

### ★CASA PATAS
FLAMENCO

Map p235 (☑91 369 04 96; www.casapatas.com; Calle de Cañizares 10; admission incl drink €38; ⊙shows 10.30pm Mon-Thu, 8pm & 10.30pm Fri & Sat; ⓂAntón Martín, Tirso de Molina) One of the top flamenco stages in Madrid, this *tablao* (choreographed flamenco show) always offers flawless quality that serves as a good introduction to the art. It's not the friendliest place in town, especially if you're only here for the show, and you're likely to be crammed in a little, but no one complains about the standard of the performances.

### ★CORRAL DE LA MORERÍA
FLAMENCO

Map p236 (☑91 365 84 46; www.corraldela moreria.com; Calle de la Morería 17; admission incl drink from €45; ⊙7pm-12.15am, shows 8.30pm & 10.20pm; ⓂÓpera) This is one of the most prestigious flamenco stages in Madrid, with 50 years of experience as a leading venue and top performers most nights. The stage area has a rustic feel, and tables are pushed up close. Set menus from €45 (additional to the admission fee).

### CAFÉ ZIRYAB
FLAMENCO

(☑91 219 29 02; www.cafeziryab.com; Paseo de la Esperanza 17; adult/child €22/8; ⊙shows 9.30pm Wed-Mon; ⓂAcacias) For a fine, well-priced flamenco show that draws as many locals as tourists, Café Ziryab is a bit out of the city centre but worth the excursion. At 11pm on Fridays, the *peña flamenca* is a jam session for those who feel the urge and, when it works, is authentic flamenco at its improvised, soul-stirring best.

### EL DESPERTAR                                   JAZZ

Map p235 (☑91 530 80 95; www.cafeeldespertar. com; Calle de la Torrecilla del Leal 18; entrance free-€6; ◎7.30pm-late Wed-Mon; ⓂAntón Martín) El Despertar is all about jazz down to its roots. Everything about this place harks back to the 1920s, with a commitment to old-style jazz and decor to match its days as a meeting point for the intelligentsia of the *barrio*. There are live performances every Friday and Saturday, most Thursdays and Sundays and many other nights. Concerts start between 8.30pm and 11pm; check the website for details.

### TEATRO VALLE-INCLÁN                         THEATRE

Map p235 (☑91 505 88 01; www.cdn.mcu.es; Plaza de Lavapiés; tickets from €15; ⓂLavapiés) The stunning refurbishment of this theatre has brought new life (and quality plays) to this once run-down corner of Lavapiés. Located on the southern end of the Plaza de Lavapiés, it is now the headquarters for the Centro Dramático Nacional (National Drama Centre) and puts on landmark plays by (mostly) Spanish playwrights such as Valle-Inclán and Fernando Arrabal.

### CONTRACLUB                               LIVE MUSIC

Map p236 (☑91 365 55 45; www.contraclub.es; Calle de Bailén 16; entrance €3-15; ◎10pm-6am Wed-Sat; ⓂLa Latina) ContraClub is a crossover live music venue and nightclub, with an eclectic mix of live music (pop, rock, indie, singer-songwriter, blues etc). After the live acts (from 10pm), resident DJs serve up equally diverse beats (indie, pop, funk and soul) to make sure you don't move elsewhere.

### TEATRO CIRCO PRICE                          THEATRE

(☑91 528 98 65; www.teatrocircoprice.es; Ronda de Atocha 35; ⓂLavapiés, Embajadores, Atocha) Just south of Lavapiés, this modern theatre does a little bit of everything from concerts and circuses to dance performances.

### LA ESCALERA DE JACOB                        THEATRE

Map p235 (☑625 721745; www.teatrolaescalera dejacob.com; Calle de Lavapiés 9; entrance €4-12; ◎6.30pm-midnight Mon-Thu, to 2am Fri, 10.30am-2am Sat, 10.30am-midnight Sun; ⓂAntón Martín, Tirso de Molina) As much a cocktail bar as a live music venue or theatre, 'Jacob's Ladder' is one of Madrid's most original stages.

Magicians, storytellers, live jazz, children's theatre and more are part of the mix. This alternative slant on life makes for some terrific live performances.

### EL RINCÓN DEL ARTE NUEVO              LIVE MUSIC

Map p236 (☑91 365 50 45; www.elrincondelarte nuevo.com; Calle de Segovia 17; entrance €5-10; ◎8.30pm-5am Sun-Thu, to 6am Fri & Sat; ⓂLa Latina) With nearly 40 years in the business, this small venue knows what its punters like and serves up a nightly feast of singer-songwriters, blues, rock and '70s, '80s and '90s tunes for an appreciative crowd. Acts here are as diverse as the genres themselves, with Melendi, Fran Postigo and Diego El Negro among those to have taken the stage. Concerts start between 9.30pm and 12.30am and sometimes stray into flamenco or pop.

### MARULA CAFÉ                             LIVE MUSIC

Map p236 (☑91 366 15 96; www.marulacafe.com; Calle de Caños Viejos 3; free-€10; ◎11pm-5am Sun-Thu, 11.30pm-6am Fri & Sat; ⓂLa Latina) The music here is all about funk, soul, jazz, the American South, Afrobeat and even a little hip hop. It's a club with attitude and always has a great rhythm. Concerts at 11.30pm, DJs until sunrise. It can be a little hard to find – it's almost under the viaduct just down the hill from Calle de la Morería.

### SALA JUGLAR                             LIVE MUSIC

Map p235 (☑91 528 43 81; www.salajuglar.com; Calle de Lavapiés 37; entrance €5-15; ◎9.30pm-3am Sun-Wed, to 3.30am Thu-Sat; ⓂLavapiés) One of the hottest spots in Lavapiés, this great venue hosts a largely bohemian crowd who come from all over the city for a fine roster leavened with flamenco (8pm Wednesday), rock and fusion. After the live acts leave the stage around midnight, it's DJ-spun tunes.

### TEATRO PAVÓN                                 THEATRE

Map p235 (☑91 528 28 19; www.teatroclasico. mcu.es; Calle de los Embajadores 9; ⓂLa Latina, Tirso de Molina) The home of the National Classical Theatre Company, this theatre has a regular calendar of classical shows by Spanish and European playwrights.

### CINE DORÉ                                     CINEMA

Map p235 (☑91 369 11 25; www.mecd.gob.es/cultura-mecd/areas-cultura/cine/mc/fe/cine-dore/programacion.html; Calle de Santa Isabel 3; ◎Tue-Sun; ⓂAntón Martín) The National Film Library offers fantastic classic and vanguard films for just €2.50.

# 🔒 SHOPPING

La Latina may be a largely after-dark and weekend affair, but its appeal to a hip, well-to-do urban crowd has attracted small boutiques, especially those specialising in designer jewellery, to the narrow streets. This is also the *barrio* that throngs with Sunday bargain hunters, drawn here by El Rastro (which tumbles down into Lavapiés), and you'll also come across curio shops.

### ★BOTERÍA JULIO RODRÍGUEZ                    ARTS & CRAFTS

(☑91 365 66 29; www.boteriajuliorodriguez.es; Calle del Águila 12; ⊙9.30am-2pm & 4.30-8pm Mon-Fri, 10am-1.30pm Sat; ⓂLa Latina) One of the last makers of traditional Spanish wineskins left in Madrid, Botería Julio Rodríguez is like a window on a fast-disappearing world. They make a great gift and, as you'd expect, they're in a different league from the cheap wineskins found in souvenir shops across downtown Madrid.

### ★HELENA ROHNER                    JEWELLERY

Map p236 (☑91 365 79 06; www.helenarohner.com.es; Calle del Almendro 4; ⊙9am-8.30pm Mon-Fri, noon-2.30pm & 3.30-8pm Sat, noon-3pm Sun; ⓂLa Latina, Tirso de Molina) One of Europe's most creative jewellery designers, Helena Rohner has a spacious boutique in La Latina. Working with silver, stone, porcelain, wood and Murano glass, she makes inventive pieces that are a regular feature of Paris fashion shows.

### EL RASTRO                    MARKET

Map p235 (Calle de la Ribera de Curtidores; ⊙8am-3pm Sun; ⓂLa Latina, Puerta de Toledo, Tirso de Molina) Welcome to what is claimed to be Europe's largest flea market. Antiques are also a major drawcard with a concentration of stores at Nuevas Galerías and Galerías Piquer; most shops open 10am to 2pm and 5pm to 8pm Monday to Saturday and not all open during El Rastro.

### ACEITUNAS JIMÉNEZ                    FOOD

Map p235 (☑91 365 46 23; Plaza del General Vara del Rey 14; ⊙10.30am-2.30pm & 3.30-8pm Mon-Thu, 10.30am-2.30pm Fri & Sat, 10.30am-3pm Sun; ⓂLa Latina) An institution on a Sunday stroll in El Rastro, this tiny shop serves up pickled olives in plastic cups and in all manner of varieties, as well as aubergines, garlic and anything else they've decided to soak in lashings of oil and/or vinegar.

### DE PIEDRA                    JEWELLERY

Map p236 (☑91 365 96 20; www.depiedracreaciones.com; Calle de la Ruda 19; ⊙11am-2pm & 5-8.30pm Mon-Sat, noon-3pm Sun; ⓂLa Latina) Necklaces, earrings, bracelets and home decorations made by a local design team fill this lovely showroom.

### LA HUERTA DE ALMERÍA                    FOOD

Map p235 (☑91 032 03 29; www.lahuertadealmeria.com; Calle de la Magdalena 25; ⊙10.30am-11.30pm; ⓂAntón Martín) The health-conscious can head here for freshly made juices, shakes and smoothies and a wide selection of organic and all-natural fruits, vegetables and dry goods. Its vegetarian or vegan meals to go are made mostly with products straight from the south of Spain.

### CARAMELOS PACO                    FOOD

Map p236 (☑91 365 42 58, 91 354 06 70; www.caramelospaco.com; Calle de Toledo 53-55; ⊙10am-2pm & 5-9pm Mon-Sat, 11am-3pm Sun; ⓂLa Latina) A sweet shop that needs to be seen to be believed, Caramelos Paco has been indulging children and adults alike since 1934 and remains unrivalled when it comes to variety – there's almost nothing you can't find here.

# 🏃 SPORTS & ACTIVITIES

### FUNDACIÓN CONSERVATORIO CASA PATAS                    DANCING

(☑91 429 84 71; www.fundacioncasapatas.com; Calle de Cañizares 10; 1hr class from €40; ⓂAntón Martín, Tirso de Molina) There's every conceivable type of flamenco instruction here, including dance, guitar, and singing.

### ACADEMIA AMOR DE DIOS                    DANCING

Map p235 (Centro de Arte Flamenco y Danza Española; ☑91 360 04 34; www.amordedios.com; 1st fl, Calle de Santa Isabel 5; ⓂAntón Martín) This is the best-known course for flamenco dancing (and probably the hardest to get into). Although it's more for budding professionals than casual visitors, it does have the odd Spanish-language *'cursillo'* (little course) that runs for a day or more.

### LETANGO TOURS                    WALKING

Map p235 (☑655 818740; www.letangospaintours.com; Calle del Mesón de Paredes 2; per person €135) Walking tours through Madrid with additional excursions to San Lorenzo de El Escorial, Segovia and Toledo.

# Sol, Santa Ana & Huertas

## Neighbourhood Top Five

**❶ Real Academia de Bellas Artes de San Fernando** (p85) Discovering the little-known artistic riches of Spain's most underrated art gallery.

**❷ Plaza de Santa Ana** (p87) Spending a lazy afternoon watching the world go by and nursing a Rioja on one of the outdoor tables.

**❸ La Venencia** (p92) Stepping back in time at this old-style sherry bar that captures the spirit of a Spain that long ago disappeared elsewhere.

**❹ Café Central** (p94) Getting into the swing of things at this art-deco salon that's internationally recognised

as one of the world's finest jazz clubs.

**❺ Barrio de las Letras** (p89) Losing yourself in the tangle of lanes that make up this storied neighbourhood with its echoes of Cervantes and Madrid's literary past.

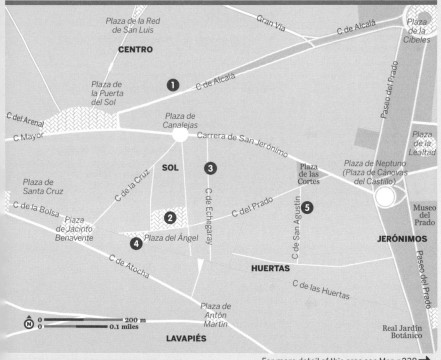

For more detail of this area see Map p238 ➡

## Lonely Planet's Top Tip

The Real Academia de Bellas Artes de San Fernando may have a collection that is the envy of many a European gallery but it's free if you come on a Wednesday. And unlike free days at other better-known Madrid art galleries, you'll see no discernible rise in visitor numbers on the day, allowing you to enjoy it in peace.

### ✕ Best Places to Eat

➡ Casa Alberto (p89)

➡ La Terraza del Casino (p91)

➡ Casa Labra (p88)

➡ Lhardy (p92)

➡ Casa Toni (p88)

For reviews, see p88.➡

### ♟ Best Places to Drink

➡ La Venencia (p92)

➡ Tartân Roof (p92)

➡ El Imperfecto (p92)

➡ La Terraza del Urban (p93)

➡ Taberna La Dolores (p92)

➡ Salmón Gurú (p92)

For reviews, see p92.➡

### ◉ Best Literary Landmarks

➡ Calle de Cervantes 2 (p89)

➡ Casa Alberto (p89)

➡ Convento de las Trinitarias (p89)

➡ Casa de Lope de Vega (p87)

➡ Plaza de Santa Ana (p87)

For reviews, see p87.➡

# Explore: Sol, Santa Ana & Huertas

Sol, Santa Ana and Huertas together make up Madrid's most clamorous corner. So many explorations of this neighbourhood begin in the Plaza de la Puerta del Sol, the pulsing heart of downtown Madrid, then move on to nearby Plaza de Santa Ana and the laneways that tumble down the hillside to the east.

And yet, there are subtle differences between the two squares. Sol is above all a crossroads, a place for people to meet before fanning out across the city. There are reasons to linger, but for the most part a sense of transience is what prevails. And Sol is always busy, no matter the hour.

Plaza de Santa Ana, on the other hand, is a destination in its own right, a stirringly beautiful square that has become emblematic of a city intent on living the good life. It is also a place of many moods. On a sunny weekday afternoon, it can be quiet (by its own rather noisy standards), a place to nurse a wine as you plot your path through the city. This is when the Barrio de las Letras is also at its most accessible, its streets suitably sedate for a *barrio* (district) rich in literary resonance. But come most nights of the week, Santa Ana and the surrounding streets crescendo into life, an explosion of noise and revelry that ripples out across the city.

# Local Life

➡ **Hang-outs** 1pm on a Sunday is known in Madrid as *la hora del vermut* (vermouth hour). Mostly this resonates in neighbouring La Latina, but Casa Alberto (p89) is arguably the real star of the hour.

➡ **Flamenco** One of the great flamenco venues of Old Madrid, the extravagantly tiled Villa Rosa (p94) has returned to its roots. It even starred in a Pedro Almodóvar movie.

➡ **Meeting point** It's a cliché whose time has passed for the in crowd, but meeting at the paving stone that marks Spain's Kilometre Zero on Plaza de la Puerta del Sol (p86) is a time-honoured local tradition.

➡ **Meeting point 2** The Plaza de Santa Ana (p87) is a wonderful place to spend an evening/afternoon/day, nursing a glass of wine and wondering why life can't always be like this.

# Getting There & Away

➡ **Metro** The Sol metro station is one of the city's most useful, with lines 1, 2 and 3 all passing through. Other useful stations are Sevilla (line 2) and Tirso de Molina and Antón Martín (both line 1).

Madrid's 'other' art gallery, the Real Academia de Bellas Artes has for centuries played a pivotal role in the artistic life of the city. As the royal fine arts academy, it has nurtured local talent, thereby complementing the royal penchant for drawing the great international artists of the day into their realm. The pantheon of former alumni reads like a who's who of Spanish art, and the collection that now hangs on the academy's walls is a suitably rich one.

**DON'T MISS**

➡ Zurbarán & El Greco

➡ 1st-Floor Masters

➡ Picasso, Sorolla & Gris

**PRACTICALITIES**

➡ Map p238, D3

➡ 📞91 524 08 64

➡ www.realacademia
bellasartessanfernando.
com

➡ Calle de Alcalá 13

➡ adult/child €8/free, Wed free

➡ 🕙10am-3pm Tue-Sun Sep-Jul

➡ Ⓜ Sol, Sevilla

## Bastion of Tradition

In any other city, this gallery would be a standout attraction, but in Madrid it often gets forgotten in the rush to the Prado, Thyssen or Reina Sofía. Nonetheless, a visit here is a fascinating journey into another age of art; when we tell you that Picasso and Dalí studied at this academy, but found it far too stuffy for their liking, you'll get an idea of what to expect. A centre of excellence since Fernando VI founded the academy in the 18th century, it remains a stunning repository of works by some of the best-loved old masters.

## Zurbarán & El Greco

The 1st floor, mainly devoted to 16th- to 19th-century paintings, is the most noteworthy of those in the academic gallery. Among relative unknowns, you come across a hall of works by Francisco de Zurbarán (especially arresting is the series of full-length portraits of white-cloaked friars) and a *San Jerónimo* by El Greco.

## Other 1st-Floor Masters

At a 'fork' in the exhibition, a sign points right to rooms 11 to 16, the main one showcasing Alonso Cano (1601–67) and José de Ribera (1591–1652). In the others, a couple of minor portraits by Velázquez hang alongside the occasional Rubens, Tintoretto and Bellini, which have somehow been smuggled in. Rooms 17 to 22 offer a space full of Bravo Murillo and last, but most captivating, 13 pieces by Goya, including self-portraits, portraits of King Fernando VII and the infamous minister Manuel Godoy, along with one depicting bullfighting.

## Modern Art

The 19th and 20th centuries are the themes upstairs. It's not the most extensive or engaging modern collection, but you'll find drawings by Picasso as well as works by Joaquín Sorolla, Juan Gris, Eduardo Chillida and Ignacio Zuloaga, in most cases with only one or two items each.

# ⊙ SIGHTS

**The Real Academia de Bellas Artes de San Fernando and the Plaza de Santa Ana capture two of Madrid's most enduring sources of appeal – the exceptional museums dedicated to fine art and the irresistible energy that dominates the city's streets. The charm and sense of history that define the intimate Barrio de las Letras is another completely different perspective on life, just as appealing and just as much a part of the Madrid experience.**

### REAL ACADEMIA DE BELLAS ARTES DE SAN FERNANDO    MUSEUM
See p85.

### ★CÍRCULO DE BELLAS ARTES    ARTS CENTRE, VIEWPOINT
Map p238 (La Azotea; ☑913605400; www.circulo bellasartes.com; Calle de Alcalá 42; admission to roof terrace €4; ☉roof terrace 9am-2am Mon-Thu, to 3am Fri, 11am-3am Sat, 11am-2am Sun; Ⓜ Banco de España, Sevilla) For some of Madrid's best views, take the lift to the 7th floor of the 'Fine Arts Circle'. You can almost reach out and touch the glorious dome of the Edificio Metrópolis and otherwise take in Madrid in all its finery, including the distant mountains. Two bars, lounge music and places to recline add to the experience. Downstairs, the centre has exhibitions, concerts, short films and book readings. There's also a fine belle-époque cafe (p93) on the ground floor.

### ★EDIFICIO METRÓPOLIS    ARCHITECTURE
Map p238 (Gran Vía; Ⓜ Banco de España, Sevilla) Among the more interesting buildings along Gran Vía is the stunning, French-designed Edificio Metrópolis, built in 1905, which marks the southern end of Gran Vía. The winged victory statue atop its dome was added in 1975 and is best seen from Calle de Alcalá or Plaza de la Cibeles. It's magnificent when floodlit.

### PLAZA DE LA PUERTA DEL SOL    SQUARE
Map p238 (Ⓜ Sol) The official centre point of Spain is a gracious, crowded hemisphere of elegant facades. It is, above all, a cross-roads: people here are forever heading somewhere else, on foot, by metro (three lines cross here) or by bus (many lines terminate and start nearby). Hard as it is to believe now, in Madrid's earliest days, the Puerta del Sol (Gate of the Sun) was the eastern gate of the city.

The main building on the square houses the regional government of the Comunidad de Madrid. The **Casa de Correos** (Map p238), as it is called, was built as the city's main post office in 1768. The clock was added in 1856 and on New Year's Eve people throng the square to wait impatiently for the clock to strike midnight, and at each gong swallow a grape – not as easy as it sounds! On the footpath outside the Casa de Correos is a plaque marking Spain's **Kilometre Zero**, the point from which Spain's network of roads is measured.

The semicircular junction owes its present appearance in part to the Bourbon king Carlos III (r 1759–88), whose **equestrian statue** (Map p238) (complete with his unmistakable nose) stands in the middle. Look out for the **statue of a bear** (Map p238) nuzzling a *madroño* (strawberry tree) at the plaza's eastern end; this is the official symbol of the city.

### CASA MUSEO DE RATÓN PEREZ    MUSEUM
Map p238 (☑91 522 69 68; www.casamuseo ratonperez.com; 1st fl, Calle de Arenal 8; €3; ☉5-8pm Mon, 11am-2pm & 5-8pm Tue-Fri, 11am-3pm & 4-8pm Sat; Ⓜ Sol) The Spanish version of the tooth fairy is a cute little mouse called 'El Ratón Perez', and this small museum close to Sol takes you into a recreation of his home. Entry is by guided tour and the commentary is only in Spanish, but it's still worth a visit as you'll see his secret door, a layout of his home inside a biscuit tin and all manner of little artefacts. Entrance is via the passageway signed 'Centro Comercial Arenal 8'.

---

### PLAZA DE CANALEJAS

It has long been one of downtown Madrid's more elegant corners, a small roundabout surrounded by elegant facades and a gateway to Plaza de Santa Ana. But there's a massive redevelopment under way, which shouldn't change the appearance – the facades are supposed to remain – but may increase the things you can do here. The northwestern corner of the square, all the way up to Calle de Alcalá, will be transformed into a luxury hotel and large shopping complex. It's due to be completed in 2018, or perhaps 2019...

# TOP SIGHT
## PLAZA DE SANTA ANA

The Plaza de Santa Ana is a delightful confluence of elegant architecture and irresistible energy. Situated in the heart of Huertas, it was laid out in 1810 during the controversial reign of Joseph Bonaparte, giving breathing space to what had hitherto been one of Madrid's most claustrophobic *barrios*. The plaza became a focal point for the intellectual life of the day, and the cafes surrounding the plaza thronged with writers, poets and artists engaging in endless *tertulias* (literary and philosophical discussions).

Echoes of this literary history survive in the statues of the 17th-century writer Calderón de la Barca and **Federíco García Lorca** (added in 1998 on the 100th anniversary of his birth), in the Teatro Español (p95) at the plaza's eastern end, and continue down into the Barrio de las Letras (p89). Culture of a very different kind – bullfighting – also took centre stage here, with many a (long-since-disappeared) bullfighting bar nearby and the Gran Victoria Hotel (now Me Meliá Reina Victoria; p176) the hotel of choice for Spain's best *toreros* (bullfighters). Apart from anything else, the plaza is the starting point for a long Huertas night; the outdoor tables that spill from the bars and restaurants onto the plaza are marvellous.

### DON'T MISS

➡ Outdoor Tables
➡ Lorca Statue
➡ Teatro Español

### PRACTICALITIES

➡ Map p238, D6
➡ Plaza de Santa Ana
➡ Ⓜ Sevilla, Sol, Antón Martín

**SOL, SANTA ANA & HUERTAS** SIGHTS

### CASA DE LOPE DE VEGA                    MUSEUM

Map p238 (☑91 429 92 16; www.casamuseo lopedevega.org; Calle de Cervantes 11; ⊘guided tours every 30min 10am-6pm Tue-Sun; ⓂAntón Martín) **FREE** Lope de Vega may be little known outside the Spanish-speaking world, but he was one of the greatest playwrights ever to write in Spanish, not to mention one of Madrid's favourite and most colourful literary sons. The house, which was restored in the 1950s, is filled with memorabilia related to his life and times. Out the back is a tranquil garden, a rare haven of birdsong.

Scandalously, he shared the house, where he lived and wrote for 25 years until his death in 1635, with a mistress and four children by three different women; Lope de Vega's house was a typical *casa de malicia* (house of ill repute).

### CONGRESO DE LOS
### DIPUTADOS                            LANDMARK

Map p238 (☑91 390 65 25; www.congreso.es; Plaza de las Cortes; ⊘guided tours noon Fri, 10.30am-12.30pm Sat Sep-Jul; ⓂSevilla) **FREE** Spain's lower house of parliament was originally a Renaissance building, but it was completely revamped in 1850 and given a facade with a neoclassical portal. The imposing lions watching over the entrance were smelted from cannons used in Spain's African wars during the mid-19th century. On the day that they were mounted outside the parliament building, one irreverent Madrid newspaper wrote, 'And what mouths they have! One might imagine them to be parliamentarians!'

### ATENEO CIENTÍFICO, LITERARIO Y
### ARTÍSTICO DE MADRID          NOTABLE BUILDING

Map p238 (☑ext 6 91 429 17 50; www.ateneo demadrid.com; Calle del Prado 21; guided-visits admission €3; ⊘guided visits 10am-1pm Mon-Fri Sep-Jul; ⓂSevilla) This venerable club of learned types was founded in 1821, although the building took on its present form in 1884. Its library prompted Benito Pérez Galdós to describe it as the most important 'intellectual temple' in Madrid and a reference point for the thriving cultural life of the Barrio de las Letras (p89). Guided visits take you into the foyer and the upstairs library, a jewel of another age, with dark timber stacks, weighty tomes and creakily quiet reading rooms dimly lit with desk lamps.

# ✗ EATING

Sol has something for everyone, but the noise surrounding Huertas' nightlife can obscure the fact that the *barrio* is a terrific place to eat out. Its culinary appeal lies in a hotchpotch of styles rather than any overarching personality. There are bastions of traditional cooking with restaurants serving Basque, Galician, Andalucian and Italian cuisine. When you factor in the fine bars and pulsing nightlife, it's difficult to find a good reason to leave the *barrio* once the sun goes down.

### CASA TONI                          SPANISH €
Map p238 (☑91 532 25 80; casatoni2@hotmail. com; Calle de la Cruz 14; mains €6-13; ⊘noon-4.30pm & 7pm-midnight; Ⓜ️Sol) Locals flock to Casa Toni, one of Madrid's best old-school Spanish bars, for simple, honest cuisine fresh off the griddle. Specialities include cuttlefish, gazpacho and offal – the crispy pork ear is out of this world. While you're there, you can try one of the local Madrid wines. The prices are great and the old Madrid charm can't be beat.

### CASA LABRA                         TAPAS €
Map p238 (☑91 532 14 05; www.casalabra.es; Calle de Tetuán 11; tapas from €1; ⊘11.30am-3.30pm & 6-11pm; Ⓜ️Sol) Casa Labra has been going strong since 1860, an era that the decor strongly evokes. Locals love their *bacalao* (cod) and ordering it here – either as deep-fried tapas (*una tajada de bacalao* goes for €1.50) or *una croqueta de bacalao* (€1.50) – is a Madrid rite of initiation. As the lunchtime queues attest, they go through more than 700kg of cod every week.

This is also a bar with history – it was where the Partido Socialista Obrero Español (PSOE; Spanish Socialist Party) was formed on 2 May 1879. It was a favourite of poet and playwright Federíco García Lorca as well as appearing in Pío Baroja's novel *La Busca*.

### VINOS GONZÁLEZ                     TAPAS, DELI €
Map p238 (☑91 429 56 18; www.casagonzalez.es; Calle de León 12; tapas from €3.50, raciones €9-15; ⊘9.30am-midnight Mon-Thu, to 1am Fri & Sat, 11am-6pm Sun; Ⓜ️Antón Martín) Ever dreamed of a deli where you could choose a tasty morsel and sit down and eat it right there? Well, the two are usually kept separate in Spain but here you can. On offer is a tempting array of local and international cheeses, cured meats and other typically Spanish delicacies. The tables are informal, cafe style and we recommend lingering.

### EL LATERAL                          TAPAS €
Map p238 (☑91 420 15 82; www.lateral.com; Plaza de Santa Ana 12; tapas €1.55-9.80, raciones €7-13; ⊘noon-midnight Sun-Wed, to 2am Thu-Sat; Ⓜ️Antón Martín, Sol) Our pick of the bars surrounding Plaza de Santa Ana, El Lateral does terrific *pinchos* (snacks), the perfect accompaniment to the fine wines on offer. Tapas are creative without being over the top (wild mushroom croquettes or sirloin with foie gras). Service is restaurant-standard, rather than your average tapas-bar brusqueness.

### LAS BRAVAS                          TAPAS €
Map p238 (☑91 522 85 81; www.lasbravas. com; Callejón de Álvarez Gato 3; raciones €4-13; ⊘12.30-4.30pm & 7.30pm-12.30am; Ⓜ️Sol, Sevilla) Las Bravas has long been the place for a *caña* (small glass of beer) and some of the best *patatas bravas* (fried potatoes with a spicy tomato sauce) in town. In fact, its version of the *bravas* sauce is so famous that it patented it. Other good orders include *calamares* (calamari) and *oreja a la plancha* (grilled pig's ear).

The antics of the bar staff are enough to merit a stop, and the distorting mirrors are a minor Madrid landmark. Elbow your way to the bar and be snappy about your orders. It also does *bravas* to take away.

### LA FINCA DE SUSANA                  SPANISH €
Map p238 (☑91 429 76 78; www.grupandilana. com; Calle del Príncipe 10; mains €8-14; ⊘1-3.45pm & 8.30-11.30pm Sun-Wed, 1-3.45pm & 8.15pm-midnight Thu-Sat; ☎; Ⓜ️Sevilla) It's difficult to find a better combination of price, quality cooking and classy atmosphere anywhere in Huertas. The softly lit dining area has a sophisticated vibe and the sometimes-innovative, sometimes-traditional food draws a hip young crowd. The duck confit with plums, turnips and couscous is a fine choice. No reservations.

### LA GLORIA DE MONTERA                SPANISH €
Map p238 (☑91 523 44 07; www.grupandilana. com; Calle del Caballero de Gracia 10; mains €8-14; ⊘1.15-11.30pm; Ⓜ️Gran Vía) La Gloria de Montera combines classy decor with eminently reasonable prices. The food isn't especially creative, but the tastes are fresh and the surroundings sophisticated. You'll get a good

## BARRIO DE LAS LETRAS

In medieval Madrid, the **Barrio de las Letras** (District of Letters; Map p238; M Antón Martín) – bordered by Plaza de Santa Ana (west), Carrera de San Jerónimo (north), Paseo del Prado (east) and Calle de Atocha (south) – was one of Madrid's most important cultural hubs.

At Calle de Cervantes 11, Lope de Vega (1562–1635), arguably Spain's premier playwright, lived and died, and his house is now a museum (p87). But the street on which Lope de Vega's house sits owes its name to an even-more-famous former resident, Miguel de Cervantes Saavedra (1547–1616). Cervantes, the author of *Don Quijote*, spent much of his adult life in Madrid and lived and died at **Calle de Cervantes 2** (Map p238; M Antón Martín); a plaque (dating from 1834) sits above the door. Sadly, the original building was torn down in the early 19th century despite a plea from King Fernando VII.

When Cervantes died, his body was interred around the corner at the **Convento de las Trinitarias** (Map p238; Calle de Lope de Vega 16; M Antón Martín), which is marked by another plaque. After centuries of mystery around exactly where his body lay, it was discovered in 2015. The convent (which is still home to cloistered nuns) is closed to casual visitors (except for Mass) but pass by to see if this has changed.

A **statue of Cervantes** stands in the Plaza de las Cortes, opposite the parliament building.

initiation into Spanish cooking without paying over the odds. It doesn't take reservations, so turn up early or be prepared to wait.

It's from the same stable as La Finca de Susana and **Ginger** (Map p238; 91 369 10 59; www.grupandilana.com; Plaza del Ángel 12; mains €7-14; 9am-11.30pm Sun-Wed, to midnight Thu-Sat; M Sol).

★ **CASA ALBERTO**                                TAPAS €€

Map p238 (91 429 93 56; www.casaalberto.es; Calle de las Huertas 18; tapas €3.25-10, raciones €7-16.50, mains €16-19; restaurant 1.30-4pm & 8pm-midnight Tue-Sat, 1.30-4pm Sun, bar noon-1.30am Tue-Sat, 12.30-4pm Sun, closed Sun Jul & Aug; M Antón Martín) One of the most atmospheric old *tabernas* (taverns) of Madrid, Casa Alberto has been around since 1827 and occupies a building where Cervantes is said to have written one of his books. The secret to its staying power is vermouth on tap, excellent tapas at the bar and fine sit-down meals. Casa Alberto's *rabo de toro* (bull's tail) is famous among aficionados, but the tavern is also known for its pig's trotters, snails, meatballs, croquettes and cod.

**LA MUCCA DE PRADO**                SPANISH, INTERNATIONAL €€

Map p238 (91 521 00 00; www.lamucca company.com/lamucca-de-prado; Calle del Prado 16; mains €9-16; 1pm-1.30am Sun-Wed, to 2am Thu, to 2.30am Fri & Sat; M Antón Martín) This wildly popular outpost of the similarly cool Malasaña La Mucca serves up terrific local dishes such as *jamón* (ham) platters, but the menu is mostly international with pizzas, steaks, burgers and salads, usually with a Spanish twist. The food is great, but there's also an irresistible buzz about this place that makes everything taste better and the night last longer.

**MARINA VENTURA**                    MEDITERRANEAN €€

Map p238 (91 429 38 10; www.marinaventura. es; Calle de Ventura de la Vega 13; mains €16-23; 1.15pm-midnight; M Sevilla) Paella and other rice dishes in all their wonderful variety – there are 18 different versions on the menu – dominate this appealing place tucked away in the Barrio de las Letras. There's the original *paella valenciana*, of course, but consider also the black rice cooked in squid ink, *arroz meloso* (a soupy seafood rice) or *arroz con bogavante* (lobster rice).

**VIETNAM**                                VIETNAMESE €€

Map p238 (91 755 31 26; www.facebook.com/ vietnamrestaurante; Calle de las Huertas 4; mains €13-18; 1-4pm & 8-11.30pm Mon, Wed & Thu, 8-11.30pm Tue, 1-4pm & 8pm-midnight Fri-Sun; M Antón Martín) Madrid's best Vietnamese restaurant does expertly prepared rice paper rolls, pho and some fabulous beef dishes using prime Argentinian beef. Service is friendly and reservations are strongly recommended on weekends. This is the real deal, not some local adaptation.

SOL, SANTA ANA & HUERTAS EATING

## DOWNTOWN PASTRY SHOPS

**La Mallorquina** (Map p238; ☑91 521 12 01; www.pastelerialamallorquina.es; Plaza de la Puerta del Sol 8; pastries from €2; ⊘9am-9.15pm; MSol) A classic pastry shop that's packed to the rafters by *madrileños* (residents of Madrid) who just couldn't pass by without stopping. Treat yourself to a takeaway *ensaimada* (a light pastry dusted with icing sugar) from Mallorca.

**Antigua Pastelería del Pozo** (Map p238; ☑91 522 38 94; Calle del Pozo 8; pastries from €1.50; ⊘9.30am-2pm & 5-8pm Tue-Sat, 9am-2pm Sun; MSol) Antigua Pastelería del Pozo has lost none of its old charm in turning out all sorts of great pastries. It has been in operation since 1830, making it the city's oldest pastry shop.

**Confitería El Riojano** (Map p238; ☑91 366 44 82; www.confiteriaelriojano.com; Calle Mayor 10; pastries from €3; ⊘10am-2pm & 5-9pm Mon-Fri, 10am-2.30pm & 5.30-9pm Sat & Sun; MSol) Founded in 1855, this place serves the usual suspects, as well as traditional Madrid offerings such as *azucarillos* (meringue-like sugar bombs) of lemon, coffee or strawberry and *bartolillos* (sweet filled pastries).

**Casa Mira** (Map p238; ☑91 429 88 95; www.casamira.es; Carrera de San Jerónimo 30; pastries from €2.50; ⊘10am-2pm & 5-9pm Mon-Sat; MSol) The turning, wedding-cake-like display in the window, laden with sweets, cakes, fat pastries and candied fruits, has to be seen to be believed. The shop is especially known for its *turrónes* (nougat).

**Brown Bear Bakery** (Map p238; ☑91 369 05 87; www.brownbearbakery.es; Calle de León 10; pastries €1.20-4; ⊘8.30am-9pm; MSol) A traditional Spanish bakery and pastry shop with a US-inspired twist, Brown Bear offers local and international favourites. With buttery *palmeras de chocolate*, croissants and muffins, or carrot cake and apple crumble from across the pond, you can sit down with a cup of coffee or take your pastries to go.

### EL DIARIO DE HUERTAS
SPANISH €€

Map p238 (☑91 429 28 00; Calle de las Huertas 69; mains €8-18; ⊘noon-midnight; MAntón Martín) This bar and restaurant has been serving old-fashioned home cooking since 1879. The menu includes typical tapas, cheeses, cured ham and sausages, and simple yet delicious classics like *gambas al ajillo* (garlic prawns) and *rabo de toro estofado* (stewed oxtail). Tables and chairs are few, so locals go on weekends to stand at the bar and share with friends.

### L'ARTISAN
FUSION €€

Map p238 (☑91 420 31 72; www.lartisanmadrid.com; Calle Ventura de la Vega 15; mains €13-18; ⊘1.30-4.30pm & 8pm-12.30am Tue-Sat; MSol) Two parallel menus, one French and one Japanese, make this restaurant a unique choice. The lunch menu changes daily, or you can enjoy a sampler for two with a selection of dishes. French specialities include creamy risotto and duck leg confit. On the Japanese side, you can try butterfish marinated with miso or *shochu* sweet potato liquor.

### EL TRICICLO
MODERN SPANISH €€

Map p238 (☑91 024 47 98; www.eltriciclo.es; Calle de Santa María 28; raciones €6-28; ⊘1-4pm & 8pm-12.30am Mon-Sat; MAntón Martín) A relative newcomer on Madrid's culinary scene, 'The Tricycle' has earned plaudits for its assured fusion cooking that places seasonal ingredients at the centre of everything it does. The approach is a broad church with some traditional staples, innovative diversions and international dishes all given space on the menu. You can order full-, half- and even one-third-sized dishes – nice idea.

### LA HUERTA DE TUDELA
SPANISH €€

Map p238 (☑91 420 44 18; www.lahuertadetudela.com; Calle del Prado 15; mains €14-22, set menus €25-37.50; ⊘1.30-4pm & 8.30-11.30pm Mon-Sat, 1.30-3.30pm Sun; MAntón Martín) A bastion of fine cooking from the northern Spanish region of Navarra, La Huerta de Tudela and its chef Ricardo Gil do excellent seasonal vegetable dishes, steaks and stews. The set menus includes one for coeliacs and another for vegetarians and vegans – typical of the thought that goes into this place. The atmosphere is formal, so dress well.

## MORATÍN VINOTECA
SPANISH, BISTRO €€

Map p238 (☑91 127 60 85; www.vinotecamoratin. com; Calle de Moratín 36; mains €12-18; ⊗1.30-4pm & 7.30pm-midnight Tue-Sat; ⓂAntón Martín) At this engaging little bistro down in the Paseo del Prado hinterland, service is both warm and knowledgable, the food is outstanding (try the octopus in olive oil with paprika and coriander on potato parmentier), and the wines are perfectly matched.

## LA CASA DEL ABUELO
TAPAS €€

Map p238 (☑902 027334; www.lacasadelabuelo. es; Calle de la Victoria 12; raciones from €9; ⊗noon-midnight Sun-Thu, to 1am Fri & Sat; ⓂSol) The 'House of the Grandfather' is an ageless, popular place that's been around for more than a hundred years. The traditional order here is a *chato* (small glass) of the heavy, sweet El Abuelo red wine (made in Toledo province) and the heavenly *gambas a la plancha* (grilled prawns) or *gambas al ajillo* (prawns sizzling in garlic on little ceramic plates).

More than 200kg of prawns are cooked here on a good day. There's another branch in Salamanca.

## MACEIRAS
GALICIAN €€

Map p238 (☑91 429 58 18; www.tabernamaceira. com; Calle de las Huertas 66; mains €6-14; ⊗1.15-4.15pm & 8pm-midnight Mon-Thu, 1.30-4.45pm & 8.30pm-1am Fri & Sat, 1.30-4.45pm & 8pm-midnight Sun; ⓂAntón Martín) Galician tapas (octopus, green peppers etc) never tasted so good as in this agreeably rustic bar down the bottom of the Huertas hill, especially

---

### BETWEEN MEALS & SPANISH FAST FOOD

If your tummy starts to rumble at a very un-Spanish hour, there are options, from *bocadillos* (filled rolls) to tapas.

**Vinos González** (p88) Deli tapas

**Enrique Tomas** (Map p238; ☑91 299 20 70; www.enriquetomas.com; Calle de la Cruz 25; bocadillos €2.50-4.50; ⊗9am-midnight Sun-Thu, to 1am Fri & Sat; ⓂSol) *Jamón* rolls

**Casa Alberto** (p89) Traditional tapas

**Los Gatos** (p91) Tapas in Huertas

**La Casa del Abuelo** (p91) Grilled prawns

---

when washed down with a crisp white Ribeiro. The simple wooden tables, loyal customers, Galician music playing in the background and handy location make it a fine place for before or after visiting the museums along the Paseo del Prado.

There's another **branch** (Map p238; www. tabernamaceira.com; Calle de Jesús 7; mains €6-14; ⊗1.15-4.15pm & 8.30pm-12.15am Mon-Fri, 1.30- 4.30pm & 8.30pm-1am Sat, 1.30-4.30pm & 8.30pm-midnight Sun; ⓂAntón Martín) around the corner.

## LOS GATOS
TAPAS €€

Map p238 (☑91 429 30 67; Calle de Jesús 2; tapas from €3.75; ⊗11am-2am; ⓂAntón Martín) Tapas you can point to without deciphering the menu and eclectic old-world decor (from bullfighting memorabilia to a fresco of skeletons at the bar) make this a popular choice down the bottom end of Huertas. The most popular orders are the *canapés* (tapas on toast), which, we have to say, are rather delicious.

## RESTAURANTE INTEGRAL ARTEMISA
VEGETARIAN €€

Map p238 (☑91 429 50 92; www.restaurantes vegetarianosartemisa.com; Calle de Ventura de la Vega 4; meals €11-16; ⊗1.30-4pm & 9pm-midnight; ☑; ⓂSevilla) With a couple of options for meat eaters, this mostly vegetarian restaurant does a brisk trade with its salads, moussaka and rice dishes. The decor is simple, the service is no-nonsense and the salads are what marks this place out as worthy of a visit. Alternatively, try the *plato degustación* (from €28) for a range of tastes.

## ★LA TERRAZA DEL CASINO
MODERN SPANISH €€€

Map p238 (☑91 532 12 75; www.casinodemadrid. es; Calle de Alcalá 15; mains €44-56, set menus €79-185; ⊗1-4pm & 9pm-midnight Mon-Sat; ⓂSevilla) Perched atop the lavish Casino de Madrid building, this temple of haute cuisine is the proud bearer of two Michelin stars and presided over by celebrity chef Paco Roncero. It's all about culinary experimentation, with a menu that changes as each new idea emerges from the laboratory and moves into the kitchen. The *menú de degustación* (€148) is a fabulous avalanche of tastes.

## ★LHARDY
SPANISH €€€

Map p238 (☑91 521 33 85; www.lhardy.com; Carrera de San Jerónimo 8; mains €24-36; ⊗1-3.30pm & 8.30-11pm Mon-Sat, 1-3.30pm Sun, closed Aug; Ⓜ Sol, Sevilla) This Madrid landmark (since 1839) is an elegant treasure trove of takeaway gourmet tapas downstairs and six dining areas upstairs that are the upmarket preserve of traditional Madrid dishes with an occasional hint of French influence. House specialities include *cocido a la madrileña* (meat-and-chickpea stew), pheasant and wild duck in an orange perfume. The quality and service are unimpeachable.

### SIDRERÍA VASCA ZERAÍN BASQUE €€€

Map p238 (☑91 429 79 09; www.restaurante-vasco-zerain-sidreria.es; Calle Quevedo 3; mains €16-30; ⊗1.30-4pm & 7.30pm-midnight Mon-Sat, 1.30-4pm Sun, closed Aug; Ⓜ Antón Martín) In the heart of the Barrio de las Letras, this sophisticated restaurant is one of the best places in town to sample Basque cuisine. The essential staples include cider, *bacalao* and wonderful steaks, while there are also a few splashes of creativity thrown in (the secret's in the sauce). We highly recommend the *menú sidrería* (cider-house menu; €37).

### A TASCA DO BACALHAU PORTUGÊS PORTUGUESE €€€

Map p238 (☑91 429 56 75; Calle de Lope de Vega 14; mains from €15.50; ⊗1.30-4pm & 8.30pm-midnight Tue-Sat, 1.30-4pm Sun, closed 1st half of Aug; Ⓜ Antón Martín) One of the few authentic Portuguese restaurants in Madrid, A Tasca do Bacalhau doesn't have a particularly extensive menu, but it's dominated by excellent *bacalhau* (cod) and rice dishes. It claims to have 412 different recipes for cod, although thankfully only a handful of these appear on the menu.

## 🍷🍸 DRINKING & NIGHTLIFE

**Huertas comes into its own after dark and stays that way until close to sunrise – this is one of the iconic neighbourhoods of the Madrid night. Bars are everywhere, from Sol down to the Paseo del Prado hinterland, but it's in Plaza de Santa Ana and along Calle de las Huertas that most of the action is concentrated. Huertas is good at any time of the night, but it's in the live jazz (and other music) venues and nightclubs that it really comes into its own.**

### ★ LA VENENCIA BAR

Map p238 (☑91 429 73 13; Calle de Echegaray 7; ⊗12.30-3.30pm & 7.30pm-1.30am; Ⓜ Sol, Sevilla) La Venencia is a *barrio* classic, with *manzanilla* (chamomile-coloured sherry) from Sanlúcar and sherry from Jeréz poured straight from the dusty wooden barrels, accompanied by a small selection of tapas with an Andalucian bent. There's no music, no flashy decorations; here it's all about you, your *fino* (sherry) and your friends.

### SALMÓN GURÚ COCKTAIL BAR

Map p238 (☑91 000 61 85; http://salmonguru.es; Calle de Echegaray 21; ⊗5pm-2.30am Wed-Sun; Ⓜ Antón Martín) When Sergi Arola's empire collapsed and the celebrated Le Cabrera cocktail bar went with it, Madrid lost one of its best cocktail maestros, Diego Cabrera. Thankfully, he's back with a wonderful multifaceted space where he serves up a masterful collection of drinks – work your way through his menu of 25 Cabrera *clasicos* to get started.

One of our favourites is the 'Tónico Sprenger', made with gin, lemon juice, cardamom tonic, cinnamon, cucumber and ginger beer.

### TARTÁN ROOF LOUNGE

Map p238 (La Azotea; www.azoteadelcirculo.com; 7th fl, Calle Marqués de Casa Riera 2; admission €4; ⊗9am-2am Mon-Thu, to 2.30am Fri, 11am-2.30am Sat & Sun) Order a cocktail, then lie down on the cushions and admire the vista from this fabulous rooftop terrace. It's a brilliant place to chill out, with the views at their best close to sunset.

### EL IMPERFECTO COCKTAIL BAR

Map p238 (Plaza de Matute 2; ⊗5pm-2.30am Mon-Thu, 3pm-2.30am Fri & Sat; Ⓜ Antón Martín) Its name notwithstanding, the 'Imperfect One' is our ideal Huertas bar, with occasional live jazz and a drinks menu as long as a saxophone, ranging from cocktails (€7, or two mojitos for €10) and spirits to milkshakes, teas and creative coffees. Its pina colada is one of the best we've tasted and the atmosphere is agreeably buzzy yet chilled.

### TABERNA LA DOLORES BAR

Map p238 (☑91 429 22 43; Plaza de Jesús 4; ⊗11am-1am; Ⓜ Antón Martín) Old bottles and beer mugs line the shelves behind the bar at this Madrid institution (1908), known for its blue-and-white-tiled exterior and for a

---

### ℹ DRINKING DRESS CODE

Going out for a drink in Madrid is generally a pretty casual affair, but to visit **Radio** or **La Terraza del Urban** you should dress well. No running shoes goes without saying, while a button-up shirt for men is close to obligatory. You might get away with jeans depending on the day and who's at the door.

---

30-something crowd that often includes the odd *famoso* (celebrity) or two. It claims to be 'the most famous bar in Madrid' – that's pushing it, but it's invariably full most nights of the week, so who are we to argue?

It serves good house wine, great anchovies and what Spaniards like to call 'well-poured beer'.

#### LA NEGRA TOMASA BAR
Map p238 (☏91 523 58 30; www.lanegratomasa. com; Calle de Cádiz 9; ☉1.30pm-4am Sun-Thu, to 5.30am Fri & Sat; ⓜSol) Bar, live music venue, restaurant and magnet for all things Cuban, La Negra Tomasa is a boisterous meeting place for the Havana set, with waitresses dressed in traditional Cuban outfits (definitely pre-Castro) and Cuban musicians playing deep into the night. Groups start at 11.30pm every night of the week, with additional performances at 3.30pm Sunday.

#### RADIO COCKTAIL BAR
Map p238 (☏91 701 60 20; www.memadrid.com; 7th fl, Plaza de Santa Ana 14; ☉7pm-2am Mon-Thu, 5pm-3am Fri, 1pm-3am Sat, 1pm-2am Sun; ⓜAntón Martín, Sol) High above the Plaza de Santa Ana, this sybaritic open-air cocktail bar has terrific views over Madrid's rooftops. It's a place for sophisticates, with chill-out areas strewn with cushions, DJs and a dress and door policy designed to sort out the classy from the wannabes.

#### JAZZ BAR BAR
Map p238 (☏91 429 70 31; Calle de Moratín 35; ☉3pm-2.30am; ⓜAntón Martín) Jazz aficionados will love this place for its endless jazz soundtrack and discreet leather booths (at last, a bar that has gone for privacy instead of trying to cram too many people in), and there's plenty of greenery to keep you cheerful. If you want live jazz, head elsewhere, but this place is like a mellow after-party for aficionados in the know.

#### LA TERRAZA DEL URBAN COCKTAIL BAR
Map p238 (☏91 787 77 70; Carrera de San Jerónimo 34, Urban Hotel; ☉noon-8pm Sun & Mon, to 3am Tue-Sat mid-May–Sep; ⓜSevilla) A strong contender for best rooftop bar in Madrid, this indulgent terrace sits atop the five-star Urban Hotel and has five-star views with five-star prices – worth every euro. It's only open while the weather's warm.

In case you get vertigo, head downstairs to the similarly high-class **Glass Bar** (Map p238; Carrera de San Jerónimo 34, Hotel Urban; ☉noon-3am; ⓜSevilla).

#### CAFÉ DEL CÍRCULO DE BELLAS ARTES CAFE
Map p238 (☏91 521 69 42; Calle de Alcalá 42; ☉9am-1am Sun-Thu, to 3am Fri & Sat; ⓜBanco de España, Sevilla) This wonderful belle-époque cafe was designed by Antonio Palacios in 1919 and boasts chandeliers and the charm of a bygone era, even if the waiters are not averse to looking aggrieved if you put them out. That said, they're friendlier than they used to be!

#### CERVECERÍA ALEMANA BAR
Map p238 (☏91 429 70 33; www.cerveceria alemana.com; Plaza de Santa Ana 6; ☉11am-12.30am Sun-Thu, to 2am Fri & Sat, closed Aug; ⓜAntón Martín, Sol) If you've only got time to stop at one bar on Plaza de Santa Ana, let it be this classic *cervecería* (beer bar), renowned for its cold, frothy beers and a wider selection of Spanish beers than is the norm. It's fine inside, but snaffle a table outside in the plaza on a summer's evening and you won't be giving it up without a fight.

Opened in 1904, this was one of Hemingway's haunts – neither the wood-lined bar nor the bow-tied waiters have changed much since his day.

#### TABERNA ALHAMBRA BAR
Map p238 (☏91 521 07 08; Calle de la Victoria 9; ☉11am-1am Sun-Wed, to 2am Thu, to 2.30am Fri & Sat; ⓜSol) There can be a certain sameness about the bars between Sol and Huertas, which is why this fine old *taberna* stands out. The striking facade and exquisite tile work of the interior are quite beautiful; however, this place is anything but stuffy and the feel is cool, casual and busy. It serves tapas and, later at night, there are some fine flamenco tunes.

### VIVA MADRID                                   BAR

Map p238 (☎91 420 35 96; www.restaurante vivamadrid.com; Calle de Manuel Fernández y González 7; ☺noon-midnight Mon-Thu, to 2am Fri & Sat; MAntón Martín, Sol) The tiled facade of Viva Madrid is one of Madrid's most recognisable and it's an essential landmark on the Huertas nightlife scene. Packed to the rafters on weekends, come here for fine mojitos and the casual, friendly atmosphere. The tapas offerings are another reason to pass by.

### DOS GARDENIAS                                 BAR

Map p238 (☎627 003571; www.facebook.com/dosgardenias.madrid; Calle de Santa María 13; ☺9.30pm-2.30am Tue-Sat; MAntón Martín) When Huertas starts to overwhelm, this tranquil little bar is the perfect antidote. The flamenco and chill-out music ensure a relaxed vibe, while sofas, softly lit colours and some of the best mojitos (and exotic teas) in the *barrio* make this the perfect spot to ease yourself into or out of the night.

## ☆ ENTERTAINMENT

### ★SALA EL SOL                          LIVE MUSIC

Map p238 (☎91 532 64 90; www.elsolmad.com; Calle de los Jardines 3; admission incl drink €10, concert tickets €6-30; ☺midnight-5.30am Tue-Sat Jul-Sep; MGran Vía) Madrid institutions don't come any more beloved than the terrific Sala El Sol. It opened in 1979, just in time for *la movida madrileña* (the Madrid scene), and quickly established itself as a leading stage for all the icons of the era, such as Nacha Pop and Alaska y los Pegamoides.

*La movida* may have mostly faded into history, but it lives on at El Sol, where the music rocks and rolls and usually resurrects the '70s and '80s, while soul and funk also get a run. Most concerts start at 11pm, though some acts take to the stage as early as 10pm. After the show, DJs spin rock, fusion and electronica from the awesome sound system. Visit the website for upcoming acts and to book.

### ★VILLA ROSA                             FLAMENCO

Map p238 (☎91 521 36 89; www.reservas.tablaoflamencovillarosa.com; Plaza de Santa Ana 15; admission incl drink adult/child €35/17; ☺11pm-6am Mon-Sat, shows 8.30pm & 10.45pm; MSol) Villa Rosa has been going strong since 1914, and in that time it has seen many manifestations. It originally made its name

as a flamenco venue and has recently returned to its roots with well-priced shows and meals that won't break the bank.

The extraordinary tiled facade (1928) is the work of Alfonso Romero, who was also responsible for the tile work in the Plaza de Toros – the facade is a tourist attraction in itself. This long-standing nightclub even appeared in the Pedro Almodóvar film *Tacones lejanos* (High Heels; 1991).

### ★CAFÉ CENTRAL                             JAZZ

Map p238 (☎91 369 41 43; www.cafecentralmadrid.com; Plaza del Ángel 10; admission €12-18; ☺12.30pm-2.30am Mon-Thu, to 3.30am Fri, 11.30am-3.30am Sat, performances 9pm; MAntón Martín, Sol) In 2011 the respected jazz magazine *Down Beat* included this art-deco bar on the list of the world's best jazz clubs, the only place in Spain to earn the prestigious accolade (said by some to be the jazz equivalent of earning a Michelin star). With well over 1000 gigs under its belt, it rarely misses a beat.

Big international names like Chano Domínguez, Tal Farlow and Wynton Marsalis have all played here and you'll hear everything from Latin jazz and fusion to tango and classical jazz. Performers usually play here for a week and then move on, so getting tickets shouldn't be a problem, except on weekends. Shows start at 9pm and tickets go on sale from 6pm before the set starts.

### ★TEATRO DE LA ZARZUELA            THEATRE

Map p238 (☎91 524 54 00; www.teatrodelazarzuela.mcu.es; Calle de Jovellanos 4; tickets €5-60; ☺box office noon-6pm Mon-Fri, 3-6pm Sat & Sun; MBanco de España, Sevilla) This theatre, built in 1856, is the premier place to see *zarzuela* (Spanish mix of theatre, music and dance). It also hosts a smattering of classical music and opera, as well as the cutting edge Compañía Nacional de Danza.

### COSTELLO CAFÉ & NITECLUB        LIVE MUSIC

Map p238 (☎91 522 18 15; www.costelloclub.com; Calle del Caballero de Gracia 10; €8-20; ☺8pm-2.30am Tue, to 3am Wed & Thu, to 3.30am Fri & Sat; MGran Vía) The very cool Costello Café & Niteclub weds smooth-as-silk ambience to an innovative mix of pop, rock and fusion in Warholesque surrounds. There's live music (pop and rock, often of the indie variety) at 9.30pm every night except Sunday and Monday, with resident and visiting DJs keeping you on your feet until closing time the rest of the week.

## CARDAMOMO
FLAMENCO

Map p238 (☑91 805 10 38; www.cardamomo.es; Calle de Echegaray 15; admission incl drink €39; ⊙10pm-3.30am & live shows 8pm & 10pm Wed-Mon; MSol, Sevilla) One of the better flamenco stages in town, Cardamomo draws more tourists than aficionados, but the flamenco is top notch. The early show lasts just 50 minutes, the latter 1½ hours.

## TEATRO ESPAÑOL
THEATRE

Map p238 (☑91 360 14 84; www.teatroespanol.es; Calle del Príncipe 25; MSevilla, Sol, Antón Martín) This theatre (formerly the Teatro del Príncipe) has been here in one form or another since the 16th century and is still one of the best places to catch mainstream Spanish drama, from the works of Lope de Vega to more recent playwrights.

## TEATRO MONUMENTAL
CLASSICAL MUSIC

Map p238 (☑91 429 10 55, 91 429 12 81; www.rtve.es/orquesta-coro; Calle de Atocha 65; ⊙ticket office 11am-2pm & 5-7pm Mon-Fri; MAntón Martín) The main concert season runs from October to March each year, when performances include those of the Banda Sinfónica Municipal Madrid, the Orquesta Sinfónica de RTVE, and occasional operas, ballets or *zarzuela* (tickets €10 to €28). It's a modern theatre with fabulous acoustics.

# 🛍 SHOPPING

**The shops in the streets surrounding Sol range from department stores and chain-clothing shops to some real gems. Shopping in Huertas is akin to being on a treasure hunt. Small, quirky shops – some run by the same family for generations, others devoted to the most specialised of niches – pop up in the most unlikely places, with especially rich pickings in the tangle of lanes that make up the Barrio de las Letras.**

## CASA DE DIEGO
FASHION & ACCESSORIES

Map p238 (☑91 522 66 43; www.casadediego.com; Plaza de la Puerta del Sol 12; ⊙9.30am-8pm Mon-Sat; MSol) This classic shop has been around since 1858, making, selling and repairing Spanish fans, shawls, umbrellas and canes. Service is old style and occasionally grumpy, but the fans are works of antique art. There's another **branch** (Map p238; ☑91 531 02 23; www.casadediego.com; Calle del los Mesoneros Romanos 4; ⊙9.30am-1.30pm & 4.45-8pm Mon-Sat; MCallao, Sol) nearby.

## LICORES CABELLO
WINE

Map p238 (☑91 429 60 88; Calle de Echegaray 19; ⊙10am-3pm & 5.30-10pm Mon-Sat; MSevilla, Antón Martín) All wine shops should be like this. This family-run corner shop really knows its wines and the interior has scarcely changed since 1913, with wooden shelves and even a faded ceiling fresco. There are fine wines in abundance (mostly Spanish, and a few foreign bottles), with some 500 labels on show or tucked away out the back.

## THE CORNER SHOP
CLOTHING

Map p238 (☑91 737 58 02; www.thecornershop.es; Calle de las Huertas 17; ⊙10.30am-9.30pm Mon-Fri, 11am-9.30pm Sat & Sun; MAntón Martín) This fine Huertas shop does a carefully curated collection of men's and women's fashions, with brand names like Scotch Soda, Blue Hole, Andy and Lucy and many others. Regardless of brands, it's always worth stopping by to check its casual street wear with a touch of style and a hint of the offbeat.

## OJALÁ MADRID
CLOTHING

Map p238 (☑91 429 65 95; www.ojala.es; Calle de las Huertas 5; ⊙11am-9.30pm; MAntón Martín) Colourful, stylish women's fashions by local designer Paloma del Pozo are well worth seeking out at the top end of Huertas. The look somehow manages to be both fun and sophisticated, a winning combination and something Spanish designers seem especially good at.

## MÁS QUE CERVEZAS
FOOD & DRINKS

Map p238 (☑91 016 41 31; www.masquecervezas.com; Calle de León 32; ⊙11am-10pm; MAntón Martín) This small, modern shop is packed floor to ceiling with bottled beers from over 30 countries, their labels bursting with bright colours. The selection is always changing, with around 500 brands at any given time.

## ALMACÉN DE PONTEJOS
CLOTHING

Map p238 (☑91 521 55 94; www.almacendepontejos.com; Plaza de Pontejos 2; ⊙9.30am-2pm & 4.30-8.15pm Mon-Fri, 9.30am-2pm Sat; MSol) Describing what this shop sells – fabrics, buttons and all manner of knick-knacks for dressmakers – only tells half the story. It's one of many such stores on the square and in the surrounding streets, an intriguing hidden subculture that dates back decades, a stone's throw from the Puerta del Sol. And it's very much alive – these shops can throng with people.

**JUSTO ALGABA**  GIFTS & SOUVENIRS

Map p238 (☑91 523 37 17; www.justoalgaba.com; Calle de la Paz 4; ☺10.30am-2pm & 5-8pm Mon-Fri, 10.30am-2pm Sat; Ⓜ Sol) This is where Spain's *toreros* (bullfighters) come to have their *traje de luces* (suit of lights, the traditional glittering bullfighting suit) made in all its intricate excess.

**TIENDA REAL MADRID**  SPORTS & OUTDOORS

Map p238 (☑91 755 45 38; www.realmadrid.com; Gran Vía 31; ☺10am-9pm Mon-Sat, 11am-9pm Sun; Ⓜ Gran Vía, Callao) The Real Madrid club shop sells replica shirts, posters, caps and just about everything else under the sun to which it could attach a club logo. In the centre of town there's a smaller **branch** (Tienda Real Madrid; Map p238; ☑91 521 79 50; www. realmadrid.com; Calle del Carmen 3; ☺10am-9pm Mon-Sat, 11am-8pm Sun; Ⓜ Sol) and, in the city's north, the stadium branch (p157).

**SANTARRUFINA**  RELIGIOUS

Map p238 (☑91 522 23 83; www.santarrufina.com; Calle de la Paz 4; ☺10am-2pm & 4.30-8pm Mon-Fri, 10am-2pm Sat; Ⓜ Sol) This gilded outpost of Spanish Catholicism has to be seen to be believed. Churches, priests and monasteries are some of the patrons of this overwhelming three-storey shop full of everything from simple rosaries to imposing statues of saints and even a litter used to carry the Virgin in processions.

**JUAN ALVAREZ**  MUSIC

Map p238 (☑91 429 20 33; www.guitarrasjuan alvarez.com; Calle de San Pedro 7, off Calle de Moratín; ☺5-8pm Mon, 10am-1.30pm & 5-8pm Tue-Fri, 10am-1.30pm Sat; Ⓜ Antón Martín) The shop and workshop may be tiny, but Juan Alvarez is one of the most celebrated guitar makers in Spain. The family business dates back to 1945 and former clients include Eric Clapton, Compay Segundo and a host of flamenco greats. Prices start from €150 and don't stop until they reach €12,000.

**JOSÉ RAMÍREZ**  MUSIC

Map p238 (☑91 531 42 29; www.guitarrasramirez. com; Calle de la Paz 8; ☺10am-2pm & 4.30-8pm Mon-Fri, 10am-2pm Sat; Ⓜ Sol) José Ramírez is one of Spain's best guitar makers and his guitars have been strummed by a host of flamenco greats and international musicians (including the Beatles). Using Honduran cedar, Cameroonian ebony and Indian or Madagascan rosewood, among other materials, based on traditions dating back over

generations, this is craftsmanship of the highest order. Out the back there's a little museum with guitars dating to 1830. Ask here about guitar classes.

**LIBRERÍA DESNIVEL**  BOOKS

Map p238 (☑91 429 12 81; www.libreriadesnivel. com; Plaza de Matute 6; ☺10am-8.30pm Mon-Fri, 11am-8pm Sat; Ⓜ Antón Martín) Although focused on mountaineering and rock-climbing, this fine bookshop has an excellent range of maps and travel books.

**LA VIOLETA**  FOOD

Map p238 (☑91 522 55 22; www.lavioletaonline. es; Plaza de Canalejas 6; ☺10am-2pm & 4.30-8.30pm Mon-Sat Sep-Jul; Ⓜ Sevilla) In the early 20th century, *violetas* (small violet-coloured sweets and frosted petals from the violet flower) took on an iconic status and remain one of the city's most typical sweets. This tiny shop evokes that era in its decor and it doesn't sell much else other than the elegantly wrapped sweets.

**MÉXICO**  ANTIQUES

Map p238 (☑91 429 94 76; Calle de las Huertas 20; ☺10.30am-2pm & 5-8pm Mon-Fri, 10.30am-2pm Sat; Ⓜ Antón Martín) A treasure chest of original old maps and drawings, this is a great place to find a unique souvenir of Spain. Some 160 folders hold antique maps of Madrid, Spain and the rest of the world. These are all originals or antique copies, not modern reprints, so prices range from a few hundred to thousands of euros.

# 🏃 SPORTS & ACTIVITIES

**TRIXI.COM**  CYCLING

Map p238 (☑91 523 15 47; www.trixi.com; Calle de los Jardines 12; 1/2/8/24hr incl helmet €4/6/12/15, tour €25; ☺10am-2pm & 4-8pm Mon-Fri, 10am-8pm Sat & Sun, tour 11am daily; Ⓜ Gran Vía) Bicycle hire and cycling tours of central Madrid.

**HAMMAM AL-ANDALUS**  SPA

Map p238 (☑91 429 90 20; http://madrid.ham mamalandalus.com; Calle de Atocha 14; treatments €33-115; ☺10am-midnight; Ⓜ Sol) Housed in the excavated cellars of old Madrid, this imitation of a traditional Arab bath offers massages and aromatherapy beneath graceful arches, accompanied by the sound of trickling water.

# El Retiro & the Art Museums

## Neighbourhood Top Five

**❶ Museo del Prado** (p99) Taking a journey through the richest centuries of Spanish and European art, beginning with Goya and Velázquez.

**❷ Centro de Arte Reina Sofía** (p108) Marvelling at the sheer genius of Picasso as you ponder the many dimensions of *Guernica,* as

well as Salvador Dalí and Joan Miró.

**❸ Museo Thyssen-Bornemisza** (p104) Ticking off just about every European master under one roof in this astonishingly rich collection.

**❹ Parque del Buen Retiro** (p110) Enjoying the peace and beauty in one of the

loveliest city parks in Europe with sweeping gardens and singularly impressive monuments sprinkled throughout.

**❺ Estado Puro** (p114) Sampling all that's innovative about the Spanish food revolution.

For more detail of this area see Map p242 ➡

## Lonely Planet's Top Tip

Avoid the free opening hours at the Museo del Prado, when crowds can really spoil your visit. First thing in the morning is the best time, and if you've purchased your ticket online and in advance, you'll skip the queues. If you're visiting the Reina Sofía and Thyssen as well, you'll save €6.40 with the 'Paseo del Arte' combined ticket – it gets you into all three galleries for €29.60.

###  Best Places to Eat

➜ Estado Puro (p114)
➜ Palacio de Cibeles (p115)
➜ Viridiana (p114)
➜ El Brillante (p114)

For reviews, see p114.➜

### ⊙ Best Architecture

➜ Plaza de la Cibeles (p112)
➜ Caixa Forum (p113)
➜ Palacio de Cristal (p111)
➜ Antigua Estación de Atocha (p114)
➜ Iglesia de San Jerónimo El Real (p113)

For reviews, see p111.➜

### ⊙ Best Art

➜ Museo del Prado (p99)
➜ Centro de Arte Reina Sofía (p109)
➜ Museo Thyssen-Bornemisza (p104)

For reviews, see p99.➜

# Explore: El Retiro & the Art Museums

The Paseo del Prado, a former river and now one of Europe's grandest boulevards, is all about the fabulous art galleries arrayed along or close to its shores. With other grand monuments and the city's botanical gardens also in residence, it's very much a daytime neighbourhood, one that all but shuts down – at least by Madrid standards – after dark. Metro stations sit at either end of the Paseo del Prado with none in between – when walking from one end to the other, take the footpaths under the trees down the centre of the Paseo, not those on the outer extremities. The *barrio* (district) of Huertas climbs up the hill to the west.

Behind the Museo del Prado and Real Jardín Botánico to the east, a gentle rise of tranquil and refined residential streets leads towards the Parque del Buen Retiro. The park is even more of a daytime experience (the gates close soon after sunset), but its moods vary with the days. On weekdays, the park is quiet and sleepy, sprinkled with enough people to feel alive but peaceful in a way that serves as an antidote to the clamour of downtown Madrid nearby. Come Saturday and Sunday, locals stream into the park – when the weather's fine on a Sunday afternoon, it can seem as if the whole city has come here to play.

# Local Life

➜ **Walk the Paseo del Prado** Every Sunday, usually from 9am to 2pm (or possibly 4pm), the eastern side of Paseo del Prado is closed to traffic between Plaza del Emperador Carlos V and Plaza de Cibeles. Walking this beautiful boulevard alongside children and bike riders is a lovely way to pass a Sunday morning.

➜ **Madrid's Left Bank** Just off the southern end of the Paseo del Prado, the Cuesta de Claudio Moyano bookstalls (p115) sell secondhand books, drawing the curious as well as serious bibliophiles.

➜ **Rent a row boat** Head out onto the lake (p111) for some aquatic fun in the heart of El Retiro.

# Getting There & Away

➜ **Metro** Banco de España metro station (line 2) to the north and Atocha station (line 1) to the south sit at either end of the Paseo del Prado. For the Parque del Buen Retiro, the most convenient station is Retiro (line 2); Ibiza (line 9) also leaves you in a good place, but it isn't as well connected to the centre.

## TOP SIGHT
# MUSEO DEL PRADO

**Welcome to one of the world's premier art galleries. The Museo del Prado's collection is like a window onto the historical vagaries of the Spanish soul, at once grand and imperious in the royal paintings of Velázquez, darkly tumultuous in Goya's *Pinturas negras* (Black Paintings) and outward looking with sophisticated works of art from all across Europe.**

## Casón del Buen Retiro

This **building** (Map p242; ☎902 107077; Calle de Alfonso XII 28; ⊙hours vary; ⓂRetiro) overlooking the Parque del Buen Retiro is run as an academic library by the nearby Museo del Prado. The Prado runs guided visits to the stunning Hall of the Ambassadors, which is crowned by the astonishing 1697 ceiling fresco *The Apotheosis of the Spanish Monarchy* by Luca Giordano.

## Edificio Jerónimos

The Prado's eastern wing (Edificio Jerónimos) is part of the Prado's stunning modern extension. Dedicated to temporary exhibitions (usually to display Prado masterpieces held in storage for decades for lack of wall space), its main attraction is the 2nd-floor cloisters. Built in 1672 with local granite, the cloisters were until recently attached to the adjacent Iglesia de San Jerónimo El Real (p113).

## Edificio Villanueva

The Prado's western wing (Edificio Villanueva) was completed in 1785 as the neoclassical Palacio de Villanueva. It served as a cavalry barracks for Napoleon's troops between 1808 and 1813. In 1814 King Fernando VII decided to use the palace as a museum. Five years later the Museo del Prado opened with 311 Spanish paintings on display.

### DON'T MISS

➤ Goya

➤ Velázquez

➤ Flemish Collection

➤ *The Garden of Earthly Delights*

➤ El Greco

➤ *Emperor Carlos V on Horseback*

➤ Edificio Villanueva

➤ Edificio Jerónimos

➤ Casón del Buen Retiro

### PRACTICALITIES

➤ Map p242, B4

➤ www.museodel prado.es

➤ Paseo del Prado

➤ adult/child €15/free, 6-8pm Mon-Sat & 5-7pm Sun free, audioguide €3.50, admission plus official guidebook €24

➤ ⊙10am-8pm Mon-Sat, to 7pm Sun

➤ ⓂBanco de España

## PRADO FLOOR PLAN

The free plan to the Prado (available at or just inside the entrance) lists the location of 50 Prado masterpieces and gives room numbers for all major artists. It's also available online.

## TICKETS

Entrance to the Prado is via the eastern Puerta de los Jerónimos; tickets must first be purchased from the **ticket office** (Puerta de Goya; Map p242; www.museo delprado.es; Calle de Felipe IV; ☉9.45am-7.30pm Mon-Sat, to 6.30pm Sun; Ⓜ Banco de España) at the northern end of the building, opposite the Hotel Ritz and beneath the Puerta de Goya.

## El Greco

This Greek-born artist (hence the name) is considered the finest of the Prado's Spanish Renaissance painters. The vivid, almost surreal works by this 16th-century master and adopted Spaniard, whose figures are characteristically slender and tortured, are perfectly executed. Two of his more than 30 paintings in the collection – *The Annunciation* and *The Flight into Egypt* – were painted in Italy before the artist arrived in Spain, while *The Trinity* and *Knight with His Hand on His Breast* are considered his most important works.

## Emperor Carlos V on Horseback (Titian)

Considered one of the finest equestrian and royal portraits in art history, this 16th-century work is said to be the forerunner to similar paintings by Diego Rodríguez de Silva Velázquez a century later. One of the great masters of the Renaissance, Titian (1488–1576) was entering his most celebrated period as a painter when he created this, and it is widely recognised as one of his masterpieces.

## Only in Madrid

Madrid must be the only city in the world where a near riot was caused by an art exhibition. John Hooper in his book *The New Spaniards* tells the story of how in 1990 the Prado brought an unprecedented number of works by Velázquez out of storage and opened its doors to the public. The exhibition was so popular that more than half a million visitors came to see the rare showing. Just before the exhibition was scheduled to end, the Prado announced that they would keep the doors open for as long as there were people wanting to enter. When the doors finally shut at 9pm, several hundred people were still outside waiting in the rain. They chanted, they shouted and they banged on the doors of this august institution with their umbrellas. The gallery was reopened, but queues kept forming and when the doors shut on the exhibition for good at 10.30pm, furious art lovers clashed with police. At midnight, there were still almost 50 people outside chanting 'We want to come in'.

## Goya

Francisco Goya is sometimes described as the first of the great Spanish masters and his work is found on all three floors of the Prado. Begin at the southern end of the ground or lower level where, in Rooms 64 and 65, Goya's *El dos de mayo* and *El tres de mayo* rank among Madrid's most emblematic paintings. In the adjacent rooms (66 and 67), his disturbing *Pinturas negras* (Black Paintings) are so named for the distorted animalesque appearance of their characters. The *Saturno devorando a su hijo* (Saturn Devouring His Son) is utterly disturbing, while *La romería de San Isidro* and *Aquelarre* or *El gran cabrón* (The Great He-Goat) are dominated by the compelling individual faces of the condemned souls. An interesting footnote to *Pinturas negras* is *El coloso*, a Goyaesque work hanging next to the *Pinturas negras* that was long considered part of the master's portfolio until the Prado's experts decided otherwise in 2008.

Up on the 1st floor, other masterful works include the intriguing *La família de Carlos IV*, which portrays the Spanish royal family in 1800; Goya portrayed himself in the background just as Velázquez did in *Las meninas*. Also present are *La maja vestida* (The Young Lady Dressed) and *La maja desnuda* (The Young Lady Undressed). These portraits of an unknown woman, commonly believed to be the Duquesa de Alba (who some think may have been Goya's lover), are identical save for the lack of clothing in the latter.

## The Flemish Collection

The Prado's outstanding collection of Flemish art includes the fulsome figures and bulbous cherubs of Peter Paul Rubens (1577–1640). His signature works are *Las tres gracias* and *Adoración de los reyes magos*. Other fine works in the vicinity include *The Triumph of Death* by Pieter Bruegel and those by Anton Van Dyck.

Van Der Weyden's 1435 painting *El descendimiento* is unusual, both for its size and for the recurring crossbow shapes in the painting's upper corners, which are echoed in the bodies of Mary and Christ (the painting was commissioned by a Crossbow Manufacturers Brotherhood). Once the central part of a triptych, the painting is filled with drama and luminous colours.

On no account miss the weird and wonderful *The Garden of Earthly Delights* (Room 56A) by Hieronymus Bosch (c 1450–1516). No one has yet been able to provide a definitive explanation for this hallucinatory work, although many have tried. The closer you look, the harder it is to escape the feeling that he must have been doing some extraordinary drugs.

*Judith at the Banquet of Holofernes,* the only painting by Rembrandt in the Prado's collection, was completed in 1634; note the artist's signature and date on the arm of the chair. The painting shows a master at the peak of his powers, with an expert use of the chiaroscuro style, and the astonishing detail in the subject's clothing and face.

## Velázquez

Velázquez's role as court painter means that his works provide a fascinating insight into 17th-century royal life and the Prado holds the richest collection of his works. Of all the works by Velázquez, *Las meninas* (The Maids of Honour; Room 12) is what most people come to see. Completed in 1656, it is more properly known as *La família de Felipe IV* (The Family of Felipe IV). It depicts Velázquez himself on the left and, in the centre, the infant Margarita. There's more to it than that: the artist in fact portrays himself painting the king and queen, whose images appear, according to some experts, in mirrors behind Velázquez. His mastery of light and colour is never more apparent than here. An interesting detail of the painting, aside from the extraordinary cheek of painting himself in royal company, is the presence of the cross of the Order of Santiago on his vest. The artist was apparently obsessed with being given a noble title. He received it shortly before his death, but in this oil painting he has awarded himself the order years before it would in fact be his!

The rooms surrounding *Las meninas* (Rooms 14 and 15) contain more fine paintings of various members of royalty who seem to spring off the canvas, many of them on horseback. Also nearby is his *La rendición de Breda* (The Surrender of Breda), while other Spanish painters worth tracking down in the neighbouring rooms include Bartolomé Esteban Murillo, José de Ribera and the stark figures of Francisco de Zurbarán.

# Museo del Prado

## PLAN OF ATTACK

Begin on the 1st floor with ① **Las meninas** by Velázquez. Although it alone is worth the entry price, it's a fine introduction to the 17th-century golden age of Spanish art; nearby are more of Velázquez' royal paintings and works by Zurbarán and Murillo. While on the 1st floor, seek out Goya's ② **La maja vestida and La maja desnuda**, with more of Goya's early works in neighbouring rooms. Downstairs at the southern end of the Prado, Goya's anger is evident in the searing ③ **El dos de mayo and El tres de mayo**, and the torment of Goya's later years finds expression in the adjacent rooms with ④ **Las pinturas negras** (the Black Paintings). Also on the lower floor, Hieronymus Bosch's weird and wonderful ⑤ **The Garden of Earthly Delights** is one of the Prado's signature masterpieces. Returning to the 1st floor, El Greco's ⑥ **Adoration of the Shepherds** is an extraordinary work, as is Peter Paul Rubens' ⑦ **Las tres gracias**, which forms the centrepiece of the Prado's gathering of Flemish masters. (Note: this painting may be moved to the 2nd floor.) A detour to the 2nd floor takes in some lesser-known Goyas, but finish in the ⑧ **Edificio Jerónimos** with a visit to the cloisters and the outstanding bookshop.

## TOP TIPS

➡ Purchase your ticket online (www.museodelprado.es) and avoid the queues.

➡ Best time to visit is as soon as possible after opening time.

➡ The website (www.museodelprado.es/coleccion/que-ver) has self-guided tours for one- to three-hour visits.

➡ Nearby are Museo Thyssen-Bornemisza and Centro de Arte Reina Sofía. Together they form an extraordinary trio of galleries.

**Las meninas (Velázquez)**
This masterpiece depicts Velázquez and the Infanta Margarita. According to some experts, the images of the king and queen appear in mirrors behind Velázquez.

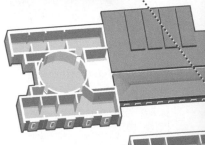

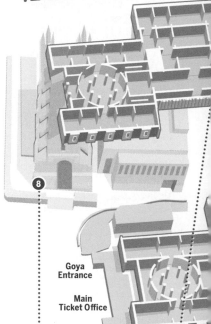

**Goya Entrance**

**Main Ticket Office**

**Edificio Jerónimos**
Opened in 2007, this state-of-the-art extension has rotating exhibitions of Prado masterpieces held in storage for decades for lack of wall space, and stunning 2nd-floor granite cloisters that date back to 1672.

**Adoration of the Shepherds (El Greco)**
There's an ecstatic quality to this intense painting. El Greco's distorted rendering of bodily forms came to characterise much of his later work.

## Las tres gracias (Rubens)

A late Rubens masterpiece, *The Three Graces* is a classical and masterly expression of Rubens' preoccupation with sensuality, here portraying Aglaia, Euphrosyne and Thalia, the daughters of Zeus.

## La maja vestida & La maja desnuda (Goya)

These enigmatic works scandalised early-19th-century Madrid society, fuelling the rumour mill as to the woman's identity and drawing the ire of the Spanish Inquisition.

DEA PICTURE LIBRARY / GETTY IMAGES ©

DEA / G. DAGLI ORTI / GETTY IMAGES ©

**Edificio Villanueva**

① ⑦ ②

## El dos de mayo & El tres de mayo (Goya)

Few paintings evoke a city's sense of self quite like Goya's portrayal of Madrid's valiant but ultimately unsuccessful uprising against French rule in 1808.

## Las pinturas negras (Goya)

*Las pinturas negras* are Goya's darkest works. *Saturno devorando a su hijo* evokes a writhing mass of tortured humanity, while *La romería de San Isidro* and *El aquelarre* are profoundly unsettling.

**Información Counter & Audioguides**

**ónimos Entrance (Main Entrance)**

**Gift Shop**

**Cafeteria**

**Murillo Entrance**

⑤ ③ ④

**Velázquez Entrance**

## The Garden of Earthly Delights (Bosch)

A fantastical painting in triptych form, this overwhelming work depicts the Garden of Eden and what the Prado describes as 'the lugubrious precincts of Hell' in exquisitely bizarre detail.

KRZYSZTOF DYDYNSKI / GETTY IMAGES ©

# TOP SIGHT
# MUSEO THYSSEN-BORNEMISZA

One of the most extraordinary collections of predominantly European art in the world, the Museo Thyssen-Bornemisza is a worthy member of Madrid's 'Golden Triangle' of art. Where the Prado or Reina Sofía enable you to study the work of a particular artist in depth, the Thyssen is a place to immerse yourself in a breathtaking breadth of artistic styles.

## 20th-Century Icons

Pablo Picasso appears in Room 45, another of the gallery's standout rooms; it includes works by Marc Chagall and Dalí's hallucinatory *Dream Caused by the Flight of a Bee Around a Pomegranate, One Second Before Waking Up.*

There's no let-up as the Thyssen builds to a stirring climax. Room 46 has Joan Miró's *Catalan Peasant with a Guitar,* Jackson Pollock's *Brown and Silver I* and the deceptively simple but strangely pleasing *Untitled (Green on Maroon)* by Mark Rothko. In Rooms 47 and 48, Francis Bacon, Roy Lichtenstein, Henry Moore and Lucian Freud, Sigmund's Berlin-born grandson, are all represented.

## Cubism & Surrealism

Down on the ground floor, in Room 41 you'll see a nice mix of the big three of cubism – Picasso, Georges Braque and Madrid's own Juan Gris – along with several other contemporaries. Wassily Kandinsky is the main drawcard in Room 43, while there's an early Salvador Dalí alongside Max Ernst and Paul Klee in Room 44.

## DON'T MISS

- ➡ Religious Art
- ➡ Rooms 5 & 10
- ➡ El Greco & Canaletto
- ➡ 2nd-Floor European Masters
- ➡ Dutch & Flemish Masters
- ➡ Rooms 31 to 35
- ➡ The Baroness Collection
- ➡ Cubism & Surrealism
- ➡ Contemporary Icons

## PRACTICALITIES

- ➡ Map p242, A3
- ➡ ☑902 760511
- ➡ www.museothyssen.org
- ➡ Paseo del Prado 8
- ➡ adult/child €12/free, Mon free
- ➡ ⊙10am-7pm Tue-Sun, noon-4pm Mon
- ➡ Ⓜ Banco de España

## The Thyssen-Bornemisza Legend

The story behind the museum's collection is almost as interesting as the paintings themselves. And it is a very Spanish story that has a celebrity love affair at its heart. The paintings held in the museum are the legacy of Baron Thyssen-Bornemisza, a German-Hungarian magnate. Madrid managed to acquire the prestigious collection when the baron married Carmen 'Tita' Cervera, a former Miss España and ex-wife of Lex Barker (of *Tarzan* fame). The deal was sealed when the Spanish government offered to overhaul the neoclassical Palacio de Villahermosa specifically to house the collection. Although the baron died in 2002, his glamorous wife has shown that she has learned much from the collecting nous of her late husband. In early 2000 the museum acquired two adjoining buildings, which have been joined to the museum to house approximately half of the collection of Carmen Thyssen-Bornemisza. She remains an important figure in the cultural life of the city – when the city authorities threatened in 2006 to tear down some 18th-century trees outside the museum to facilitate the rerouting of the Paseo del Prado, the Baroness threatened to chain herself to one of the trees in protest. The plan was quietly shelved.

## Rooms 28 to 35

If all that sounds impressive, the 1st floor is where the Thyssen really shines. There's a Gainsborough in Room 28 and a Goya in Room 31. The latter's *Asensio Julià* is believed to be dedicated to Goya's friend and fellow artist, the eponymous Valencian painter who worked with Goya on the frescoes in the Ermita de San Antonio de la Florida (p148). Art historians also single out this painting's confident brushstrokes as a forerunner to the Romantic movement. Also in Room 31, one of the Thyssen's lesser-known masterpieces, the 19th-century *Dresden Easter Morning* by Caspar David Friedrich, is a haunting study in light and texture by one of the leading figures in the German Romantic movement. The painting is rich in symbolism – the moon and dawn evoke death and resurrection – and the shades of colour portray shifts of extraordinary subtlety.

If you've been skimming the surface, Room 32 is the place to linger over every painting. The astonishing texture of Van Gogh's *Les Vessenots* is a masterpiece, but the same applies to Manet's *Woman in Riding Habit,* Monet's *The Thaw at Vétheuil,* Renoir's *Woman with a Parasol in a Garden* and Pissarro's *Rue Saint-Honoré in the Afternoon.* Simply extraordinary.

### THE MASTERS

Don't come here expecting a large number of paintings from a single master, but instead expect single paintings from a large number of masters.

### RELIGIOUS ART

The 2nd floor, which is home to medieval art, includes some real gems hidden among the mostly 13th- and 14th-century and predominantly Italian, German and Flemish religious paintings and triptychs. Much of it is sacred art that won't appeal to everyone, but it somehow captures the essence of medieval Europe.

EL RETIRO & THE ART MUSEUMS MUSEO THYSSEN-BORNEMISZA

There's no time to catch your breath, because Room 33 is similarly something special with Cézanne, Gauguin, Toulouse-Lautrec and Degas all on show. The big names continue in Room 34 (Picasso, Matisse and Modigliani) and 35 (Edvard Munch and Egon Schiele).

## Rooms 5 & 10

Unless you have a specialist's eye for the paintings that fill the first four rooms, pause for the first time in Room 5, still on the 2nd floor, where you'll find one work by Italy's Piero della Francesca (1410–92) and the instantly recognisable *Portrait of King Henry VIII* by Holbein the Younger (1497–1543). In Room 8 *Jesus Among the Doctor*s by Albrecht Dürer, a leading figure in the German Renaissance, is an exceptional, vaguely disturbing work; note Dürer's anagram on the slip of paper emerging from the book in the painting's foreground. Continue on to Room 10 for the evocative 1586 *Massacre of the Innocents* by Lucas Van Valckenborch.

## Spain & Venice

Room 11 is dedicated to El Greco (with three pieces) and his Venetian contemporaries Tintoretto and Titian, while Caravaggio and the Spaniard José de Ribera dominate Room 12. A single painting each by Murillo and Zurbarán add further Spanish flavour in the two rooms that follow, while the exceptionally rendered views of Venice by Canaletto (1697–1768) should on no account be missed. Few paintings have come to be the iconic image of a city quite like Canaletto's *View of Piazza San Marco* – the painter's use of line and angle, and the intense detail in even the smallest of the painting's figures give a powerful sense of atmosphere and movement.

## The Baroness Collection I

Best of all on the top floor is the extension (Rooms A to H), which houses the collection of Carmen Thyssen-Bornemisza; the rest belonged to Baron Thyssen-Bornemisza, a German-Hungarian magnate and her late husband. Room C houses paintings by Canaletto, Constable and Van Gogh, while the stunning Room H includes works by Monet, Sisley, Renoir, Pissarro and Degas.

## The Baroness Collection II

In the 1st floor's extension (Rooms I to P), Room K has works by Monet, Pissarro, Sorolla and Sisley, while Room L is the domain of Gauguin (including his iconic *Mata Mua*), Degas and Toulouse-Lautrec. Rooms M (Munch), N (Kandinsky), O (Matisse and Georges Braque) and P (Picasso, Matisse, Edward Hopper and Juan Gris) round out an outrageously rich journey.

# MUSEO THYSSEN-BORNEMISZA

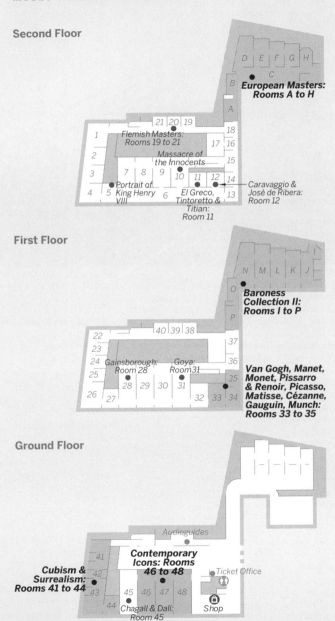

**Second Floor**

European Masters:
Rooms A to H

Flemish Masters:
Rooms 19 to 21

Massacre of
the Innocents

Portrait of
King Henry
VIII

El Greco,
Tintoretto &
Titian:
Room 11

Caravaggio &
José de Ribera:
Room 12

**First Floor**

Baroness
Collection II:
Rooms I to P

Gainsborough:
Room 28

Goya:
Room 31

Van Gogh, Manet,
Monet, Pissarro
& Renoir, Picasso,
Matisse, Cézanne,
Gauguin, Munch:
Rooms 33 to 35

**Ground Floor**

Audioguides

Contemporary
Icons: Rooms
46 to 48

Ticket Office

Cubism &
Surrealism:
Rooms 41 to 44

Chagall & Dalí:
Room 45

Shop

EL RETIRO & THE ART MUSEUMS MUSEO THYSSEN-BORNEMISZA

## TOP SIGHT
# CENTRO DE ARTE REINA SOFÍA

Home to Picasso's *Guernica*, arguably Spain's single-most famous artwork, and a host of other important Spanish artists, the Centro de Arte Reina Sofía is Madrid's premier collection of contemporary art. In addition to plenty of paintings by Picasso, other major drawcards are works by Salvador Dalí and Joan Miró. The collection spans the 20th century up to the 1980s.

## Contemporary Spanish Artists

The Reina Sofía offers a terrific opportunity to learn more about lesser-known 20th-century Spanish artists. Among these are: Miquel Barceló (b 1957); *madrileño* artist José Gutiérrez Solana (1886–1945); the renowned Basque painter Ignacio Zuloaga (1870–1945); and Benjamín Palencia (1894–1980), whose paintings capture the turbulence of Spain in the 1930s.

The late Barcelona painter Antoni Tàpies (1923–2012), for years one of Spain's most creative talents, is represented, as are the pop art of Eduardo Arroyo (b 1937), abstract painters such as Eusebio Sempere (1923–85) and members of the Equipo 57 group (founded in 1957 by a group of Spanish artists in exile in Paris), including Pablo Palazuelo (1916–2007).

## Edificio Nouvel

Beyond its artwork, the Reina Sofía is an important architectural landmark, adapted from the shell of an 18th-century hospital with eye-catching external glass lifts. The stunning extension (the Edificio Nouvel), which spreads along the western tip of the Plaza del Emperador Carlos V, hosts temporary exhibitions, auditoriums, the bookshop, a cafe and the museum's library.

## DON'T MISS

➡ Picasso's *Guernica*
➡ Juan Gris & Georges Braque
➡ Joan Miró
➡ Salvador Dalí
➡ Contemporary Spanish art collection
➡ Eduardo Chillida's sculptures
➡ Edificio Nouvel
➡ Librería la Central bookshop

## PRACTICALITIES

➡ Map p242, A6
➡ www.museoreina sofia.es
➡ Calle de Santa Isabel 52
➡ adult/concession €10/free, 1.30-7pm Sun, 7-9pm Mon & Wed-Sat free, tickets cheaper if purchased online
➡ ⊙10am-9pm Mon & Wed-Sat, to 7pm Sun
➡ Ⓜ Atocha

## Joan Miró

The work of Joan Miró (1893–1983) is defined by often delightfully bright primary colours. After his paintings became a symbol of the Barcelona Olympics in 1992, his work began to receive the international acclaim it so richly deserved and the museum is a fine place to view a representative sample of his innovative style.

## Other Cubist Masters

Picasso may have been the brainchild behind the cubist form, but he was soon joined by others who saw its potential. Picasso is said to have been influenced by the mask traditions of Africa, and these elements can also be discerned in the work of Madrid-born Juan Gris (1887–1927) or Georges Braque (1882–1963), two of the masters of the genre.

## Picasso's Guernica

Claimed by some to be the most important artwork of the 20th century, Pablo Picasso's *Guernica* (1937) measures 3.5m by 7.8m and is an icon of the cubist style for which Picasso became famous. You could easily spend hours studying the painting; take the time to both examine the detail of its various constituent elements and step back to gain an overview of this extraordinary canvas.

To deepen your understanding of *Guernica,* don't neglect the sketches that Picasso painted as he prepared to execute his masterpiece. They're in the rooms surrounding Room 206. They offer an intriguing insight into the development of this seminal work.

## Salvador Dalí

The Reina Sofía is home to around 20 canvases by Salvador Dalí, of which the most famous is perhaps the surrealist extravaganza *El gran masturbador* (1929); at once disturbing and utterly compelling, this is one of the museum's standout paintings. Look also for a strange bust of a certain *Joelle* done by Dalí and his friend Man Ray.

## Sculptures

Of the sculptors, watch for Pablo Gargallo (1881–1934), whose work in bronze includes a bust of Picasso, and the renowned Basque sculptors Jorge Oteiza (1908–2003) and Eduardo Chillida (1924–2002); Chillida's forms rendered in rusted wrought iron are among Spanish art's most intriguing forms.

### GUERNICA'S MAKING

*Guernica* was Picasso's response to the bombing of Gernika (Guernica) in the Basque Country by Hitler's Legión Condor, at the request of Franco, on 26 April 1937. At least 200 died in the attack and much of the town was destroyed. The painting subsequently migrated to the US and only returned to Spain in 1981, in keeping with Picasso's wish that the painting return to Spanish shores (first to Picasso's preferred choice, the Museo del Prado, then to its current home) once democracy had been restored.

**The museum's Guide to the Collection (€22), available from the gift shop, takes a closer look at 80 of the museum's signature works.**

EL RETIRO & THE ART MUSEUMS CENTRO DE ARTE REINA SOFÍA

# TOP SIGHT
# PARQUE DEL BUEN RETIRO

The glorious gardens of El Retiro are as beautiful as any you'll find in a European city. Littered with marble monuments, landscaped lawns, the occasional elegant building and abundant greenery, it's quiet and contemplative during the week but comes to life on weekends. Put simply, this is one of our favourite places in Madrid.

## Ermita de San Isidro

In the northeastern corner of El Retiro, the small country chapel is the **Ermita de San Isidro** (Map p242; Paseo del Quince de Mayo 62; MRetiro), among the few, albeit modest, examples of extant Romanesque architecture in Madrid. Parts of the wall, a side entrance and part of the apse were restored in 1999 and are all that remain of the 13th-century building. When it was built Madrid was a little village more than 2km away.

Just south of the Ermita de San Isidro, amid sculpted hedgerows and wandering peacocks, is **La Casa de Fieras**, Madrid's former zoo, which was once home to the same camels that played a starring role in *Lawrence of Arabia*.

## Jardín de los Planteles & Madrid's Oldest Tree

Occupying much of the southwestern corner of the park is the **Jardín de los Planteles** (Map p242; MRetiro), one of the least-visited sections of El Retiro, where quiet pathways lead beneath an overarching canopy of trees. Nearby, just inside the Retiro's Puerta de Felipe IV, stands what is thought to be **Madrid's oldest tree** (Map p242; MRetiro), a Mexican conifer *(ahuehuete)* planted in 1633. With a trunk circumference of 52m, it was used by French soldiers during the Napoleonic Wars in the early 19th century as a cannon mount.

## La Rosaleda & El Ángel Caído

At the southern end of the park is **La Rosaleda** (Rose Garden; Map p242; MRetiro, Atocha) with its more than 4000 roses. Not far away is a statue of **El Ángel Caído** (Map p242; MRetiro). Strangely, it sits 666m above sea level...

## Monument to Alfonso XII & El Estanque

The focal point for so much of El Retiro's life is the artificial *estanque* (lake), which is watched over by the massive ornamental structure of the **Monument to Alfonso XII** (Map p242; MRetiro) on the east side, complete with marble lions. As sunset approaches on a Sunday afternoon in summer, the crowd grows, bongos sound out across the park and people start to dance.

On the southern end of the lake, the odd structure decorated with sphinxes is the **Fuente Egipcia** (Egyptian Fountain; Map p242; ☉6am-midnight May-Sep, to 10pm Oct-Apr; MRetiro): legend has it that an enormous fortune buried in the park by Felipe IV in the mid-18th century rests here. Just down the hill and south of the lake, the sober 1883 **Palacio de Velázquez** (Map p242; www.museoreinasofia.es; admission varies; ☉10am-10pm May-Sep, to 7pm Oct, to 6pm Nov-Apr) is used for temporary exhibitions organised by the Centro de Arte Reina Sofía.

## DON'T MISS

- ➡ El Estanque & Monument to Alfonso XII
- ➡ Palacio de Cristal
- ➡ Ermita de San Isidro
- ➡ La Rosaleda
- ➡ El Ángel Caído
- ➡ Boat Ride
- ➡ Fuente Egipcia
- ➡ Palacio de Velázquez
- ➡ Madrid's Oldest Tree

## PRACTICALITIES

- ➡ Map p242, C3
- ➡ Plaza de la Independencia
- ➡ ☉6am-midnight May-Sep, to 10pm Oct-Apr
- ➡ MRetiro, Príncipe de Vergara, Ibiza, Atocha

Palacio de Cristal

## Palacio de Cristal

Hidden among the trees south of the lake is the **Palacio de Cristal** (Map p242; ☑91 574 66 14; www.museoreinasofia.es; ☉10am-10pm Apr-Sep, to 7pm Oct, to 6pm Nov-Mar; ⓂRetiro), a magnificent metal-and-glass structure that is arguably El Retiro's most beautiful architectural monument. It was built in 1887 as a winter garden for exotic flowers and is now used for temporary exhibitions organised by the Centro de Arte Reina Sofía (p109).

## Park Activities

Most visitors are content to explore El Retiro on foot, but there are plenty of alternatives on offer. Renting a **row boat** (per 45min weekdays/weekends €6/8; ☉10am-8.30pm Apr-Sep, to 5.45pm Oct-Mar; ⓂRetiro) on the lake is a very Madrid thing to do. Cycling and rollerblading are terrific ways to range far and wide across El Retiro; the north–south Paseo del Duque de Fernán Núñez on the park's eastern side is the favoured haunt of rollerbladers. To rent bikes, visit **DiverBikes** (☑91 431 34 24; www.diverbikes.es; Ave Menendez Pelayo 9; per hr from €4; ☉10am-9pm; ⓂPríncipe de Vergara), just across the road from the Retiro's northeastern corner.

There are quite a few children's playgrounds, including one close to the park's entrance on Plaza de la Independencia and another at the eastern end of the park, just off (and visible from) the Paseo del Duque de Fernán Núñez.

## Royal History

El Retiro wasn't always so accessible. Laid out in the 17th century by Felipe IV as the preserve of royalty, the park was opened to the public in 1868 and ever since *madrileños* have gathered here to stroll, read the Sunday papers in the shade, take a boat ride or nurse a cool drink at the numerous outdoor *terrazas* (open-air cafes).

# ◉ SIGHTS

Some of Madrid's most memorable sights inhabit this *barrio*, with most of them on or within short walking distance of the Paseo del Prado. The three world-class art museums (the Prado, Thyssen and Reina Sofía) get most of the attention, and rightly so. But the Parque del Buen Retiro is a stunning oasis in the heart of the city, at once expansively green and studded with stirring monuments. Throw in a handful of other museums and a daring exhibition space (Caixa Forum) and you've reason enough to spend two or three days in this neighbourhood alone.

**MUSEO DEL PRADO**  MUSEUM
See p99.

**MUSEO THYSSEN-BORNEMISZA**  MUSEUM
See p104.

**CENTRO DE ARTE REINA SOFÍA**  MUSEUM
See p109.

**PARQUE DEL BUEN RETIRO**  GARDENS
See p110.

**MIRADOR DE MADRID**  VIEWPOINT
Map p242 (www.centrocentro.org; 8th fl, Palacio de Comunicaciones, Plaza de la Cibeles; adult/child €2/0.50; ☺10.30am-1.30pm & 4-7pm Tue-Sun; Ⓜ Banco de España) The views from the summit of the Palacio de Comunicaciones are among Madrid's best, sweeping out over Plaza de la Cibeles, up the hill towards the sublime Edificio Metrópolis and out to the mountains. Buy your ticket up the stairs then take the lift to the 6th floor, from where the gates are opened every half hour. You can either take another lift or climb the stairs up to the 8th floor.

**PLAZA DE LA CIBELES**  SQUARE
Map p242 (Ⓜ Banco de España) Of all the grand roundabouts that punctuate the Paseo del Prado, Plaza de la Cibeles most evokes the splendour of imperial Madrid. The jewel in the crown is the astonishing Palacio de Comunicaciones. Other landmark buildings around the plaza's perimeter include the Palacio de Linares and Casa de América (p122), the **Palacio Buenavista** (Map p250; Plaza de la Cibeles; Ⓜ Banco de España) and the national **Banco de España** (Map p242; Calle de Alcalá 48). The spectacular fountain of the goddess Cybele at the centre of the plaza is one of Madrid's most beautiful.

Ever since it was erected by Ventura Rodríguez in 1780, the fountain has been a Madrid favourite. Carlos III liked it so much he tried to have it moved to the royal gardens of the Granja de San Ildefonso, on the road to Segovia, but *madrileños* kicked up such a fuss that he let it be.

There are fine views east from Plaza de la Cibeles towards the Puerta de Alcalá or, even better, west towards the Edificio Metrópolis (p86).

**CENTROCENTRO**  ARTS CENTRE
Map p242 (✆91 480 00 08; www.centrocentro.org; Plaza de la Cibeles 1; ☺10am-8pm Tue-Sun; Ⓜ Plaza de España) **FREE** One of Madrid's more surprising and diverse cultural spaces, CentroCentro is housed in the grand Palacio de Comunicaciones. It has cutting-edge exhibitions covering 5000 sq metres over four floors (floors 1, 3, 4 and 5), as well as quiet reading rooms and some stunning architecture, especially in the soaring Antiguo Patio de Operaciones on the 2nd floor. On the 8th floor is the Mirador de Madrid.

**PUERTA DE ALCALÁ**  MONUMENT
Map p242 (Plaza de la Independencia; Ⓜ Retiro) This imposing triumphal gate was once the main entrance to the city (its name derives from the fact that the road that passed under it led to Alcalá de Henares) and was surrounded by the city's walls. It was here that the city authorities controlled access to the capital and levied customs duties.

---

**FOOTBALL PLAZA CELEBRATIONS**

The battle for football supremacy in Madrid is rarely confined to the stadiums. Whenever Real Madrid wins a major trophy, crowds head for **Plaza de la Cibeles** to celebrate in their hundreds and thousands. To protect the fountain, the city council boards up the statue and surrounds it with police on the eve of important matches. A little further down Paseo del Prado, **Plaza de Neptuno** (Plaza de Cánovas del Castillo; Map p242; Ⓜ Banco de España) is where fans of Atlético de Madrid hold equally popular (and every bit as destructive) celebrations.

The first gate to bear this name was built in 1599, but Carlos III was singularly unimpressed and had it demolished in 1764 to be replaced by another, the one you see today. It's best appreciated from the east for fine views through the arch down towards central Madrid. Our only complaint? It could do with a clean.

Twice a year, in autumn and spring, cars abandon the roundabout and are replaced by flocks of sheep being transferred in an age-old ritual from their summer to winter pastures (and vice versa). And the Puerta de Alcalá was immortalised in the cultural lexicon in 1986 when Ana Belén and Victor Manuel's strangely catchy song 'La Puerta de Alcalá' became an unlikely smash hit.

### REAL FÁBRICA DE TAPICES       LANDMARK
Map p242 (Royal Tapestry Workshop; ✍91 434 05 50; www.realfabricadetapices.com; Calle de Fuenterrabía 2; adult/child €5/3.50; ☺10am-2pm Mon-Fri Sep-Jul, guided tours hourly; Ⓜ Atocha Renfe, Menéndez Pelayo) If a wealthy Madrid nobleman ever wanted to impress, he went to the Real Fábrica de Tapices, where royalty commissioned the pieces that adorned their palaces and private residences. The Spanish government, Spanish royal family and the Vatican were the biggest patrons of the tapestry business: Spain alone is said to have collected four million tapestries. With such an exclusive clientele, it was a lucrative business and remains so, 300 years after the factory was founded.

Goya began his career here, first as a cartoonist and later as a tapestry designer. Given such an illustrious history, it is, therefore, somewhat surprising that coming here today feels like visiting a carpet shop, with small showrooms strewn with fine tapestries. There is a permanent exhibition on show and a sales area. If you're lucky, you'll get to see how they're made.

The guided tours at noon are in English.

### REAL JARDÍN BOTÁNICO       GARDENS
Map p242 (Royal Botanical Garden; ✍91 420 04 38; www.rjb.csic.es; Plaza de Bravo Murillo 2; adult/child €4/free; ☺10am-9pm May-Aug, to 8pm Apr & Sep, to 7pm Mar & Oct, to 6pm Nov-Feb; Ⓜ Atocha) Madrid's botanical gardens are a leafy oasis in the centre of town, though they're not as expansive or as popular as the Parque del Buen Retiro. With some 30,000 species crammed into a relatively small 8-hectare area, it's more a place to wander at leisure than laze under a tree, although

there are benches dotted throughout the gardens where you can sit.

### MUSEO NAVAL       MUSEUM
Map p242 (✍91 523 87 89; Paseo del Prado 5; €3; ☺10am-7pm Tue-Sun Sep-Jul, to 3pm Tue-Sun Aug; Ⓜ Banco de España) This museum will appeal to those who always wondered what the Spanish Armada really looked like. On display are quite extraordinary models of ships from the earliest days of Spain's maritime history to the 20th century. Lovers of antique maps will also find plenty of interest, especially Juan de la Cosa's parchment map of the known world, put together in 1500. The accuracy of Europe and Africa is astounding, and it's supposedly the first map to show the Americas.

### CAIXA FORUM       MUSEUM, ARCHITECTURE
Map p242 (✍91 330 73 00; https://obrasocialla caixa.org/en/cultura/caixaforum-madrid/que-hacemos; Paseo del Prado 36; adult/child €4/free; ☺10am-8pm; Ⓜ Atocha) This extraordinary structure is one of Madrid's most eye-catching landmarks. Seeming to hover above the ground, the brick edifice is topped by an intriguing summit of rusted iron. On an adjacent wall is the *jardín colgante* (hanging garden), a lush (if thinning) vertical wall of greenery almost four storeys high. Inside there are four floors of exhibition space awash in stainless steel and with soaring ceilings. The exhibitions here are always worth checking out and include photography, contemporary painting and multimedia shows.

Caixa Forum's shop (mostly books) is outstanding. You can visit the shop without paying the entrance fee.

### IGLESIA DE SAN
### JERÓNIMO EL REAL       CHURCH
Map p242 (✍91 420 35 78; Calle de Ruiz de Alarcón; ☺10am-1pm & 5-8.30pm; Ⓜ Atocha, Banco de España) FREE Tucked away behind Museo del Prado, this chapel was traditionally favoured by the Spanish royal family, and King Juan Carlos I was crowned here in 1975 upon the death of Franco. The sometimes-sober, sometimes-splendid mock-Isabelline interior is actually a 19th-century reconstruction that took its cues from Iglesia de San Juan de los Reyes in Toledo; the original was largely destroyed during the Peninsular War. What remained of the former cloisters has been incorporated into Museo del Prado.

EL RETIRO & THE ART MUSEUMS SIGHTS

## IGLESIA DE JESÚS DE MEDINACELI
CHURCH

Map p242 (☑91 429 93 75; Plaza de Jesús 2; ☺7am-1.30pm & 5-9pm Mon-Thu, 6.30am-11pm Fri, 8.30am-1.30pm & 5-9pm Sat, 8.30am-2pm & 5-9pm Sun; Ⓜ Banco de España) Up to 100,000 people crowd Iglesia de Jesús de Medinaceli on the first Friday of Lent to kiss the right foot of a wooden sculpture of Christ (*besapié;* kissing of the foot). Pilgrims make three wishes to Jesus, of which he is said to grant one.

## ANTIGUA ESTACIÓN DE ATOCHA
NOTABLE BUILDING

Map p242 (Old Atocha Train Station; Plaza del Emperador Carlos V; Ⓜ Atocha Renfe) In 1992 the northwestern wing of the Antigua Estación de Atocha was given a stunning overhaul. The structure of this grand iron-and-glass relic from the 19th century was preserved, while its interior was artfully converted into a light-filled tropical garden with more than 500 plant species. The project was the work of architect Rafael Moneo, and his landmark achievement was to create a thoroughly modern space that resonates with the stately European train stations of another age.

In the modern northeastern corner of the station, the **11 March 2004 Memorial** (Map p242; 1st fl, Estación de Atocha; ☺11am-2pm & 5-7pm Tue-Sun Apr-Feb, 10am-8pm daily Mar; Ⓜ Atocha Renfe) **FREE** is a moving monument to the victims of the 2004 terrorist attack at the station. Although partially visible from Paseo de la Infanta Isabel, the memorial is best viewed from below. A glass panel shows the names of those killed, while the airy glass-and-perspex dome is inscribed with the messages of condolence and solidarity left by well-wishers in a number of languages in the immediate aftermath of the attack. The 12m-high dome is designed so that the sun highlights different messages at different times of the day, while the effect at night is akin to flickering candles.

## MUSEO DE ARTES DECORATIVAS
MUSEUM

Map p242 (☑91 532 64 99; www.mecd.gob.es/mnartesdecorativas/portada.html; Calle de Montalbán 12; adult/child, student & senior €3/1.50, Sun free; ☺9.30am-3pm Tue-Sat, 10am-3pm Sun Jul & Aug, 9.30am-3pm Tue, Wed, Fri & Sat, 9.30am-3pm & 5-8pm Thu, 10am-3pm Sun Sep-Jun; Ⓜ Retiro) Those who love sumptuous period furniture, ceramics, carpets, tapestries and the like will find themselves passing a worthwhile hour or two here. There's

plenty to catch your eye and the ceramics from around Spain are a definite feature, while the recreations of kitchens from several regions are curiosities. Reconstructions of regal bedrooms, women's drawing rooms and 19th-century salons also help shed light on how the privileged classes of Spain have lived through the centuries.

# 🍴 EATING

**In the discreet residential enclave between Parque del Buen Retiro and Paseo del Prado you'll find a handful of exclusive restaurants where eating is taken seriously, classic charm is the pervasive atmosphere, and limousines wait outside to ferry the well-heeled back home. On the western shore of the *paseo* is one of Madrid's most exciting tapas bars.**

## EL BRILLANTE
SPANISH €

Map p242 (☑91 528 69 66; Plaza del Emperador Carlos V; bocadillos €4.50-7, raciones €7.50-13; ☺7.30am-2.30am Sep-Jul; Ⓜ Atocha) Just by the Centro de Arte Reina Sofía, this breezy, no-frills bar-eatery is a Madrid institution for its *bocadillos* (filled rolls) – the *bocadillo de calamares* has been a favourite for more than half a century – and no-nonsense *raciones* (large tapas servings). It's also famous for serving *chocolate con churros* or *porras* (chocolate with deep-fried doughnuts) in the wee hours after a hard night on the tiles.

## ⭐ ESTADO PURO
TAPAS €€

Map p242 (☑91 330 24 00; www.tapasenestadopuro.com; Plaza de Neptuno/Plaza de Cánovas del Castillo 4; tapas €4.50-12.50, mains €14-20; ☺noon-midnight; Ⓜ Banco de España, Atocha) A slick but casual tapas bar, Estado Puro serves up fantastic tapas, such as the *tortilla española siglo XXI* (21st-century Spanish omelette, served in a glass...), quail eggs in soy sauce or pig's trotters with cuttlefish noodles. The kitchen is overseen by Paco Roncero, head chef at La Terraza del Casino (p91), who learned his trade with master chef Ferran Adrià.

## ⭐ VIRIDIANA
MODERN SPANISH €€€

Map p242 (☑91 523 44 78; www.restauranteviridiana.com; Calle de Juan de Mena 14; mains €28-39, menú de degustación €100; ☺1.30-4pm & 8pm-midnight; Ⓜ Banco de España) Chef Abraham García is a much-celebrated Madrid figure and his larger-than-life personality is reflected in Viridiana's menu. Many influences are brought to bear on the cooking here, among them international innovations and ingredients and well-considered seasonal variations.

**PALACIO DE CIBELES** SPANISH €€€
Map p242 (☑91 523 14 54; www.palaciodecibeles.com; 6th fl, Plaza de la Cibeles 1; mains €16-39, set menus €38.50-55; ☺1-4pm & 8pm-midnight; ⓂBanco de España) High in the iconic Palacio de Comunicaciones on Plaza de la Cibeles, this much-loved restaurant by Adolfo Muñoz takes Spanish staples, gives them a twist from the Castilla-La Mancha region, and then riffs a little wherever the urge takes him.

 **DRINKING & NIGHTLIFE**

**Drinking and nightlife are not really a part of the El Retiro or Paseo del Prado experience. A handful of *terrazas* in Parque del Buen Retiro is probably your best bet. Then again, Tatro Kapital is one of the city's most famous nightclubs and Huertas with its many bars is just up the hill.**

**TEATRO KAPITAL** CLUB
Map p242 (☑91 420 29 06; www.grupo-kapital.com; Calle de Atocha 125; admission from €17; ☺midnight-6am Thu-Sat; ⓂAtocha) One of the most famous megaclubs in Madrid, this seven-storey venue has something for everyone, from cocktail bars and dance music to karaoke, salsa, hip hop, chilled spaces and an open-air rooftop. There's even a 'Kissing Room'. Door staff have their share of

attitude and don't mind refusing entrance if you give them any lip.

It's such a big place that a cross-section of Madrid society (VIPs and the Real Madrid set love this place) hangs out here without ever getting in each other's way.

 **SHOPPING**

**The best shops close to Paseo del Prado tend to be those book/gift shops attached to the art museums – those at Caixa Forum and La Central (at Centro de Arte Reina Sofía) are especially good. And there's always the historic bookstalls that line Cuesta de San Moyano, at the southern end of Paseo del Prado.**

**LIBRERÍA LA CENTRAL** BOOKS
Map p242 (☑91 787 87 82; www.lacentral.com/museoreinasofia; Ronda de Atocha 2; ☺10am-9pm Mon & Wed-Sat, to 2.30pm Sun; ⓂAtocha) Part of the stunning extension to Centro de Arte Reina Sofía, La Central is perhaps Madrid's best gallery bookshop, with a range of posters, postcards and artistic stationery items as well as extensive sections on contemporary art, design, architecture and photography.

**CUESTA DE CLAUDIO MOYANO BOOKSTALLS** BOOKS
Map p242 (Cuesta de Claudio Moyano; ☺hours vary; ⓂAtocha) Madrid's answer to the booksellers that line the Seine in Paris, these secondhand bookstalls are an enduring Madrid landmark. Most titles are in Spanish, but there's a handful of offerings in other languages. Opening hours vary from stall to stall, and some of the stalls close at lunch.

 **SPORTS & ACTIVITIES**

**CENTRO DEPORTIVO LA CHOPERA** GYM
Map p242 (☑91 420 11 54; Parque del Buen Retiro; 1/10 sessions €5/40, court hire per adult €6.90; ☺8.30am-8.45pm Mon-Fri, to 2.30pm Sat & Sun, closed Aug; ⓂAtocha) With a fine workout centre, several football fields and a few tennis courts, this *centro deportivo* (sports centre and gym) in the southwestern corner of Parque del Buen Retiro is one of Madrid's most attractive and central. It also has tennis courts, but you'll need your own racquet.

1. *El tres de mayo* (Goya) 2. *La rendición de Breda* (Velázquez) 3. *Las meninas* (Velázquez)

# Masterpieces in Madrid

See the following grand materpieces of Spanish painting and you've drawn near to greatness. All except *Guernica* are in the Museo del Prado (p99).

## El jardín de las delicias (Bosch)

Amid the Prado's accumulation of dark and sometimes brooding paintings, Hieronymus Bosch's *The Garden of Earthly Delights* seems to spring from an entirely different place. Weird, wonderful and unforgettable, it's a surreal work of art that rewards lengthy inspection.

## El tres de mayo (Goya)

Goya's genius for capturing human drama is nowhere more evident than in *El tres de mayo,* with all the intensity and despair of Madrid's failed 1808 rebellion against Napoleon laid bare on canvas.

## Guernica (Picasso)

Epic in scale, compelling in its original detail, *Guernica* is the spectacular symbol of the cubist style perfected by Picasso and arguably the most famous painting of the 20th century. It can be found in the Centro de Arte Reina Sofía (p108).

## La rendición de Breda (Velázquez)

Best known for the intimacy of his royal portraits, Velázquez takes on the drama of a city's surrender in this piece (The Surrender of Breda). In doing so he brings to the canvas his perfect understanding of light, colour and the individuality of human faces.

## Las meninas (Velázquez)

This intriguing royal scene (The Maids of Honour) is Velázquez' most recognisable painting, a marriage of a painter at the peak of his powers and a subject matter (royal life) that he made his own.

# Salamanca

## Neighbourhood Top Five

**1 Agatha Ruiz de la Prada** (p125) Shopping for Spanish fashions along Calle de Serrano, one of the most prestigious shopping boulevards in Europe, beginning with this signature store brimful with colour.

**2 Museo Lázaro Galdiano** (p120) Gaining an insight into the old-money Salamanca world by visiting this extraordinary art collection housed in a noble mansion.

**3 Plaza de Toros** (p121) Finding out more about bullfighting by taking a tour at the city's elegant bullring.

**4 Platea** (p124) Catching the buzz of Spanish culinary innovation in the stunning converted theatre that has taken Salamanca dining by storm.

**5 Oriol Balaguer** (p126) Discovering a whole new world of chocolates in the boutique of Spain's master chocolatier.

For more detail of this area see Map p244 ➡

# Explore: Salamanca

One of the larger *barrios* (districts) that we cover, Salamanca can look daunting on a map, but it's easily navigated for the most part on foot. Calle de Serrano and Calle de José Ortega y Gasset are the two main shopping strips, and if you're in town to shop then there's very little of interest that's more than a short detour from these two main axes. For the Museo Lázaro Galdiano, it's a stiff uphill climb from the rest of the neighbourhood, while the Plaza de Toros, out in the east of the neighbourhood, is a 30-minute walk from Calle de Serrano, also uphill for much of the way. For both of these major attractions, consider hopping on the metro.

Although you will find bars and nightclubs here, Salamanca is very much a daytime *barrio*. Salamanca's tapas bars and restaurants overflow with a busy lunchtime crowd during the week when eating is often a pit stop on part of a shopping itinerary. We suggest you do likewise to really get under Salamanca's skin. By evening, things are much quieter, with many people coming specifically to eat before heading elsewhere in Madrid to continue their night.

## Local Life

→ **Hang-out** José Luis (p124), close to the Museo Lázaro Galdiano, is beloved by a wealthy crowd, its outdoor tables invariably inhabited by suits lingering over bottled mineral water.

→ **Picnic** Mallorca (p123) has some fantastic takeaway foods, and it's ideal if you're planning a picnic in the Parque del Buen Retiro, which borders Salamanca to the south.

→ **Slice of Andalucía** At **El Nuevo Rincón de Jerez** (☑91 819 29 99; www.elnuevorincondejerez.es; Calle de Rufino Blanco 5; raciones €7-15; ☺1-4.30pm & 7pm-midnight Tue-Sun Sep-Jul; Ⓜ Manuel Bacerra) they sing *La Salve Rociera*, a song with deep roots in the flamenco and Catholic traditions of the south. Breathtaking.

## Getting There & Away

→ **Metro** Serrano and Velázquez (both line 4) or Núñez de Balboa (lines 4 and 5) are the most convenient metro stations; the last means a downhill walk to most of the *barrio*. Gregorio Marañón (lines 7 and 10) is best for the Museo Lázaro Galdiano. Ventas (lines 2 and 5) is the station for the Plaza de Toros.

## Lonely Planet's Top Tip

María Luisa Banzo, the owner of La Cocina de María Luisa (p125), was formerly a prominent figure in the government of conservative Popular Party Prime Minister José María Aznar – keep an eye out for the former PM (also from Castilla y León) and other prominent politicians in her restaurant.

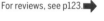 **Best Places to Eat**

→ Platea (p124)

→ Biotza (p124)

→ La Colonial de Goya (p124)

→ La Cocina de María Luisa (p125)

→ Astrolabius (p123)

For reviews, see p123.

🍷 **Best Places to Drink**

→ Geographic Club (p125)

→ Almonte (p125)

→ Gabana 1800 (p125)

For reviews, see p125.

🛍 **Best Places to Shop**

→ Agatha Ruiz de la Prada (p125)

→ Manolo Blahnik (p126)

→ Oriol Balaguer (p126)

→ Mantequería Bravo (p126)

For reviews, see p125.

## José Lázaro Galdiano

Born in Navarra in northeastern Spain, José Lázaro Galdiano (1862–1947) moved to Madrid as a young man. He would later become a hugely significant figure in the cultural life of the city. During WWI he was an important supporter of the Museo del Prado, and later built his own private collection by buying up Spanish artworks in danger of being sold overseas and bringing home those that had already left. He lived in exile during the Civil War, but continued to collect and upon his return he set up a respected artistic foundation in his former palace that would ultimately house the museum.

## Old Masters

It can be difficult to believe the breadth of masterpieces that Galdiano gathered during his lifetime, and there's enough here to merit this museum's inclusion among Madrid's best art galleries. The highlights include works by Francisco de Zurbarán, Claudio Coello, Hieronymus Bosch, Bartolomé Esteban Murillo, El Greco, Lucas Cranach and John Constable, and there's even a painting in Room 11 attributed to Diego Rodríguez de Silva Velázquez.

### DON'T MISS

- Old Masters
- Goya Paintings
- Curio Collection
- Frescoes & Textiles

### PRACTICALITIES

- Map p244, B1
- ☑91 561 60 84
- www.flg.es
- Calle de Serrano 122
- adult/concession/child €6/3/free, last hour free
- ◷10am-4.30pm Tue-Sat, to 3pm Sun
- ⓂGregorio Marañón

## Goya

As is often the case, Goya belongs in a class of his own. He dominates Room 13, while the ceiling of the adjoining Room 14 features a collage from some of his more famous works. Some that are easy to recognise include *La maja desnuda, La maja vestida* and the frescoes of the Ermita de San Antonio de la Florida (p148).

## Curio Collection

This remarkable collection ranges beyond paintings to sculptures, bronzes, miniature figures, jewellery, ceramics, furniture, weapons...clearly Galdiano was a man of wide interests. The ground floor is largely given over to a display setting the social context in which he lived, with hundreds of curios from all around the world on show. There are more on the top floor.

## Frescoes & Textiles

The lovely 1st floor, which contains many of the Spanish artworks, is arrayed around the centrepiece of the former ballroom and beneath lavishly frescoed ceilings. On no account miss the top floor's Room 24, which contains some exquisite textiles.

## TOP SIGHT
# PLAZA DE TOROS & MUSEO TAURINO

## Architecture

One of the largest rings in the bullfighting world, Las Ventas can hold 25,000 spectators, and has a grand Mudéjar (a Moorish architectural style) exterior and a suitably coliseum-like arena surrounding the broad sandy ring.

## Puerta de Madrid

The grand and decidedly Moorish Puerta de Madrid symbolises the aspiration of all bullfighters and, suitably, it's known colloquially as the 'gate of glory'. Madrid's bullfighting crowd is known as the most demanding in Spain – if they carry a *torero* (bullfighter) out through the gate (usually clutching an ear or a tail – other trophies awarded to an elite few), it's because he has performed exceptionally.

## Museo Taurino

The **Museo Taurino** (☑91 725 18 57; www.las-ventas.com; Calle de Alcalá 237; ☺10am-5.30pm; Ⓜ Ventas) FREE inhabits a newly renovated space dedicated to bullfighting legend Manolete, as well as a curious collection of paraphernalia, costumes (the *traje de luces*, or suit of lights, is one of bullfighting's most recognisable props), photos and other bullfighting memorabilia up on the top floor above one of the two courtyards by the ring. It's a fascinating insight into the whole subculture that surrounds bullfighting.

## Guided Tour

Although you can visit the ring without taking a tour, we strongly recommend that you take one of the **guided visits** (☑687 739032; www.lasventastour.com; adult/child €13/10; ☺10am-5.30pm, days of bullfight 10am-1.30pm; Ⓜ Ventas), which take you out onto the sand and into the royal box. Tours are in English and Spanish and must be booked in advance.

### DON'T MISS

➡ Mudéjar Architecture
➡ Puerta de Madrid
➡ Museo Taurino

### PRACTICALITIES

➡ ☑91 356 22 00
➡ www.las-ventas.com
➡ Calle de Alcalá 237
➡ admission free
➡ ☺10am-5.30pm
➡ Ⓜ Ventas

# ◉ SIGHTS

In the *barrio* of Salamanca, the unmistakeable whiff of old money mingles comfortably with the aspirations of Spain's nouveau riche. In short, it's the sort of place to put on your finest clothes, regardless of your errand, and simply be seen. Sights are thinly spread but worth tracking down, with a focus on the arts, architecture and the very Spanish passion of bullfighting.

**MUSEO LÁZARO GALDIANO**            MUSEUM
See p120.

**PLAZA DE TOROS &**
**MUSEO TAURINO**            STADIUM, MUSEUM
See p121.

**MUSEO AL AIRE LIBRE**            SCULPTURE
Map p244 (Paseo de la Castellana; ⊘24hr; MRubén Darío) FREE This fascinating open-air collection of 17 abstract sculptures includes works by renowned Basque artist Eduardo Chillida, Catalan master Joan Miró, as well as Eusebio Sempere and Alberto Sánchez, among Spain's foremost sculptors of the 20th century. The sculptures are beneath the overpass where Paseo de Eduardo Dato crosses Paseo de la Castellana, but somehow the hint of traffic grime and pigeon shit only adds to the appeal. All but one are on the eastern side of Paseo de la Castellana.

**MUSEO ARQUEOLÓGICO**
**NACIONAL**            MUSEUM
Map p244 (✐91 577 79 12; www.man.es; Calle de Serrano 13; admission €3, 2-8pm Sat & 9.30am-noon Sun free; ⊘9.30am-8pm Tue-Sat, to 3pm Sun; MSerrano) The showpiece National Archaeology Museum contains a sweeping accumulation of artefacts behind its towering facade. Daringly redesigned within, the museum ranges across Spain's ancient history and the large collection includes stunning mosaics taken from Roman villas across Spain, intricate Muslim-era and Mudéjar handiwork, sculpted figures such as the *Dama de Ibiza* and *Dama de Elche,* examples of Romanesque and Gothic architectural styles and a partial copy of the prehistoric cave paintings of Altamira (Cantabria).

**PALACIO DE LINARES**            NOTABLE BUILDING
Map p244 (✐91 595 48 00, ticket reservations 902 221424; www.casamerica.es; Plaza de la Cibeles 2; adult/student & senior/child €8/5/free; ⊘guided tours 11am, noon & 1pm Sat & Sun Sep-Jul, shorter hours Aug, ticket office 10am-3pm & 4-8pm Mon-Fri; MBanco de España) So extraordinary is the Palacio de Comunicaciones on Plaza de la Cibeles that many visitors fail to notice this fine 19th-century pleasure dome that stands watch over the northeastern corner of the plaza. Built in 1873, the Palacio de Linares is a worthy member of the line-up of grand facades on the plaza, while its interior is notable for the copious use of Carrara marble. Tours take an hour and you can purchase tickets at the ticket office.

Tickets can also be reserved by phone or online at www.entradas.com; they often sell out in advance, so don't leave it until the last minute. In the palace's grounds is the **Casa de América**, a modern exhibition centre, which also hosts all sorts of events and concerts.

---

### SALAMANCA'S DIFFICULT BIRTH

When Madrid's authorities were looking to expand beyond the newly inadequate confines of the medieval capital, the Marqués de Salamanca, a 19th-century aristocrat and general with enormous political clout, heard the call. He threw everything he had into the promotion of his *barrio* (district) in the 1870s, buying up land cheaply, which he hoped to sell later for a profit. He was ahead of his time: the houses he built contained Madrid's first water closets, the latest in domestic plumbing and water heating for bathrooms and kitchens, while he also inaugurated horse-drawn tramways. In the year of his death, 1883, the streets got electric lighting. Hard as it is now to imagine, there was little enthusiasm for the project and the *marqués* quickly went bankrupt. Towards the end of his life, he wrote, 'I have managed to create the most comfortable *barrio* in Madrid and find myself the owner of 50 houses, 13 hotels and 18 million feet of land. And I owe more than 36 million *reales* on all of this. The task is completed but I am ruined.' It was only later that *madrileños* (people of Madrid) saw the error of their ways.

**BIBLIOTECA NACIONAL
& MUSEO DEL LIBRO**  LIBRARY, MUSEUM
Map p244 (☑91 580 78 05; www.bne.es; Paseo de
los Recoletos 20; ☺library 9am-9pm Mon-Fri, to
2pm Sat mid-Sep–mid-Jun, 9am-7.30pm Mon-Fri
mid-Jun–mid-Sep, museum 10am-8pm Tue-Sat,
to 2pm Sun; ⓂColón) FREE Perhaps the most
impressive of the grand edifices erected
along the Paseo de los Recoletos in the
19th century, the 1892 Biblioteca Nacional
(National Library) dominates the southern
end of Plaza de Colón. Downstairs, and entered via a separate entrance, the fascinating museum is a must for bibliophiles, with
interactive displays on printing presses and
other materials, illuminated manuscripts,
the history of the library, and literary cafes.

Our favourite exhibits are the 1626 map
of Spain and Picasso's *Mademoiselle Léonie
en un sillón* in the Sala de las Musas. There's
not an e-book in sight.

**FUNDACIÓN JUAN MARCH**  CULTURAL CENTRE
Map p244 (☑91 435 42 40; www.march.es; Calle
de Castelló 77; ☺11am-8pm Mon-Sat, 10am-2pm
Sun & holidays; ⓂNúñez de Balboa) FREE This
foundation organises some of the better
temporary exhibitions in Madrid each year
and it's always worth checking its website
to see what's on or around the corner. It
also stages concerts (p125) across a range of
musical genres and other events throughout
the year.

# ✖ EATING

**Eating out in Salamanca is generally
a suave affair and restaurants here
invite you to rub shoulders with the
young, the beautiful and the very well
dressed – in most places you'll need
to dress accordingly – while celebrity
chefs occasionally tug the city's most
conservative *barrio* in new culinary
directions.**

**EL LATERAL**  TAPAS €
Map p244 (☑91 435 06 04; www.lateral.com;
Calle de Velázquez 57; tapas €1.55-9.80, raciones
€7-13; ☺noon-1am Sun-Wed, to 2am Thu-Sat;
ⓂVelázquez, Núñez de Balboa) El Lateral does
terrific *pinchos* (tapas), which serve as the
ideal accompaniment to the fine wines
on offer. Tapas are creative without being
over the top (wild mushroom croquettes

or sirloin with foie gras). This being Salamanca, they draw a pretty upmarket crowd,
but you'd be surprised how rapidly the ties
loosen after work.

There's another branch in **Malasaña** (Map
p246; ☑91 531 68 77; www.lateral.com; Calle de
Fuencarral 43; tapas €1.50-10, raciones €7-13;
☺noon-midnight Sun-Wed, to 2am Thu-Sat; ⓂTri-
bunal) and a bar-restaurant in Huertas (p88).

**MALLORCA**  BAKERY €
Map p244 (☑91 577 18 59; www.pasteleria-
mallorca.com; Calle de Serrano 6; mains €7-12;
☺9am-9pm; ⓂRetiro) For fine takeaway food,
head to Mallorca, a Madrid institution.
Everything here, from gourmet mains to
snacks and sweets, is delicious.

**VIANDAS DE SALAMANCA**  SPANISH €
Map p244 (☑91 577 99 12; www.viandasde
salamanca.es; Calle de Goya 43; bocadillos from
€4; ☺9.30am-9.30pm Mon-Sat, to 8pm Sun; ⓂVe-
lázquez) This outpost of the hugely successful
cured-meats delis serves up the usual *bocadillos de jamón* (rolls filled with ham) as well
as all manner of other takeaway cured meats.
It's handy for between-meal munchies.

**★ASTROLABIUS**  FUSION €€
Map p244 (☑91 562 06 11; www.astrolabius
madrid.com; Calle de Serrano 118; mains €10-25;
☺1-4pm & 8.30pm-midnight Tue-Sat, closed Aug;
ⓂNúñez de Balboa) This terrific family-run
place in Salamanca's north is a simple
philosophy – take grandmother's recipes
and filter them through the imagination of
the grandchildren. The result is a beguiling
mix of flavours, such as scallops of the world
in garlic, or the prawn croquettes. The atmosphere is edgy and modern, but casual in
the best Madrid sense.

## ★PLATEA
SPANISH €€

Map p244 (☑91 577 00 25; www.plateamadrid.com; Calle de Goya 5-7; ⊘12.30pm-12.30am Sun-Wed, to 2.30am Thu-Sat; ⓂSerrano, Colón) The ornate Carlos III cinema opposite the Plaza de Colón has been artfully transformed into a dynamic culinary scene with more than a hint of burlesque. There are 12 restaurants, three gourmet food stores and cocktail bars.

Working with the original theatre-style layout, the multilevel seating has been used to array a series of restaurants that seem at once self-contained yet connected to the whole through the soaring open central space, with all of them in some way facing the stage area where cabaret-style or 1930s-era performances or live cooking shows provide a rather glamorous backdrop. It's where food court meets haute cuisine, a daring combination of lunch or dinner with the occasional floor show without the formality that usually infuses such places.

## JOSÉ LUIS
SPANISH €€

Map p244 (☑91 563 09 58; www.joseluis.es; Calle de Serrano 89; tapas from €5; ⊘8.30am-1am Mon-Fri, 9am-1am Sat, 12.30pm-1am Sun; ⓂGregorio Marañón) With numerous branches around Madrid, José Luis is famous for its fidelity to traditional Spanish recipes. It wins many people's vote for Madrid's best *tortilla de patatas* (Spanish potato omelette), but it's also good for *croquetas* and *ensaladilla rusa* (Russian salad). This outpost has a slightly stuffy, young-men-in-suits feel to it, which is, after all, *very* Salamanca.

## TEPIC
MEXICAN €€

Map p244 (☑91 522 08 50; www.tepic.es; Calle de Ayala 14; mains €12-18; ⊘1-11.30pm Mon-Thu, to midnight Fri & Sat, to 5pm Sun; ⓂSerrano) Recently moved from Chueca, Tepic offers 'Urban Mexican Food' in chic dining rooms and with friendly service. Tepic's signature dish is the Acapulco Tropical, a cheese taco with meat and pineapple, but it's all good here and leaves you with none of that heavy after-dinner feel that can spoil the aftermath of many Mexican meals.

The *menú de degustación* (€28) is outstanding, there are lots of Mexican beers to choose from and the margaritas are spectacular. Although the kitchen closes around midnight, you can linger for an hour or two more over your margarita (or, better still, order another), depending on the night.

## BIOTZA
TAPAS, BASQUE €€

Map p244 (☑91 781 03 13; Calle de Claudio Coello 27; pintxos €2.80-3.40, raciones from €6, set menus from €18; ⊘1-4.30pm & 8.30pm-midnight Mon-Sat; ⓂSerrano) This breezy Basque tapas bar is one of the best places in Madrid to sample the creativity of bite-sized *pintxos* (Basque tapas) as only the Basques can make them. It's the perfect combination of San Sebastián–style tapas, Madrid-style pale-green/red-black decoration and unusual angular benches. The prices quickly add up, but it's highly recommended nonetheless.

## LA COLONIAL DE GOYA
TAPAS €€

Map p244 (☑91 575 63 06; www.lacolonialdegoya.com; Calle de Jorge Juan 34; mains €13-20; ⊘1-4pm & 8pm-midnight; ⓂVelázquez) Other better-known places have come and gone around here, but La Colonial de Goya has stood the test of time. The food is occasionally creative but is more often traditional (such as warm *canapés* and *croquetas*). The atmosphere is casual, while the all-white decor of wood and exposed brick walls is as classy as the neighbourhood.

## RESTAURANTE ESTAY
TAPAS €€

Map p244 (☑91 578 04 70; www.estayrestaurante.com; Calle de Hermosilla 46; tapas €1.90-4.40, 6-tapas set menu from €15; ⊘8am-midnight Mon-Thu, to 1.30am Fri, 9am-1.30am Sat; ⓂVelázquez) Restaurante Estay is partly a standard Spanish bar, where besuited waiters serve *café con leche,* and also one of the best-loved tapas bars in this part of town. The long list of hot and cold tapas concentrates mostly on Spanish staples, with a handful of more adventurous combinations. It also does breakfasts. It's a rather odd mix, but somehow it works.

## LA MARUCA
CANTABRIAN €€

Map p244 (☑91 781 49 69; www.restaurantelamaruca.com; Calle de Velázquez 54; mains €13-22; ⊘11am-1am; ⓂVelázquez) This classy and fresh space is dedicated to the cooking of Spain's northern Cantabria region and it's extremely popular among Salamanca's young and wealthy. While Cantabria means the best *anchoas* (anchovies) in the country and other fruits of the sea, La Maruca is unusual in that it focuses as much on the Cantabrian interior – think meatballs and hearty stews.

**LA COCINA DE MARÍA LUISA** CASTILIAN €€€
Map p244 (☑91 781 01 80; www.lacocinademaria
luisa.es; Calle de Jorge Juan 42; mains €18-27;
☺1.30-4pm & 9pm-midnight Mon-Sat Sep-Jul;
ⓂVelázquez) The home kitchen of former
parliamentarian María Luisa Banzo has one
of Salamanca's most loyal followings. The
cooking is a carefully charted culinary journey through Castilla y León, accompanied
by well-chosen regional wines and rustic decor that add much warmth to this welcom-
ing place. The house speciality comes from
María Luisa's mother – pig's trotters filled
with meat and black truffles from Soria.

The chance to choose half-sized versions
of most dishes will appeal to many.

#  DRINKING & NIGHTLIFE

**Salamanca is the land of the beautiful
people and it's all about gloss and
glamour. As you glide among the *pijos*
(beautiful people or yuppies), keep your
eyes peeled for Real Madrid players and
celebrities. Although places do exist in
Salamanca's otherwise quiet streets
that enable you to spend the whole night
here, there are far better *barrios* to get
a feel for Madrid's famous nightlife. And
many of Salamanca's celebrities would
appear to agree – the clubs and cocktail
bars of Malasaña and Chueca are also
popular haunts.**

**GABANA 1800** CLUB
Map p244 (☑91 575 18 46; www.gabana.es; Calle
Velázquez 6; admission €15; ☺midnight-5.30am
Wed-Sat; ⓂRetiro) With its upmarket crowd
that invariably includes a few *famosos*
(famous people), Gabana 1800 is very Salamanca. That this place has lasted the distance where others haven't owes much to
the fabulous array of drinks, rotating cast
of first-class DJs and fairly discerning door
policy – dress to impress.

**ALMONTE** CLUB
Map p244 (☑91 563 25 04; www.almontesalaro
ciera.com; Calle de Juan Bravo 35; ☺11pm-5am
Sun-Fri, 10pm-6am Sat; ⓂNúñez de Balboa,
Diego de León) If flamenco has captured
your soul, but you're keen to do more than
watch, head to Almonte. Live acts kick off
the night, paying homage to the flamenco
roots of Almonte in Andalucía's deep south.
The young and the beautiful who come here

have *sevillanas* (a flamenco dance style) in
their soul and in their feet.

Head downstairs to see the best dancing.
Dance if you dare.

**GEOGRAPHIC CLUB** BAR
Map p244 (☑91 578 08 62; www.thegeographic
club.es; Calle de Alcalá 141; ☺1pm-2am Sun-Thu,
to 3am Fri & Sat; ⓂGoya) With its elaborate
stained-glass windows, ethno-chic from all
over the world and laid-back atmosphere,
the Geographic Club is an excellent choice
in Salamanca for an early-evening drink
– try one of the 30-plus tropical cocktails.
We like the table built around an old hot-
air-balloon basket almost as much as the
cavern-like pub downstairs.

#  ENTERTAINMENT

**FUNDACIÓN JUAN MARCH** CONCERT VENUE
Map p244 (☑91 435 42 40; www.march.es; Calle
de Castelló 77; ⓂNúñez de Balboa) A foundation
dedicated to promoting music and culture
(as well as exhibitions), the Juan March
Foundation stages free concerts throughout the year. Performances range from solo
recitals to themed concerts dedicated to a
single style or composer.

# 🛍 SHOPPING

**Salamanca is the ideal place to take the
pulse of Spain's fashion scene and you'll
likely find it in top shape. Here you'll
discover that there's so much more to
Spanish fashion than Zara and Mango.
Fashions range from classically elegant
to cool and cutting-edge, from both
leading and upcoming Spanish designers
and the big names in international
fashion. Shopping here is a social event,
where people put on their finest and
service is often impeccable, if a little
stuffy. Throw in a sprinkling of gourmet
food shops and you could easily spend
days doing little else but shopping.**

★**AGATHA RUIZ
DE LA PRADA** FASHION & ACCESSORIES
Map p244 (☑91 319 05 01; www.agatharuizdela
prada.com; Calle de Serrano 27; ☺10am-8.30pm
Mon-Sat; ⓂSerrano) This boutique has to be
seen to be believed, with pinks, yellows and
oranges everywhere you turn. It's fun and
exuberant, but not just for kids. It also has

## SPANISH WINES

Spanish wine is subject to a complicated system of wine classification with a range of designations marked on the bottle. Most importantly, wines are labelled according to region or classificatory status rather than grape variety. If an area meets certain strict standards for a given period and covers all aspects of planting, cultivating and ageing, it receives Denominación de Origen (DO; Denomination of Origin) status. There are currently over 60 DO-recognised wine-producing areas in Spain.

An outstanding wine region gets the much-coveted Denominación de Origen Calificada (DOC). At present, the only DOC wines come from La Rioja in northern Spain and the small Priorat area in Catalonia.

Other important indications of quality depend on the length of time a wine has been aged, especially if in oak barrels. The best wines are often, therefore, *crianza* (aged for one year in oak barrels), *reserva* (two years ageing, at least one of which is in oak barrels) and *gran reserva* (two years in oak and three in the bottle).

serious and highly original fashion. Agatha Ruiz de la Prada is one of the enduring icons of *la movida madrileña,* Madrid's 1980s outpouring of creativity.

### BOMBONERÍAS SANTA — FOOD & DRINKS

Map p244 (☎91 576 76 25; www.bomboneriassanta.com; Calle de Serrano 56; ⌚10am-2pm & 5-8.30pm Mon, 10am-8.30pm Tue-Sat, shorter hours Jul & Aug; Ⓜ Serrano) If your style is as refined as your palate, the exquisite chocolates in this tiny shop will satisfy. The packaging is every bit as pretty as the *bombones* (chocolates) within, but they're not cheap – count on paying around €60 per kilo of chocolate.

### ORIOL BALAGUER — FOOD

Map p244 (☎91 401 64 63; www.oriolbalaguer.com; Calle de José Ortega y Gasset 44; ⌚9am-8.30pm Mon-Fri, 10am-8.30pm Sat, 10am-2.30pm Sun; Ⓜ Núñez de Balboa) Catalan pastry chef Oriol Balaguer has a formidable CV – he's worked in the kitchens of Ferran Adrià in Catalonia, won the prize for the World's Best Dessert (the 'Seven Textures of Chocolate') and his croissants once won the title of Spain's best. His chocolate boutique is presented like a small art gallery dedicated to exquisite chocolate collections and cakes.

You'll never be able to buy ordinary chocolate again.

### MANTEQUERÍA BRAVO — FOOD & DRINKS

Map p244 (☎91 575 80 72; www.bravo1931.com; Calle de Ayala 24; ⌚9.30am-2.30pm & 5.30-8.30pm Mon-Fri, 9.30am-2.30pm Sat; Ⓜ Serrano) Behind the attractive old facade lies a connoisseur's paradise, filled with local cheeses, sausages, wines and coffees. The products here are great for a gift, but everything's so good that you won't want to share. Not that long ago, Mantequería Bravo won the prize for Madrid's best gourmet food shop or delicatessen.

### MANOLO BLAHNIK — SHOES

Map p244 (☎91 575 96 48; www.manoloblahnik.com; Calle de Serrano 58; ⌚10am-2pm & 4-8pm Mon-Sat; Ⓜ Serrano) Nothing to wear to the Oscars? Do what many Hollywood celebrities do and head for Manolo Blahnik. The showroom is exclusive and each shoe is displayed like a work of art.

### BALENCIAGA — FASHION & ACCESSORIES

Map p244 (☎91 419 99 00; www.balenciaga.com; Calle de Lagasca 75; ⌚10.30am-8pm Mon-Sat; Ⓜ Núñez de Balboa) Flagship store for the celebrated Basque Balenciaga brand, with a stunning limestone-and-marble interior.

### ISOLÉE — FOOD, FASHION

Map p244 (☎902 876136; www.isolee.com; Calle de Claudio Coello 55; ⌚11am-8.30pm Mon-Fri, to 9pm Sat; Ⓜ Serrano) Multipurpose lifestyle stores were late in coming to Madrid, but they're now all the rage and there's none more stylish than Isolée, which has outlasted them all. It sells a select range of everything from clothes and shoes (Andy Warhol to Adidas) to CDs and food.

### LOEWE — FASHION & ACCESSORIES

Map p244 (☎91 426 35 88; www.loewe.com; Calle de Serrano 26 & 34; ⌚10am-8.30pm Mon-Sat; Ⓜ Serrano) Born in 1846 in Madrid, Loewe is arguably Spain's signature line in high-end fashion. Classy handbags and accessories are the mainstays and prices can be jaw-droppingly high, but it's worth stopping by here, even if you don't plan to buy.

**EKSEPTION & EKS**  FASHION & ACCESSORIES
Map p244 (☑91 361 97 76; www.ekseption.es; Calle de Velázquez 28; ⊙10.30am-2.30pm & 4.30-8.30pm Mon-Sat; ⓂVelázquez) This elegant showroom store consistently leads the way with the latest trends, spanning catwalk designs alongside a look that is more informal, though always sophisticated. The unifying theme is urban chic and its list of designer brands includes Balenciaga, Givenchy, Marc Jacobs and Dries van Noten.

Next door, Eks, which was being renovated when we visited, is the preserve of younger, more casual lines, including a fantastic selection of jeans.

**CAMPER**  SHOES
Map p244 (☑91 578 25 60; www.camper.com; Calle de Serrano 24; ⊙10am-9pm Mon-Sat, noon-8pm Sun; ⓂSerrano) Spanish fashion is not all haute couture, and this world-famous cool and quirky shoe brand from Mallorca offers bowling-shoe chic with colourful, fun designs that are all about quality coupled with comfort. There are other outlets throughout the city, including a Malasaña shop (p136).

**PURIFICACIÓN GARCÍA**  FASHION & ACCESSORIES
Map p244 (☑91 435 80 13; www.purificaciongarcia.com; Calle de Serrano 28; ⊙10am-8.30pm Mon-Sat; ⓂSerrano) Fashions may come and go but Puri consistently manages to keep ahead of the pack. Her signature style for men and women is elegant and mature designs that are just as at home in the workplace as at a wedding.

**ABC SERRANO**  SHOPPING CENTRE
Map p244 (☑91 577 50 31; www.abcserrano.com; Calle de Serrano; ⊙10am-9pm Mon-Sat; ⓂNúñez de Balboa) Elegant shopping centre with mainstream Spanish brands.

**MERCADO DE LA PAZ**  MARKET
Map p244 (☑91 435 07 43; www.mercadolapaz.es; off Calle de Ayala; ⊙9am-2.30pm & 5-8pm Mon-Fri, 9am-2.30pm Sat; ⓂSerrano) One of few Madrid markets not to have been gentrified in recent years, Mercado de la Paz remains a thoroughly local market. Fresh produce, meat and fish are the mainstays, but there are plenty of things to buy and eat as you go (cured meats and cheeses, for example).

**DE VIAJE**  BOOKS
Map p244 (☑91 577 98 99; www.deviaje.com; Calle de Serrano 41; ⊙10am-8.30pm Mon-Fri, 10.30am-2.30pm & 5-8pm Sat; ⓂSerrano) Whether you're after a guidebook, a coffee-table tome or travel literature, De Viaje, Madrid's largest travel bookshop, probably has it. Covering every region of the world, it has mostly Spanish titles, but some in English as well.

**LAVINIA**  WINE
Map p244 (☑91 650 33 92; www.lavinia.es; Calle de José Ortega y Gasset 16; ⊙10am-9pm Mon-Sat; ⓂNúñez de Balboa) 🖉 Although we love the intimacy of old-style Spanish wine shops, they can't match the selection of Spanish and international wines available at Lavinia, which has more than 4000 bottles to choose from. It also organises wine courses, tastings and excursions to nearby bodegas (wineries).

**CUARTO DE JUEGOS**  TOYS
Map p244 (☑91 435 00 99; www.cuartodejuegos.es; Calle de Jorge Juan 42; ⊙10am-8.30pm Mon-Fri, 10.30am-2pm & 5-8pm Sat; ⓂVelázquez, Príncipe de Vergara) We're not sure if it's an official rule, but batteries seem to be outlawed at this traditional toy shop, where all kinds of old-fashioned board games and puzzles are still sold. Yes, there's Ludo, Chinese checkers and backgammon, but there's so much more here and they're not just for kids.

# 🏃 SPORTS & ACTIVITIES

**LAB ROOM SPA**  SPA
Map p244 (☑91 431 21 98; www.thelabroom.com; Calle de Claudio Coello 13; ⊙11am-8pm Mon-Fri, to 7pm Sat; ⓂRetiro) An exclusive spa and beauty parlour whose past clients include Penélope Cruz, Jennifer Lopez, Gwyneth Paltrow and Gael García Bernal, the Lab Room is close to the ultimate in pampering for both men and women. It offers a range of make-up sessions, massages and facial and body treatments; prices can be surprisingly reasonable.

**CHI SPA**  SPA
Map p244 (☑91 578 13 40; www.thechispa.com; Calle del Conde de Aranda 6; ⊙9am-9pm Mon-Fri, 10am-6pm Sat & Sat; ⓂRetiro) Wrap up in a robe and slippers and prepare to be pampered in one of Spain's best day spas. There are separate areas for men and women, and services include a wide range of massages, facials, manicures and pedicures. Now, what was it you were stressed about?

# Malasaña & Conde Duque

## Neighbourhood Top Five

**❶ Museo de Historia** (p130) Passing under the fabulous doorway and spending an hour or two delving into Madrid's past.

**❷ Flamingos Vintage Kilo** (p136) Shopping for retro fashions in the true rebellious spirit of Malasaña, starting along Calle de Velarde before moving on to Calle de Espíritu Santo.

**❸ Albur** (p131) Kicking back in true Malasaña style in one of the *barrio's* best restaurants along Calle de Manuela Malasaña.

**❹ Gran Vía** (p130) Strolling down the newly pedestrianised boulevard, one of Madrid's grandest, and admiring the extraordinary architecture.

**❺ Teatro Flamenco Madrid** (p135) Enjoying topclass flamenco then stepping out into the heart of retro Malasaña along iconic Calle de Pez.

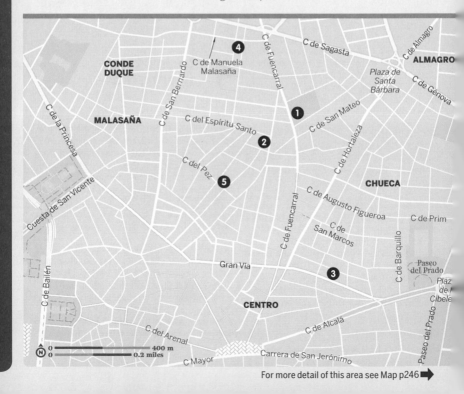

For more detail of this area see Map p246 ➡

# Explore: Malasaña & Conde Duque

The gritty inner-city neighbourhood of Malasaña is Madrid at its least gentrified, a *barrio* (district) that became famous for its hard-rock spirit during Madrid's wild 1980s and still largely resists the urge to grow up. The shopping is outstanding and there are a handful of pretty squares. But Malasaña is at its best on weekends or on most evenings and into the night – other than a flurry of activity around lunchtime as people hurry to and from their favourite tapas bar or restaurant, Malasaña lives for the night.

Calle de Fuencarral, a narrow but nonetheless major city thoroughfare that has been pedestrianised for much of its length, is most people's gateway to the neighbourhood. West of that line in Malasaña, shopfronts announce names like 'True Love Tattoo' and 'Retro City' alongside graffiti and posters of heavy-rocking bands that have become an integral part of its gritty urban charm. Plaza del Dos de Mayo is Malasaña's heartbeat. Slightly more refined and less clamorous, the sub-*barrio* of Conde Duque, to the west, has the best of Malasaña without quite the same grit and noise.

## Local Life

➔**Neighbourhood hub** Plaza del Dos de Mayo is Malasaña's epicentre, at its best late afternoon when children pour out of nearby schools to play while their parents order beer and wine at adjacent outdoor tables.

➔**Gran Vía walk** As of 2018, Madrid's grandest and most heavily trafficked thoroughfare will be a car-free zone. Walking its length makes it easier than ever to experience its fab architecture.

➔**Calle de Fuencarral** Lined with shops, pedestrian-friendly Calle de Fuencarral is a classic Madrid shopping experience and a brilliant way to transition into Malasaña's gritty tangle of streets.

## Getting There & Away

➔**Metro** Tribunal (lines 1 and 10) sits in the heart of Malasaña and most of the *barrio* (district) is a downhill walk from there. Noviciado (lines 2 and 10) is also good for Conde Duque, as well as Calle de Pez. Other convenient metro stations around the perimeter include San Bernardo, Bilbao, Gran Vía and Santo Domingo.

## Lonely Planet's Top Tip

In order to make the most of their popularity, some restaurants in Malasaña offer two sittings on Friday and Saturday nights, usually around 9pm and 11pm. Unless you can't wait (yes, we know that eating at 11pm and finishing dinner after midnight takes some getting used to), we recommend reserving a table for the second sitting – otherwise you'll often get the feeling that they're trying to hurry you along.

 **Best Places to Eat**

➔ Albur (p131)
➔ Pez Tortilla (p130)
➔ Casa Julio (p131)
➔ La Tasquita de Enfrente (p133)

For reviews, see p130.➔

⊙ **Best Literary Cafes**

➔ Café Comercial (p133)
➔ Café Manuela (p135)

For reviews, see p133.➔

⊙ **Best Architecture**

➔ Antiguo Cuartel del Conde Duque (p130)
➔ Museo de Historia (p130)

For reviews, see p130.

# ◉ SIGHTS

### GRAN VÍA STREET

Map p246 (ⓂGran Vía, Callao) It's difficult to imagine Madrid without Gran Vía, the grand boulevard lined with towering belle-époque facades that climbs up through the centre of Madrid from Plaza de España then down to Calle de Alcalá. But it has only existed since 1910, when it was bulldozed through a labyrinth of old streets. Fourteen streets disappeared off the map, as did 311 houses, including one where Goya had once lived. In 2018, Gran Vía will be transformed into a largely pedestrian thoroughfare.

Plans for the boulevard were first announced in 1862 and so interminable were the delays that a famous *zarzuela* (Spanish mix of theatre, music and dance), *La Gran Vía*, first performed in 1886, was penned to mock the city authorities. It may have destroyed whole *barrios*, but Gran Vía is still considered one of the most successful examples of urban planning in central Madrid since the late 19th century.

One eye-catching building, the **Edificio Carrión** (Map p232; cnr Gran Vía & Calle de Jacometrezo; ⓂCallao) was Madrid's first pre-WWI tower-block apartment hotel. Also dominating the skyline about one-third of the way along Gran Vía is the 1920s-era **Telefónica building** (Map p246; ⓂGran Vía), which was for years the highest building in the city. During the civil war, when Madrid was besieged by Franco's forces and the boulevard became known as 'Howitzer Alley' due to the artillery shells that rained down upon it, the Telefónica building was a favoured target.

Among the more interesting buildings is the stunning, French-designed Edificio Metrópolis (p86), built in 1907, which marks the southern end of Gran Vía. The winged victory statue atop its dome was added in 1975 and is best seen from Calle de Alcalá or Plaza de la Cibeles. A little up the boulevard is the **Edificio Grassy** (Map p238; Gran Vía 1; ⓂBanco de España, Sevilla), with the Rolex sign and built in 1916. With its circular 'temple' as a crown, and profusion of arcs and slender columns, it's one of the most elegant buildings along Gran Vía.

Otherwise Gran Vía is home to around twice as many businesses (over 1050 at last count) as homes (nearly 600); over 13,000 people work along the street; and up to 60,000 vehicles pass through every day (including almost 185 buses an hour during peak periods). There are over 40 hotels on Gran Vía, but, sadly, just three of the 15 cinemas for which Gran Vía was famous remain.

### MUSEO DE HISTORIA MUSEUM

Map p246 (☑91 701 16 86; www.madrid.es/museo dehistoria; Calle de Fuencarral 78; ◷10am-8pm Tue-Sun; ⓂTribunal) `FREE` The fine Museo de Historia (formerly the Museo Municipal) has an elaborate and restored baroque entrance, raised in 1721 by Pedro de Ribera. Behind this facade, the collection is dominated by paintings and other memorabilia charting the historical evolution of Madrid. The highlights are Goya's *Allegory of the City of Madrid* (on the 1st floor); the caricatures lampooning Napoleon and the early-19th-century French occupation of Madrid (1st floor); and the expansive model of Madrid as it was in 1830 (basement).

### MUSEO MUNICIPAL DE ARTE CONTEMPORÁNEO MUSEUM

Map p246 (☑91 588 59 28; www.madrid.es/museo artecontemporaneo; Calle del Conde Duque 9-11; ◷10am-2pm & 5.30-8.30pm Tue-Sat, 10.30am-2pm Sun; ⓂVentura Rodríguez) `FREE` This rich collection of modern Spanish art includes mostly paintings and graphic art with a smattering of photography, sculpture and drawings. Highlights include Eduardo Arroyo and Basque sculptor Jorge Oteiza. Running throughout the collection are creative interpretations of Madrid's cityscape – avant-garde splodges and almost old-fashioned visions of modern Madrid side by side, among them a typically fantastical representation of the Cibeles fountain by one-time icon of *la movida madrileña* (the Madrid scene), Ouka Leele.

The museum is inside the **Antiguo Cuartel del Conde Duque** (Map p246; ⓂPlaza de España, Ventura Rodríguez, San Bernardo).

# ✖️ EATING

### ⭐PEZ TORTILLA TAPAS €

Map p246 (☑653 919984; www.peztortilla.com; Calle del Pez 36; tapas from €4; ◷noon-midnight Sun, 6.30pm-2am Mon-Wed, noon-2am Thu, noon-2.30am Fri & Sat; ⓂNoviciado) Every time we come here, this place is full to bursting, which is not surprising given its philosophy of great tortilla (15 kinds!), splendid *croquetas* (croquettes) and craft beers (more than

70 varieties, with nine on tap). The *croquetas* with black squid ink or the tortilla with truffle brie and *jamón* (ham) are two stars among many.

### ★CASA JULIO

SPANISH €

Map p246 (☑91 522 72 74; Calle de la Madera 37; 6/12 croquetas €6/12; ☺1-3.30pm & 6.30-11pm Mon-Sat Sep-Jul; ⓂTribunal) A citywide poll for the best *croquetas* in Madrid would see half of those polled voting for Casa Julio and the remainder not doing so only because they haven't been yet. They're that good that celebrities and mere mortals from all over Madrid come here to sample the traditional *jamón* variety or more creative versions such as spinach with gorgonzola.

Strangely, the place acquired a certain celebrity when U2 chose the bar for a photo shoot some years back.

### 80 GRADOS

SPANISH €

Map p246 (☑91 445 83 51; Calle de Manuela Malasaña 10; tapas €2.30-6.60; ☺1.30-4pm & 8.30pm-midnight Sun-Wed, 1.30-4pm & 8.30pm-2am Thu-Sat; ⓂBilbao) Excellent tapas cooked at 80°C (try the toasted pork rib sandwich with honey mustard), cold tapas (tomato stuffed with duck, bacon and blue cheese) and an excellent wine list are the secrets to this place's considerable success. The warm decor and buzzing crowd add to its popularity. Set menus, and dishes for pregnant women and coeliacs, are also available.

### CARMENCITA BAR

AMERICAN €

Map p246 (☑91 523 80 73; www.carmencitabar.es; Calle de San Vicente Ferrer 51; mains €8-11; ☺noon-5pm & 7pm-1am Mon-Sat, 11am-5pm Sun; ⓂNoviciado) Tucked away on a quiet corner and full of light from the large-pane windows, Carmencita Bar attracts a young international crowd with a daily brunch menu – as well as hearty burgers, sumptuous cakes, coffee, cocktails and mimosas. The interior is inviting and casual, with worn wooden chairs and small tables where you can grab a seat with friends.

### HANSO CAFÉ

CAFE €

Map p246 (☑91 137 54 29; www.facebook.com/hansocafe; Calle del Pez 20; coffees €1.50-3.50, pastries & sandwiches €2-7; ☺9am-8pm Tue-Fri, 10am-8pm Sat & Sun; ⓂNoviciado) This vintage-style cafe takes coffee and cakes seriously. Try something sweet like the banana or cranberry bread, or one of the Asian-influenced cakes with flavours such as red

bean, mango and green tea. Or if you prefer, some toast with avocado or a sandwich, crepe or bagel. There's also a selection of espresso drinks, teas and chai lattes.

### BAR PALENTINO

TAPAS €

Map p246 (☑91 532 30 58; Calle del Pez 8; bocadillos €2.50; ☺7am-2pm Mon-Sat; ⓂNoviciado) Formica tables, not a single attention to decor detail, and yet... This ageless Malasaña bar is a reminder of an important lesson in eating Spanish style: don't be fooled by appearances. Wildly popular with young and old alike, Bar Palentino has an irresistible charm, thanks in large part to its owners María Dolores (who claims to be 'the house speciality') and Casto.

And the food? Simple traditional tapas and *bocadillos* (filled rolls) that have acquired city-wide fame, not least for their price.

### BODEGA DE LA ARDOSA

TAPAS €

Map p246 (☑91 521 49 79; www.laardosa.es; Calle de Colón 13; tapas & raciones €4-12; ☺8.30am-2am Mon-Fri, 12.45pm-2.30am Sat & Sun; ⓂTribunal) Going strong since 1892, the charming, wood-panelled bar of Bodega de la Ardosa is brimful with charm. To come here and not try the *salmorejo* (cold tomato soup made with bread, oil, garlic and vinegar), *croquetas* or *tortilla de patatas* (potato and onion omelette) would be a crime. On weekend nights there's scarcely room to move.

### BEHER DE GUIJELO

SPANISH, FAST FOOD €

Map p246 (☑91 521 27 41; www.beher.com; Calle de Fuencarral 106; bocadillos €4; ☺10am-11pm Sun-Thu, to midnight Fri & Sat; ⓂBilbao) Part of the wave of Spanish fast food sweeping the capital, Beher follows the same winning formula as other longer-established examples of the genre – cured meats in vacuum-sealed packs and takeaway options such as paper cones and *bocadillos* filled with *jamón*.

### ★ALBUR

TAPAS €€

Map p246 (☑91 594 27 33; www.restaurantealbur.com; Calle de Manuela Malasaña 15; mains €13-18; ☺12.30-5pm & 7.30pm-midnight Mon-Thu, 12.30-5pm & 7.30pm-1.30am Fri, 1pm-1.30am Sat, 1pm-midnight Sun; ☎; ⓂBilbao) One of Malasaña's best deals, this place has a wildly popular tapas bar and a classy but casual restaurant out the back. The restaurant waiters never seem to lose their cool, and their extremely well-priced rice dishes are the stars of the show, although in truth you could order anything here and leave well satisfied.

## BETWEEN MEALS & SPANISH FAST FOODS

If your stomach is struggling to adjust to Spain's notoriously late eating hours, and/or you're looking for a quick meal without resorting to junk food, there are plenty of options in Malasaña.

**Bodega de La Ardosa** (p131) Great tapas

**Bar Palentino** (p131) Old-style bar food

**La Mucca de Pez** (p132) Tapas and more

**Maricastaña** (p132) Modern Spanish meals

**La Musa** (p132) Creative tapas.

### FEDERAL CAFÉ INTERNATIONAL €€

Map p246 (☑91 532 84 24; www.federalcafe. es; Plaza de las Comendadoras 9; mains €7-13; ☺9am-midnight Mon-Thu, to 1am Fri & Sat, to 5pm Sun; ⓜNoviciado) One of the best places to see and be seen, Federal has an extensive international menu including breakfast, brunch, sandwiches, drinks and more. It's been serving eggs Benedict since before it was cool, and the young international crowd is there all day, with groups of friends having lunch, and people working on laptops at the long tables in back.

### ZOMBIE BAR BURGERS €€

Map p246 (☑91 011 19 52; www.zombiebar.es; Calle del Pez 7; mains €9-15; ☺noon-midnight Sun-Thu, to 2am Fri & Sat; ⓜNoviciado) Madrid's passion for burgers shows no signs of abating. If anything, the quality just keeps getting better. Zombie Bar, on Malasaña's most happening street, has a cool space flooded with natural light and lined with stone walls and serves burgers based around the best patties and rustic breads.

### MARICASTAÑA SPANISH €€

Map p246 (☑91 082 71 42; www.maricastana madrid.com; Corredera Baja de San Pablo 12; mains €9-19; ☺9am-2am Mon-Thu, to 2.30am Fri & Sat, 10am-2am Sun; ⓜCallao) This fabulous find sits in the increasingly cool corner of Malasaña that is flourishing just off the back of Gran Vía. The decor is quite lovely, all potted plants, creative lighting, iron pillars and rustic brickwork, and the food is

simple but excellent – try the pumpkin croquettes or the tuna pieces with bean shoots and strawberries.

### LA MUCCA DE PEZ TAPAS €€

Map p246 (☑91 521 00 00; www.lamucca.es; Plaza Carlos Cambronero 4; mains €9-16; ☺noon-1.30am Sun-Wed, 1pm-2am Thu, 1pm-2.30am Fri & Sat; ⓜCallao) The only problem with this place is that it's such an agreeable spot to spend an afternoon it can be impossible to snaffle a table. An ample wine list complements the great salads, creative pizzas and a good mix of meat and seafood mains, and the atmosphere simply adds to the overall appeal.

### LA GASTROCROQUETERÍA DE CHEMA TAPAS €€

Map p246 (☑91 364 22 63; www.gastrocroqueteria. com; Calle del Barco 7; tapas & mains €4-17; ☺9pm-midnight Mon-Fri, 2-4.30pm & 9pm-midnight Sat & Sun; ⓜTribunal) *Croquetas* in all their glory are what this place is all about. Try any number of riffs on the croquette theme (with foie gras, oxtail and caramelised onion, or prawns with kimchi, for example). It also does other tapas and more substantial mains and *raciones*.

### LA T GASTROBAR TAPAS, MODERN SPANISH €€

Map p246 (☑91 531 14 06; www.latgastrobar.es; Calle del Molino de Viento 4; mains €10-18; ☺1pm-2am Tue-Thu, to 2.30am Fri & Sat, 1.30-5pm Sun; ⓜCallao) This slick split-level place does variations on Spanish classics, such as squid-ink risotto croquettes, as well as smoked-duck carpaccio. The atmosphere is classy yet casual in the finest Madrid tradition.

### LA MUSA SPANISH, FUSION €€

Map p246 (☑91 448 75 58; www.grupolamusa. com; Calle de Manuela Malasaña 18; tapas €3-7, mains €11-17; ☺9am-1am Mon-Thu, to 2am Fri, 1pm-2am Sat, 1pm-1am Sun; ⓜSan Bernardo) Snug, loud and unpretentious, La Musa is all about designer decor, lounge music and memorably fun food. The menu is divided into three types of tapas – Spanish, international and those from a wood-fired oven. Try the *degustación de tapas* (€30) for two.

### ★LA TASQUITA DE ENFRENTE MODERN SPANISH €€€

Map p246 (☑91 532 54 49; Calle de la Ballesta 6; mains €16-32, set menus €45-70; ☺1.30-4.30pm & 8.30pm-midnight Mon-Sat; ⓜGran Vía) It's difficult to overstate how popular this place is among people in the know in Madrid's food scene. The seasonal menu prepared by chef Juanjo López never ceases to surprise while also combining simple Spanish staples to stunning effect. The *menú de degustación* (tasting menu; €50) or *menú de Juanjo* (€65) would be our choice for first-timers. Reservations are essential.

# 🍷 DRINKING & 🍸 NIGHTLIFE

### CAFÉ COMERCIAL CAFE

Map p246 (📞91 088 25 25; www.cafecomercial madrid.com; Glorieta de Bilbao 7; ⏱7.30am-midnight Mon-Fri, 8.30am-midnight Sat & Sun; 📶; Ⓜ️Bilbao) The city's oldest cafe has a special place in the hearts of many *madrileños*. Open for more than a century, it's still pulsing with life. Any day of the week you can enjoy a coffee or some food at one of the old marble-topped tables and feel like you're part of Madrid's literary and cultural scene.

### LA TAPE CRAFT BEER

Map p246 (📞91 593 04 22; www.latape.com; Calle de San Bernardo 88; ⏱10am-2am; Ⓜ️Bilbao, San Bernardo) Long before craft or artisan beers took hold in Madrid, La Tape was onto it. The menu has 22 Spanish and international beers, as well as a strong selection of gluten-free beers. With plenty on tap to choose from, it's a beer-lover's pleasure to come here.

### NICE TO MEET YOU BAR

Map p246 (📞638 908559; www.dearhotelmadrid. com/en/nice-to-meet-you; Gran Vía 80, 14th fl, Dear Hotel; ⏱7.30am-2am; Ⓜ️Plaza de España) This rooftop bar occupying the top floor of Dear Hotel has a spectacular view of Plaza España and Malasaña. Come any time of day to sit down with a cocktail and enjoy the view, or try something to eat – food specialities include Mediterranean staples like cod and ox steak.

### 1862 DRY BAR COCKTAIL BAR

Map p246 (📞609 531151; www.facebook. com/1862DryBar; Calle del Pez 27; ⏱3.30pm-2am Mon-Thu, to 2.30am Fri & Sat, to 10.30pm Sun; Ⓜ️Noviciado) Great cocktails, muted early-20th-century decor and a refined air make this one of our favourite bars down Malasaña's southern end. Prices are reasonable, the cocktail list extensive and new cocktails appear every month.

### GORILA BAR

Map p246 (📞91 007 08 88; www.facebook.com/gorilamadrid; Calle de la Corredera Baja de San Pablo 47; ⏱10am-1am; Ⓜ️Tribunal) Gorila is one of those multipurpose Malasaña bars that's as good for breakfast as for a night-time beer or cocktail. The split-level space is watched over by a giant painted gorilla and populated by a casual Malasaña crowd.

### CASA CAMACHO BAR

Map p246 (📞91 531 35 98; Calle de San Andrés 4; ⏱1.30pm-1.30am Mon-Wed, 12.30pm-2am Thu-Sat; Ⓜ️Tribunal) Little has changed at Casa Camacho since it opened in 1929. It's tiny: a short bench in a corner is the only seating, and the rest is standing room for a couple of dozen locals looking for an aperitivo or quick tapa (cold plates €3 to €10). Elbow up to the bar for a vermouth on tap or the house special 'yayo' – gin, vermouth and soda.

### IRREALE BAR

Map p246 (📞91 172 28 02; www.facebook.com/irrealemadrid; Calle de Manuela Malasaña 20; ⏱6pm-1am Sun-Wed, to 2am Thu, 1pm-2.30am Fri & Sat; Ⓜ️Bilbao) It's not that long ago that you entered any Madrid bar and ordered *una cerveza* (a beer). There was only one kind. But craft beers have now taken hold and Irreale has a particularly strong selection with a changing roster of around 10 beers on tap and dozens by the bottle. It's a great place to start your Malasaña night.

### LATA DE SARDINAS BAR

Map p246 (📞91 548 73 71; Calle del Limón 12; ⏱1.30-4pm & 8.30pm-midnight Tue-Sat, 1.30-4pm Sun; Ⓜ️Plaza de España, Ventura Rodríguez) This intimate Conde Duque haunt is known for its good food, but we like it more for its passion for that old Madrid favourite, *vermut* (vermouth). Here it's served it the old way – with four ice cubes and a slice of orange – but the bartenders are not averse to throwing in the odd cinnamon stick or splash of ginger.

### CORAZÓN BAR COCKTAIL BAR

Map p246 (📞91 025 78 96; www.saloncorazon. com; Calle de Valverde 44; ⏱7pm-3am Sun-Thu, to 3.30am Fri & Sat; Ⓜ️Tribunal) Like all good cocktail bars, Corazón has the right mix of quantity (more than 100 cocktails), mystery (they love their secret ingredients) and a select choice of beers for those easing themselves into the night. Dark wood and velvet sofas keep things nice and serious.

### THE PASSENGER BAR

Map p246 (✆91 169 49 76; www.facebook.com/the passengermadrid; Calle del Pez 16; ⊘6pm-4am; Ⓜ Noviciado) Quietly sophisticated coffee shop by day, hipster rock bar by night, the Passenger has the appearance of a train in motion (cabin interior, screens with moving images for the windows) and great drinks. Live music sometimes livens things up in the evenings; check the Facebook page for upcoming gigs.

### EL JARDÍN SECRETO BAR

Map p246 (✆91 541 80 23; www.eljardinsecreto madrid.com; Calle del Conde Duque 2; ⊘5.30pm-12.30am Sun-Wed, 6.30pm-1.30am Thu, 6.30pm-2.30am Fri & Sat; Ⓜ Plaza de España) 'The Secret Garden' is intimate and romantic in a *barrio* that's one of Madrid's best-kept secrets. Lit by Spanish designer candles, draped in organza from India and serving up chocolates from the Caribbean, El Jardín Secreto ranks among our most favoured drinking corners in Conde Duque.

### STUYCK CO BEER HALL

Map p246 (✆91 466 92 98; www.thestuyckco.com; Calle Corredera Alta de San Pablo 33; ⊘6.30pm-midnight Mon-Fri, 1pm-midnight Sat & Sun; Ⓜ Tribunal) With a list of craft beers on tap that changes weekly, Stuyck Co is one of the best places in town for connoisseurs to sip a pint or two. The bare brick walls and rough beams give the place the feel of an abandoned warehouse, but the furniture is modern, the service is good and the pub-grub is tasty.

### FÁBRICA MARAVILLAS BREWERY

Map p246 (✆91 521 87 53; www.fmaravillas.com; Calle de Valverde 29; ⊘6pm-midnight Mon-Wed, to 1am Thu, to 2am Fri, 12.30pm-2am Sat, 12.30pm-midnight Sun; Ⓜ Tribunal, Gran Vía) Spain has taken its time getting behind the worldwide trend of boutique and artisan beers, but it's finally starting to happen. The finest example of this in Madrid is Fábrica Maravillas, a microbrewery known for its 'Malasaña Ale'.

### LA PALMERA BAR

Map p246 (✆630 884470; Calle de la Palma 67; ⊘7.30pm-2am Mon-Sat, noon-4pm Sun; Ⓜ Noviciado) Tucked away in the quiet-by-day laneways of Conde Duque, this tiny unprepossessing place is covered in blue and yellow tiles and has an antique bar that looks like a huge bathtub. La Palmera draws an artsy crowd who come to sit at the small

wooden tables and nurse a drink or two. The atmosphere is very low key.

### TUPPERWARE BAR, CLUB

Map p246 (✆91 446 42 04; www.tupperwareclub.com; Calle de la Corredera Alta de San Pablo 26; ⊘9pm-3am Mon-Wed, 8pm-3.30am Thu-Sat, 8pm-3am Sun; Ⓜ Tribunal) A Malasaña stalwart and prime candidate for the bar that best catches the enduring *rockero* (rocker) spirit of Malasaña, Tupperware draws a 30-something crowd, spins indie rock with a bit of soul and classics from the '60s and '70s, and generally revels in its kitsch (eyeballs stuck to the ceiling, and plastic TVs with action-figure dioramas lined up behind the bar).

### CAFÉ DE MAHÓN CAFE

Map p246 (✆91 532 47 56; www.facebook.com/cafedemahon; Plaza del Dos de Mayo 4; ⊘noon-1.30am Mon-Thu, to 3am Fri-Sun; Ⓜ Bilbao) If we had to choose our favourite slice of Malasaña life, this engaging little cafe, with outdoor tables that watch over Plaza del Dos de Mayo, would be a prime candidate. It's beloved by *famosos* (celebrities) as much as by the locals catching up for a quiet drink with friends. It has a habit of opening and closing whenever the whim takes it.

### MOLOKO SOUND CLUB BAR, CLUB

Map p246 (✆626 529967; www.molokosoundclub.com; Calle de Quiñones 12; ⊘10.30pm-3.30am Wed-Sat; Ⓜ San Bernardo) With its walls plastered with old concert flyers and the odd art-house movie poster, Moloko remains an excellent middle-of-the-night option in the Conde Duque area of western Malasaña. The music – indie, rock, soul, garage and '60s – is consistently good, which is why people return here again and again.

### CAFÉ MANUELA CAFE
Map p246 (☎91 531 70 37; www.facebook.com/CafeManuela; Calle de San Vicente Ferrer 29; ☺4pm-2am Sun-Thu, to 2.30am Fri & Sat; Ⓜ Tribunal) Stumbling into this graciously restored throwback to the 1950s along one of Malasaña's grittier streets is akin to discovering hidden treasure. There's a luminous quality to it when you come in out of the night and, like so many Madrid cafes, it's a surprisingly multifaceted space.

### LOLINA VINTAGE CAFÉ CAFE
Map p246 (☎91 523 58 59; www.lolinacafe.com; Calle del Espíritu Santo 9; ☺10am-midnight Sun-Thu, to 2.30am Fri & Sat; Ⓜ Tribunal) Lolina Vintage Café seems to have captured the essence of the *barrio* in one small space, with its studied retro look (comfy old-style chairs and sofas, gilded mirrors and 1970s-era wallpaper). It's low-key, full from the first breakfast to closing, and it caters to every taste with salads and cocktails.

### LA VÍA LÁCTEA BAR, CLUB
Map p246 (☎91 446 75 81; www.facebook.com/lavialacteabar; Calle de Velarde 18; ☺8pm-3am Sun-Thu, to 3.30am Fri & Sat; Ⓜ Tribunal) A living, breathing and delightfully grungy relic of *la movida madrileña* (the Madrid scene), La Vía Láctea remains a Malasaña favourite for a mixed, informal crowd who seems to live for the 1980s. The music ranges across rock, pop, garage, rockabilly and indie.

### BAR EL 2D BAR
Map p246 (☎91 445 88 39; Calle de Velarde 24; ☺noon-2am; Ⓜ Tribunal) One of the enduring symbols of *la movida madrileña,* El 2D's fluted columns, 1970s-brown walls and 1980s music suggest that it hasn't quite arrived in the 21st century yet. No one seems to care.

### JOSÉ ALFREDO COCKTAIL BAR
Map p246 (☎91 521 49 60; www.josealfredobar.com; Calle de Silva 22; cocktails from €9; ☺7pm-3am Sun-Thu, to 3.30am Fri & Sat; Ⓜ Callao) This American-style cocktail bar just off Gran Vía is an institution. It plays indie music and does fabulous cocktails – try the 'Lazy Bitch' (rum, banana liqueur, cinnamon liqueur and lime juice) or the 'José Alfredo' (tequila, curaçao, grenadine, lime and pineapple and orange juice).

### YA'STA CLUB
Map p246 (☎91 521 88 33; www.yastaclub.net; Calle de Valverde 10; €10; ☺11.45pm-6am Wed-Sat; Ⓜ Gran Vía) Going strong since 1985 and the height of *la movida madrileña*, Ya'sta is a stalwart of the Malasaña night. Everything gets a run here, from techno, trance and electronica to indie pop.

### CAFÉ PEPE BOTELLA BAR
Map p246 (☎91 522 43 09; Calle de San Andrés 12; ☺10am-2am Sun-Thu, to 2.30am Fri & Sat; ☏; Ⓜ Tribunal) Pepe Botella has hit on a fine formula for success. As good in the hours around midnight as it is in the afternoon when its wi-fi access draws the laptop-toting crowd, it's a classy bar with green-velvet benches, marble-topped tables, and old photos and mirrors covering the walls.

## ☆ ENTERTAINMENT

### ★ TEATRO FLAMENCO MADRID FLAMENCO
Map p246 (☎91 159 20 05; www.teatroflamencomadrid.com; Calle del Pez 10; adult/student & senior/child €25/16/12; ☺6.45pm & 8.15pm; Ⓜ Noviciado) This flamenco venue is an excellent deal. With a focus on quality flamenco (dance, song and guitar) rather than the more formal meal-and-floor-show package of the *tablaos* (choreographed flamenco shows), and with a mixed crowd of locals and tourists, this place generates a terrific atmosphere most nights for the hour-long show.

### BARCO LIVE MUSIC
Map p246 (☎91 521 24 47; www.barcobar.com; Calle del Barco 34; entrance free-€15; ☺9pm-5.30am Sun-Thu, to 6am Fri & Sat; Ⓜ Tribunal) Located just before Malasaña spills over into the seedy backend of Gran Vía, BarCo is an outstanding live venue with jazz, flamenco, Latin music, funk, rock and blues. Concerts start between 9pm and midnight and there's room to dance if the mood takes you.

### CAFÉ LA PALMA LIVE MUSIC, DANCE
Map p246 (☎91 522 50 31; www.cafelapalma.com; Calle de la Palma 62; free-€15; ☺5pm-3am Sun, Wed & Thu, to 3.30am Fri & Sat; Ⓜ Noviciado) It's amazing how much variety Café La Palma has packed into its labyrinth of rooms. Live shows featuring hot local bands are held at the back, while DJs mix it up at the front.

# 🛍 SHOPPING

**Malasaña is one of Madrid's quirkiest *barrios* in which to shop, home to edgy clothing stores and shops where mainstream designers show off their street cred. The eastern end of Calle de Velarde has become a real hub for vintage clothing.**

### EL MODERNO                                    HOMEWARES

Map p246 (✆91 348 31 94; www.facebook.com/elmodernoconceptstore; Calle de la Corredera de San Pablo 19; ⊘11am-9pm Sun-Wed, to 10pm Thu-Sat; MCallao, Gran Vía) This concept store down the Gran Vía end of Malasaña is the epitome of style, although it's less Malasaña retro than a slick new-Madrid look. Designer homewares, quirky gifts and shapely furnishings, all laid out in an open gallery space allow you to indulge your inner interior designer.

### SPORTIVO                                           CLOTHING

Map p246 (✆91 542 56 61; www.sportivostore.com; Calle del Conde Duque 20; ⊘10am-9pm Mon-Sat, noon-4pm Sun; MPlaza de España) It's rare to find a Madrid store that focuses solely on men's fashions, but this place bucks the trend. Brands like Carven, YMC and Commune of Paris draw an appreciative crowd.

### LA COMPAÑIA POLAR            CLOTHING, ACCESORIES

Map p246 (✆91 559 46 49; Calle del Conde Duque 5; ⊘11am-2pm & 5-8.30pm Mon-Fri, 11am-3pm & 4-8.30pm Sat; MPlaza de España) Mostly men's fashions and accessories dominate this Conde Duque store that has been around since 2003. Hawaiian shirts and more sedate looks bookend a range that hovers close to the mainstream without losing its alternative slant.

### FLAMINGOS VINTAGE KILO               VINTAGE

Map p246 (✆649 877198; www.vintagekilo.com; Calle del Espíritu Santo 1; ⊘11am-9pm Mon-Sat; MTribunal) Flamingos sells vintage clothing for men and women, including a selection of old denim, cowboy boots, leather jackets, Hawaiian shirts and more. Some articles have a set price, while others are sold by the kilo. The first of its kind in Madrid, it's a great place to browse for the cool and unexpected from the '70s, '80s and '90s.

### KARIBU MALASAÑA               GIFTS & SOUVENIRS

Map p246 (✆91 115 36 74; www.tiendakaribu.com; Calle de Manuela Malasaña 29; ⊘11am-2.30pm & 4.30-8.30pm Mon-Sat; MSan Bernardo, Bilbao)

Quirky gift items dominate this lovely little boutique, which spans the full range of pop art, retro, vintage and the tastefully modern. There are must-have gadgets (magnetic key holders, portable LP record player), kitchen items (retro toasters) and the purely decorative.

### CURIOSITE                            GIFTS & SOUVENIRS

Map p246 (✆91 287 21 77; www.curiosite.es; Calle de la Corredera Alta de San Pablo 28; ⊘11am-9pm Mon-Sat; MTribunal) Some of Madrid's more original gifts are on offer in this quirky shop that combines old favourites (eg Star Wars speakers, retro Polaroid cameras) and a sideways glance at mundane household items. It's fun and modern and retro all at once, which makes it a perfect fit for Malasaña.

### CAMPER                                             SHOES

Map p246 (✆91 531 23 47; www.camper.com; Calle de Fuencarral 42; ⊘10am-8pm Mon-Sat; MGran Vía, Tribunal) Spanish fashion is not all haute couture, and this world-famous cool and quirky shoe brand from Mallorca offers bowling-shoe chic with colourful, fun designs that are all about quality coupled with comfort.

### DIVINA PROVIDENCIA        FASHION & ACCESSORIES

Map p246 (✆91 521 10 95; www.divinaprovidencia.com; Calle de Fuencarral 42; ⊘10am-2.30pm & 5-8pm Mon-Sat; MTribunal, Gran Vía) Divina Providencia has moved seamlessly from fresh new face on the Madrid fashion scene to almost mainstream stylishness, with fun clothes for women and strong retro and Asian influences.

### SNAPO                              FASHION & ACCESSORIES

Map p246 (✆91 017 16 72; www.snaposhoponline.com; Calle del Espíritu Santo 6; ⊘11am-2pm & 5-8.30pm Mon-Sat; MTribunal) Snapo is rebellious Malasaña to its core, thumbing its nose at the niceties of fashion respectability – hardly surprising given that one of its lines of clothing is called Fucking Bastardz Inc. It does jeans, caps and jackets, but its T-shirts are the Snapo trademark.

### RETRO CITY                                       CLOTHING

Map p246 (Calle de Corredera Alta de San Pablo 4; ⊘noon-2.30pm & 5.30-9pm Mon-Sat; MTribunal) Retro City lives for the colourful '70s and '80s and proclaims its philosophy to be all about 'vintage for the masses'. Whereas other such stores in the *barrio* have gone for an angry, thumb-your-nose-at-society aesthetic, Retro City just looks back with nostalgia.

# Chueca

## Neighbourhood Top Five

**1** **Bazaar** (p139) Taking your pick for lunch along one of Madrid's best culinary streets, starting perhaps with this cool-as-Chueca *barrio* icon.

**2** **Museo Chicote** (p142) Following the footsteps of Hemingway and other *famosos* (celebrities) by

ordering a mojito at this legendary cocktail bar.

**3** **Sociedad General de Autores y Editores** (p139) Seeking out one of Madrid's most unusual buildings, an extravagant confection devoted to Modernisme.

**4** **Plaza de Chueca** (p142) Learning what Madrid's clamorous nightlife is all

about on a Saturday night when the square and surrounding streets throng with people.

**5** **Calle del Almirante** (p144) Shopping for stylish Spanish designer fashions in some of Madrid's most exclusive boutiques.

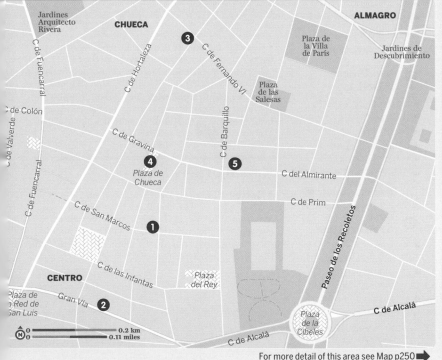

For more detail of this area see Map p250 ➡

### Lonely Planet's Top Tips

➡ Avoid driving in Chueca at all costs. A complex system of one-way streets, the often-gridlocked Calle de Horteleza and narrow lanes with nowhere to park all make this a neighbourhood to explore by metro and, once in Chueca, on foot.

➡ Bookings are essential in Chueca's restaurants, especially on Friday and Saturday nights. Tapas bars are also full to bursting – unless you're after atmosphere, consider coming on another night.

### ✖ Best Places to Eat

➡ Bazaar (p139)
➡ La Carmencita (p140)
➡ Yakitoro by Chicote (p140)
➡ Bocaito (p141)
➡ Celso y Manolo (p141)
➡ La Buena Vida (p142)

For reviews, see p139. ➡

### 🍷 Best Places to Drink

➡ Museo Chicote (p142)
➡ Bar Cock (p143)
➡ Del Diego (p143)
➡ Café Belén (p142)
➡ Mamá Inés (p144)
➡ Gran Café de Gijón (p142)

For reviews, see p142. ➡

### ⊙ Best Architecture

➡ Sociedad General de Autores y Editores (p139)
➡ Casa de las Siete Chimeneas (p139)
➡ Museo del Romanticismo (p139)

For reviews, see p139. ➡

## Explore: Chueca

Chueca is one of downtown Madrid's most appealing *barrios* (districts), a curious mix of throbbing nightlife, cool places to eat and brilliant shopping. In these and so many other ways, it carries the essence of Madrid's modern appeal – good times and with largely devoted to enjoying all the good things in life.

Chueca wears its heart on its sleeve, a *barrio* that the gay and lesbian community has transformed into one of the coolest places in Spain. Sometimes it's in your face, but more often it's what locals like to call 'hetero-friendly'. It's the sort of place where little is left to the imagination but it's never threatening, just good (mostly) clean fun and with plenty of reasons to visit at any time of the day.

As a general rule, the further east you go, the more sophisticated Chueca becomes. Down on Calle del Almirante and Calle del Conde de Xiquena, it's all about classy restaurants and designer boutiques, while around Plaza de Chueca, Chueca's heartbeat and meeting place of choice, it's loud by night and has loads of fab places to eat.

## Local Life

➡ **Hang-out** Antigua Casa Ángel Sierra (p143), right on Plaza de Chueca, has seen it all in almost a century of Chueca life and the crowds here stand six or seven deep on a busy Saturday night.

➡ **Cocktail calle** Calle de la Reina, a block north of Gran Vía in Chueca's south, has one of the richest collections of storied cocktail bars in Europe. Start with Bar Cock (p143).

➡ **Secret shops & galleries** Calle de Santa Teresa and the quiet streets that surround it are something of a local favourite with stunning boutiques like Malababa and small private art galleries.

## Getting There & Away

➡ **Metro** Chueca metro station (line 5) sits right in the heart of Chueca. At Chueca's northern end, Alonso Martínez (lines 4, 5 and 10) has good connections to elsewhere in the city, while Gran Vía (lines 1 and 5) serve a similar purpose to the south. Banco de España (line 2) is handy for Chueca's southeast.

# ◉ SIGHTS

### SOCIEDAD GENERAL DE
### AUTORES Y EDITORES                    ARCHITECTURE
Map p250 (General Society of Authors & Editors; Calle de Fernando VI 4; Ⓜ Alonso Martínez) This swirling, melting wedding cake of a building is as close as Madrid comes to the work of Antoni Gaudí, which so illuminates Barcelona. It's a joyously self-indulgent ode to Modernisme (an architectural and artistic style, influenced by art nouveau and sometimes known as Catalan modernism) and is virtually one of a kind in Madrid. Casual visitors are actively discouraged, but what you see from the street is impressive enough. The only exceptions are on the first Monday of October, International Architecture Day, when its interior staircase alone is reason enough to come and look inside.

### CASA DE LAS
### SIETE CHIMENEAS                       ARCHITECTURE
Map p250 (Plaza del Rey; Ⓜ Banco de España) A block northwest of the Plaza de la Cibeles is the Casa de las Siete Chimeneas, a 16th-century mansion that takes its name from the seven chimneys it still boasts. They say that the ghost of one of Felipe II's lovers still runs about here in distress on certain evenings. Nowadays, it's home to the Ministry of Education, Culture and Sport.

### MUSEO DEL ROMANTICISMO             MUSEUM
Map p250 (☑91 448 10 45; www.mecd.gob.es/mromanticismo/inicio.html; Calle de San Mateo 13; adult/student/child €3/1.50/free; ◷9.30am-8.30pm Tue-Sat, 10am-3pm Sun May-Oct, shorter hours Nov-Apr; Ⓜ Tribunal) This intriguing museum is devoted to the Romantic period of the 19th century. It houses a minor treasure trove of mostly 19th-century paintings, furniture, porcelain, books, photos and other bits and bobs from a bygone age and offers an insight into what upper-class houses were like in the 19th century. The best-known work in the collection is Goya's *San Gregorio Magno, Papa*.

### MUSEO DE CERA                         MUSEUM
Map p250 (☑91 319 93 30; www.museocera madrid.com; Paseo de los Recoletos 41; adult/child €19/12; ◷10am-2.30pm & 4.30-8.30pm Mon-Fri, 10am-8.30pm Sat & Sun; Ⓜ Colón) This wax museum, with more than 450 characters, is a fairly standard version of the genre. Models range from the Beatles to Bart Simpson, and from Cristiano Ronaldo to Cervantes, Dalí

> ### SMALL PRIVATE GALLERIES
> For those with an interest in contemporary art that extends beyond what you'll find at the Centro de Arte Reina Sofía (p108), central Madrid is studded with small galleries showcasing both up-and-coming and longer-established painters, sculptors and photographers. For a near-complete list, check out **Arte Madrid** (www.artemadrid. com); its brochure of the same name, available online in PDF format, contains a map and program of upcoming exhibitions.

and Picasso – it's a typically broad-ranging collection of international and Spanish figures down through the centuries. If you're drawn to the darker side of life, there's everything from the Inquisition to Freddy Krueger, while the Tren del Terror is not for the faint-hearted.

# ✕ EATING

### ★ BAZAAR                      MODERN SPANISH €
Map p250 (☑91 523 39 05; www.restaurant bazaar.com; Calle de la Libertad 21; mains €7.50-13; ◷1.15-4pm & 8.30-11.30pm Sun-Wed, 1.15-4pm & 8.15pm-midnight Thu-Sat; 🛜; Ⓜ Chueca) Bazaar's popularity among the well-heeled Chueca set shows no sign of abating. Its pristine white interior design, with theatre-style lighting and wall-length windows, may draw a crowd that looks like it's stepped out of the pages of *¡Hola!* magazine, but the food is extremely well priced and innovative, and the atmosphere is casual.

Reservations are available only for dinner Sunday to Thursday. At all other times, get there early or be prepared to wait, regardless of whether you're famous or not. The cocktail list is long and prices start at just €5!

### XANACUK                       HEALTH FOOD €
Map p250 (☑91 521 22 70; www.xanacuk.com; Calle de Augo Figueroa 13; sandwiches from €2.55; ◷9.30am-10.15pm Mon-Sat, to 8.30pm Sun; ☑; Ⓜ Chueca) This juice and salad bar is very veggie-friendly and locals and tourists alike enjoy stopping in for a healthy boost. With options for vegetarians and vegans, you can design your own salad and stick around, or grab a pre-made sandwich or wrap to go.

## COOKING COURSES

There are plenty of places in Madrid to learn Spanish cooking. In most cases, you'll need at least passable Spanish, but some run special classes for English speakers.

**Alambique** (p68) Cooking classes in Spanish, with a handful of English- and French-speaking courses.

**Apunto – Centro Cultural del Gusto** (p145) This engaging little bookstore runs cooking classes across a range of cuisines.

**Cooking Club** (p157) The regular, respected program of classes encompasses a vast range of cooking styles.

**Kitchen Club** (Map p246; ☑91 522 62 63; www.kitchenclub.es; Calle de Ballesta 8; ⓜGran Vía, Callao) Offers a top-notch range of courses just off the back of Gran Vía in the city centre.

**LA DUQUESITA** BAKERY €

Map p250 (☑91 308 02 31; www.laduquesita. es; Calle de Fernando VI 2; pastries from €2.50; ⓗ8.30am-8.30pm Mon-Fri, 10am-8.30pm Sat & Sun; ⓜAlonso Martínez) A lavish step back in time with wonderful traditional pastries.

**BACO Y BETO** TAPAS €

Map p250 (☑91 522 84 41; Calle de Pelayo 24; tapas from €4; ⓗ8pm-1am Mon-Fri, 2-4.30pm & 8.30pm-1am Sat; ⓜChueca) Some of the tastiest tapas in Madrid are what you'll find here. Tapas might include quail's eggs with *salmorejo cordobés* (cold, tomato-based soup from Córdoba), or *raciones* (larger tapas servings), such as aubergine with parmesan. The clientele is predominantly gay.

**MAGASAND** SANDWICHES €

Map p250 (☑91 319 68 25; www.magasand.com; Travesía de San Mateo 16; sandwiches €4-11, salads €4.20-9; ⓗ9.30am-10pm Mon-Fri, noon-8pm Sat; ⓢ; ⓜAlonso Martínez) Comfy sofas, bar stools, free wi-fi and designer magazines elevate this above your average sandwich bar. Creative sandwiches, bagels, salads and hot soups make the menu.

**CELICIOSO** BAKERY €

Map p246 (☑91 531 88 87; www.celicioso. com; Calle de Hortaleza 3; pastries €2.80-4.40; ⓗ10.30am-9.30pm; ⓜGran Vía) Gluten-free options are rare in Madrid, but Celicioso makes up for that lack with its selection of coeliac-friendly pastries. You can grab a table and stick around for breakfast, coffee or brunch and enjoy the quiet interior, or take a few cupcakes to go. It even has gluten-free lasagna, as well as sugar- and egg-free options.

**TIENDA DE VINOS** SPANISH €

Map p250 (El Comunista; ☑91 521 70 12; Calle de Augo Figueroa 35; mains €8-12; ⓗ1pm-12.30am; ⓜChueca) This place with a wonderful old facade opposite the Mercado de San Antón earned its name as a bastion of left-wing sympathies (hence its better-known name of 'El Comunista') and for no-nonsense Spanish cooking. The latter still holds sway, with grilled fish, croquettes and other homemade specialities for very reasonable prices.

★**YAKITORO BY CHICOTE** JAPANESE, SPANISH €€

Map p250 (☑91 737 14 41; www.yakitoro.com; Calle de la Reina 41; tapas €3-8; ⓗ1pm-midnight; ⓜBanco de España) Based around the idea of a Japanese tavern, driven by a spirit of innovation and a desire to combine the best in Spanish and Japanese flavours, Yakitoro is a hit. Apart from salads, it's all built around brochettes cooked over a wood fire, with wonderful combinations of vegetable, seafood and meat.

★**LA CARMENCITA** SPANISH €€

Map p250 (☑91 531 09 11; www.tabernalacarmen cita.es; Calle de la Libertad 16; mains €13-27; ⓗ9am-2am; ⓜChueca) Around since 1854, La Carmencita is the bar where legendary poet Pablo Neruda was once a regular. The folk of La Carmencita have taken 75 of their favourite traditional Spanish recipes and brought them to the table, sometimes with a little updating but more often safe in the knowledge that nothing needs changing.

There's everything from roast baby goat to razor clams or anchovies, with plenty of salads to lighten things up. Backed up by what they call 'wines with soul', it's hard to resist this place.

## CELSO Y MANOLO
TAPAS, SPANISH €€

Map p250 (☑91 531 80 79; www.celsoymanolo.
es; Calle de la Libertad 1; raciones €7.50-12; ☺1-
4.30pm & 8pm-2am; Ⓜ Banco de España) One of
Chueca's best bars, Celso y Manolo serves up
*tostadas* for those looking to snack, oxtail for
those looking for a touch of the traditional,
and a host of dishes from Spain's north and
northwest. There are also good wines, good
coffee, even better cocktails and an artfully
restored interior.

## BOCAITO
TAPAS €€

Map p250 (☑91 532 12 19; www.bocaito.com; Calle
de la Libertad 4-6; tapas €2.50-8, mains €11-28;
☺1-4pm & 8.30pm-midnight Mon-Sat; Ⓜ Chueca,
Sevilla) Film-maker Pedro Almodóvar once
described this traditional bar and restaurant as 'the best antidepressant'. Forget
about the sit-down restaurant (though well
regarded) and jam into the bar, shoulder-
to-shoulder with the casual crowd, order a
few Andalucian *raciones* off the menu and
slosh them down with some gritty red or a
*caña* (small glass of beer). Enjoy the theatre
in which the busy bartenders excel. Specialities include the *tostas* (toasts), *bocaitos* (small
filled rolls) and the mussels with béchamel,
*canapés* and fried fish.

## TUK TUK ASIAN STREET FOOD
ASIAN €€

Map p250 (☑91 523 25 56; www.tuktukstreet
food.es; Calle Barquillo 26; mains €8-14; ☺1-4pm
& 8-11pm; Ⓜ Chueca) A hard hitter in Madrid's
street-food revolution, Tuk Tuk cooks up
authentic comfort food from Thailand, In-
donesia, Singapore and more. Also served:
signature dishes like Nathan Road Noodles,
a twist on a Chinese favourite with udon
noodles, chicken or prawns and the flavours
of basil, coriander and chilli marmalade. Interiors are colourful and service is friendly.

## FRIDA
INTERNATIONAL €€

Map p250 (☑91 704 82 86; www.fridamadrid.com;
Calle de San Gregorio 8; mains €9-20; ☺9am-1am
Mon-Fri, 10am-2am Sat & Sun; Ⓜ Chueca) What a
lovely little spot this is. Set on a tiny square,
its wooden tables flooded with natural light
through the big windows, Frida is ideal for
a casual meal, a quietly intimate encounter
or simply an afternoon spent reading the
papers. Food is simple but tasty – designer
pizzas, tajine, kebab...

## CERVECERÍA SANTA BÁRBARA
SPANISH €€

Map p250 (☑91 319 04 49; www.cerveceriasanta
barbara.com; Plaza de Santa Bárbara 8; mains

€8-14; ☺noon-11.30pm Sun-Thu, to 1am Fri & Sat;
Ⓜ Alonso Martínez) This old-school Spanish
bar has been around in some form since
1815 and is the place to come to see what all
Spanish bars used to be like. It's especially
popular for what locals call an *afterwork*
or an *aperitivo*, with strongly traditional
dishes like *jamón* (ham) or homemade potato chips.

## LA PAELLA DE LA REINA
MEDITERRANEAN €€

Map p250 (☑91 531 18 85; www.lapaelladelareina.
com; Calle de la Reina 39; mains €14-21; ☺1-4pm
& 7.30-11.30pm; Ⓜ Banco de España) Madrid
is not renowned for its paella (Valencia is
king in that regard), but *valencianos* who
can't make it home are known to frequent
La Paella de la Reina. Like any decent paella
restaurant, you need two people to make an
order but, with that requirement satisfied,
you've plenty of choice. The typical Valencia
paella is cooked with beans, chicken and
rabbit.

## RESTAURANTE MOMO
SPANISH €€

Map p250 (☑91 532 73 48; Calle de la Libertad 8;
mains €8-11, lunch/dinner set menu €12/16; ☺1-
4pm & 9pm-midnight Mon-Sat; Ⓜ Chueca) Momo
is a Chueca beacon of reasonably priced
home cooking for a casual crowd. It has an
artsy vibe and is ideal for those who want
a hearty meal without too much elabora-
tion. Unusually, the well-priced three-course
set menus spill over into the evening. It's a
mostly gay crowd, but everyone's welcome.

## JANATOMO
JAPANESE €€

Map p250 (☑91 521 55 66; Calle de la Reina 27;
mains €12-19; ☺1.30-4.30pm Sun & Tue-Thu,
1.30-4.30pm & 8.30pm-12.30am Fri & Sat Sep-
Jul; Ⓜ Gran Vía) Restaurateurs Tomoyuki and
Eiko Ikenaga arrived in Spain in the 1950s
and have watched Spaniards slowly become
accustomed to foreign cuisines – sushi bars
are now all the rage here. Their patience has
paid off and now their restaurant, Janato-
mo, has undergone a style overhaul, adding
a Zen ambience to its splendid Japanese
cooking.

## MERCADO DE SAN ANTÓN
TAPAS €€

Map p250 (☑91 330 07 30; www.mercadosanan
ton.com; Calle de Augo Figueroa 24; tapas from
€1.50, mains €5-20; ☺10am-midnight; Ⓜ Chueca)
Spain's fresh food markets make for an interesting alternative to bars and restaurants.
Many have been transformed to meet all of
your food needs at once. Downstairs is all

CHUECA EATING

---

### BETWEEN MEALS & SPANISH FAST FOOD

Chueca has some excellent places to eat if you're caught between Spanish restaurant opening times.

**Yakitoro by Chicote** (p140) Mini-brochettes

**Magasand** (p140) All-day sandwiches

**Olivia Te Cuida** (p142) Light fusion meals

**Mercado de San Antón** (p141) International market food

---

about fresh produce, but upstairs there's all manner of appealing tapas varieties from Japan, the Canary Islands and other corners of the country/globe.

#### RIBEIRA DO MIÑO                SEAFOOD €€

Map p250 (☑91 521 98 54; www.marisqueria ribeiradomino.com; Calle de la Santa Brigida 1; mains €11.50-19; ⊙1-4pm & 8pm-midnight Tue-Sun Sep-Jul; Ⓜ Tribunal) This riotously popular seafood bar and restaurant is where *madrileños* with a love for seafood go to indulge. The *mariscada de la casa* (€38 for two) is a platter of seafood so large that even the hungriest of visitors will be satisfied. Leave your name with the waiter and be prepared to wait up to an hour for a table on weekends.

#### OLIVIA TE CUIDA                CAFE €€

Map p250 (☑91 702 00 66; Calle de Santa Teresa 8; mains €9-14; ⊙9am-6pm Mon-Sat; Ⓜ Alonso Martínez) One of Chueca's most agreeably intimate little spaces, 'Olivia Looks After You' serves up a constantly changing seasonal menu at its communal wooden tables. Typical are the light meals (such as couscous with mint, or the carrot-and-mango salad) from mostly organic produce.

#### ★LA BUENA VIDA                SPANISH €€€

Map p250 (☑91 531 31 49; www.restaurantela buenavida.com; Calle del Conde de Xiquena 8; mains €25-28; ⊙1-4pm & 9-11.30pm Tue-Thu, 1.30-4pm & 9pm-12.30am Fri & Sat; Ⓜ Chueca, Colón) A cross between a Parisian bistro and an old-school upmarket Madrid restaurant, this prestigious Chueca place is popular with a well-heeled, knowledgable crowd. The menu is seasonal and leans towards classic Spanish tastes, although dishes like the red tuna sirloin with guacamole and sesame seeds suggest that the chefs are not averse to the odd playful interpretation. It's consistently one of Madrid's best.

## 🍷 DRINKING & NIGHTLIFE

### ★MUSEO CHICOTE                COCKTAIL BAR

Map p250 (☑91 532 67 37; www.grupomercado delareina.com/en/museo-chicote-en; Gran Vía 12; ⊙7pm-3am Mon-Thu, to 4am Fri & Sat, 4pm-1am Sun; Ⓜ Gran Vía) This place is a Madrid landmark, complete with its 1930s-era interior, and its founder is said to have invented more than 100 cocktails, which the likes of Ernest Hemingway, Ava Gardner, Grace Kelly, Sophia Loren and Frank Sinatra have all enjoyed at one time or another.

### ★CAFÉ BELÉN                BAR

Map p250 (☑91 308 27 47; www.elcafebelen. com; Calle de Belén 5; ⊙3.30pm-3am Tue-Thu, to 3.30am Fri & Sat, to midnight Sun; 🛜; Ⓜ Chueca) Café Belén is cool in all the right places – lounge and chill-out music, dim lighting, a great range of drinks (the mojitos are especially good) and a low-key crowd that's the height of casual sophistication. It's one of our preferred Chueca watering holes.

### CAFÉ-RESTAURANTE EL ESPEJO                CAFE

Map p250 (☑91 308 23 47; Paseo de los Recoletos 31; ⊙8am-midnight; Ⓜ Colón) Once a haunt of writers and intellectuals, this architectural gem blends Modernista and art-deco styles, and its interior could well overwhelm you with all the mirrors, chandeliers and bow-tied service of another era. The atmosphere is suitably quiet and refined, although our favourite corner is the elegant glass pavilion out on Paseo de los Recoletos.

### GRAN CAFÉ DE GIJÓN                CAFE

Map p250 (☑91 521 54 25; www.cafegijon.com; Paseo de los Recoletos 21; ⊙7am-1.30am; Ⓜ Chueca, Banco de España) This graceful old cafe has been serving coffee and meals since 1888 and has long been favoured by Madrid's literati for a drink or a meal – *all* of Spain's great 20th-century literary figures came here for coffee and *tertulias* (literary and philosophical discussions). You'll find yourself among intellectuals, conservative Franco diehards and young *madrileños* looking for a quiet drink.

## ANGELITA
WINE BAR

Map p246 (📞915 21 66 78; www.madrid-angelita.
es; Calle de la Reina 4; ⊙9pm-2am Mon, 1.30pm-
2am Tue-Thu, 2pm-2am Fri & Sat; Ⓜ Gran Vía) Just
back from Gran Vía, Angelita has one of the
best wine lists of any bar in Madrid, with
more than 20 choices by the glass and nearly 500 different bottles if you'd like to go all
the way. A terrific choice that combines traditional Madrid (marble bartop) with slick
modern decor. Great cocktails, too.

## GIN CLUB
COCKTAIL BAR

Map p250 (El Mercado de la Reina; 📞91 521 31
98; www.grupomercadodelareina.com; Gran Vía
12; ⊙1.30pm-2am Sun-Thu, to 2.30am Fri & Sat;
Ⓜ Banco de España) As you'd expect, it's all
about gin here, with more than 40 different
types available including gin with coffee (El
Gin Coffee). There's a bar to sit at or a low-
table salon.

## BAR COCK
COCKTAIL BAR

Map p250 (📞91 532 28 26; www.barcock.com;
Calle de la Reina 16; ⊙7pm-3am Sun-Thu, to 3.30am
Fri & Sat; Ⓜ Gran Vía) With a name like this, Bar
Cock could go either way, but it's definitely
cock as in 'rooster'. The decor evokes an old
gentlemen's club and the feeling is more elegant and classic than risqué. It's beloved by
A-list celebrities and A-list wannabes, and
a refined 30-something crowd who come
here for the lively atmosphere and great
cocktails.

## CLUB 54 STUDIO
CLUB

Map p250 (📞615 126807; www.studio54madrid.
com; Calle de Barbieri 7; ⊙11am-3.30am Wed-Sun;
Ⓜ Chueca) Modelled on the famous New York
club Studio 54, this nightclub draws a predominantly gay crowd, but its target market
is more upmarket than many in the *barrio*.
Unlike other Madrid clubs where paid danc-
ers up on stage try to get things moving,
here they let the punters set the pace.

## AREIA
LOUNGE

Map p250 (📞91 310 03 07; www.areiachillout.
com; Calle de Hortaleza 92; ⊙2pm-3am Mon-Fri,
1pm-3am Sat & Sun; Ⓜ Chueca, Alonso Martínez)
The ultimate lounge bar by day (cushions,
chill-out music and dark secluded corners
where you can hear yourself talk or even
snog quietly), this place is equally enjoyable
by night. That's when DJs take over (from
11pm Sunday to Wednesday, and from 9pm
the rest of the week).

## DIURNO
CAFE

Map p250 (📞91 522 00 09; www.grupomercado
delareina.com/en/diurno-en; Calle de San Mar-
cos 37; ⊙10am-1am Sun-Thu, to 2am Fri & Sat;
Ⓜ Chueca) One of the most important hubs
of *barrio* life in Chueca, this cafe (with
DVD store attached) has become to modern
Chueca what the grand literary cafes were
to another age. It's always full with a fun local crowd relaxing amid the greenery. Well-
priced meals and snacks are served if you
can't bear to give up your seat.

## DEL DIEGO
COCKTAIL BAR

Map p250 (📞91 523 31 06; www.deldiego.com;
Calle de la Reina 12; ⊙7pm-3am Mon-Thu, to
3.30am Fri & Sat; Ⓜ Gran Vía) Del Diego is one
of the city's most celebrated cocktail bars.
The decor blends old-world cafe with New
York style, and it's the sort of place where
music rarely drowns out the conversation.
Even with around 75 cocktails to choose
from, we'd still order the signature 'El Diego'
(vodka, advocaat, apricot brandy and lime).

## WHY NOT?
CLUB

Map p250 (📞91 521 80 34; Calle de San Bartolomé 7; entrance €10; ⊙10.30pm-6am; Ⓜ Chueca)
Underground and packed with bodies, gay-
friendly Why Not? is the sort of place where
nothing's left to the imagination (the gay
and straight crowd who come here are pretty amorous) and it's full nearly every night
of the week. Pop and Top 40 music are the
standard, and the dancing crowd is mixed
but all serious about having a good time.

## ANTIGUA CASA ÁNGEL SIERRA
TAVERNA

Map p250 (📞91 531 01 26; http://tabernadeangel
sierra.es; Calle de Gravina 11; ⊙noon-1am; Ⓜ Chueca) This historic old *taberna* (tavern) is the
antithesis of modern Chueca chic – it has
hardly changed since it opened in 1917. As
Spaniards like to say, the beer on tap is very
'well poured' here and it also has vermouth
on tap. It can get pretty lively weekend evenings when it not so much spills over onto
the vibrant Plaza de Chueca as takes it over.

## LA TERRAZA DE ARRIBA
LOUNGE

Map p250 (Splash Óscar; Plaza de Vázquez de
Mella 12; ⊙6.30pm-2.30am Wed & Thu, 4.30pm-
2.30am Fri-Sun mid-May–mid-Sep; Ⓜ Gran Vía)
One of Madrid's stunning rooftop terraces,
this chilled space atop Hotel Óscar (p178),
with gorgeous skyline views and a small
swimming pool, has become something of
a retreat among A-list celebrities.

**MAMÁ INÉS** GAY

Map p250 (☑91 523 23 33; www.mamaines.com; Calle de Hortaleza 22; ☉9am-1.30am Sun-Thu, to 2.30am Fri & Sat; ⓂChueca) A gay meeting place, this cafe-bar has a laid-back ambience by day and a romantic (never sleazy) air by night. You can get breakfast, yummy pastries and the word on where that night's hot spot will be. There's a steady stream of people coming and going.

**CAFÉ ACUARELA** CAFE

Map p250 (☑91 522 21 43; Calle de Gravina 10; ☉11am-2am Sun-Thu, to 3am Fri & Sat; ⓂChueca) A few steps up the hill from Plaza de Chueca, this longtime centrepiece of gay Madrid – a huge statue of a nude male angel guards the doorway – is an agreeable, dimly lit salon decorated with, among other things, religious icons. It's ideal for quiet conversation and catching the weekend buzz as people plan their forays into the more clamorous clubs in the vicinity.

## ☆ ENTERTAINMENT

**THUNDERCAT** LIVE MUSIC

Map p250 (☑654 511457; www.thundercatclub.com; Calle de Campoamor 11; ☉10pm-6am Thu-Sat; ⓂAlonso Martínez) They keep it simple at Thundercat – it's rock, as classic as they can find it, with live gigs beginning after midnight and rolling on through the night. There's a jam session at 11.30pm Thursday.

**EL JUNCO JAZZ CLUB** JAZZ

Map p250 (☑91 319 20 81; www.eljunco.com; Plaza de Santa Bárbara 10; €6-15; ☉11pm-5.30am Tue-Thu, to 6am Fri & Sat; ⓂAlonso Martínez) El Junco has established itself on the Madrid nightlife scene by appealing as much to jazz aficionados as to clubbers. Its secret is high-quality live jazz gigs from Spain and around the world, followed by DJs spinning funk, soul, nu jazz, blues and innovative groove beats. There are also jam sessions at 11pm in jazz (Tuesday) and blues (Sunday).

**BOGUI JAZZ** JAZZ

Map p250 (☑91 521 15 68; www.boguijazz.com; Calle de Barquillo 29; €6-15; ☉10pm-6am Wed-Sat; ⓂChueca) One of Madrid's best-loved jazz clubs has finally reopened its doors after years of being closed (it fell foul of a council crackdown on licensing laws). It's picked up right where it left off, with 10.30pm live jazz shows from Thursday to Saturday, followed by rock DJs until dawn.

### GAY CHUECA

If you're eager to tap into the gay networks of Chueca, Mamá Inés is the place to start – apart from being a gay meeting place *par excellence,* its bar staff have their finger on the pulse. Also outstanding is **Librería Berkana** (Map p250; ☑91 522 55 99; www.libreria berkana.com; Calle de Hortaleza 62; ☉10.30am-9pm Mon-Fri, 11.30am-9pm Sat, noon-2pm & 5-9pm Sun; ⓂChueca), where you'll find the biweekly *Shanguide* (jammed with listings and contact ads), *Shangay Express* (better for articles) and possibly the *Mapa Gaya de Madrid,* which lists gay bars, discos and saunas.

## 🛍 SHOPPING

Chueca caters as much for gay clubbers as for a refined gay sensibility. Where Chueca eases gently down the hill towards Paseo de los Recoletos and beyond to Salamanca, especially in Calle del Conde de Xiquena and Calle del Almirante, niche designers take over with exclusive boutiques and the latest individual fashions.

**LOEWE** FASHION & ACCESSORIES

Map p250 (☑91 522 68 15; www.loewe.com; Gran Vía 8; ☉10am-8.30pm Mon-Sat, 11am-8pm Sun; ⓂGran Vía) Born in 1846 in Madrid, Loewe is arguably Spain's signature line in high-end fashion and its landmark store on Gran Vía is one of the most famous and elegant stores in the capital. Classy handbags and accessories are the mainstays. Prices can be jaw-droppingly high, but it's worth stopping by, even if you don't plan to buy. There's another branch in Salamanca (p126).

**PATRIMONIO COMUNAL OLIVARERO** FOOD

Map p250 (☑91 308 05 05; www.pco.es; Calle de Mejía Lequerica 1; ☉10am-2pm & 5-8pm Mon-Fri, 10am-2pm Sat Sep-Jun, 9am-3pm Mon-Sat Jul; ⓂAlonso Martínez) For picking up some of the country's olive-oil varieties (Spain is the world's largest producer), Patrimonio Comunal Olivarero is perfect. With examples of the extra-virgin variety (and nothing else) from all over Spain, you could spend ages agonising over the choices. Staff know their oil and are happy to help out if you speak a little Spanish.

### XOAN VIQUEIRA
FASHION & ACCESSORIES

Map p250 (☑91 173 70 29; www.xoanviqueira.com; Calle de Gravina 22; ☉11am-2pm & 5-8.30pm Mon-Fri, 11am-2pm Sat; ⓂChueca) We love the playfulness of this designer Chueca store where screenprinting artist Xoan Viqueira throws his creativity at everything from *alpargatas* (traditional Spanish rope-soled shoes) to clothing and homewares.

### MONKEY GARAGE
FASHION & ACCESSORIES

Map p250 (☑91 137 73 98; www.facebook.com/monkeygarage11; Calle de la Santa Brigida 11; ☉noon-9.30pm Mon-Thu, 12.30-10pm Fri & Sat; ⓂTribunal) Inhabiting an old mechanics workshop, this edgy, stylish shop sells clean-lined Scandivanian fashions, designer jewellery and modern artworks.

### MACCHININE
TOYS

Map p250 (☑91 701 05 18; www.facebook.com/macchinine; Calle de Barquillo 7; ☉10am-2pm & 4.30-8.30pm Mon-Sat; ⓂBanco de España) Packed with nearly 5000 miniature cars, macchinine is a mecca for toy car enthusiasts. The likeable owners are just as passionate about connecting hobbyists with hard-to-find classic cars as they are showing visitors around their museum-like automobile wonderland. From antique models to modern hot rods, there are prices for all budgets (and browsing is fine, too).

### ISOLÉE
FOOD, FASHION

Map p250 (☑902 876136; www.isolee.com; Calle de las Infantas 19; ☉11am-9pm Mon-Sat; ⓂGran Vía) This long-standing concept-and-lifestyle store sells a select range of everything from clothes and shoes (Andy Warhol to Adidas) to CDs and food. Another branch is in Salamanca (p126).

### MALABABA
FASHION & ACCESSORIES

Map p250 (☑91 203 59 51; www.malababa.com; Calle de Santa Teresa 5; ☉10.30am-8.30pm Mon-Thu, to 9pm Fri & Sat; ⓂAlonso Martínez) This corner of Chueca is one of Madrid's happiest hunting grounds for the style-conscious shopper who favours individual boutiques with personality above larger stores. One such place, light-filled Malababa features classy Spanish-made accessories, including jewellery, handbags, shoes, purses and belts, all beautifully displayed.

### CASA POSTAL
ANTIQUES

Map p250 (☑91 532 70 37; Calle de la Libertad 37; ☉10am-2pm & 5-7.30pm Mon-Fri, 11am-2pm Sat; ⓂChueca) Old postcards, posters, books and other period knick-knacks fill this treasure cave to the rafters.

### CACAO SAMPAKA
FOOD

Map p250 (☑91 319 58 40; www.cacaosampaka.com; Calle de Orellana 4; ☉10am-9pm Mon-Sat; ⓂAlonso Martínez) If you thought chocolate was about fruit 'n' nut, think again. This gourmet chocolate shop is a chocoholic's dream, with more combinations to go with humble cocoa than you ever imagined possible. There's also a cafe that's good for lunch.

### LURDES BERGADA
FASHION & ACCESSORIES

Map p250 (☑91 531 99 58; www.lurdesbergada.es; Calle del Conde de Xiquena 8; ☉10am-2.30pm & 4.30-8.30pm Mon-Sat; ⓂChueca) Lurdes Bergada and Syngman Cucala, a mother-and-son designer team from Barcelona, offer classy and original men's and women's fashions using neutral colours and all-natural fibres. They've developed something of a cult following and it's hard to leave without finding something that you just have to have. There's another branch in **Malasaña** (Map p250; ☑91 521 88 18; www.lurdesbergada.es).

### PONCELET
FOOD

Map p250 (☑91 308 02 21; www.poncelet.es; Calle de Argensola 27; ☉10.30am-2.30pm & 5-8.30pm Mon-Thu, 10.30am-8.30pm Fri & Sat; ⓂAlonso Martínez) With 80 Spanish and 240 European cheese varieties, this fine cheese shop is the best of its kind in Madrid. The range is outstanding and the staff really know their cheese.

### RESERVA Y CATA
WINE

Map p250 (☑91 319 04 01; www.reservaycata.com; Calle del Conde de Xiquena 13; ☉11am-2pm & 5.30-8.30pm Mon-Fri, 11am-2pm Sat; ⓂColón, Chueca) This old-style shop stocks an excellent range of local wines, and the knowledgable staff can help you pick out a great one for your next dnner party or a gift for a friend back home. It specialises in quality Spanish wines.

## 🏃 SPORTS & ACTIVITIES

### APUNTO – CENTRO CULTURAL DEL GUSTO
COOKING

Map p250 (☑91 702 10 41; www.apuntolibreria.com; Calle de Hortaleza 64; per person from €55; ⓂChueca) This engaging little bookstore runs fun yet professional cooking classes across a range of cuisines.

# Parque del Oeste & Northern Madrid

## Neighbourhood Top Five

**1 Ermita de San Antonio de la Florida** (p148) Visiting the stunning collection of frescoes that remain exactly where Goya painted them; it's one of Madrid's best-kept secrets.

**2 Museo Sorolla** (p149) Surrounding yourself with paintings infused with the clear light of the Mediterranean in a marvellous architectural showpiece.

**3 Bodega de la Ardosa** (p152) Propping up the bar and ordering *patatas bravas* (fried potatoes with a spicy tomato sauce) and a vermouth at this ageless *barrio* bar.

**4 DiverXo** (p154) Discovering the weird-and-wonderful world of Spanish nouvelle cuisine by dining at one of the world's most unusual restaurants.

**5 Estadio Santiago Bernabéu** (p155) Watching Real Madrid play in front of 80,000 passionate fans at this temple to footballing success.

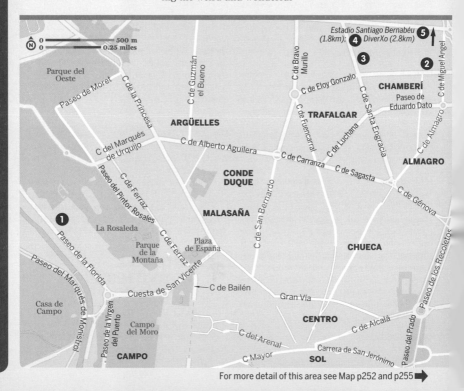

For more detail of this area see Map p252 and p255 ➡

# Explore: Parque del Oeste & Northern Madrid

Ranged around central Madrid to the north and west, these neighbourhoods cover a vast area and visiting requires careful planning. Chamberí is worth a trip in its own right, a reasonably self-contained *barrio* (district) with enough sights, shops and restaurants to warrant at least half a day. Chamberí is good at any time of the day or night, but to understand its appeal as one of the more accessible slices of Madrid life away from the tourist crowds, late afternoon is our favourite time of the day.

The rest of the attractions are thinly spread. Catch the metro to Moncloa metro station, and then follow Parque del Oeste roughly south and then on down to Templo de Debod on the cusp of the city centre. Ermita de San Antonio de la Florida is more of a dedicated (though easily made) excursion – catch the metro to Príncipe Pío and walk to the hermitage, before returning via the same route.

Northern Madrid follows the path of that great Madrid artery, known for much of its length as Paseo de la Castellana. Again, you're more likely to come here as part of a surgical strike on a particular sight or restaurant, but metro connections are good.

## Local Life

➡ **Meeting point** Plaza de Olavide is the heart and soul of Chamberí, from the old-timers sitting on park benches watching the world go by to the children in the playgrounds and the outdoor tables that encircle the plaza.

➡ **Hang-out** Bodega de la Ardosa (p152) is one of the best places in Madrid to understand the appeal of the neighbourhood bar – utterly unpretentious, serving great food and drawing a cast of regulars; it's Madrid in microcosm.

➡ **Traditional shops** A Chamberí speciality is the shops that have been serving the *barrio* for decades, places such as Calzados Cantero (p157), Papelería Salazar (p156) and Relojería Santolaya (p157).

## Getting There & Away

➡ **Metro** The most convenient metro stations for Chamberí are Bilbao (lines 1 and 4), Quevedo (line 2) and Iglesia (line 1). Other useful stations include Príncipe Pío (lines 6 and 10) for Ermita de San Antonio de la Florida, and Moncloa (lines 3 and 6), Argüelles (lines 3 and 4) and Plaza de España (lines 2, 3 and 10). Metro line 10 connects northern Madrid to the rest of Madrid.

## Lonely Planet's Top Tip

From 8am to around 2pm on Sunday, Calle de Fuencarral between the Glorieta de Quevedo and Glorieta de Bilbao is closed to traffic and all the *barrio* comes out to play. It's a nice alternative to touristy Madrid and you'll mingle with kids on bicycles and rollerblades, and see occasional jumping castles, puppet shows and the like. This has been a *barrio* tradition for over four decades. It also occurs on public holidays.

### ✖ Best Places to Eat

➡ DiverXo (p154)

➡ Santceloni (p155)

➡ La Favorita (p153)

➡ Mama Campo (p153)

➡ Costa Blanca Arrocería (p154)

➡ Cheese Bar (p153)

For reviews, see p152.➡

### ⊖ Best Places to Drink

➡ Bodega de la Ardosa (p152)

➡ Real Café Bernabéu (p155)

➡ La Violeta (p155)

➡ La Vaquería Montañesa (p155)

For reviews, see p155.➡

### ◉ Best Museums

➡ Ermita de San Antonio de la Florida (p148)

➡ Museo Sorolla (p149)

➡ Museo de América (p151)

➡ Templo de Debod (p152)

For reviews, see p148.➡

PARQUE DEL OESTE & NORTHERN MADRID

## TOP SIGHT
# ERMITA DE SAN ANTONIO DE LA FLORIDA

**This hermitage ranks alongside Madrid's finest art galleries. Also known as the Panteón de Goya, the chapel has frescoed ceilings as painted by Goya in 1798 on the request of Carlos IV. It's one of the few places to see Goya masterworks in their original setting.**

### An 18th-Century Madrid Crowd

As interesting as the miracle that forms the fresco's centrepiece, a typical Madrid crowd swarms around the saint. It was customary in such works that angels and cherubs appear in the cupola, above all the terrestrial activity, but Goya, never one to let himself be confined within the mores of the day, places the human above the divine.

### Fiesta de San Antonio

Young women (traditionally seamstresses) flock to the hermitage on 13 June to petition for a partner. Whether spiritually inclined or not, the attitude seems to be 'why take a chance?'

### Goya's Tomb

The painter is buried in front of the altar. His remains were transferred in 1919 from Bordeaux (France), where he had died in self-imposed exile in 1828. Oddly, the skeleton that was exhumed in Bordeaux was missing one important item – the head.

### The Miracle of St Anthony

Figures on the dome depict the miracle of St Anthony. The saint heard word from his native Lisbon that his father had been unjustly accused of murder. The saint was whisked miraculously to his hometown from northern Italy, where he tried in vain to convince the judges of his father's innocence. He then demanded that the corpse of the murder victim be placed before the judges. Goya's painting depicts the moment in which St Anthony calls on the corpse (a young man) to rise up and absolve his father.

## DON'T MISS

➡ The Miracle of St Anthony
➡ An 18th-century Madrid crowd
➡ Goya's tomb
➡ Fiesta de San Antonio

## PRACTICALITIES

➡ Panteón de Goya
➡ Map p255, B4
➡ 📞 91 542 07 22
➡ www.sanantoniodelaflorida.es
➡ Glorieta de San Antonio de la Florida 5
➡ admission free
➡ ⏱9.30am-8pm Tue-Sun, hours vary Jul & Aug
➡ Ⓜ Príncipe Pío

# ◉ SIGHTS

Madrid's north has some remarkable sights. The Ermita de San Antonio de la Florida is one of the city's richest treasures, while the Estadio Santiago Bernabéu is an icon in the world of sport. The only problem is that the many attractions are pretty far-flung, so be prepared to spend some time on the metro hopping from one to the other. The cluster of sights out west – Parque del Oeste, Faro de Madrid, Museo de América, Templo de Debod and Museo de Cerralbo – are an exception, not to mention wonderfully diverse.

### MUSEO NACIONAL DE CIENCIAS NATURALES
MUSEUM

(✆91 411 13 28; www.mncn.csic.es; Calle de José Gutiérrez Abascal 2; adult/child €6/3; ⊙10am-5pm Tue-Fri, to 8pm Sat & Sun Sep-Jul, 10am-5pm Tue-Fri, to 3pm Sat & Sun Aug; Ⓜ Gregorio Marañón) The Museum of Natural Sciences is a favourite for families, with permanent exhibitions including dinosaur skeletons, rocks and minerals, and fossils of animals large and small. Visitors can also see displays on human evolution and biodiversity. The collection has existed for more than 200 years, making it one of the oldest of its kind in the world.

### PLAZA DE OLAVIDE
PLAZA

Map p252 (Ⓜ Bilbao, Iglesia, Quevedo) Plaza de Olavide is one of Madrid's most agreeable public spaces, a real *barrio* special. But it hasn't always had its current form. From 1934 the entire plaza was occupied by a covered, octagonal market. In November 1974, the market was demolished in a spectacular controlled explosion, opening up the plaza. To see the plaza's history told in pictures, step into Bar Méntrida at No 3 to have a drink and admire the photos on the wall.

### MUSEO SOROLLA
GALLERY

Map p252 (✆91 310 15 84; www.mecd.gob.es/msorolla; Paseo del General Martínez Campos 37; adult/child €3/free; ⊙9.30am-8pm Tue-Sat, 10am-3pm Sun; Ⓜ Iglesia, Gregorio Marañón) The Valencian artist Joaquín Sorolla immortalised the clear Mediterranean light of the Valencian coast. His Madrid house, a quiet mansion surrounded by lush gardens that he designed himself, was inspired by what he had seen in Andalucía and now contains the most complete collection of the artist's works.

On the ground floor there's a cool *patio cordobés*, an Andalucian courtyard off which is a room containing collections of Sorolla's drawings. The 1st floor, with the main salon and dining areas, was mostly decorated by the artist himself. On the same floor are three separate rooms that Sorolla used as studios. In the second one is a collection of his Valencian beach scenes. The third was where he usually worked. Upstairs, works spanning Sorolla's career are organised across four adjoining rooms.

Admission is free 2pm to 8pm Saturday and all day Sunday.

### ESTACIÓN DE CHAMBERÍ
MUSEUM

Map p252 (Andén 0; www.museomadrid.com/tag/anden-0-horario; cnr Calles de Santa Engracia & de Luchana; ⊙11am-1pm & 5-7pm Fri, 10am-2pm Sat & Sun; Ⓜ Iglesia, Bilbao) FREE Estación de Chamberí, the long-lost ghost station of Madrid's metro, is now a museum piece that recreates the era of the station's inauguration in 1919 with advertisements from that time (including Madrid's then-four-digit phone numbers), ticket offices and other memorabilia almost a century old. It's an engaging journey down memory lane.

For years, *madrileños* (residents of Madrid) wondered what happened to the Chamberí metro station – they knew it existed, yet it appeared on no maps and no trains ever stopped there. The answer was that Chamberí station lay along line 1, between the stops of Bilbao and Iglesia, until 1966 when Madrid's trains (and, where possible, platforms) were lengthened. Logistical difficulties meant that Chamberí could not be extended and the station was abandoned. In 2008 the Estación de Chamberí finally reopened to the public (just not for trains).

### FARO DE MADRID
VIEWPOINT

Map p255 (✆91 544 81 04; Avenida de los Reyes Católicos; adult/concession/child €3/1.50/free; ⊙9.30am-8pm Tue-Sun; Ⓜ Moncloa) After a decade closed, this supremely ugly Madrid landmark just in front of Museo de América reopened in 2015. It looks out over the northern corner of the Parque del Oeste and has sweeping views of western Madrid. It was built in 1992 to commemorate the 500th anniversary of the discovery of America and to celebrate Madrid's role that year as the European Capital of Culture. Sunset is the perfect time to visit.

## TOP SIGHT
# ESTADIO SANTIAGO BERNABÉU

Football fans and budding Madridistas (Real Madrid supporters) will want to make a pilgrimage to the Estadio Santiago Bernabéu, a temple to all that's extravagant and successful in football. For a tour of the stadium, buy your ticket at window 10 (next to Gate 7). The self-guided tours take you up into the stands for a panoramic view of the stadium, then pass through the presidential box, press room, dressing rooms, players' tunnel and even onto the pitch itself. The tour ends in the extraordinary Exposición de Trofeos (trophy exhibit), probably the sporting world's most dazzling collection of silverware.

Better still, attend a game alongside 80,000 delirious fans. For bigger games, tickets are difficult to find unless you're willing to take the risk with scalpers. For less important matches, you shouldn't have too many problems. Tickets can be purchased online, by phone or in person from the ticket office at Gate 42 on Avenida de Concha Espina; for the last option, turn up early in the week before a scheduled game (eg a Monday morning for a Sunday game).

### DON'T MISS

➜ Live game
➜ Guided tour
➜ Tienda Real Madrid
➜ Exposición de Trofeos

### PRACTICALITIES

➜ ⏺tickets 902 324324, tours ⏺91 398 43 00/70
➜ www.realmadrid.com
➜ Avenida de Concha Espina 1
➜ tours adult/child €25/18
➜ ⏱tours 10am-7pm Mon-Sat, 10.30am-6.30pm Sun, except match days
➜ Ⓜ Santiago Bernabéu

You're allowed to enter every half-hour from 9.30am to 1.30pm, whereafter it's less restrictive.

### TELEFÉRICO                                    CABLE CAR

Map p255 (⏺91 541 11 18; www.teleferico.com; cnr Paseo del Pintor Rosales & Calle de Marqués de Urquijo; one-way/return €4.20/5.90; ⏱noon-9pm May-Aug, reduced hours Sep-Apr; Ⓜ Argüelles) One of the world's most horizontal cable cars (it never hangs more than 40m above the ground), the Teleférico putters out from the slopes of Parque del Oeste. The 2.5km journey takes you into the depths of the Casa de Campo, Madrid's enormous green open space (although more a dry olive hue in summer), to the west of the city centre. The views on the way are splendid and there's a decent children's playground near the Casa de Campo station.

Try to time it so you can settle in for a cool lunch or an evening tipple on one of the *terrazas* (open-air cafes) along Paseo del Pintor Rosales.

### MUSEO TIFOLÓGICO                               MUSEUM

(Museum for the Blind; ⏺91 589 42 19; www. museo.once.es; Calle de la Coruña 18; ⏱10am-2pm & 5-8pm Tue-Fri, 10am-2pm Sat, closed Aug; Ⓜ Estrecho) FREE One attraction specifically for visually impaired travellers and Spaniards is the Museo Tifológico. Run by the National Organisation for the Blind (ONCE), its exhibits (all of which may be touched) include paintings, sculptures and tapestries, as well as more than 40 scale models of world monuments, including Madrid's Palacio Real and Cibeles fountain, as well as La Alhambra in Granada and the aqueduct in Segovia. It also provides leaflets in Braille and audioguides to the museum.

### CASA DE CAMPO                                    PARK

Map p255 (Ⓜ Batán) Sometimes called the 'lungs of Madrid', this 17-sq-km stand of greenery stretches west of the Río Manzanares. There are prettier and more central parks in Madrid but its scope is such that there are plenty of reasons to visit. And visit the *madrileños* do, nearly half a million of them every weekend, celebrating the fact that the short-lived Republican government of the 1930s opened the park to the public (it was previously the exclusive domain of royalty).

For city-bound *madrileños* with neither the time nor the inclination to go further afield, it has become the closest they get to nature, despite the fact that cyclists, walkers and picnickers overwhelm the byways and trails that criss-cross the park. There are tennis courts and a swimming pool, as well as the **Zoo Aquarium de Madrid** (☎902 345014; www.zoomadrid.com; adult/child €23/19; ⊙10.30am-10pm Sun-Thu, to midnight Fri & Sat Jul & Aug, shorter hours Sep-Jun; 🚌37 from Intercambiador de Príncipe Pío, Ⓜ Casa de Campo) and the **Parque de Atracciones** (☎91 463 29 00; www.parquedeatracciones.es; adult/child €32/25; ⊙noon-midnight Jul & Aug, hours vary Sep-Jun). The Teleférico also takes you here with good views en route. At Casa de Campo's southern end, restaurants specialise in wedding receptions, ensuring plenty of bridal parties roaming the grounds in search of an unoccupied patch of greenery where they can take photos. Also in the park, the Andalucian-style ranch known as Batán is used to house the bulls destined to do bloody battle in the Fiestas de San Isidro Labrador.

### MUSEO DE CERRALBO — MUSEUM

Map p255 (☎91 547 36 46; www.mecd.gob.es/mcerralbo; Calle de Ventura Rodríguez 17; adult/concession €3/free; ⊙9.30am-3pm Tue, Wed, Fri & Sat, 9.30am-3pm & 5-8pm Thu, 10am-3pm Sun; Ⓜ Ventura Rodríguez) Huddled beneath the modern apartment buildings northwest of Plaza de España, this noble old mansion is a reminder of how wealthy *madrileños* (people from Madrid) once lived. The former home of the 17th Marqués de Cerralbo (1845–1922) – politician, poet and archaeologist – is a study in 19th-century opulence. The upper floor boasts a gala dining hall and a grand ballroom. The mansion is jammed with the fruits of the collector's eclectic meanderings – from Oriental pieces to religious paintings and clocks.

On the main floor are suits of armour from around the world, while the Oriental room is full of carpets, Moroccan kilims, tapestries, musical instruments and 18th-century Japanese suits of armour, much of it obtained at auction in Paris in the 1870s. The music room is dominated by a gondola of Murano glass and pieces of Bohemian crystal. The house is also replete with porcelain, including Sèvres, Wedgwood, Meissen and local ceramics.

Clearly the *marqués* was a man of diverse tastes and it can all be a little overwhelming, especially once you factor in artworks by Zurbarán, Ribera, van Dyck and El Greco.

Admission is free 2pm to 3pm Saturday, 5pm to 8pm Thursday and all day Sunday.

> ### ℹ METRO LINE 10
> Two of the neighbourhood's top sights – the Ermita de San Antonio de la Florida (p148) and Estadio Santiago Bernabéu – may seem far-flung but they're actually connected by metro line 10. En route between the two, the line also has stops at Plaza de España and Tribunal, which are handy stations for the rest of the *barrio* (district).

### MUSEO DE AMÉRICA — MUSEUM

Map p255 (☎91 549 26 41; www.mecd.gob.es/museodeamerica/el-museo.html; Avenida de los Reyes Católicos 6; adult/concession €3/1.50, free Sun; ⊙9.30am-3pm Tue, Wed, Fri & Sat, 9.30am-7pm Thu, 10am-3pm Sun; Ⓜ Moncloa) Empire may have become a dirty word but it defined how Spain saw itself for centuries. Spanish vessels crossed the Atlantic to the Spanish colonies in Latin America, carrying adventurers one way and gold and other looted artefacts from indigenous cultures on the return journey. These latter pieces – at once the heritage of another continent and a fascinating insight into imperial Spain – are the subject of this excellent museum.

The two levels of the museum show off a representative display of ceramics, statuary, jewellery and instruments of hunting, fishing and war, along with some of the paraphernalia of the colonisers. The display is divided into five thematic zones: **El Conocimiento de América**, which traces the discovery and exploration of the Americas; **La Realidad de América**, a big-screen summary of how South America wound up as it has today; and others on society, religion and language, which each explore tribal issues, the clash with the Spanish newcomers and its results. The Colombian gold collection, dating as far back as the 2nd century AD, is particularly eye-catching.

### PARQUE DEL OESTE — GARDENS

Map p255 (Avenida del Arco de la Victoria; Ⓜ Moncloa) Sloping down the hill behind the Moncloa metro station, Parque del Oeste is quite beautiful, with plenty of shady corners where you can recline under a tree in the heat of the day and enjoy fine views out to

## TOP SIGHT
# TEMPLO DE DEBOD

Yes, that *is* an Egyptian temple in downtown Madrid. No matter which way you look at it, there's something incongruous about finding the Templo de Debod in the Parque de la Montaña northwest of Plaza de España. The temple was saved from the rising waters of Lake Nasser in southern Egypt when Egyptian president Gamal Abdel Nasser built the Aswan High Dam. After 1968 it was sent block by block to Spain as a gesture of thanks to Spanish archaeologists in the Unesco team that worked to save the monuments that would otherwise have disappeared forever.

Begun in 2200 BC and completed over many centuries, the temple was dedicated to the god Amon of Thebes, about 20km south of Philae in the Nubian desert of southern Egypt. According to some authors of myth and legend, the goddess Isis gave birth to Horus in this very temple, although obviously not in Madrid.

Rather than treating the temple as a sight on its own, consider a stroll in the surrounding parkland from where the views towards the Palacio Real are some of Madrid's prettiest.

### DON'T MISS

➡ Temple interior
➡ Parque de la Montaña and Royal Palace views

### PRACTICALITIES

➡ Map p255, C4
➡ Paseo del Pintor Rosales
➡ admission free
➡ ⊘10am-8pm Tue-Sun
➡ Ⓜ Ventura Rodríguez

the west towards Casa de Campo. It has been a *madrileño* favourite ever since its creation in 1906.

The Paseo de Camoens, a main thoroughfare running through the park, is closed to vehicular traffic from 11pm on Friday until 6am on Monday to deter prostitution, which was once a problem here.

**CEMENTERIO DE LA FLORIDA**   CEMETERY
Map p255 (Calle de Francisco Jacinto y Alcantara; Ⓜ Príncipe Pío) Across the train tracks east of the Ermita de San Antonio de la Florida is the cemetery where 43 rebels executed by Napoleon's troops are buried. They were killed on the nearby Montaña del Príncipe Pío in the predawn of 3 May 1808, after the Dos de Mayo uprising. The event was immortalised by Goya in *El dos de mayo* and *El tres de mayo*, which hang in the Museo del Prado (p99). The forlorn cemetery, established in 1796, is often closed.

 **EATING**

**The good thing about eating in this part of town is that you're more likely to be joined by locals than by other tourists. Chamberí in particular has dozens of** appealing **choices. The business and well-to-do clientele who eat in the restaurants of northern Madrid know their food and they're happy to pay for it. These restaurants are often a fair metro, taxi or chauffeur-driven limousine ride north of the centre, but they're well worth it for a touch of class.**

**BODEGA DE LA ARDOSA**   TAPAS €
Map p252 (⚡91 446 58 94; Calle de Santa Engracia 70; raciones from €7.50; ⊘9am-3pm & 6-11.30pm Thu-Tue; Ⓜ Iglesia) Tucked away in a fairly modern corner of Chamberí, this fine relic has an extravagantly tiled facade complete with shrapnel holes dating back to the Spanish Civil War. For decades locals have been coming here for their morning tipple and some of the best traditional Spanish *patatas bravas* (fried potatoes with spicy tomato sauce) in town. It also has vermouth on tap.

**CASA MINGO**   ASTURIAN €
Map p255 (⚡91 547 79 18; www.casamingo.es; Paseo de la Florida 34; raciones €2.70-11, pollo asado €11; ⊘11am-midnight; Ⓜ Príncipe Pío) Opened in 1888, Casa Mingo is a well known and vaguely cavernous Asturian cider house. Things are kept simple, focusing primarily on the signature dish of *pollo asado* (roast

chicken, cut in quarters) accompanied by a bottle of cider. *Chorizo a la sidra* (chorizo cooked with cider), *queso cabrales* (blue cheese from Asturias) and a weekday lunch *cocido a la madrileña* (meat-and-chickpea stew) in winter are other favourites.

### VIANDAS DE SALAMANCA
SPANISH €

Map p252 (☑91 593 40 77; www.viandasdesala manca.es; Calle de Fuencarral 156; bocadillos €3.75; ☺9.30am-9.30pm Mon-Sat, to 8pm Sun; MQuevedo) Across Madrid you'll find delis from Spain's *jamón*-producing regions selling *jamón* (ham), chorizo and the like. But Viandas de Salamanca was one of the first to see their potential as simple but filling and quintessentially Spanish fast food. This shop, a few steps off the Glorieta de Quevedo, sells *bocadillos de jamón*, little paper cones filled with *jamón* and *jamón*-filled pastries.

### CERVECERÍA 100 MONTADITOS
FAST FOOD €

Map p252 (http://spain.100montaditos.com; Calle de Fuencarral 145; mini-rolls €1-3.50; ☺noon-midnight; MQuevedo) This bar with outlets all across the city serves up no fewer than 100 different varieties of mini-*bocadillos* (filled rolls) that span the full range of Spanish staples, such as chorizo, *jamón*, tortilla and a variety of cheeses and seafood, in more combinations than you could imagine. You order at the counter and your name is called in no time. Menus are available in English.

### ★MAMA CAMPO
SPANISH €€

Map p252 (☑91 447 41 38; www.mamacampo. es; Plaza de Olavide; mains €7-15; ☺1.30-4pm & 8.30pm-midnight Tue-Sat, 1.30-4pm Sun; MBilbao, Iglesia, Quevedo) Mama Campo breaks the mould of sameness that unites the bars surrounding Plaza de Olavide. Positioning itself as an ecofriendly take on the Spanish *taberna* (tavern), it's gone for a winning white decor within and a fresh approach to Spanish staples, always with an emphasis on fresh, organic ingredients. It also has tables on one of our favourite squares.

Next door it has a new bar, known as La Cantina, and just around the corner in Calle de Trafalgar it also has a health food store, and even a cooking school/workshop for kids (where the Mama Campo empire began).

### ★LA FAVORITA
SPANISH €€

Map p252 (☑91 448 38 10; www.restaurantela favorita.com; Calle de Covarrubias 25; mains €12-26, set menus €50-70; ☺1.30-4pm & 9pm-midnight Mon-Fri, 9pm-midnight Sat; MAlonso Martínez) Set in a delightful old mansion, La Favorita is famous for its opera arias throughout the night, sung by professional opera singers masquerading as waiters. The outdoor garden courtyard is delightful on a summer's evening, while the music and food (which leans towards the cuisine of the northeastern Spanish region of Navarra) are top drawer.

### LE QUALITÉ TASCA
TAPAS €€

(☑91 014 69 20; www.lequalitetasca.com; Calle de Ponzano 48; raciones €8-19; ☺1-11pm Sun, 8.30-11.30pm Tue & Wed, 1pm-midnight Thu, 1pm-1.30am Fri & Sat; MRíos Rosas) For a tapas experience with scarcely a tourist in sight, Le Qualité Tasca, in Chamberí's north, is an excellent choice. The menu ranges from classic cured meats and cheeses to innovative takes on old ideas, from *tortilla en tres texturas* (Spanish omelette in three textures) to *croquetas de camarón y quisquilla* (two-shrimp croquettes). Terrific wines, too.

### LA GIRALDA
ANDALUCIAN €€

Map p252 (☑91 445 77 79; www.restauranteslagir alda.com; Calle de Hartzenbusch 12; tapas from €2.50, mains €10-19; ☺1-4pm & 8.30pm-midnight Mon-Sat, 1.30-4pm Sun; MBilbao) Around since 1981, this Andalucian gem has tiled walls, an excellent collection of nearly 80 sherries from Jerez, and cuisine that springs from Seville and Cádiz – think rices, squid meatballs and lightly fried seafood. Tapas at the bar are reliably traditional with *jamón*, *canapés* and *tortillita de camarones* (deep-fried, baby-shrimp omelette).

### CHEESE BAR
CHEESE €€

Map p252 (☑91 399 25 50; www.ponceletcheese bar.es; Calle de José Abascal 61; mains €12-19; ☺noon-midnight Tue-Sat, to 4pm Sun; MGregorio Marañón) By the people who brought you Madrid's best cheese shop, Poncelet (p145), Cheese Bar does many things but the cheese platters from Poncelet's considerable repertoire, as well as the fondues and raclettes, are the undoubted stars of the show. Craft beers round out a fine package.

### GOIKO GRILL
BURGERS €€

Map p252 (☑91 060 11 41; www.goikogrill.com; Glorieta de Bilbao 3; burgers €10-15; ☺1-5pm & 8-11.30pm Mon-Wed, to midnight Thu-Sat; MBilbao) A strong player on Madrid's burgeoning burger scene, Goiko Grill has several locations around the city. The modern, minimal design puts the emphasis where it should

PARQUE DEL OESTE & NORTHERN MADRID EATING

## BETWEEN MEALS & SPANISH FAST FOOD

If you just can't wait until restaurants open, try the following:

**Plaza de Olavide** Most bars and restaurants around the square don't close their kitchens between lunch and dinner.

**Viandas de Salamanca** (p153) Rolls filled with *jamón* throughout the day.

**Cervecería 100 Montaditos** (p153) Mini-rolls with all manner of fillings.

be: on serving unique hamburgers to true fans. Toppings are a mix of Spanish and US influences. Most of the time they're packed, so it's best to call ahead for a reservation.

### COSTA BLANCA ARROCERÍA    SPANISH €€

Map p252 (✒91 448 58 32; Calle de Bravo Murillo 3; mains €11-23; ⊗1.30-4pm Mon, 1.30-4pm & 8.30-11.30pm Tue-Fri, 2-4pm & 8.30-11.30pm Sat & Sun; Ⓜ Quevedo) Even if you don't have plans to be in Chamberí, it's worth a trip across town to this bar-restaurant that offers outstanding rice dishes, including paella. The quality is high and prices are among the cheapest in town. Start with *almejas a la marinera* (baby clams) and follow it up with *paella de marisco* (seafood paella) for the full experience.

As always in such places, you'll need two people to make up an order.

### SAGARETXE    TAPAS €€

Map p252 (✒91 446 25 88; www.sagaretxe.com; Calle de Eloy Gonzalo 26; tapas €2.20, set menus €15.50-31; ⊗noon-5pm & 7pm-midnight; Ⓜ Iglesia) One of the best *pintxos* (Basque tapas) bars in Madrid, Sagaretxe takes the stress out of eating tapas, with around 20 varieties lined up along the bar (and more than 100 that can be prepared in the kitchen upon request). Simply point and any of the wonderful selection will be plated up for you.

### LAS TORTILLAS DE GABINO    SPANISH €€

Map p252 (✒91 319 75 05; www.lastortillasde gabino.com; Calle de Rafael Calvo 20; tortillas €10.50-15.50, mains €14-22; ⊗1.30-4pm & 9-11.30pm Mon-Sat; Ⓜ Iglesia) It's a brave Spanish chef that fiddles with the iconic *tortilla de patatas* (potato omelette), but the results here are delicious. All manner of surprising combinations are available

including tortilla with octopus. This place also gets rave reviews for its *croquetas*. The service is excellent and the bright yet classy dining area adds to the sense of a most agreeable eating experience.

### EL PEDRUSCO DE ALDEALCORVO    SPANISH €€

Map p252 (✒91 446 88 33; www.elpedruscode aldealcorvo.es; Calle de Juan de Austria 27; mains €19-44; ⊗1.30-4pm Tue-Sun; Ⓜ Iglesia) If you haven't time to visit one of the *asadores* (restaurants specialising in roasted meats) of Segovia, head to this fine restaurant where the *cochinillo asado* (roast suckling pig) and ¼ *lechazo* (quarter roast lamb) are succulent and as good as any in Madrid.

A salad is a must to counterbalance all that meat and you'll be delighted to see a vegetable.

### ★DIVERXO    MODERN SPANISH €€€

(✒91 570 07 66; www.diverxo.com; Calle de Padre Damián 23; set menus €195-250; ⊗2-3.30pm & 9-10.30pm Tue-Sat, closed three weeks in Aug; Ⓜ Cuzco) Madrid's only three-Michelin-starred restaurant, DiverXo in northern Madrid is one of Spain's most unusual culinary experiences. Chef David Muñoz is something of the *enfant terrible* of Spain's cooking scene. Still in his 30s, he favours what he has described as a 'brutal' approach to cooking – his team of chefs appear as you're mid bite to add surprising new ingredients.

The carefully choreographed experience centres on the short (2½-hour, seven-course) or long (four-hour, 11-course) menus, or the 'Wow' and 'Glutton Wow' menus, and is utterly unlike the more formal upmarket dining options elsewhere. The nondescript suburban setting and small premises (chefs sometimes end up putting the finishing touches to dishes in the hallway) only add to the whole street-smart atmosphere.

### ZALACAÍN    BASQUE, NAVARRAN €€€

Map p252 (✒91 561 48 40; www.restaurante zalacain.com; Calle de Álvarez de Baena 4; mains €29-48, set menu €90; ⊗1.15-4pm & 9pm-midnight Mon-Fri, 9pm-midnight Sat, closed Aug & Easter; Ⓜ Gregorio Marañón) Where most other fine-dining experiences centre on innovation, Zalacaín is a bastion of tradition, with a refined air and loyal following. The pig's trotters filled with mushrooms and lamb is a house speciality, as is the lobster salad. The wine list is purported to be one of the city's best (with an estimated 35,000 bottles and 1200 different varieties).

Everyone who's anyone in Madrid, from the king down, has eaten here since the doors opened in 1973; it was the first restaurant in Spain to receive three Michelin stars – it now has one. You should certainly dress to impress (men will need a tie and a jacket).

A major 2017 renovation has brought the atmosphere up a notch, but little else has changed, about which Madrid's great and good breathed a huge sigh of relief.

**PUERTA 57**                                    SPANISH €€€

(☑91 457 33 61; www.grupolamaquina.es; Gate 57, Estadio Santiago Bernabéu, Calle de Padre Damián; mains & raciones €9-25; ☉1-4pm & 8.30pm-midnight; ⓂSantiago Bernabéu) There are many reasons to recommend this place, but the greatest novelty lies in its location – inside the home stadium of Real Madrid; its Salón Madrid (one of a number of dining rooms) looks out over the playing field. The cuisine is traditional Spanish with an emphasis on seafood and it gets rave reviews from its predominantly business clientele.

Needless to say, you'll need to book a long time in advance for a meal during a game.

**SANTCELONI**                                    CAIALAN €€€

Map p252 (☑91 210 88 40; www.restaurante santceloni.com; Paseo de la Castellana 57; mains €48-72, set menu €175; ☉2-4pm & 9-11pm Mon-Fri, 9-11pm Sat Sep-Jul; ⓂGregorio Marañón) The Michelin-starred Santceloni is one of Madrid's best restaurants, with luxurious decor, faultless service, fabulous wines and nouvelle cuisine from the kitchen of chef Óscar Velasco. The menu changes with the seasons and each dish is a work of art; the *menús gastronómicos* are worthwhile to really sample the breadth of surprising tastes.

# 🍷 DRINKING & NIGHTLIFE

**Memorable bars are fairly thin on the ground out here. You can drink while overlooking one of the world's most famous football grounds or pick any bar among those that encircle the Plaza de Olavide in Chamberí – this is a real local favourite and drinking here almost makes you an honorary *madrileño*. A couple of vermouth bars round out an enticing package.**

**LA VIOLETA**                                    BAR

Map p252 (☑667 058644; www.lavioletavermut. com; Calle Vallehermoso 62; ☉7pm-1am Tue-Thu, 1-4.30pm & 7pm-2am Fri, 1pm-2am Sat, 1-5pm Sun; ⓂCanal) This breezy little Chamberí bar has many calling cards – among them, great music and a sense of being a real old-style Madrid neighbourhood bar. But we like it for its *vermut* (vermouth), one of the city's favourite drinks. Unusually, there are more than 20 different versions to try and staff are adept at pairing the perfect tapa (snack) with each variety.

**LA VAQUERÍA MONTAÑESA**                          BAR

Map p252 (☑91 138 71 06; www.lavaqueria montanesa.es; Calle de Blanca de Navarra 8; ☉1pm-1am Fri & Sat; ⓂAlonso Martínez) Inhabiting an old dairy and tucked away in a little-visited corner of Chamberí like some hidden Madrid treasure, La Vaquería Montañesa does terrific food but it's the vermouth, served in a martini glass, that really draws us back.

**THE DASH**                                    COCKTAIL BAR

Map p252 (☑687 949064; www.facebook.com/ thedashmadrid; Calle de Murillo 5; ☉4pm-2am Tue-Thu, to 2.30am Fri & Sat, 1-11pm Sun; ⓂIglesia) This neighbourhood cocktail bar with its big marble bar top evokes the classic cocktail bars of Madrid's past but it's a casual place with few pretensions. There's a terrific mix of cocktails with few surprises but all expertly mixed.

**REAL CAFÉ BERNABÉU**                          BAR

(☑91 458 36 67; www.realcafebernabeu.es; Gate 30, Estadio Santiago Bernabéu, Avenida de Concha Espina; ☉10am-2am; ⓂSantiago Bernabéu) Overlooking one of the most famous football fields on earth, this trendy cocktail bar will appeal to those who live and breathe football or those who simply enjoy mixing with the beautiful people. Views of the stadium are exceptional, although it closes two hours before a game and doesn't open until an hour after. There's also a good restaurant.

# ⭐ ENTERTAINMENT

★**ESTADIO SANTIAGO BERNABÉU**                    FOOTBALL

(☑902 324324; www.realmadrid.com; Avenida de Concha Espina 1; tickets from €40; ⓂSantiago Bernabéu) Watching Real Madrid play is one of football's greatest experiences, but tickets are difficult to find. They can be purchased online, by phone or in person from the ticket office at Gate 42 on Av de Concha Espina; turn up early in the week before a scheduled game. Numerous online ticketing agencies also sell tickets. Otherwise, you'll need to take a risk with scalpers.

The football season runs from September (or the last weekend in August) until May, with a two-week break just before Christmas until early in the New Year.

### SALA CLAMORES
LIVE MUSIC

Map p252 (☑91 445 79 38; www.clamores.es; Calle de Alburquerque 14; admission free-€15; ☺6.30pm-2am Sun-Thu, to 5.30am Fri & Sat; ⓜBilbao) Clamores is a one-time classic jazz cafe that has morphed into one of the most diverse live music stages in Madrid. Jazz is still a staple, but flamenco, blues, world music, singer-songwriters, pop and rock all make regular appearances. Live shows can begin as early as 7pm on weekends but sometimes really only get going after 1am.

On the rare nights when there's nothing live, a DJ takes over, spinning pop, indie and funk.

### AUDITORIO NACIONAL DE MÚSICA
CLASSICAL MUSIC

(☑91 337 01 40; www.auditorionacional.mcu.es; Calle del Príncipe de Vergara 146; ⓜCruz del Rayo) When it's not playing the Teatro Real, Madrid's Orquesta Sinfónica plays at this modern venue, which also attracts famous conductors from all across the world. It's usually fairly easy to get your hands on tickets at the box office.

### TEATROS DEL CANAL
THEATRE

Map p252 (☑91 308 99 99; www.teatroscanal.com; Calle de Cea Bermúdez 1; ⓜCanal) A state-of-the-art theatre complex, Teatros del Canal does major theatre performances, as well as musical and dance concerts. It's also a popular festival venue.

### CINES PRINCESA
CINEMA

Map p255 (☑91 541 41 00, 902 229122; www.cinesrenoir.com; Calle de la Princesa 3; tickets from €4; ⓜPlaza de España) Screens all kinds of original-version films, from Hollywood blockbusters to arty flicks, with (unusually) subtitles in Spanish.

### HONKY TONK
LIVE MUSIC

Map p252 (☑91 445 61 91; www.clubhonky.com; Calle de Covarrubias 24; admission free-€5; ☺9.30pm-5am Sun-Thu, to 6am Fri & Sat; ⓜAlon-

so Martínez, Bilbao) Despite the name, this is a great place to see blues or local rock, though many acts have a little country, jazz or R&B thrown into the mix too. It's a fun vibe in a smallish club that's been around since the heady 1980s; arrive early as it fills up fast.

### GALILEO GALILEI
LIVE MUSIC

Map p252 (☑91 534 75 57; www.salagalileogalilei.com; Calle de Galileo 100; admission free-€18; ☺6pm-4.30am; ⓜIslas Filipinas) There's no telling what will be staged here next, but it's sure to be good; past performers include Jackson Browne, El Cigala, Kiko Veneno, Niña Pastori and Brazilian songstress Cibelle, among others. The program changes nightly, with singer-songwriters, jazz, flamenco, folk, fusion, indie, world music and even comedians.

### MOBY DICK
LIVE MUSIC

(☑91 555 76 71; www.mobydickclub.com; Avenida del Brasil 5; admission free-€20; ☺9pm-3am Wed, to 5am Thu, to 6am Fri & Sat; ⓜSantiago Bernabéu) In a corner of Madrid that works hard by day and parties even harder on weekends, Moby Dick is an institution on the live music circuit, mostly hosting well-known rock bands who can't quite fill the 25,000-seater venues.

### CINESA PROYECCIONES
CINEMA

Map p252 (☑902 333231; www.cinesa.es; Calle de Fuencarral 136; tickets from €4; ⓜBilbao, Quevedo) Wonderful art-deco exterior; modern cinema within.

## 🛍 SHOPPING

**You wouldn't come to Madrid's north for the shopping, but Chamberí, especially in the streets close to the Plaza de Olavide, is a notable exception. Here you'll find a handful of the old-world shops that were once such a feature of Madrid, but which are slowly disappearing elsewhere. Even if you don't come to buy, they're a treasured window on the city's past.**

### PAPELERÍA SALAZAR
BOOKS, STATIONERY

Map p252 (☑91 446 18 48; www.papeleriasalazar.es; Calle de Luchana 7-9; ☺9.30am-1.30pm & 4.30-8pm Mon-Fri, 10am-1.30pm Sat; ⓜBilbao) Opened in 1905, Papelería Salazar is Madrid's oldest stationery store and is now run by the fourth generation of the Salazar family. It's a treasure trove that combines items of interest only to locals (old-style Spanish bookplates, First Communion invitations) with useful items like Faber-Castell pens and pencils, maps, notebooks and drawing supplies. It's a priceless relic of the kind that is slowly disappearing in Madrid.

### RELOJERÍA SANTOLAYA ANTIQUES

Map p252 (⌨91 447 25 64; www.relojeriasantolaya.com; Calle Murillo 8; ☉10am-1pm & 5-8pm Mon-Fri; Ⓜ Quevedo, Iglesia, Bilbao) Founded in 1867, this timeless old clock repairer just off Plaza de Olavide is the official watch repairer to Spain's royalty and heritage properties. There's not much for sale here, but stop by the tiny shopfront and workshop to admire the dying art of timepiece repairs, with not a digital watch in sight.

### BAZAR MATEY GIFTS & SOUVENIRS

Map p252 (⌨91 446 93 11; www.matey.com; Calle de la Santísima Trinidad 1; ☉9.30am-1.30pm & 4.30-8pm Mon-Sat, closed Sat afternoons Jul & Aug; Ⓜ Iglesia, Quevedo) Bazar Matey is a wonderful store catering to collectors of model trains, aeroplanes and cars, and all sorts of accessories. The items here are the real deal, with near-perfect models of everything from old Renfe trains to obscure international airlines. Prices can be sky high, but that doesn't deter the legions of collectors who stream in from all over Madrid on Saturday.

### CALZADOS CANTERO SHOES

Map p252 (⌨91 447 07 35; Plaza de Olavide 12; ☉9.45am-2pm & 4.45-8.30pm Mon-Fri, 9.45am-2pm Sat; Ⓜ Iglesia) A charming old-world shoe store, Calzados Cantero sells a range of shoes at rock-bottom prices. But it's most famous for its rope-soled *alpargatas* (espadrilles), which start from €8. This is a *barrio* classic, the sort of store to which parents bring their children as their own parents did a generation before.

### PASAJES LIBRERÍA
### INTERNACIONAL BOOKS

Map p252 (⌨91 310 12 45; www.pasajeslibros.com; Calle de Génova 3; ☉10am-8.30pm Mon-Sat; Ⓜ Alonso Martínez) One of the best bookshops in Madrid, Pasajes has an extensive English section (downstairs at the back), which includes high-quality fiction (if it's a new release, it'll be the first bookshop in town to have it), as well as history, Spanish subject matter, travel, and a few literary magazines.

### TIENDA REAL MADRID SPORTS & OUTDOORS

(⌨91 458 72 59; www.realmadrid.com; Gate 55, Estadio Santiago Bernabéu, Av de Concha Espina 1; ☉10am-9pm Mon-Sat, 11am-7.30pm Sun; Ⓜ Santiago Bernabéu) The club shop of Real Madrid sells the full gamut of football memorabilia. From the shop window, you can see down onto the stadium itself.

### EL DRAGÓN LECTOR BOOKS

Map p252 (⌨91 448 60 15; www.eldragonlector.com; Calle de Sagunto 20; ☉10am-2pm & 5-8pm Mon-Fri, 10.30am-2pm Sat; Ⓜ Iglesia) Tucked away in a quiet corner of Chamberí, this fab little bookstore for little people has mostly Spanish titles, but some English-language ones as well.

### LA TIENDA VERDE MAPS, BOOKS

(⌨91 535 38 10; www.tiendaverde.es; Calle de Maudes 23; ☉10am-2pm & 5-8pm Mon-Fri, 10am-2pm Sat; Ⓜ Cuatro Caminos) La Tienda Verde sells hiking maps (the best Spanish ones are *Prames* and *Adrados*) and guides.

### MERCADILLO MARQUÉS
### DE VIANA MARKET

(El Rastrillo; Calle del Marqués de Viana; ☉9am-2pm Sun; Ⓜ Tetuán) This calmer version of rowdy El Rastro (p72) is located in northern Madrid.

## 🏃 SPORTS & ACTIVITIES

### ROLAND SCHWEGLER MASSAGE

Map p252 (⌨658 023261; www.rolandfisio.com; Calle del Castillo 13; 25/50min €27/38; ☉10am-8pm Mon-Fri; Ⓜ Iglesia) For an excellent massage at a very reasonable price, German-turned-*madrileño* Roland Schwegler is experienced in all types of massage and speaks Spanish, German and English.

### INTERNATIONAL HOUSE LANGUAGE

Map p252 (⌨902 141517; www.ihmadrid.es; Calle de Zurbano 8; Ⓜ Alonso Martínez) Intensive courses lasting two/four weeks cost €420/740 (20 hours per week) to €540/1040 (30 hours per week). Staff can organise accommodation with local families.

### COOKING CLUB COOKING

(⌨91 323 29 58; Calle de Veza 33; per person from €55; Ⓜ Valdeacederas) This respected program of classes encompasses a vast range of cooking styles.

# Day Trips from Madrid

### San Lorenzo de El Escorial p159

One of Spain's grandest monuments, this Unesco World Heritage–listed palace-monastery complex combines a cool mountain setting with the imposing grandeur of imperial Spain.

### Toledo p161

Toledo is a beautifully sited, architecturally distinguished city with signposts to its glory days as a crossroads of civilisation.

### Segovia p164

A Roman aqueduct, a castle that inspired Disney and a colour scheme of sandstone and warm terracotta make Segovia one of the most agreeable towns close to Madrid.

### Ávila p166

Surrounded by the finest medieval walls in Spain, Ávila is an evocative Castilian city that's the spiritual home to the cult of Santa Teresa.

### Aranjuez p168

A royal getaway down through the centuries, Aranjuez has an extraordinary palace and expansive gardens grafted onto a delightfully small-town canvas.

### Chinchón p168

Home to one of the prettiest town squares in Spain, Chinchón is a world away from downtown Madrid, with fabulous food thrown in.

MARQUES/SHUTTERSTOCK ©

## TOP SIGHT
# SAN LORENZO DE EL ESCORIAL

Home to the majestic (and Unesco World Heritage–listed) monastery and palace complex of San Lorenzo de El Escorial, this one-time royal getaway is one of Madrid's most worthwhile excursions. First built on the orders of King Felipe II in the 16th century as both a royal palace and as a mausoleum for Felipe's parents, Carlos I and Isabel, it's an extraordinary place filled with art and surrounded by glorious gardens.

### First Steps
Resist the rush to the heart of the complex and linger over the monastery's main entrance on the western side of the complex. Above the gateway a statue of St Lawrence stands watch, holding a symbolic gridiron, the instrument of his martyrdom (he was roasted alive on one).

### Patio de los Reyes
After passing St Lawrence and grimacing at his fate, you'll first enter the Patio de los Reyes (Patio of the Kings), which houses the statues of the six kings of Judah. Admiring these statues, it's difficult not to marvel at the arrogance of the Spanish royals who saw nothing amiss in comparing themselves to the great kings of the past.

### Basilica
Directly ahead of the Patio de los Reyes lies the sombre basilica. As you enter, look up at the unusual flat vaulting by the choir stalls. Once inside the church proper, turn left to view Benvenuto Cellini's white Carrara marble statue of Christ crucified (1576) – it's one of the most underrated masterpieces of the complex.

## DON'T MISS
- ➡ Patio de los Reyes
- ➡ Basílica
- ➡ El Greco Paintings
- ➡ Museums
- ➡ Salas Capitulares
- ➡ Jardín del Príncipe

## PRACTICALITIES
- ➡ ☑91 890 78 18
- ➡ www.patrimonio nacional.es
- ➡ adult/concession €10/5, guide/audioguide €4/3, EU citizens free last 3 hours Wed & Thu
- ➡ ☉10am-8pm Apr-Sep, to 6pm Oct-Mar, closed Mon

## EL GRECO

The ground floor contains various treasures, including some tapestries and an El Greco painting. Impressive as the painting is, it's a far cry from El Greco's dream of decorating the whole complex; he actually came to Spain from Greece in 1577 hoping to get a job decorating El Escorial, although Felipe II rejected him as a court artist.

## Two Museums

After wondering at what might have been had El Greco been given a free hand, head downstairs to the northeastern corner of the complex. You pass through the Museo de Arquitectura and the Museo de Pinturaf. The former tells (in Spanish) the story of how the complex was built, the latter contains 16th-and17th-century Italian, Spanish and Flemish art.

## Up & Down

The route through the monastery takes you upstairs into a gallery known as the Palacio de Felipe II or Palacio de los Austrias. You'll then descend to the 17th-century Panteón de los Reyes (Crypt of the Kings), where almost all Spain's monarchs since Carlos I are interred. It's a sober, domed and slightly claustrophobic structure with royal tombs piled four-high around the walls. Backtracking a little, you're in the Panteón de los Infantes (Crypt of the Princesses), with its white marble tombs.

## Salas Capitulares

Stairs lead up from the cloistered Patio de los Evangelistas (Patio of the Gospels) to the Salas Capitulares (chapterhouses) in the southeastern corner of the monastery. These bright, airy rooms, whose ceilings are richly frescoed, contain a treasure chest of works by El Greco, Titian, Tintoretto, José de Ribera and Hieronymus Bosch (known as El Bosco to Spaniards).

## Huerta de los Frailes

Just south of the monastery is the **Huerta de los Frailes** (Friars Garden; ☺10am-8pm Apr-Sep, to 6pm Oct-Mar, closed Mon), which merits a stroll. As royal gardens go, it's fairly modest, but can be a wonderfully tranquil spot when the rest of the complex is swarming with visitors.

## Jardín del Príncipe

The **Prince's Garden** (☺10am-8pm Apr-Sep, to 6pm Oct-Mar, closed Mon) **FREE**, which leads down to the town of El Escorial (and the train station), is a lovely monumental garden. It contains the **Casita del Príncipe** (www.patrimonionacional.es; €5; ☺10am-8pm Apr-Sep, to 6pm Oct-Mar, closed Mon), a little neoClassical gem built in 1772 by Juan de Villanueva under Carlos III for his heir, Carlos IV.

# Toledo

## Explore

Toledo is truly one of Spain's most magnificent cities. Dramatically sited atop a gorge overlooking the Río Tajo, it was known as the 'city of three cultures' in the Middle Ages, a place where – legend has it – Christian, Muslim and Jewish communities peacefully coexisted. Unsurprisingly, rediscovering the vestiges of this unique cultural synthesis remains modern Toledo's most compelling attraction. Horseshoe-arched mosques, Sephardic synagogues and one of Spain's finest Gothic cathedrals cram into its dense historical core. But the layers go much deeper. Further sleuthing will reveal Visigothic and Roman roots. Toledo's other forte is art, in particular the haunting canvases of El Greco, the influential, impossible-to-classify painter with whom the city is synonymous. Justifiably popular with day trippers, try to stay overnight to really appreciate the city in all its haunting glory.

## The Best...

➡ **Sight** Catedral

➡ **Place to Eat** Alfileritos 24 (p163)

➡ **Place to Shop Casa Cuatero** (☑925 22 26 14; www.casacuartero.com; Calle Hombre de Palo 5; ☺10am-2pm & 5-8pm Mon-Fri, 10am-3pm & 4-8pm Sat)

## Top Tip

If you don't feel like taking the bus up into the old town from down below and would like to walk, the worst of the climb can be avoided by taking the *remonte peatonal* (escalator), which starts near the Puerta de Alfonso VI and ends near the Monasterio de Santo Domingo El Antiguo.

## Getting There & Away

➡ **Bus** From Toledo's **bus station** (☑925 21 58 50; www.alsa.es; Bajada Castilla La Mancha), buses depart for Madrid's Plaza Elíptica (from €5.50, one to 1¾ hours) roughly every half-hour; some are direct, some via villages. There are also daily services to Cuenca (€15, 3¼ hours).

➡ **Train** From the pretty **train station** (☑902 240202; www.renfe.es; Paseo de la Rosa), high-speed Alta Velocidad Española (AVE) trains run every hour or so to Madrid (€13, 30 minutes).

## Need to Know

➡ **Location** 71km southwest of Madrid

➡ **Tourist Office** Main Tourist Office (☑925 25 40 30; www.toledo-turismo. com; Plaza Consistorio 1; ☺10am-6pm), Regional Tourist Office (☑925 22 08 43; www. turismocastillalamancha.es; Puerta de Bisagra; ☺10am-2pm & 3-7pm Mon-Fri, 10am-3pm & 4-6pm Sat, 10am-3pm Sun)

# ◉ SIGHTS

★**CATEDRAL DE TOLEDO**          CATHEDRAL
(☑925 22 22 41; www.catedralprimada.es; Plaza del Ayuntamiento; adult/child €12.50/free, incl Museo de Textiles y Orfebrería admission; ☺10am-6pm Mon-Sat, 2-6pm Sun) Toledo's illustrious main church ranks among the top 10 cathedrals in Spain. An impressive example of medieval Gothic architecture, its humongous interior is full of the classic characteristics of the style, rose windows, flying buttresses, ribbed vaults and pointed arches among them. The cathedral's sacristy is a veritable art gallery of old masters, with works by Velázquez, Goya and – of course – El Greco.

From the earliest days of the Visigothic occupation, the current site of the cathedral has been a centre of worship. During Muslim rule, it contained Toledo's central mosque, converted into a church in 1085, but ultimately destroyed 140 years later. Dating from the 1220s and essentially a Gothic structure, the cathedral was rebuilt from scratch in a melting pot of styles, including Mudéjar and Renaissance. The Visigothic influence continues today in the unique celebration of the Mozarabic Rite, a 6th-century liturgy that was allowed to endure after Cardinal Cisneros put its legitimacy to the test by burning missals in a fire of faith; they survived more or less intact. The rite is celebrated in the Capilla Mozarabe at 9am Monday to Saturday, and at 9.45am on Sunday.

The high altar sits in the extravagant **Capilla Mayor**, the masterpiece of which is the *retablo* (altarpiece), with painted wooden sculptures depicting scenes from the lives of Christ and the Virgin Mary; it's flanked by royal tombs. The oldest of the cathedral's magnificent stained-glass pieces is the rose window above the Puerta del Reloj. Behind the main altar lies a mesmerising piece of 18th-century churrigueresque (lavish baroque ornamentation), the **Transparente**, which is illuminated by a light well carved into the dome above.

In the centre of things, the *coro* (choir stall) is a feast of sculpture and carved wooden stalls. The 15th-century lower tier depicts the various stages of the conquest of Granada.

The *tesoro,* however, deals in treasure of the glittery kind. It's dominated by the extraordinary **Custodia de Arfe**: with 18kg of pure gold and 183kg of silver, this 16th-century processional monstrance bristles with some 260 statuettes. Its big day out is the Feast of Corpus Christi, when it is paraded around Toledo's streets.

Other noteworthy features include the sober cloister, off which is the 14th-century **Capilla de San Blas**, with Gothic tombs and stunning frescoes; the gilded **Capilla de Reyes Nuevos**; and the *sala capitular* (chapter house), with its remarkable 500-year-old *artesonado* (wooden Mudéjar ceiling) and portraits of all the archbishops of Toledo.

The highlight of all, however, is the *sacristía* (sacristy), which contains a gallery with paintings by such masters as El Greco, Zurbarán, Caravaggio, Titian, Raphael and Velázquez. It can be difficult to appreciate the packed-together, poorly lit artworks, but it's a stunning assemblage in a small space. In an adjacent chamber, don't miss the spectacular Moorish standard captured in the Battle of Salado in 1340.

An extra €3 gets you entrance to the upper level of the cloister, and the bell tower, which offers wonderful views over the centre of historic Toledo.

★ALCÁZAR     FORTRESS
(Museo del Ejército; ☎925 22 30 38; Calle Alféreces Provisionales; adult/child €5/free, Sun free; ⊙10am-5pm Thu-Tue) At the highest point in the city looms the foreboding Alcázar. Rebuilt under Franco, it has been reopened as a vast military museum. The usual displays of uniforms and medals are here, but the best part is the exhaustive historical section, with an in-depth overview of the nation's history in Spanish and English. The exhibition is epic in scale but like a well-run marathon, it's worth the physical (and mental) investment.

MONASTERIO SAN
JUAN DE LOS REYES     MONASTERY
(☎925 22 38 02; www.sanjuandelosreyes.org; Plaza de San Juan de los Reyes 2; €2.80; ⊙10am-6.30pm Jun-Sep, to 5.30pm Oct-May) This imposing 15th-century Franciscan monastery and church was provocatively founded in the heart of the Jewish quarter by the Catholic monarchs Isabel and Fernando to demonstrate the supremacy of their faith. The rulers had planned to be buried here but eventually ended up in their prize conquest, Granada. The highlight is the amazing two-level cloister, a harmonious fusion of late ('flamboyant') Gothic downstairs and Mudéjar architecture upstairs, with superb statuary, arches, vaulting, elaborate pinnacles and gargoyles surrounding a lush garden.

IGLESIA DE SANTO TOMÉ     CHURCH
(☎925 25 60 98; www.santotome.org; Plaza del Conde; adult/child €2.80/free; ⊙10am-6.45pm mid-Mar–mid-Oct, 10am-5.45pm mid-Oct–mid-Mar) Iglesia de Santo Tomé contains El

## EL GRECO IN TOLEDO

Few artists are as closely associated with a city as El Greco is with Toledo. Born in Crete in 1541, Domenikos Theotokopoulos (El Greco; the Greek) moved to Venice in 1567 to be schooled as a Renaissance artist. Under the tutelage of masters such as Tintoretto, he learned to express dramatic scenes with few colours, concentrating the observer's interest in the faces of his portraits and leaving the rest in relative obscurity, a characteristic that remained one of his hallmarks.

El Greco came to Spain in 1577 hoping to get a job decorating El Escorial, but Felipe II rejected him as a court artist. In Toledo, the painter managed to cultivate a healthy clientele and command good prices. He had to do without the patronage of the cathedral administrators, who were the first of many clients to haul him to court for his obscenely high fees.

As Toledo's fortunes declined, so did El Greco's personal finances, and although the works of his final years are among his best, he often found himself unable to pay the rent. He died in 1614, leaving his works scattered about the city.

Greco's most famous masterpiece *El entierro del conde de Orgaz* (The Burial of the Count of Orgaz), which is accessed by a separate entrance on Plaza del Conde. When the count was buried in 1322, Sts Augustine and Stephen supposedly descended from heaven to attend the funeral. El Greco's work depicts the event, complete with miracle guests including himself, his son and Cervantes.

### MUSEO DE SANTA CRUZ                    MUSEUM

(☑925 22 10 36; Calle de Cervantes 3; adult/child €5/free; ⊘9.45am-6.15pm Mon-Sat, 10am-2.30pm Sun) It's hard to imagine that this 16th-century building was once a hospital. If only modern hospitals were equipped with the kind of ornate plateresque portico that welcomes you to this beautiful arts and ceramics museum. The pièce de résistance is the huge ground-floor gallery laid out in the shape of a cross. The various art and sculpture exhibits are backed up by interesting explanatory boards that place all the pieces into their historical context.

### ★SINAGOGA DEL TRÁNSITO            SYNAGOGUE, MUSEUM

(☑925 22 36 65; http://museosefardi.mcu.es; Calle Samuel Leví; adult/child €3/1.50, after 2pm Sat & all day Sun free; ⊘9.30am-7.30pm Tue-Sat Mar-Oct, to 6pm Tue-Sat Nov-Feb, 10am-3pm Sun year-round) This magnificent synagogue was built in 1355 by special permission from Pedro I. The synagogue now houses the **Museo Sefardí** (☑925 22 36 65; http://museo sefardi.mcu.es; ⊘9.30am-6pm Mon-Sat, 10am-3pm Sun). The vast main prayer hall has been expertly restored and the Mudéjar decoration and intricately carved pine ceiling are striking. Exhibits provide an insight into the history of Jewish culture in Spain, and include archaeological finds, a memorial garden, costumes and ceremonial artefacts.

### MEZQUITA DEL CRISTO DE LA LUZ                          MOSQUE

(☑925 25 41 91; Calle del Cristo de la Luz; adult/child €2.80/free; ⊘10am-2pm & 3.30-5.45pm Mon-Fri, 10am-5.45pm Sat & Sun) On the northern slopes of town you'll find a modest, yet beautiful, mosque (the only one remaining of Toledo's 10) where architectural traces of Toledo's medieval Muslim conquerors are still in evidence. Built around AD 1000, it suffered the usual fate of being converted into a church (hence the religious frescoes), but the original vaulting and arches survived.

### MUSEO DEL GRECO                MUSEUM, GALLERY

(☑925 22 44 05; www.mecd.gob.es/mgreco; Paseo del Tránsito; adult/child €3/1.50, from 2pm Sat & all day Sun free; ⊘9.30am-7.30pm Tue-Sat Mar-Oct, to 6pm Nov-Feb, 10am-3pm Sun) In the early 20th century, an aristocrat bought what he thought was El Greco's house and did a meritorious job of returning it to period style. He was wrong – El Greco never lived here – but the museum remains. As well as the house itself, there are fascinating excavated cellars from a Jewish-quarter palace and a good selection of paintings, including a Zurbarán, a set of the apostles by El Greco and works by his son and followers.

## ✖ EATING & DRINKING

### ★ALFILERITOS 24            MODERN SPANISH €€

(☑925 23 96 25; www.alfileritos24.com; Calle de los Alfileritos 24; mains €19-20, bar food €4.50-12; ⊘9.30am-midnight Sun-Thu, to 1am Fri & Sat) The 14th-century surroundings of columns, beams and barrel-vault ceilings are snazzily coupled with modern artwork and bright dining rooms in an atrium space spread over four floors. The menu demonstrates an innovative flourish in the kitchen, with dishes such as green rice with quail or loins of venison with baked-in-the-bag Reineta apple.

### LA ABADÍA                        CASTILIAN, TAPAS €€

(☑925 25 11 40; www.abadiatoledo.com; Plaza de San Nicolás 3; raciones €7-15; ⊘bar 8am-midnight, restaurant 1-4pm & 8.30pm-midnight) In a former 16th-century palace, this atmospheric bar and restaurant has arches, niches and coloured bottles lined up as decoration, spread throughout a warren of brick-and-stone-clad rooms. The menu includes lightweight dishes and tapas, but the three-course 'Menú de Montes de Toledo' (€20) is a fabulous collection of tastes from the nearby mountains, including partridge, wild mushrooms and almonds.

### ★ADOLFO                   MODERN EUROPEAN €€€

(☑925 22 73 21; www.adolforestaurante.com; Callejón Hombre de Palo 7; mains €25-28, set menu €76; ⊘1-4pm & 8pm-midnight Mon-Sat, 1-4pm Sun) Toledo doffs its hat to fine dining at this temple of good food and market freshness. Run by notable La Mancha–born chef Adolfo Muñoz, the restaurant has been around for over 25 years, and in that time has morphed into one of Spain's best gourmet establishments. Partridge is the speciality.

★**LIBRO TABERNA EL
INTERNACIONAL**                    BAR, CAFE
(☑925 67 27 65; www.facebook.com/librotaberna
toledo; Calle de la Ciudad 15; ☺8pm-1.30am Tue-
Thu, noon-1.30am Fri & Sat, noon-4pm Sun) 🌿
If you think Toledo is more touristy than
trendy, you clearly haven't dipped your hipster detector into the cool confines of El Internacional, a proud purveyor of slow food,
overflowing bookcases, rescued 1970s armchairs and, of course, beards.

# Segovia

## Explore

Unesco World Heritage–listed Segovia has
always had a whiff of legend about it, not
least in the myths that the city was founded
by Hercules or by the son of Noah. It may
also have something to do with the fact that
nowhere else in Spain has such a stunning
monument to Roman grandeur (the soaring
aqueduct) surviving in the heart of a vibrant modern city. Or maybe it's because art
really has imitated life Segovia-style – Walt
Disney is said to have modelled Sleeping
Beauty's castle in California's Disneyland on
Segovia's Alcázar. Whatever it is, the effect
is stunning: a magical city of warm terracotta and sandstone hues set amid the rolling hills of Castilla, against the backdrop of
the Sierra de Guadarrama.

## The Best...

➡ **Sight** Acueducto
➡ **Place to Eat** Casa Duque
➡ **Place to Drink** Bodega del Barbero

## Top Tip

Unless you're in a hurry to get back, consider taking the slow train to Madrid. From
Segovia it climbs up through the quiet villages of the Sierra de Guadarrama foothills,
before dropping down to Madrid.

## Getting There & Away

➡ **Bus** The bus station is just off Paseo de
Ezequiel González. **La Sepulvedana** (☑902
119699; www.lasepulvedana.es) buses run half-
hourly to Segovia from Madrid's Paseo de
la Florida bus stop (€7.89, 1½ hours). Buses
also depart to Ávila (€6.80, one hour, eight

daily) and Salamanca (€16, 2½ hours, four
daily), among other destinations.
➡ **Car & Motorcycle** Of the two main roads
down to the AP6, which links Madrid and
Galicia, the N603 is the prettier.
➡ **Train** There are a couple of services by
train operated by **Renfe** (☑902 240202; www.
renfe.es): just three normal trains run daily
from Madrid to Segovia (€8.25, two hours),
leaving you at the main train station 2.5km
from the aqueduct. The faster option is
the high-speed Avant (€12.90, 28 minutes),
which deposits you at the newer Segovia-
Guiomar station, 5km from the aqueduct.

## Need to Know

➡ **Location** 90km northwest of Madrid
➡ **Tourist Office** Centro de Recepción de
Visitantes (☑921 46 67 21; www.turismo
desegovia.com; Plaza del Azoguejo 1; ☺10am-
8pm Mon-Sat, to 7pm Sun Apr-Sep, 10am-6.30pm
Mon-Sat, to 5pm Sun Oct-Mar) Regional Tourist
Office (☑921 46 60 70; www.segoviaturismo.es;
Plaza Mayor 10; ☺9.30am-2pm & 5-8pm Mon-Sat,
9.30am-5pm Sun Jul–mid-Sep, 9.30am-2pm &
4-7pm Mon-Sat, 9.30am-5pm Sun mid-Sep–Jun)

## ⊙ SIGHTS

★**ACUEDUCTO**                    LANDMARK
Segovia's most recognisable symbol is El
Acueducto (Roman Aqueduct), an 894m-
long engineering wonder that looks like an
enormous comb plunged into Segovia. First
raised here by the Romans in the 1st century
AD, the aqueduct was built with not a drop
of mortar to hold the more than 20,000 uneven granite blocks together. It's made up of
163 arches and, at its highest point in Plaza
del Azoguejo, rises 28m high.

★**ALCÁZAR**                    CASTLE
(☑921 46 07 59; www.alcazardesegovia.com; Plaza de la Reina Victoria Eugenia; adult/concession/
child under 6yr €5.50/5/free, tower €2.50,
audioguides €3; ☺10am-6.30pm Oct-Mar, to
7.30pm Apr-Sep; 👶) Rapunzel towers, turrets
topped with slate witches' hats and a deep
moat at its base make the Alcázar a pro-
totype fairy-tale castle – so much so that
its design inspired Walt Disney's vision of
Sleeping Beauty's castle. Fortified since Roman days, the site takes its name from the
Arabic *al-qasr* (fortress). It was rebuilt in the
13th and 14th centuries, but the whole lot
burned down in 1862. What you see today

## THE DEVIL'S WORK

Although no one really doubts that the Romans built the aqueduct, a local legend asserts that two millennia ago a young girl, tired of carrying water from the well, voiced a willingness to sell her soul to the devil if an easier solution could be found. No sooner said than done. The devil worked through the night, while the girl recanted and prayed to God for forgiveness. Hearing her prayers, God sent the sun into the sky earlier than usual, catching the devil unawares with only a single stone lacking to complete the structure. The girl's soul was saved, but it seems like she got her wish anyway. Perhaps God didn't have the heart to tear down the aqueduct.

is an evocative, over-the-top reconstruction of the original.

### ★CATEDRAL                                    CATHEDRAL

(🖉921 46 22 05; www.turismodesegovia.com; Plaza Mayor; adult/concession €3/2, Sun morning free, tower tour €5; ⊗9am-9pm Mon-Sat, 1.15-9pm Sun Apr-Oct, 9.30am-5.30pm Mon-Sat, 1.15-5.30pm Sun Nov-Mar, tower tours 10.30pm & 12.30pm year-round, plus 4.30pm Apr-Oct, 4pm Nov-Mar) Started in 1525 on the site of a former chapel, Segovia's cathedral is a powerful expression of Gothic architecture that took almost 200 years to complete. The austere three-nave interior is anchored by an imposing choir stall and enlivened by 20-odd chapels, including the **Capilla del Cristo del Consuelo**, with its magnificent Romanesque doorway, and the **Capilla de la Piedad**, containing an important altarpiece by Juan de Juni. Join an hour-long guided tour to climb the tower for fabulous views.

### PLAZA MAYOR                                    SQUARE

The shady Plaza Mayor is the nerve centre of old Segovia, lined by an eclectic assortment of buildings, arcades and cafes and with an open pavilion in its centre. It's also the site of the *catedral* and the regional tourist office.

### PLAZA DE SAN MARTÍN                            SQUARE

This is one of the most captivating small plazas in Segovia. The square is presided over by a statue of Juan Bravo; the 14th-century **Torreón de Lozoya** (🖉921 46 24 61; Plaza de San Martín 5; ⊗5-9pm Tue-Fri, noon-2pm & 5-9pm

Sat & Sun) FREE, a tower that now houses exhibitions; and the **Iglesia de San Martín** (⊗before & after Mass), a Romanesque jewel with a Mudéjar tower and arched gallery.

### IGLESIA DE VERA CRUZ                          CHURCH

(🖉921 43 14 75; Carretera de Zamarramala; €2; ⊗10.30am-1.30pm & 4-7pm Tue-Sun Apr-Sep, 4-6pm Tue, 10.30am-1.30pm & 4-6pm Wed-Sun Oct-Mar) This 12-sided church is one of the best preserved of its kind in Europe. Built in the early 13th century by the Knights Templar and based on Jerusalem's Church of the Holy Sepulchre, it once housed a piece of the Vera Cruz (True Cross), which now rests in the nearby village church of Zamarramala (on view only at Easter). The curious two-storey chamber in the circular nave (the inner temple) is where the knights' secret rites took place.

## ✖ EATING & DRINKING

### ★CASA DUQUE                              SPANISH €€€

(🖉921 46 24 87; www.restauranteduque.es; Calle de Cervantes 12; mains €19.50-24, set menus €35-40; ⊗12.30-4.30pm & 8.30-11.30pm) *Cochinillo asado* (roast suckling pig) has been served at this atmospheric *mesón* (tavern) since the 1890s. For the uninitiated, try the *menú de degustación* (€40), which includes *cochinillo*. Downstairs is the informal *cueva* (cave), where you can get tapas (snacks) and full-bodied *cazuelas* (stews). Reservations recommended.

### ★MESÓN JOSÉ MARÍA                        CASTILIAN €€

(🖉921 46 11 11; www.restaurantejosemaria.com; Calle del Cronista Lecea 11; mains €14-26; ⊗restaurant 1-4pm & 8-11.30pm, bar 9am-1am Sun-Thu, 10am-2am Fri & Sat; 🐾) Offers fine bar tapas and five dining rooms serving exquisite *cochinillo asado* and other local specialities – most of which, including the suckling pig, are displayed in the window. The bar is standing-room only at lunchtime.

### ★RESTAURANTE EL FOGÓN SEFARDÍ              JEWISH €€

(🖉921 46 62 50; www.lacasamudejar.com; Calle de Isabel la Católica 8; tapas from €2.50, mains €12-26, set menus €19-25; ⊗1.30-4.30pm & 7.30-11.30pm) Located within the Hospedería La Gran Casa Mudéjar, this is one of the most original places in town. Sephardic Jewish cuisine is served either on the intimate patio or in the splendid dining hall with original

15th-century Mudéjar flourishes. The theme in the bar is equally diverse. Stop here for a taste of the award-winning tapas.

### BODEGA DEL BARBERO
WINE BAR

(📞921 46 27 70; Calle Alhóndiga 2; ⊙10am-1am Mon-Fri, noon-1am Sat & Sun) Tucked down a narrow street, this intimate bar has a wide range of vino by the glass, good tapas, regular art exhibitions and live music on the outside terrace on summer weekends.

### LA TASQUINA
WINE BAR

(📞921 46 39 14; Calle de Valdeláguila 3; ⊙9pm-late) This wine bar draws crowds large enough to spill out onto the pavement, nursing their wines, *cavas* (sparkling wines) and cheeses.

# Ávila

## Explore

Ávila's old city, surrounded by imposing city walls comprising eight monumental gates, 88 watchtowers and more than 2500 turrets, is one of the best-preserved medieval bastions in Spain. In winter, when an icy wind whistles in off the plains, the old city huddles behind the high stone walls as if seeking protection from the harsh Castilian climate. At night, when the walls are illuminated to magical effect, you'll wonder if you've stumbled into a fairy tale. It's a deeply religious city that for centuries has drawn pilgrims to the cult of Santa Teresa de Ávila, with its many churches, convents and high-walled palaces. As such, Ávila is the essence of Castilla and the epitome of old Spain.

## The Best...

➜ **Sight** Murallas
➜ **Place to Eat** Soul Kitchen (p168)
➜ **Place to Drink** La Bodeguita de San Segundo (p168)

## Top Tip

Ávila is one of the coldest and windiest cities in Spain and winter snow is always a possibility. If you're coming in winter, come prepared.

## Getting There & Away

➜ **Bus** Frequent services run from the **bus station** (📞920 25 65 05; Avenida de Madrid 2) to Segovia (€6.80, one hour), Salamanca

(€7.95, 1½ hours, five daily) and Madrid (€11, 1½ hours); a couple of daily buses also head for the main towns in the Sierra de Gredos.

➜ **Car & Motorcycle** From Madrid the driving time is around one hour; the toll costs €9.35.

➜ **Train** There are **Renfe** (📞902 240202; www.renfe.es) services to Madrid (from €12.25, 1¼ to two hours, up to 17 daily), Salamanca (from €12.25, 1¼ hours, eight daily) and León (from €21.90, three to four hours, five daily).

## Need to Know

➜ **Location** 101km west of Madrid
➜ **Tourist Office Centro de Recepción de Visitantes** (📞920 35 40 00, ext 370; www.avilaturismo.com; Avenida de Madrid 39; ⊙9am-8pm Apr-Sep, to 5.15pm Oct-Mar)

# ◉ SIGHTS

### ★MURALLAS
WALLS

(www.muralladeavila.com; adult/child under 12yr €5/free; ⊙10am-8pm Apr-Oct, to 6pm Nov-Mar; 🅿) Ávila's splendid 12th-century walls stretch for 2.5km atop the remains of earlier Roman and Muslim battlements and rank among the world's best-preserved medieval defensive perimeters. Two sections of the walls can be climbed – a 300m stretch that can be accessed from just inside the **Puerta del Alcázar**, and a longer (1300m) stretch from **Puerta de los Leales** that runs the length of the old city's northern perimeter. The admission price includes a multilingual audioguide.

### ★CATEDRAL DEL SALVADOR
CATHEDRAL

(📞920 21 16 41; Plaza de la Catedral; admission incl audioguide €5; ⊙10am-7pm Mon-Fri, 10am-8pm Sat, noon-6.30pm Sun Apr-Sep, 10am-5pm Mon-Fri, 10am-6pm Sat, noon-5pm Sun Oct-Mar) Ávila's 12th-century cathedral is both a house of worship and an ingenious fortress: its stout granite apse forms the central bulwark in the historic city walls. The sombre, Gothic-style facade conceals a magnificent interior with an exquisite early-16th-century **altar frieze** showing the life of Jesus, plus Renaissance-era carved choir stalls and a **museum** with an El Greco painting and a splendid silver monstrance by Juan de Arfe. (Push the buttons to illuminate the altar and the choir stalls.)

## WHO WAS SANTA TERESA?

Teresa de Cepeda y Ahumada, probably the most important woman in the history of the Spanish Catholic Church (after the Virgin Mary of course…), was born in Ávila on 28 March 1515, one of 10 children of a merchant family. Raised by Augustinian nuns after her mother's death, she joined the Carmelite order at age 20. After her early, undistinguished years as a nun, she was shaken by a vision of hell in 1560, which crystallised her true vocation: she would reform the Carmelites.

In stark contrast to the opulence of the church in 16th-century Spain, her reforms called for the church to return to its roots, taking on the suffering and simple lifestyle of Jesus Christ. The Carmelites demanded the strictest of piety and even employed flagellation to atone for their sins. Not surprisingly, all this proved extremely unpopular with the mainstream Catholic Church.

With the help of many supporters, Teresa founded convents all over Spain and her writings proved enormously popular. She died in 1582 and was canonised by Pope Gregory XV in 1622.

### MONASTERIO DE SANTO TOMÁS
MONASTERY, MUSEUM

(✆920 22 04 00; www.monasteriosantotomas. com; Plaza de Granada 1; €4; ◷10.30am-9pm Jul & Aug, 10.30am-2pm & 3.30-7.30pm Sep-Jun) Commissioned by the Reyes Católicos (Catholic Monarchs), Fernando and Isabel, and completed in 1492, this monastery is an exquisite example of Isabelline architecture, rich in historical resonance. Three interconnected cloisters lead to the church that contains the alabaster **tomb of Don Juan**, the monarchs' only son. There's also the impressive **Museo Oriental** (Oriental Museum), with 11 rooms of Far Eastern art, plus a more modest **Museo de Historia Natural** (Natural History Museum); both are included in the admission price.

### MONASTERIO DE LA ENCARNACIÓN
MONASTERY

(✆920 21 12 12; Calle de la Encarnación; church free, museum €2; ◷9.30am-1pm & 4-7pm Mon-Fri, 10am-1pm & 4-7pm Sat & Sun May-Sep, 9.30am-1.30pm & 3.30-6pm Mon-Fri, 10am-1pm & 4-6pm Sat & Sun Oct-Apr) North of the city walls, this unadorned Renaissance monastery is where Santa Teresa fully took on the monastic life and lived for 27 years. One of the three main rooms open to the public is where the saint is said to have had a vision of the baby Jesus. Also on display are relics, such as the piece of wood used by Teresa as a pillow (ouch!) and the chair upon which St John of the Cross made his confessions.

### BASÍLICA DE SAN VICENTE
CHURCH

(✆920 25 52 30; www.basilicasanvicente.es; Plaza de San Vicente; admission incl audioguide €2.30; ◷10am-6.30pm Mon-Sat, 4-6pm Sun Apr-Oct, 10am-1.30pm & 4-6.30pm Mon-Sat, 4-6pm Sun Nov-Mar) This graceful church is a masterpiece of Romanesque simplicity: a series of largely Gothic modifications in sober granite contrasted with the warm sandstone of the Romanesque original. Work started in the 11th century, supposedly on the site where three martyrs – Vicente and his sisters, Sabina and Cristeta – were slaughtered by the Romans in the early 4th century. Their canopied **cenotaph** is an outstanding piece of Romanesque style, with nods to the Gothic.

### CONVENTO DE SANTA TERESA
CHURCH, MUSEUM

(✆920 21 10 30; www.teresadejesus.com; Plaza de la Santa; church & relic room free, museum €2; ◷9.30am-1.30pm & 3.30-8pm Tue-Sun) Built in 1636 around the room where the saint was born in 1515, this is the epicentre of the cult surrounding Teresa. There are three attractions in one here: the church, a relics room and a museum. Highlights include the gold-adorned **chapel** (built over the room where she was born), the baroque **altar** and the (albeit macabre) **relic** of the saint's ring finger, complete with ring. Apparently Franco kept it beside his bedside throughout his rule.

### IGLESIA DE SANTO TOMÉ EL VIEJO
CHURCH

(Plaza de Italia; admission incl Museo Provincial €1.20, Sat & Sun free; ◷10am-2pm & 5-8pm Tue-Sat, 10am-2pm Sun Jul-Sep, 10am-2pm & 4-7pm Tue-Sat, 10am-2pm Sun Oct-Jun) This church dates from the 13th century, and it was from this pulpit that Santa Teresa was castigated most vehemently for her reforms. It has been restored to house mostly Roman foundation stones and a splendid **floor mosaic**.

**WORTH A DETOUR**

## ARANJUEZ & CHINCHÓN

Aranjuez was founded as a royal pleasure retreat, away from the riff-raff of Madrid, and it remains a place to escape the rigours of city life. The **Palacio Real** (☑91 891 07 40; www.patrimonionacional.es; palace adult/concession €9/4, guide/audioguide €4/3, EU citizens last 3hr Wed & Thu free, gardens free; ⊙palace 10am-8pm Apr-Sep, to 6pm Oct-Mar, gardens 8am-9.30pm mid-Jun–mid-Aug, shorter hours mid-Aug–mid-Jun) started as one of Felipe II's modest summer palaces but took on a life of its own as a succession of royals lavished money upon it. The obligatory guided tour (in Spanish) provides insight into the palace's art and history. In the lush gardens, you'll find the Casa de Marinos, which contains the **Museo de Falúas** (⊙10am-5.15pm Oct-Mar, to 6.15pm Apr-Sep), a museum of royal pleasure boats from days gone by. The 18th-century neoclassical **Casa del Labrador** (☑91 891 03 05; €5; ⊙10am-8pm Apr-Sep, to 6pm Oct-Mar) is also worth a visit. If you're here for lunch, try the Michelin-starred **Casa José** (☑91 891 14 88; www.casajose.es; Calle de Abastos 32; mains €14-29, set menu €75; ⊙1.45-3.30pm & 9-11.30pm Tue-Sat, 1.45-3.30pm Sun Sep-Jul) or the more informal **Casa Pablete** (☑918 91 03 81; Calle de Stuart 108; tapas from €3, mains €12-22; ⊙1.30-4pm & 8.30-11pm Wed-Sun, 1.30-4pm Mon). Aranjuez is accessible from Madrid aboard C3 *cercanía* (local trains serving suburbs and nearby towns) that leave every 15 or 20 minutes from Madrid's Atocha station (€3.40).

Another fine day trip is to Chinchón, just 45km from Madrid yet worlds away. Visiting here is like stepping back into a charming, ramshackle past, with most of the appeal concentrated around the glorious **Plaza Mayor**. **Café de la Iberia** (☑91 894 08 47; www.cafedelaiberia.com; Plaza Mayor 17; mains €14-26; ⊙12.30-4.30pm & 8-10.30pm) is the pick of the restaurants serving roasted meats surrounding the square. To get here, the La Veloz bus 337 leaves half-hourly to Chinchón from Avenida del Mediterráneo in Madrid, 100m west of Plaza del Conde de Casal. The 50-minute ride costs €3.35.

★**LOS CUATRO POSTES**                VIEWPOINT

Northwest of the city, on the road to Salamanca, Los Cuatro Postes provides the best views of Ávila's walls. It also marks the place where Santa Teresa and her brother were caught by their uncle as they tried to run away from home (they were hoping to achieve martyrdom at the hands of the Muslims). The best views are at night.

## ✖ EATING & DRINKING

★**SOUL KITCHEN**                CASTILIAN €€

(☑920 21 34 83; www.soulkitchen.es; Calle de Caballeros 13; mains €9-23; ⊙10am-midnight Mon-Fri, 11am-2am Sat, 11am-midnight Sun) This place has the kind of energy that can seem lacking elsewhere. The eclectic menu changes regularly and ranges from salads with dressings like chestnut and fig to hamburgers with cream of *setas* (oyster mushrooms). Lighter dishes include bruschetta with tasty toppings. Live music, poetry readings (and similar) happen in summer.

**MESÓN DEL RASTRO**                CASTILIAN €€

(☑920 35 22 25; www.elrastroavila.com; Plaza del Rastro 1; mains €11-24; ⊙1-4pm & 9-11pm) The dark-wood-beamed interior announces immediately that this is a bastion of robust Castilian cooking, which it has been since 1881. Expect delicious mainstays such as *judías del barco de Ávila* (white beans, often with chorizo, in a thick sauce) and *cordero asado* (roast lamb), mercifully light salads and, regrettably, the occasional coach tour.

★**LA BODEGUITA DE SAN SEGUNDO**                WINE BAR

(☑920 25 73 09; Calle de San Segundo 19; ⊙11am-midnight Wed-Mon) Situated in the 16th-century Casa de la Misericordia, this superb wine bar is standing-room only most nights, though more tranquil in the quieter afternoon hours. Its wine list is renowned throughout Spain, with over a thousand wines to choose from and tapas-sized creative servings of cheeses and cured meats as the perfect accompaniment.

# Sleeping

*Madrid has high-quality accommodation at prices that haven't been seen in the centre of other European capitals in decades. Five-star temples to good taste and a handful of buzzing hostels bookend a fabulous collection of midrange hotels; most of the midrangers are creative originals, blending high levels of comfort with an often-quirky sense of style.*

## Hotels

Madrid's accommodation scene keeps getting better. The best of the old have survived, upgrading their facilities while adhering to old-style values of discretion and hospitality, but they have been joined by modern designer hotels that capture the essence of Spain's style revolution.

Many of these newcomers have taken the shells of charming traditional architecture and converted their interiors into chic, high-tech accommodation that blends the casual and the classy – two essential elements in the irresistible personality of contemporary Spain. These *hoteles con encanto* (hotels with charm) share the market with stylish, modern monuments to 21st-century fashions that seem to push the boundaries of design in ways that were once the preserve of Barcelona, that eternal rival up the road.

It's in the midrange price category that you'll find the best examples of this revolution. At surprisingly reasonable prices and devoid of stuffiness, hotels in this category enable you to feel pampered without the price tag of a five-star hotel – the choice can be seemingly endless and examples are to be found in every Madrid neighbourhood. And if the top end is your piece of the market, you'll be able to choose between the grand old dames that are counted among Europe's elite of luxury hotels and newly minted boutique hotels.

## Hostales

The Spanish *hostal* is a cross between a cheap hotel and a hostel and usually represents outstanding value. The better ones can be bright and spotless, with private rooms featuring full en suite bathroom (*baño completo;* most often with a shower – *ducha* – rather than bathtub), usually a TV and air-conditioning and/or heating. Some are new and slick, but the overwhelming majority are family run, adhering to old-style decor and warmth.

## Hostels

At the budget end of the market, Madrid has its share of hostel-style accommodation with multibed (usually bunk) dorms and busy communal areas. They're cheap, usually plugged in to the local nightlife scene and are terrific places to meet other travellers.

SLEEPING

## NEED TO KNOW

### Price Ranges
The following price ranges refer to a double room with bathroom:

| € | under €75 |
| €€ | €75–€200 |
| €€€ | over €200 |

### Useful Websites
**Centro de Turismo de Madrid** (www.esmadrid. com) Good for an overview of the accommodation scene.

**Spain Select** (www. spain-select.com) Dozens of apartments across Madrid for short or long stays.

**Atrapalo** (www.atrapalo. com) Spanish-language booking service for flights and hotels.

**Lonely Planet** (www. lonelyplanet.com/spain/ madrid/hotels) Reviews and online booking.

## Lonely Planet's Top Choices

**Central Palace Madrid** (p172) Palace views and gorgeous rooms.

**Hotel Silken Puerta América** (p178) Landmark hotel with rooms designed by world-famous architects.

**Praktik Metropol** (p175) Quirky decor, fine views and high levels of comfort.

**Hotel Orfila** (p178) Arguably Madrid's top address and best service.

**ApartoSuites Jardines de Sabatini** (p178) Perfect combination of location and style.

## Best by Budget

### €
**Madrid City Rooms** (p174) Outstanding service and excellent rooms in the centre.

**Lapepa Chic B&B** (p176) Fabulous budget B&B with attention to detail.

**Hostal Main Street Madrid** (p177) Central and very cool *hostal*.

**Flat 5 Madrid** (p177) One of Madrid's best deals away from the tourist hordes.

**Hostal Madrid** (p172) Renovated rooms and friendly service downtown.

### €€
**Posada del León de Oro** (p174) La Latina at its most atmospheric.

**Catalonia Las Cortes** (p175) Great rooms, service and Huertas location.

**NH Collection Palacio de Tepa** (p175) Palace on the outside, stylish rooms within.

### €€€
**Hotel Ritz** (p176) Quite simply one of Europe's grandest hotels.

**Villa Magna** (p177) Refined Salamanca address for the well heeled.

**Westin Palace** (p176) Near faultless five-star address.

**Hotel Urban** (p175) Swish downtown temple to modern luxury.

## Best for Contemporary Cool

**Only You Hotel** (p178) Designer rooms with unexpected extras.

**Hotel One Shot Luchana 22** (p178) Converted Chamberí palace in a modern style.

**Artrip** (p174) Artsy location with stylish rooms.

**VP El Madroño** (p176) Salamanca's swishest address in a quiet setting.

**Hotel Alicia** (p174) Huertas' coolest address, right on Plaza de Santa Ana.

## Best Rooms with a View

**ApartoSuites Jardines de Sabatini** (p178) Views over the gardens to the palace.

**Hotel Vincci Capitol** (p172) Grab a room with views down the grand old boulevard.

**Me Melía Reina Victoria** (p176) Perfect vantage point for Plaza de Santa Ana.

**Praktik Metropol** (p175) Fab downtown views high above Gran Vía.

## Best Apartments

**Hostal Madrid** (p172) Rambling collection of apartments, old and new.

**60 Balconies Atocha** (p176) Architect-designed digs with fine views.

**Apartasol** (p175) Modern apartments across the city centre.

# Where to Stay

| NEIGHBOURHOOD | FOR | AGAINST |
| --- | --- | --- |
| **Plaza Mayor & Royal Madrid** | Walking distance to most attractions, as well as shopping and restaurants; good metro connections elsewhere. | Can be noisy, although generally from night-time revellers rather than traffic. |
| **La Latina & Lavapiés** | Excellent central location, combining medieval architecture with terrific restaurants and tapas bars. | Uphill walk from the art galleries; can be noisy in the evening (less so later at night). |
| **Sol, Santa Ana & Huertas** | Close to most attractions and excellent eating, drinking and entertainment options. | Possibly Madrid's noisiest neighbourhood, with all-night revellers, especially on weekends; steep hills can test weary legs. |
| **El Retiro & the Art Museums** | You're right next door (or just around the corner) from Madrid's big three art galleries. | Traffic noise can be a problem; most restaurants at least a 10-minute walk away. |
| **Salamanca** | Puts you in the heart of fantastic shopping and close to good eating options; quieter by night than most Madrid neighbourhoods. | A decent walk from the rest of the city. |
| **Malasaña & Chueca** | Lively streets and wonderful places to eat and drink; sense of Madrid beyond the tourist crowds; gay friendly (Chueca). | Another noisy night-time neighbourhood. |
| **Parque del Oeste & Northern Madrid** | Removed from clamour of downtown but a short metro ride away; immersion in local Madrid life. | Attractions more thinly spread. |

# 🛏 Plaza Mayor & Royal Madrid

## HOSTAL MADRID
HOSTAL, APARTMENT €

Map p232 (☎91 522 00 60; www.hostal-madrid. info; Calle de Esparteros 6; s €35-75, d €45-115, d apt €45-150; ❋🛜; Ⓜ Sol) The 24 rooms at this well-run *hostal* have exposed brickwork, updated bathrooms and a look that puts many three-star hotels to shame. They also have terrific apartments (ageing in varying stages of gracefulness and ranging in size from 33 sq metres to 200 sq metres) which have fully equipped kitchens, their own sitting area and bathroom.

Larger apartments (room 51 on the 5th floor is one of the best) have an expansive terrace with good views over the rooftops of central Madrid. It's a favoured haunt of writers (Günter Grass wrote one of his novels in room 53). Fabulous value all round.

## HOSTAL PATRIA
HOSTAL €

Map p232 (☎91 366 21 87; www.hostalpatria.com; 4th fl, Calle Mayor 10; s/d €35/48; ❋🛜; Ⓜ Sol) Simple rooms with parquetry floor are a cut above your *hostal* average and staff are helpful – it's a winning combination. The location, a few steps from the Puerta del Sol, is terrific. Noise can be an issue, but that can be said about most cheaper places in the centre.

## HOTEL JC ROOMS PUERTA DEL SOL
HOTEL €

Map p232 (☎91 559 40 14; www.jchoteles-puerta delsol.com; Calle de la Flora; r €40-62; ❋@🛜; Ⓜ Ópera) Colourful rooms adorned with large photos of Madrid's attractions are reason enough to stay here, with the central location and outrageously reasonable prices added bonuses. Some of the rooms are a bit small, but otherwise it's an excellent choice.

## ★CENTRAL PALACE MADRID
HOTEL €€

Map p232 (☎91 548 20 18; www.centralpalace madrid.com; Plaza de Oriente 2; d without/with view €90/160; ❋🛜; Ⓜ Ópera) Now here's something special. The views alone would be reason enough to come to this hotel and definitely worth paying extra for – rooms with balconies look out over the Palacio Real and Plaza de Oriente. The rooms themselves are lovely and light filled, with tasteful, subtle faux-antique furnishings, comfortable beds, light wood floors and plenty of space.

## HOTEL VINCCI CAPITOL
HOTEL €€

(☎91 521 83 91; www.vinccihoteles.com; Gran Vía 41; r €125-215; ❋🛜🏊; Ⓜ Callao) Located in the landmark Edificio Carrión, this modern hotel has large rooms with muted tones, and some even have the novelty of circular beds. But what makes the hotel stand out are the views – straight down Gran Vía, with its life and grandeur. Not all rooms have views, but there's a 9th-floor viewing area for guests.

One local newspaper gave the hotel a '9' for architecture, a '4' for decoration and a '6' for the comfort of the rooms; they're being a little harsh, but we know what they mean.

## HOTEL MENINAS
BOUTIQUE HOTEL €€

Map p232 (☎91 541 28 05; www.hotelmeninas. com; Calle de Campomanes 7; s/d from €85/95; ❋🛜; Ⓜ Ópera) This is a classy, cool choice. The colour scheme is blacks, whites and greys, with dark-wood floors and splashes of fuchsia and lime green. Flat-screen TVs in every room, modern bathroom fittings, and even a laptop in some rooms, round out the clean lines and latest innovations. Past guests include Viggo Mortensen and Natalie Portman. Some rooms are on the small side.

## PETIT PALACE POSADA DEL PEINE
BOUTIQUE HOTEL €€

(☎91 523 81 51; www.petitpalace.com; Calle de Postas 17; r €105-145; ❋🛜; Ⓜ Sol) This hotel combines a splendid historic building (dating to 1610), brilliant location (just 50m from Plaza Mayor) and modern hi-tech rooms. Rooms are beautifully appointed, bathrooms sparkle with stunning fittings and hydromassage showers, and many historical architectural features remain in situ in the public areas. It's just a pity some of the rooms aren't larger.

## HOTEL JC ROOMS SANTO DOMINGO
HOTEL €€

Map p232 (☎91 547 48 88; www.jchoteles-santo domingo.com; Cuesta de Santo Domingo 16; r €40-75; ❋@🛜; Ⓜ Santo Domingo) Part of the growing JC Rooms portfolio, the Hotel JC Rooms Santo Domingo has smallish themed rooms brimful with colour and with large photos of Madrid and other Spanish attractions. The quality is high and the prices make this a terrific deal. We like the location, too, tucked away between Sol, Ópera and Gran Vía.

### MARIO ROOM MATE · BOUTIQUE HOTEL €€

Map p232 (☑91 548 85 48; www.room-matehotels.com; Calle de Campomanes 4; s/d from €75/85; ❄🕙; ⓂÓpera) Entering this swanky boutique hotel is like crossing the threshold of Madrid's latest nightclub, with staff dressed in all black, black walls and swirls of red lighting in the lobby. Rooms can be small, but have high ceilings, simple furniture and light tones contrasting smoothly with muted colours and dark surfaces. Some rooms are pristine white; others have splashes of colour with zany murals.

### HOTEL FRANCISCO 1 · BOUTIQUE HOTEL €€

Map p232 (☑91 548 02 04; www.hotelfrancisco.com; Calle del Arenal 15; s/d from €85/95; ❄@🕙; ⓂSol, Ópera) This recently overhauled hotel has a wonderful range of rooms, most with hardwood floors, some with design features such as the building's original stone arches, and others with private terraces and a vaguely Japanese aesthetic. The most appealing rooms are those at the upper end, but they're all good in the heart of town.

### HOTEL PRECIADOS · BUSINESS HOTEL €€

Map p232 (☑91 454 44 00; www.preciadoshotel.com; Calle de Preciados 37; r from €97; ❄🕙; ⓂSanto Domingo, Callao) With a classier feel than many of the other business options around town, the Preciados gets rave reviews for its service. Soft lighting, light shades and plentiful glass personalise the rooms and provide an intimate feel.

### THE HAT MADRID · HOTEL, HOSTEL €€

Map p232 (☑91 772 85 72; www.thehatmadrid.com; Calle Imperial 9; dm/r/apt from €20/65/110; ❄@🕙; ⓂSol, La Latina) The Hat Madrid is an excellent choice just down the hill from Plaza Mayor and manages to span all budgets without cheapening the experience. The dorms are lovely and light-filled and you're not made to feel like a second-class citizen. Equally the rooms and apartments have a lovely fresh look. Friendly service rounds out a wonderful experience in a couldn't-be-more-central location.

### CASA DE MADRID · HOTEL €€€

Map p232 (☑91 559 57 91; www.casademadrid.com; 2nd fl, Calle de Arrieta 2; s/d from €200/265, ste from €400; 🕙; ⓂÓpera) Refined, extravagantly decorated rooms make Casa de Madrid a luxurious choice overlooking the Teatro Real. Rooms, in an 18th-century building, are awash with antique furnishings and marble busts, with each built around a theme (eg Japan, India). It's a little like staying at the Ritz, but more discreet.

### GRAN MELIA PALACIO DE LOS DUQUES · HOTEL €€€

Map p232 (☑91 276 47 47; www.melia.com; Cuesta de Santo Domingo 5; d from €280; ⓂSanto Domingo) With a marvellous sense of light and space that you rarely find in Madrid's downtown hotels, the Gran Melia Palacio de Los Duques is a five-star belle. Rooms have a white-and-gold colour scheme that won't be to everyone's tastes, but with supreme levels of comfort, a Thai wellness centre and gorgeous public areas, not to mention faultless service, it's difficult to complain.

### BARCELÓ TORRE DE MADRID · HOTEL €€€

Map p232 (☑91 524 23 99; www.barcelo.com; Plaza de España 18; d €180-310; @🕙🏊; ⓂPlaza de España) This five-star hotel occupies nine floors of Torre Madrid, one of the city's most iconic buildings. With views of the Royal Palace and Gran Vía, a modern design and large comfortable rooms and suites, it's for the discerning traveller. Guests can enjoy the wellness centre, and anyone can stop into the bright and inviting lobby bar for a drink.

## 🛏 La Latina & Lavapiés

### MAD HOSTEL · HOSTEL €

Map p235 (☑91 506 48 40; www.madhostel.com; Calle de la Cabeza 24; dm incl breakfast €24-30; ❄@🕙; ⓂAntón Martín) From the people who brought you **Cat's Hostel** (Map p235; ☑91 369 28 07; www.catshostel.com; Calle de Cañizares 6; dm €12-27; ❄@🕙; ⓂAntón Martín), Mad Hostel is similarly filled with life. The 1st-floor courtyard – with retractable roof – recreates an old Madrid *corrala* (traditional internal or communal patio) and is a wonderful place to chill, while the four-to eight-bed dorm rooms are smallish but clean. There's a small, rooftop bar.

### MOLA! HOSTEL · HOSTEL €

Map p235 (☑663 624143; www.molahostel.com; Calle de Atocha 16; dm €15-20, d from €53; ❄@🕙; ⓂSol, Tirso de Molina) This sparkling new hostel overlooking the Plaza de Jacinto Benavente in the heart of town is a terrific deal. Rooms are colourful, warmly decorated and well sized, and dorms (with four to 10 beds) are rather stylish. It's a friendly place where the staff are eager to connect you with other travellers and for you to make the most of your time in Madrid.

### HOSTAL FONDA HORIZONTE HOSTAL €

Map p235 (☑91 369 09 96; www.hostalhorizonte. com; 2nd fl, Calle de Atocha 28; s/d €45/62 with shared bathroom €33/50; ☎; ⓂAntón Martín) Billing itself as a *hostal* run by travellers for travellers, Hostal Horizonte is a well-run place. Rooms have far more character than your average *hostal,* with high ceilings, deliberately old-world furnishings and modern bathrooms. The King Alfonso XII room is especially well presented.

### ★POSADA DEL LEÓN DE ORO BOUTIQUE HOTEL €€

Map p236 (☑91 119 14 94; www.posadadelleon deoro.com; Calle de la Cava Baja 12; d/ste from €102/155; ❋☎; ⓂLa Latina) This rehabilitated inn has muted colour schemes and generally large rooms. There's a *corrala* (traditional internal or communal patio) at its core and thoroughly modern rooms along one of Madrid's best-loved streets. The downstairs bar is terrific.

### POSADA DEL DRAGÓN BOUTIQUE HOTEL €€

Map p236 (☑91 119 14 24; www.posadadeldragon. com; Calle de la Cava Baja 14; s/d from €73/85; ❋☎; ⓂLa Latina) At last a boutique hotel in the heart of La Latina. This restored 19th-century *posada* sits on one of our favourite Madrid streets, and rooms either look out over it or the pretty internal patio. Most of rooms are on the small side but have extremely comfortable beds and bold, brassy colour schemes and designer everything.

### ARTRIP BOUTIQUE HOTEL €€

Map p235 (☑91 539 32 82; www.artriphotel.com; Calle de Valencia 11; d/ste from €125/155; ❋☎; ⓂLavapiés) For an alternative but supremely comfortable take on Madrid life, Artrip is close to the big-three art museums and surrounded by plenty of private art galleries in the heart of multicultural Lavapiés. Rooms are dazzling white offset by strong splashes of colour and artful use of wooden beams.

## 🛏 Sol, Santa Ana & Huertas

### HOSTAL ADRIANO HOSTAL €

Map p238 (☑91 521 13 39; www.hostaladriano. com; 4th fl, Calle de la Cruz 26; s/d from €50/60; ❋☎; ⓂSol) They don't come any better than

this bright and friendly hostel wedged in the streets that mark the boundary between Sol and Huertas. Most rooms are well sized and each has its own colour scheme. Indeed, more thought has gone into the decoration than in your average *hostal,* from the bed covers to the pictures on the walls.

On the same floor, the owners run the **Hostal Adria Santa Ana** (Map p238; ☑91 521 13 39; www.hostaladriasantaana.com; 4th fl, Calle de la Cruz 26; s/d €65/75; ❋☎; ⓂSol), which is a step up in price, style and comfort. Both *hostales* drop their prices in summer.

### HOSTAL LUIS XV HOSTAL €

Map p238 (☑91 522 10 21; www.hrluisxv.net; 8th fl, Calle de la Montera 47; s/d/tr €58/73/88; ❋☎; ⓂGran Vía) The spacious rooms, attention to detail and pretty much everything else makes this family-run *hostal* feel pricier than it is. You'll find it hard to tear yourself away from the balconies outside every exterior room, from where the views are superb (especially from the triple in room 820). You're so high up that noise is rarely a problem.

### HOSTAL ACAPULCO HOSTAL €

Map p238 (☑91 531 19 45; www.hostalacapulco. com; 4th fl, Calle de la Salud 13; s/d from €50/60; ❋☎; ⓂGran Vía, Callao) A cut above many other hostels in Madrid, this immaculate little *hostal* has marble floors, renovated bathrooms (with bathtubs), double-glazed windows and comfortable beds. Street-facing rooms have balconies overlooking a sunny plaza and are flooded with natural light. The staff are also friendly and always more than happy to help you plan your day in Madrid. There's also a coffee machine.

### MADRID CITY ROOMS B&B €

Map p238 (☑91 360 44 44; www.madridcity rooms.com; 2nd fl, Calle de la Cruz 6; s/d from €40/55; ❋☎; ⓂSol) Don't let the exterior fool you because the simple yet colourful rooms, all with balconies and double-glazing, make for an excellent downtown budget bolt-hole. The friendly service is also a plus and the overall look is a touch more polished than your average *hostal.*

### ★HOTEL ALICIA BOUTIQUE HOTEL €€

Map p238 (☑91 389 60 95; www.room-matehoteles. com; Calle del Prado 2; d €125-175, ste from €200; ❋☎; ⓂSol, Sevilla, Antón Martín) One of the landmark properties of the designer Room Mate chain of hotels, Hotel Alicia overlooks

Plaza de Santa Ana with beautiful, spacious rooms. The style (the work of designer Pascua Ortega) is a touch more muted than in other Room Mate hotels, but the supermodern look remains intact, the downstairs bar is oh-so-cool, and the service is young and switched on.

### ★PRAKTIK METROPOL BOUTIQUE HOTEL €€
Map p238 (☑91 521 29 35; www.praktikmetropol. com; Calle de la Montera 47; s/d from €90/100; ❄️🛜; MGran Vía) You'd be hard-pressed to find better value anywhere in Europe than here in this overhauled hotel. Rooms have a fresh, contemporary look with white wood furnishings, and some (especially the corner rooms) have brilliant views down to Gran Vía and out over the city. It's spread over six floors and there's a roof terrace if you don't have a room with a view.

### NH COLLECTION PALACIO DE TEPA HOTEL €€
Map p238 (☑91 389 64 90; www.nh-collection. com; Calle de San Sebastián 2; d from €175; ❄️🛜; MAntón Martín) Inhabiting a 19th-century palace a stone's throw from Plaza de Santa Ana, this flagship property of the respected NH chain has modern designer rooms with hardwood floors and soothing colours. Service is professional and the location is outstanding. The premium rooms and junior suites in particular have real class.

### CATALONIA LAS CORTES HOTEL €€
Map p238 (☑91 389 60 51; www.hoteles-catalonia. es; Calle del Prado 6; s/d from €150/175; ❄️🛜; MAntón Martín) Occupying an 18th-century palace and renovated in a style faithful to the era, this elegant hotel is a terrific choice right in the heart of Huertas. It's something of an oasis surrounded by the nonstop energy of the streets in this *barrio*. Service is discreet and attentive and the hotel gets plenty of return visitors, which is just about the best recommendation we can give.

### SUITE PRADO HOTEL HOTEL €€
Map p238 (☑91 420 23 18; www.suiteprado.com; Calle de Manuel Fernández y González 10; s/d ste from €95/110; ❄️🛜; MSevilla) The spacious modern suites at this centrally located hotel have plenty of space and are semi-luxurious. All have sitting rooms and good bathrooms and kitchenettes.

### HOTEL PLAZA MAYOR HOTEL €€
Map p238 (☑91 360 06 06; www.h-plazamayor. com; Calle de Atocha 2; s/d/ste from €55/77/120; ❄️🛜; MSol, Tirso de Molina) We love this place. Sitting just across from Plaza Mayor, here you'll find stylish decor, helpful staff and charming original elements of this 150-year-old building. Rooms are attractive, some with a light colour scheme and wrought-iron furniture. The pricier attic rooms boast dark wood and designer lamps, and have lovely little terraces with wonderful rooftop views of central Madrid.

### HOTEL VINCCI SOHO HOTEL €€
Map p238 (☑91 141 41 00; www.vinccihoteles.com; Calle del Prado 18; d from €145; ❄️🛜; MSevilla, Antón Martín) A refined sense of style permeates everything about this hotel, from the subtly lit common areas to the rooms that combine vaguely Zen aesthetics with blood-red bathrooms. As ideal a base for the museums along the Paseo del Prado as for the clamour of central Madrid, it gets most things right.

### APARTASOL APARTMENT €€
(☑91 828 95 11; www.apartasol.com; apt €50-130) If you'll be in Madrid for more than a few days and you'd like the comfort and space of your own apartment, consider Apartasol. This traveller-friendly agency has well-equipped modern apartments scattered around the vicinity of the Puerta del Sol and Gran Vía. Prices are first rate and discounts are available for longer stays.

### HOTEL SENATOR HOTEL €€
Map p238 (☑91 531 41 51; www.playasenator.com; Gran Vía 21; s/d from €80/90; ❄️🛜; MGran Vía) One of central Madrid's prettiest facades conceals some of the most attractive four-star accommodation in the city centre. Unusually, only one room on each floor doesn't face onto the street and the views down Gran Vía from the corner rooms are brilliant. Rooms are sophisticated and come with armchairs and, wait for it, reclinable beds.

### HOTEL URBAN LUXURY HOTEL €€€
Map p238 (☑91 787 77 70; www.derbyhotels. com; Carrera de San Jerónimo 34; r from €230; ❄️🛜📶; MSevilla) This towering glass edifice is the epitome of art-inspired designer cool. It boasts original artworks from Africa and

Asia; dark-wood floors and dark walls are offset by plenty of light; and the dazzling bathrooms have wonderful designer fittings – the washbasins are sublime. The rooftop swimming pool is one of Madrid's best and the gorgeous terrace is heaven on a candlelit summer's evening.

**ME MELÍA REINA
VICTORIA**          LUXURY HOTEL €€€

Map p238 (☑91 701 60 00; www.melia.com; Plaza de Santa Ana 14; r from €175; ✻⊛; ⓂSol, Antón Martín) Once the landmark Gran Victoria Hotel, the Madrid home of many a famous bullfighter, this audacious hotel is a landmark of a different kind. Overlooking the western end of Plaza de Santa Ana, this luxury hotel is decked out in minimalist white with curves and comfort in all the right places.

# 🛏 El Retiro & the Art Museums

### ★LAPEPA CHIC B&B          B&B €

Map p242 (☑648 474742; www.lapepa-bnb.com; 7th fl, Plaza de las Cortes 4; s/d from €58/64; ✻⊛; ⓂBanco de España) A short step off Paseo del Prado and on a floor with an art-nouveau interior, this fine little B&B has lovely rooms with a contemporary, clean-line look so different from the dour *hostal* furnishings you'll find elsewhere. Modern art or even a bedhead lined with flamenco shoes gives the place personality in bucketloads. It's worth paying extra for a room with a view.

### ★60 BALCONIES ATOCHA          APARTMENT €€

Map p242 (☑91 755 39 26; www.60balconies.com; Plaza del Emperador Carlos V 11; apt €125-255; ✻⊛; ⓂAtocha) As convenient for Atocha train station as for the city's major art galleries, and well-connected to the rest of the city on foot or by Metro, 60 Balconies is an exciting new project by a dynamic young architectural team. The apartments range from 31-sq-metre studios up to 103-sq-metre, three-bedroom apartments, all stylish, spacious and a wonderful alternative to hotels. Another similarly excellent property is over in Chueca (p178).

### ★HOTEL RITZ          LUXURY HOTEL €€€

Map p242 (☑91 701 67 67; www.mandarinoriental.com; Plaza de la Lealtad 5; d/ste from €265/470; ✻⊛; ⓂBanco de España) The grand old lady of Madrid, the Hotel Ritz is the height of exclusivity. One of the most lavish buildings in the city, it has classic style and impeccable service that is second to none. Unsurprisingly, it's the favoured hotel of presidents, kings and celebrities. The public areas are palatial and awash with antiques, while rooms are extravagantly large, opulent and supremely comfortable.

In the Royal Suite, the walls are covered with raw silk and there's a personal butler to wait upon you. We challenge you to find a more indulgent hotel experience anywhere in Spain.

### WESTIN PALACE          LUXURY HOTEL €€€

Map p242 (☑91 360 80 00; www.westinpalacemadrid.com; Plaza de las Cortes 7; d/ste from €200/470; ✻⊛; ⓂBanco de España, Antón Martín) An old Madrid classic, this former palace of the Duque de Lerma opened as a hotel in 1911 and was Spain's second luxury hotel. Ever since it has looked out across Plaza de Neptuno at its rival, the Ritz, like a lover unjustly scorned. It may not have the world-famous cachet of the Ritz, but it's not called the Palace for nothing.

# 🛏 Salamanca

### VP EL MADROÑO          BOUTIQUE HOTEL €€

Map p244 (☑91 198 30 92; www.madrono-hotel.com; Calle del General Díaz Porlier 101; d/tr from €105/125; ✻⊛; ⓂDiego de León) You're a long way from touristy Madrid out here, not far from the bullring, and therein lies part of this swish place's appeal. All of the rooms have been renovated, either in a vaguely classic style or with more contemporary designer flair. It also has family rooms and there's even a lovely garden out back.

### PETIT PALACE ART GALLERY          HOTEL €€

Map p244 (☑91 435 54 11; www.petitpalaceartgallerymadrid.com; Calle de Jorge Juan 17; d from €90; ✻⊛; ⓂSerrano) Occupying a stately 19th-century Salamanca building, this landmark property of the Petit Palace chain is a lovely designer hotel that combines hi-tech facilities with an artistic aesthetic with loads of original works dotted around the public spaces and even in some of the rooms. Hydro-massage showers, laptops and exercise bikes in many rooms are just some of the extras, and the address is ideal for the best of Salamanca.

**VILLA MAGNA** · HOTEL €€€
Map p244 (☏91 587 12 34; www.villamagna.es; Paseo de la Castellana 22; d €335-420, ste from €450; P ❄ 🛜; MRubén Dario) This is a very Salamanca address, infused as it is with elegance and impeccable service. The look is brighter than you might imagine with the use of Empire chairs, Bauhaus ideas and even Chinese screens. Rooms are studiously classic in look with supremely comfortable furnishings and plenty of space. No expense has been spared in the rooftop suites.

## 🛏 Malasaña & Conde Duque

### ★HOSTAL MAIN STREET MADRID · HOSTAL €
Map p246 (☏91 548 18 78; www.mainstreetmadrid.com; 5th fl, Gran Vía 50; r from €55; ❄ 🛜; MCallao, Santo Domingo) Excellent service is what travellers rave about here, but the rooms – modern and cool in soothing greys – are also some of the best *hostal* rooms you'll find anywhere in central Madrid. It's an excellent package, and not surprisingly, they're often full, so book well in advance.

### FLAT 5 MADRID · HOSTAL €
Map p246 (☏91 127 24 00; www.flat5madrid.com; 5th fl, Calle de San Bernardo 55; s/d with private bathroom €55/70, r with shared bathroom from €48; ❄ 🛜; MNoviciado) Unlike so many other hostels in Madrid where the charm depends on a time-worn air, Flat 5 Madrid has a fresh, clean-line look with bright colours, flat-screen TVs and flower boxes on the window sills. Even the rooms that face onto a patio have partial views over the rooftops.

### LIFE HOTEL · HOTEL €
Map p246 (☏91 531 42 96; www.hotellifemadrid.es; Calle de Pizarro 16; s/d from €42/58; ❄ 🛜; MNoviciado) If only all places to stay were this good. This place inhabits the shell of an historic Malasaña building, but the rooms are slick and contemporary with designer bathrooms. You're also just a few steps up the hill from Calle del Pez, one of Malasaña's most happening streets. It's an exceptionally good deal, even when prices head upwards.

### HOTEL ABALÚ · BOUTIQUE HOTEL €€
Map p246 (☏91 531 47 44; www.hotelabalu.com; Calle del Pez 19; d €75-120, ste from €150; ❄ 🛜; MNoviciado) Malasaña's very own boutique hotel is starting to age and the word on the

street is that it's not what it was. We know what they mean but the rooms are still good, it's located on cool Calle del Pez and each room (some on the small side) has its own design drawn from the imagination of designer Luis Delgado.

## 🛏 Chueca

### HOSTAL LA ZONA · HOSTAL €
Map p246 (☏91 521 99 04; www.hostallazona.com; 1st fl, Calle de Valverde 7; s €38-58, d €50-70, all incl breakfast; ❄ 🛜; MGran Vía) Catering primarily to a gay clientele, the stylish Hostal La Zona has exposed brickwork, subtle colour shades and wooden pillars. We like a place where a sleep-in is encouraged – breakfast is served from 9am to noon, which is exactly the understanding Madrid's nightlife merits. Arnaldo and Vincent are friendly hosts.

### HOSTAL DON JUAN · HOSTAL €
Map p250 (☏91 522 31 01; www.hostaldonjuan.net; 2nd fl, Plaza de Vázquez de Mella 1; s/d/tr €40/56/75; ❄ 🛜; MGran Vía) Paying cheap rates for your room doesn't mean you can't be treated like a king. This elegant two-storey *hostal* is filled with original artworks and antique furniture that could grace a royal palace, although mostly it resides in the public areas. Rooms are large and simple but luminous; most have a street-facing balcony.

### CASA CHUECA · HOSTAL €
Map p250 (☏91 523 81 27; www.casachueca.com; 2nd fl, Calle de San Bartolomé 4; s/d from €45/62; 🛜; MGran Vía) If you don't mind lugging your bags up to the 2nd floor, Casa Chueca is outstanding. Rooms are modern, colourful and a cut above your average *hostal;* in keeping with the *barrio* that it calls home, Casa Chueca places a premium on style. Add casual, friendly service and you'd be hard-pressed to find a better price-to-quality ratio anywhere in central Madrid.

### HOSTAL AMÉRICA · HOSTAL €
Map p246 (☏91 522 64 48; www.hostalamerica.net; 5th fl, Calle de Hortaleza 19; s/d from €40/60; ❄ 🛜; MGran Vía) Run by a lovely mother-and-son team, the América has superclean, spacious and IKEA-dominated rooms. As most rooms face on to the usual interior 'patio' of the building, you should get a good night's sleep despite the busy area. For the rest of the time, there's a roof terrace – quite a luxury for a *hostal* in downtown Madrid – with tables, chairs and a coffee machine.

★**60 BALCONIES**
**RECOLETOS** APARTMENT €€
Map p250 (☑91 755 39 26; www.60balconies.com; Calle del Almirante 17; apt €132-212; ❋ ☎; ⓜChueca) In a classy corner of Chueca, these architect-designed apartments, ranging from 45 sq metre up to 130 sq metre, are stylish and make you feel like you've found your own Madrid pad. They're a similar deal to their Atocha property (p176) and rank among the best apartment choices in town.

**ONLY YOU HOTEL** BOUTIQUE HOTEL €€
Map p250 (☑91 005 22 22; www.onlyyouhotels.com; Calle de Barquillo 21; d €200-280; ❋ @ ☎; ⓜChueca) This stunning boutique hotel makes perfect use of a 19th-century Chueca mansion. The look is classy and contemporary thanks to respected interior designer Lázaro Rosa-Violán. Nice touches include all-day à la carte breakfasts and a portable router that you can carry out into the city to stay connected.

**HOTEL ÓSCAR** BOUTIQUE HOTEL €€
Map p250 (☑91 701 11 73; www.room-matehoteles.com; Plaza de Vázquez de Mella 12; d €90-195, ste from €150; ❋ ☎; ⓜGran Vía) Hotel Óscar belongs to the highly original Room Mate chain of hotels. Designer rooms ooze style and sophistication, some with floor-to-ceiling murals. The lighting is always funky, and the colour scheme has splashes of pinks, lime greens, oranges or more-minimalist black and white.

**THE PRINCIPAL MADRID** HOTEL €€€
Map p250 (☑915 21 87 43; www.theprincipal madridhotel.com; Calle Marqués de Valdeiglesias 1; r €210-360, ste from €460; ❋ @ ☎; ⓜSevilla) Just off the pretty end of Gran Vía and within sight of one of its more charming landmarks, the Edificio Metrópolis, the Principal is a fine, central choice. Some of the standard rooms are on the small side for a five-star hotel, but those with views towards Gran Vía are splendid.

## 🛌 Parque del Oeste & Northern Madrid

★**APARTOSUITES**
**JARDINES DE SABATINI** APARTMENT €€
Map p255 (☑91 198 32 90; www.jardinesdesabatini.com; Cuesta de San Vicente 16; studio without/with views from €85/110; ste without/with views from €125/150; ❋ ☎; ⓜPlaza de España, Príncipe Pío) Modern, spacious studios and suites are only half the story at this terrific property just down the hill from Plaza de España. Definitely pay extra for a room with a view and the studios with a balcony and uninterrupted views over the lovely Jardines de Sabatini to the Palacio Real – simply brilliant. The Campo del Moro is just across the road.

★**HOTEL ONE SHOT**
**LUCHANA 22** HOTEL €€
Map p252 (☑91 292 29 40; www.hoteloneshot luchana22.com; Calle de Luchana 22; r €105; ❋ ☎; ⓜBilbao) Classy, contemporary rooms in an early-20th-century, neoclassical palace close to Plaza de Olavide in Chamberí make for a pleasant alternative to staying downtown. The wrap-around loft has abundant light and a modern four-poster bed.

★**HOTEL ORFILA** HOTEL €€€
Map p252 (☑91 702 77 70; www.hotelorfila.com; Calle de Orfila 6; r from €225; ℗ ❋ ☎; ⓜAlonso Martínez) One of Madrid's best hotels, Hotel Orfila has all the luxuries of any five-star hotel – supremely comfortable rooms, for a start – but it's the personal service that elevates it into the upper echelon; regular guests get bathrobes embroidered with their own initials. An old-world elegance dominates the decor, and the quiet location and sheltered garden make it the perfect retreat at day's end.

**HOTEL AC SANTO MAURO** HOTEL €€€
Map p252 (☑91 319 69 00; www.achotels.marriott.com; Calle de Zurbano 36; d/ste from €230/450; ❋ ☎ ❋; ⓜAlonso Martínez) Everything about this place oozes exclusivity and class, from the address – one of the elite patches of Madrid real estate – to the 19th-century mansion that's the finest in a *barrio* of many. It's a place of discreet elegance and warm service, and rooms are suitably lavish.

★**HOTEL SILKEN**
**PUERTA AMÉRICA** LUXURY HOTEL €€€
(☑91 744 54 00; www.hoteles-silken.com; Avenida de América 41; d/ste from €140/275; ℗ ❋ ☎; ⓜCartagena) Given the location of their hotel (halfway between the city and the airport) the owners knew they had to do something special – to build a self-contained world so innovative and luxurious that you'd never want to leave. Their idea? Give 22 of architecture's most creative names (eg Zaha Hadid, Norman Foster, Ron Arad, David Chipperfield, Jean Nouvel) a floor each to design.

# Understand Madrid

# Madrid Today

Emerging from *la crisis* with its customary sense of energy and optimism, and with a can-do mayor taking the city in a whole new direction, Madrid has recovered its *mojo*. New restaurants are opening, the local economy leads the national recovery and life feels good. That's not to say there aren't problems – a new, equally unsustainable boom may be taking hold, and the rivalry with Barcelona seems more intense than ever. But Madrid's still a wonderful place to be.

## Best on Film

**Pepi, Luci, Bom y otras chicas del montón** (1980) Early Almodóvar film showcasing 1980s Madrid in all its madness.
**La colmena** (1982) Faithful rendering of Camilo José Cela's Madrid during the grim 1950s.
**La comunidad** (2000) Cheerfully off-the-wall tale of greed in a Madrid apartment block.
**Los fantasmas de Goya** (2006) Goya, the Spanish Inquisition and the painter's many scandals.
**Volver** (2006) Heart-warming Almodóvar film starring Penélope Cruz.

## Best in Print

**Madrid: A Travellers Reader** (Hugh Thomas; 2018) An excellent anthology of writings about Madrid by a respected historian.
**A Heart So White** (Javier Marías; 1992) A tale of subtle family intrigue.
**Winter in Madrid** (CJ Sansom; 2006) Easy-to-read spy thriller set in post–Civil War Madrid.
**The Anatomy of a Moment** (Javier Cercas; 2009) Masterful retelling of the attempted coup that rocked Spain on 23 February 1981.
**A Load of Bull: An Englishman's Adventures in Madrid** (Tim Parfitt; 2006) Humorous love letter to Madrid in the 1980s and beyond.

## On the Up

Catalonia may claim to be Spain's economic engine, but when it comes to economic progress, the rest of the country looks to Madrid for leadership, and not just because this is the seat of the national government. Spain's financial recovery, halting at first, is unmistakeable now, and Madrid is at the centre of it. Retail revenues are up, property sales are gathering pace and unemployment is falling, all adding to a sense that Madrid's worst days are behind it. The numbers are good, but they're only playing catch-up with a city whose people have been bringing a buzz back to the city's streets. Walk down Calle de Serrano or Calle de Fuencarral and it's plain to see that things are on the upswing. Those businesses that clung on during the hard times are reaping their rewards, and new places are opening up all the time. In short, Madrid is back in business.

## A New Political Direction

In the depths of the economic downturn, Madrid was one of the first cities to try and reclaim their political future. It began in May 2011 with the *indignados* (the indignant) taking over the Plaza de la Puerta del Sol. Whereas the rejection of mainstream party politics has led to uncertainty, political deadlock or right-wing populist idealogues elsewhere, Madrid's version was always going to be different and the city turned towards a left-leaning mayor, former judge Manuela Carmena, who rides the metro to work and who has quickly earned herself a reputation for getting things done. Common-sense policies designed to get *madrileños* back onto the streets (the closure of Gran Vía to traffic and the partial closure of the Paseo del Prado, for example) have been matched by modernising policies (such as the upgrading of the city's transport ticketing system, and a retreat from government support for bullfighting) and a more compassionate approach to those hit hardest by the crisis have all won her plaudits. The conservative forces are preparing their fightback, but the mayoress remains popular.

## The Catalonia Question

In stark contrast to Barcelona, Madrid is a city highly suspicious of parochialism and one that, historically, simply doesn't care where you're from. In Madrid, everybody comes from somewhere else – to find anyone whose four grandparents come from Madrid is more difficult than you might imagine. The reaction to immigrants from poorer regions – whether Latin America, Morocco or Romania – has been more complicated, but it remains true that, unlike elsewhere in Europe, extreme-right, anti-immigration political parties haven't even managed a minor foothold here.

The result of this tolerance to outsiders is a city that celebrates its inclusiveness, its oft-heard refrain '*si estas en Madrid, eres de Madrid*' (if you're in Madrid, you're from Madrid). All of which means there is a genuine sense of bewilderment and lack of comprehension as to why Catalonia – with its strong sense of Catalan identity and desire to go its own way – might want to leave the Spanish fold. And therein lies part of the problem – the powers-that-be in Madrid simply don't understand the separatist impulse, and the conservative reaction to Catalonia's 2017 referendum only made matters worse. In contrast, on the streets, many *madrileños* told us they'd be happy for Catalonia to vote in a referendum. Most just couldn't understand why they'd want to.

## A Football-Led Recovery

Enough locals are obsessed with football for the results of the city's two football teams – Real Madrid and Atlético de Madrid – to genuinely affect the city's mood. Even those who don't follow football gritted their teeth in frustration as an all-conquering Barcelona swept Real Madrid aside during the barren years that followed Real Madrid's Champions League victory in 2002. But normal service (as far as *madrileños* are concerned) has been restored, with historic back-to-back Champions League victories in 2016 and 2017, and the return to form of Atléti, who've even moved to a new, world-class stadium. The fact that the rise in Madrid's footballing fortunes has coincided with the economic recovery should serve as a reminder that this is the natural order of things, as so many locals would have you believe.

## if Madrid were 100 people

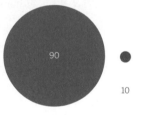

90 would be Spanish
10 would be other nationalities

## belief systems
(% of population)

90

10

Catholic          Other religion

## population per sq km

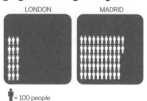

♦ ≈ 100 people

# History

Founded as a Muslim garrison town in the 9th century, Madrid took centre stage in 1561 when it was unexpectedly chosen as Spain's capital. As the centre of a global empire and the seat of the Spanish royal court, Madrid was transformed into Spain's most important city. In the centuries that followed, it accumulated prestige, people from across Spain and beyond, and the trappings of power and wealth. The end result is the most Spanish of all Spain's major cities.

## Muslim Mayrit

When the Muslim army of Tariq ibn Ziyad crossed the Strait of Gibraltar in the 8th century, it sparked an upheaval that would convulse the Iberian Peninsula for more than 700 years. In 756 the emirate of Córdoba was established in the south in what the Muslims called Al-Andalus and its soldiers and administrators would occupy much of the peninsula until the beginning of the 9th century.

As Iberia's Christians began the Reconquista (Reconquest) – the centuries-long campaign by Christian forces to reclaim the peninsula – the Muslims of Al-Andalus constructed a chain of fortified positions through the heart of Iberia. One of these forts was built by Muhammad I, emir of Córdoba, in 854, on the site of what would become Madrid. They called the new settlement Mayrit (or Magerit), which comes from the Arabic word *majira,* meaning water channel. As the Reconquista gathered strength, forts such as Mayrit grew in significance as part of a defensive line against Christian incursion. Recognising that Mayrit lacked natural fortifications to the east, Muhammad I constructed a defensive wall within whose boundaries only Muslims could live; Mayrit's small Christian community lived outside, near what is now the Iglesia de San Andrés. The last remaining fragment of the Muralla Árabe sits below the modern Catedral de Nuestra Señora de la Almudena.

**Books on Madrid**

*A Traveller's Companion to Madrid (Hugh Thomas)*

*Hidden Madrid: A Walking Guide (Mark and Peter Besas)*

*Madrid: The History (Jules Stewart)*

| TIMELINE | 1st–5th centuries AD | 854 | End 9th century |
|---|---|---|---|
| | The Roman Empire subdues the Celtiberian tribes. The Roman road that connects Mérida with Toledo (Toletum), Segovia, Alcalá de Henares and Zaragoza (Cesaraugusta) runs close to Madrid. | Muhammad I, emir of Córdoba, establishes Mayrit (Magerit) fortress, one of many across the so-called Middle March, a frontier land connecting Al-Andalus with the northern Christian kingdoms. | Muhammad I orders the construction of a wall along the ridgeline, enclosing the current Catedral de Nuestra Señora de la Almudena and what is now Plaza de Oriente. |

Mayrit's strategic location in the centre of the peninsula drew an increasing number of soldiers and traders. To accommodate the many newcomers, Mayrit grew into a town. The main mosque was built on what is now the corner of Calle Mayor and Calle de Bailén, although only the smallest fragment remains. Even so, Mayrit was dispensable to its far-off Muslim rulers. As the armies of Muslim and Christian Spain battled for supremacy elsewhere, Mayrit was not considered one of the great prizes and ultimately passed into Christian hands without a fight. In 1083 Toledo's ruler gave Mayrit to King Alfonso VI of Castilla during a period of rare Muslim-Christian entente.

## A Medieval Christian Outpost

Madrid never again passed into Muslim hands, although the city was often besieged by Muslim forces. As the frontline gradually pushed south, Christian veterans from the Reconquista and clerics and their orders flooded into Madrid and forever changed the city's character. A small Muslim community remained and to this day the warren of streets around Las Vistillas, where they lived, is known as La Morería (the Moorish quarter). Nearby, Plaza de la Paja was the site of the city's main market. By the end of the 13th century, a new city wall – bordered by what are now Calle Arenal, Cava de San Miguel, Calle de la Cava Baja, Plaza de la Puerta de Moros and Calle de Bailén – was built. Where Plaza Mayor, Plaza de España and Plaza de la Puerta del Sol now stand lay beyond the walls.

Madrid may have been growing, but its power was negligible and the city existed in the shadow of the more established cities of Segovia and Toledo. Left largely to their own devices, a small number of local families set about governing themselves, forming Madrid's first town council, the Consejo de Madrid. The travelling Cortes (royal court and parliament) sat in Madrid for the first time in 1309. This first sign of royal favour was followed by others – Madrid was an increasingly popular residence with the Castilian monarchs, particularly Enrique IV (r 1454–74). They found it a relaxing base from which to set off on hunting expeditions, especially for bears in the El Pardo district.

Despite growing evidence of royal attention, medieval Madrid remained dirt-poor and small-scale. In 1348 the horrors of the Black Death struck, devastating the population, and a handful of local families ran a feudal system of government, lording it over the peasants who worked the surrounding *tierra* (land). As one 15th-century writer observed, 'in Madrid there is nothing except what you bring with you'. It simply bore no comparison with other major Spanish, let alone European, cities.

The remains of Roman villas and inns have been found in the Madrid region. The small Roman outpost known as Miacum, close to modern Madrid, was an obscure way-station on the important Roman road that crossed the Iberian Peninsula.

| Around 1070 | 1083 | 1110 | 1222 |
| --- | --- | --- | --- |
| Madrid's patron saint, San Isidro Labrador, is born among the small community of Christians clustered around the Iglesia de San Andrés (where he was buried in 1130) in Muslim Mayrit. | Mayrit passes into the hands of King Alfonso VI of Castilla without a fight, ending Muslim rule over Mayrit, in return for the king's assistance in capturing Valencia. | Almoravid Muslims attack Madrid in an attempt to wrest the city back from Christian rule. They succeed in destroying Madrid's walls but are unable to seize the *alcázar* (fortress). | Madrid's emblem of seven stars and a bear nuzzling a *madroño* (strawberry tree) appears for the first time in historical records. A statue of it now stands in the Plaza de la Puerta del Sol. |

## A Tale of Two Cities

When Carlos I's son and successor, Felipe II, ascended the Spanish throne in 1556, Madrid was surrounded by walls that boasted 130 towers and six stone gates. Although it sounds impressive, these fortifications were largely built of mud and were designed more to impress than provide any meaningful defence of the city. Such modest claims to significance notwithstanding, Madrid was chosen by Felipe II as the capital of Spain in 1561.

Felipe II was more concerned with the business of empire and building his monastic retreat, the Real Monasterio de San Lorenzo at San Lorenzo de El Escorial than he was in developing Madrid. Despite a handful of elegant churches, the imposing *alcázar* and a smattering of noble residences, Madrid consisted, for the most part, of precarious, whitewashed houses that were little more than mud huts. They lined chaotic, ill-defined and largely unpaved lanes and alleys. The monumental Paseo del Prado, which now provides Madrid with so much of its grandeur, was nothing more than a small creek. Even so, Madrid went from having just 2000 homes in 1563 to more than 7000 just 40 years later as opportunists, impoverished rural migrants, would-be princes and fortune-seekers flocked to the city hoping for a share of the glamour and wealth that came from being close to royalty.

The sumptuous Palacio del Buen Retiro was completed in 1630 and replaced the *alcázar* as the prime royal residence (the former Museo del Ejército building and Casón del Buen Retiro are all that remain). Countless grand churches, convents and mansions were also built and, thanks to royal patronage, this was the golden age of art in Spain: Velázquez, El Greco, José de Ribera, Zurbarán, Murillo and Coello were all active in

---

### BEAR NECESSITIES

Madrid's emblem, a bear nuzzling a *madroño* (strawberry tree, so named because its fruit looks like strawberries), framed by seven five-point stars and topped by a crown – is one of the most photographed corners of the Plaza de la Puerta del Sol (p86). When Alfonso VI accepted Mayrit from the Muslims in 1083, it was seen as an example of things to come for Christian forces hoping to sweep across Spain from the north. Taking the theme further, a group of seven stars that lies close to the North Star in the northern hemisphere forms a shape known as the Ursa Minor, or small she-bear. Thus the bear (once a common sight in the El Pardo area north of the city) and seven stars came to symbolise Madrid. The five points of the stars later came to represent the five provinces that surround Madrid (Segovia, Ávila, Toledo, Cuenca and Guadalajara).

---

| 1309 | 1348 | 1426 | 1478 |
|---|---|---|---|
| The Cortes sits for the first time in Madrid. During the sitting, the royals declare war on Granada; the Reconquista's demands ensure that the royal court often travels throughout Spain. | The Black Death sweeps across Spain, killing King Alfonso XI and countless compatriots. Estimates suggest that the plague kills anywhere between 20% and 50% of Madrid's population. | During a devastating drought, devout *madrileños* take the body of San Isidro, Madrid's patron saint, out onto the streets, whereupon it begins to rain. | Isabel and Fernando, the Reyes Católicos (Catholic Monarchs), stir up religious bigotry and establish the Spanish Inquisition; thousands will be killed up until its abolition in 1834. |

Madrid in the 17th century. For the first time, Madrid began to take on the aspect of a city.

By the middle of the 17th century Madrid had completely outgrown its capacity to cope: it was home to 175,000 people, making it the fifth-largest city in Europe. But if you took away the court, the city amounted to nothing, and when Pedro Teixeira drew the first map of the city in 1656, the place was still largely a cesspit of narrow, squalid lanes.

## The Bourbons Leave Their Mark

After King Carlos II died in 1700 without leaving an heir, the 12-year War of the Spanish Succession convulsed Europe. While Europe squabbled over the Spanish colonial carcass, Felipe V (grandson of Louis XIV of France and Maria Teresa, a daughter of Felipe IV) ascended the throne in 1702 as the first member of the Bourbon dynasty, which remains at the head of the Spanish state today. Felipe's centralisation of state control and attempts at land reform are viewed by some historians as the first steps in making Spain a modern European nation, and the former clearly cemented Madrid's claims to being Spain's pre-eminent city. He preferred to live outside the noisy and filthy capital, but when in 1734 the *alcázar* was destroyed in a fire, the king laid down plans for a magnificent new royal palace, Palacio Real, to take its place.

His immediate successors, especially Carlos III (r 1759–88), also gave Madrid and Spain a period of comparatively commonsense governance. Carlos (his equestrian statue dominates the Puerta del Sol) came to be known as the best 'mayor' Madrid had ever had. By introducing Madrid's first program of sanitation and public hygiene, he cleaned up a city that was, by all accounts, the filthiest in Europe. Carlos III was so successful that, near the end of his reign, France's ambassador in Madrid described the city as one of the cleanest capitals in Europe. Mindful of his legacy, Carlos III also completed the Palacio Real, inaugurated the city's botanical gardens, the Real Jardín Botánico, and carried out numerous other public works. His stamp upon Madrid's essential character was also evident in his sponsorship of local and foreign artists, among them Goya and Tiepolo. Carlos III also embarked on a major road-building program.

## Napoleon & El Dos de Mayo

Within a year of Carlos III's death Europe was again in uproar, this time as the French Revolution threatened to sweep away the old order of privileged royals and inherited nobility. Through the machinations of Carlos IV, the successor to Carlos III, and his self-serving minister, Manuel

When, in the 17th century, all home owners were ordered to reserve the second storey of their homes for government bureaucrats and clergy newly arrived in the city, *madrileños* instead built homes with just a single-storey facade at street level, building additional storeys out the back, away from prying eyes.

| 1479–81 | 1492 | 1520 | 1561 |
| --- | --- | --- | --- |
| Isabel, Queen of Castilla, marries Fernando, King of Aragón. A Madrid edict declares Muslims to be second-class citizens, forcing them to wear signs identifying their religion, among other indignities. | The last Muslim rulers of Al-Andalus are defeated by Christian armies in Granada, uniting the peninsula for the first time in seven centuries. Jews are expelled from the peninsula. | Madrid joins Toledo in the rebellion of the Comuneros against Carlos I, a disastrous decision that prompts the victorious king to rein in Madrid's growing independence. | Against all the odds, Felipe II establishes his permanent court at Madrid, which was, in Felipe II's words, 'a city fulfilling the function of a heart located in the middle of the body'. |

## A CAPITAL CHOICE

When Felipe II decided to make Madrid Spain's capital in 1561, you could almost hear the collective gasp of disbelief from Spain's great and good, few of whom lived in Madrid. Madrid was home to just 30,000 people, whereas Toledo and Seville each boasted more than 80,000. Even Valladolid, the capital of choice for Isabel and Fernando, had 50,000 inhabitants. What's more, in the 250 years since 1309, Madrid had hosted Spain's travelling road show of royalty just 10 times, far fewer than Spain's other large cities.

Madrid's apparent obscurity may, however, explain precisely why Felipe II chose it as his capital. Valladolid was considered to be of questionable loyalty. Toledo, which, like Madrid, stands close to the geographical heart of Spain, was known for its opinionated nobles and powerful clergy who had shown an annoying tendency to oppose the king's whims and wishes. In contrast, more than one king had described Madrid as 'very noble and very loyal'. By choosing Madrid Felipe II was choosing the path of least resistance. Felipe II also wanted the capital to be 'a city fulfilling the function of a heart located in the middle of the body'.

In 1601 Felipe III, tired of Madrid, moved the court to Valladolid. Within five years, the population of Madrid halved. The move was so unpopular, however, that the king, realising the error of his ways, returned to Madrid. 'Sólo Madrid es corte' (roughly, 'Only Madrid can be home to the court') became the catchcry and thus it has been ever since.

Godoy, Spain incurred the wrath of both the French and the British. The consequences were devastating. First, Nelson crushed the Spanish fleet in the Battle of Trafalgar in 1805. Next, Napoleon convinced a gullible Godoy to let French troops enter Spain on the pretext of a joint attack on Portugal, whereby General Murat's French detachment took control of Madrid. By 1808 the French presence had become an occupation and Napoleon's brother, Joseph Bonaparte, was crowned king of Spain.

Madrid did not take kindly to foreign rule and, on the morning of 2 May 1808 *madrileños* (people from Madrid), showing more courage than their leaders, attacked French troops around the Palacio Real and what is now Plaza del Dos de Mayo in Malasaña. Murat moved quickly and by the end of the day the rebels were defeated. Goya's masterpieces, *El dos de mayo* and *El tres de mayo,* today on display in the Museo del Prado, poignantly evoke the hope and anguish of the ill-fated rebellion.

Although reviled by much of Madrid's population, Joseph Bonaparte's contribution to Madrid in five short years should not be underestimated. Working hard to win popular support, Bonaparte staged numerous free *espectáculos* – bullfights, festivals of food and drink, and religious processions. He also transformed Madrid with a host of

| 1601 | 1622 | Mid-17th century | 1702 |
|---|---|---|---|
| In the last serious challenge to Madrid's position as capital, Felipe III moves Spain's capital to Valladolid, but popular discontent convinces him to return the royal court to Madrid. | Seville-born Diego Rodríguez de Silva Velázquez moves to Madrid, takes up a position as a painter in the royal court and becomes synonymous with the golden age of Spanish art. | Madrid's population swells to 175,000 people, up from just 30,000 a century before. Only London, Paris, Constantinople and Naples can boast larger populations in Europe. | Felipe V is crowned king, beginning the Bourbon dynasty that still rules Spain and, save for four decades of the 20th century, has done so from Madrid. |

measures necessary in a city that had grown up without any discernible sense of town planning. These measures included widening streets and the destruction of various churches and convents to create public squares (such as the Plaza de Oriente, Plaza de Santa Ana, Plaza de San Miguel, Plaza de Santa Bárbara, Plaza de Tirso de Molina and Plaza de Callao). He also conceived the viaduct that still spans Calle de Segovia. Under Bonaparte sanitation was also improved and cemeteries were moved to the outskirts of the city.

The French were finally evicted from Spanish territory in 1813 as a result of the Guerra de la Independencia (War of Independence, or Peninsular War). But when the autocratic King Fernando VII returned in 1814, Spain was in disarray. Though far from Spain's most distinguished ruler, Fernando was responsible for opening to the public the Parque del Buen Retiro, which had been largely destroyed during the war, and founding an art gallery in the Prado.

## Capital of a Country Divided

For much of the 19th century, Spain and Madrid were in turmoil, with no less than three civil wars (the Carlist Wars between liberals and conservatives as the royal family squabbled over the spoils of succession), and a series of coups and counter coups. At the heart of it all, Madrid was incredibly backward, although the *desmortización* (disentailment) of Church property in 1837, the emergence of a middle class and growing entrepreneurial activity finally enabled Madrid's ordinary inhabitants to emerge from the shadow of royalty and powerful clergy.

In 1851 the city's first railway line, operating between Madrid and Aranjuez, opened. Seven years later the Canal de Isabel II, which still supplies the city with water from the Sierra de Guadarrama, was inaugurated. Street paving, the sewage system and rubbish collection were improved and gas lighting was introduced. More importantly, foreign (mostly French) capital was beginning to fill the investment vacuum. In the years that followed, a national road network radiating from the capital was built and public works, ranging from the reorganisation of the Puerta del Sol to the building of the Teatro Real, Biblioteca Nacional and Congreso de los Diputados (lower house of parliament), were carried out. In the 1860s the first timid moves to create an Ensanche, or extension of the city, were undertaken. The initial spurt of building took place around Calle de Serrano, where the enterprising Marqués de Salamanca (see box p122) bought up land and built high-class housing.

In 1873 Spain was declared a republic, but the army soon intervened to restore the Bourbon monarchy. Alfonso XII, Isabel's son, assumed power. In the period of relative tranquillity that ensued, the expansion

Madrileños never forgave Bonaparte his foreign origins and the brutality with which he suppressed uprisings against his rule, mocking his yearning for legitimacy by calling him names that included the Cucumber King, Pepe Botella and King of the Small Squares.

For medieval travellers to Madrid, the impression was of streets 'which would be beautiful if it were not for the mud and filth'. Houses were 'bad and ugly and almost all made of mud'. Rubbish and human excrement were thrown from balconies, 'a thing which afterwards creates an insupportable odour'.

| 1734 | 1759–88 | 1808 | 1812 |
|---|---|---|---|
| Medieval Madrid's most enduring symbol, the *alcázar*, is destroyed by fire. Plans begin almost immediately for a lavish royal palace to take its place. | Carlos III, King of Spain and patron of Madrid, cleans up the city, lays out the Parque del Buen Retiro and sponsors Goya, transforming Madrid into a sophisticated European capital. | Napoleon's troops under General Murat march into Madrid and Joseph Bonaparte, Napoleon's brother, is crowned King of Spain, after an uprising by Madrid's citizen-defenders against foreign rule. | Thirty thousand *madrileños* die from hunger caused by fighting against the French in the lead-up to the War of Independence. The French are expelled from Spanish soil a year later. |

## A CITY OF IMMIGRANTS

In a country where regional nationalisms abound – even Barcelona, that most European of cities, is fiercely and parochially Catalan – Madrid is notable for its absence of regional sentiment. If you quiz *madrileños* as to why this is so, they often reply, 'but we're *all* from somewhere else'. It has always been thus in Madrid. In the century after the city became the national capital in 1561, the population swelled by more than 500%, from 30,000 to 175,000. Most were Spaniards (peasants and would-be nobles) who left behind the impoverished countryside and were drawn by the opportunities that existed on the periphery of the royal court.

During the first three decades of the 20th century Madrid's population doubled from half a million to around one million; in 1930 a study found that less than 40% of the capital's population was from Madrid. The process continued in the aftermath of the civil war, and in the 1950s alone more than 600,000 arrived from elsewhere in Spain. In the late 20th century the process of immigration took on a new form, as Spain became the EU's largest annual recipient of immigrants. Between 15% and 20% of Madrid's population are foreigners, more than double the national average.

Unsurprisingly, true *madrileños* are something of a rare breed. Those who can claim four grandparents born in the city are dignified with the name *gatos* (cats). The term dates from when one of Alfonso VI's soldiers artfully scaled Muslim Mayrit's formidable walls in 1083. 'Look,' cried his comrades, 'he moves like a cat!'

of the Ensanche gathered momentum, the city's big train stations were constructed and the foundation stones of a cathedral were laid. Another kind of 'cathedral', the Banco de España, was completed and opened its doors in 1891. By 1898 the first city tramlines were electrified and in 1910 work began on the Gran Vía. Nine years later the first metro line started operating.

The 1920s was a period of frenzied activity, not just in urban construction but in intellectual life. As many as 20 newspapers circulated on the streets of Madrid, and writers and artists (including Lorca, Dalí and Buñuel) converged on the capital, which hopped to the sounds of American jazz and whose grand cafes resounded with the clamour of lively *tertulias* (literary discussions). The '20s roared as much in Madrid as elsewhere in Europe.

## In the Eye of the Storm

In 1923 the captain-general of Catalonia and soon-to-be dictator, General Miguel Primo de Rivera, seized power and held it until Alfonso XIII had him removed in 1930. Madrid erupted in joyful celebration, but it would prove to be a false dawn. By now, the Spanish capital, home to

| 1819 | 1833 | 1873 | 1881 |
|---|---|---|---|
| Fernando VII opens the Museo del Prado. Originally conceived as a storehouse for royal art accumulated down through the centuries, it later becomes one of Europe's most important art galleries. | King Fernando VII dies, leaving three-year-old Isabel II as heir-apparent. Her mother, María Cristina, rules as regent and Spain descends into the Carlist civil wars, which devastated Madrid. | Spain's first, short-lived republic is declared in February, although the Bourbon monarchy returns to power in Madrid's Palacio Real with help from the army in December of the following year. | The Partido Socialista Obrero Español (PSOE; Spanish Socialist Workers' Party) is founded in a backroom of Casa Labra, still one of Madrid's most prestigious tapas bars. |

more than one million people, had become the seething centre of Spain's increasingly radical politics, and the rise of the socialists in Madrid, as well as anarchists in Barcelona and Andalucía, sharpened tensions throughout the country.

Municipal elections in Madrid in April 1931 brought a coalition of republicans and socialists to power. Three days later a second republic was proclaimed and Alfonso XIII fled. The republican government opened up to the public the Casa de Campo – until then serving as a private royal playground – and passed numerous reformist laws, but divisions within the government enabled a right-wing coalition to assume power in 1933. Again the pendulum swung and in February 1936 the left-wing Frente Popular (Popular Front) barely defeated the right's Frente Nacional (National Front) to power. General Francisco Franco was exiled, supposedly out of harm's way, to the Canary Islands, but with the army supporting the right-wing parties and the extreme left clamouring for revolution, the stage was set for a showdown. In July 1936 garrisons in North Africa revolted, quickly followed by others on the mainland. The Spanish Civil War had begun.

Having stopped Franco's nationalist troops advancing from the north, Madrid found itself in the sights of Franco's forces moving up from the south. Take Madrid, Franco reasoned, and Spain would be his. By early November 1936 Franco was in the Casa de Campo. The republican government escaped to Valencia, but the resolve of the city's defenders, a mix of hastily assembled and poorly trained recruits, sympathisers from the ranks of the army and air force, the International Brigades and Soviet advisers, held firm. Madrid became an international *cause célèbre*, drawing luminaries as diverse as Ernest Hemingway and Willy Brandt in defence of the city. For all the fame of the brigades, the fact remains, however, that of the 40,000 soldiers and irregulars defending Madrid, more than 90% were Spaniards.

Madrid's defenders held off a fierce nationalist assault in November 1936, with the fighting heaviest in the northwest of the city, around Argüelles and the Ciudad Universitaria. Soldiers loyal to Franco inside Madrid were overpowered by local militias and 20,000 Franco supporters sought protection inside the walls of foreign embassies. Faced with republican intransigence – symbolised by the catchphrase *'No pasarán!'* ('They shall not pass!') coined by the communist leader Dolores Ibárruri – Franco besieged Madrid, bombarded the city from the air and waited for the capital to surrender. It didn't.

German bombers strafed Madrid, one of the first such campaigns of its kind in the history of warfare, although the Salamanca district was spared, allegedly because it was home to a high proportion of Franco

Madrid was a candidate for the 2012 and 2016 Olympics, coming third and second, respectively. Madrid's bid for the 2020 Olympics was a familiar story, as it came in third behind Istanbul and eventual winners Tokyo, leaving it as the only major European capital never to have hosted the Games.

| 1898 | 1919 | 1920s | 1931 |
|---|---|---|---|
| Spain loses its remaining colonies of Cuba, Puerto Rico and the Philippines to the US, setting off a period of national angst. In the same year, Madrid's tramlines are electrified. | Madrid's first metro line opens, crossing the city from north to south, with eight stations and a total length of 3.5km from Puerta del Sol to Cuatro Caminos. | Madrid enjoys a cultural revival with Salvador Dalí, Federico García Lorca and Luis Buñuel bringing high culture and mayhem to a city in love with jazz and *tertulias* (literary discussions). | After a period of right-wing dictatorship, Spain's Second Republic is proclaimed and King Alfonso XIII flees, leaving Spain in political turmoil and planting the seeds for civil war. |

supporters. The Museo del Prado was not so fortunate and most of its paintings were evacuated to Valencia. As many as 10,000 people died in the Battle of Madrid; Franco's approach was summed up by his promise that 'I will destroy Madrid rather than leave it to the Marxists'.

By 1938 Madrid was in a state of near famine, with food, clothes and ammunition in short supply. As republican strongholds fell elsewhere across Spain, Madrid's republican defenders were divided over whether to continue the resistance. After a brief internal power struggle, those favouring negotiations won. On 28 March 1939 an exhausted Madrid finally surrendered.

## Franco's Madrid

Mindful that he was occupying a city that had hardly welcomed him with open arms, Franco considered shifting the capital south to the more amenable Seville. As if to punish Madrid for its resistance, he opted instead to remake Madrid in his own image and transform the city into a capital worthy of its new master. Franco and his right-wing Falangist Party maintained a heavy-handed repression, and Madrid in the early 1940s was impoverished and battle scarred.

In the Francoist propaganda of the day, the 1940s and '50s were the years of *autarquía* (economic self-reliance), a policy that owed more to Spain's international isolation post-WWII due to its perceived support for Hitler than any principled philosophy. For most Spaniards, however, these were the *años de hambre* (the years of hunger). Throughout the 1940s, tens of thousands of suspected republican sympathisers were harassed, imprisoned, tortured and shot. Thousands of political prisoners were shipped off to Nazi concentration camps. Many who remained were put to work in deplorable conditions.

The dire state of the Spanish economy forced hundreds of thousands of starving *campesinos* (peasants) to flock to Madrid, increasing the already enormous pressure for housing. Most contented themselves with erecting *chabolas* (shanty towns) in the increasingly ugly satellite suburbs that began to ring the city.

By the early 1960s, known as the *años de desarollo* (years of development), industry was taking off in and around Madrid. Foreign investment poured in and the services and banking sector blossomed. Factories of the American Chrysler motor company were Madrid's single biggest employers in the 1960s. In 1960 fewer than 70,000 cars were on the road in Madrid; 10 years later more than half a million clogged the capital's streets.

For all the signs of development in Madrid, Franco was never popular in his own capital and an improved standard of living did little to

During the Madrid siege, Francoist general Emilio Mola assured a journalist that he would take Madrid with his four columns of soldiers massed on the city's outskirts and with the help of his 'fifth column', a phrase that has since remained in the popular lexicon and referred to Franco's right-wing sympathisers in Madrid.

| 1936–39 | 1960s | 1973 | 1975–78 |
|---|---|---|---|
| The Spanish Civil War breaks out. Nationalist forces bombard Madrid from the air and with artillery, besieging it for three years, before the exhausted city surrenders on 28 March 1939. | After two decades of extreme economic hardship, the decade becomes known as the *años de desarollo* (years of development), with investment and rural immigrants flooding into Madrid. Opposition begins to grow. | Admiral Carrero Blanco, Franco's prime minister and designated successor, is assassinated by ETA in a car-bomb attack in Salamanca after leaving Mass at the Iglesia de San Francisco de Borga. | Franco dies in Madrid on 20 November 1975, after 39 years in power. Without an obvious successor to Franco, Spain returns to democratic rule three years later. |

diminish *madrileños'* disdain for a man who held the capital in an iron grip. In the Basque Country the terrorist group Euskadi Ta Askatasuna (ETA; Basque Homeland and Freedom) began to fight for Basque independence. Their first important action outside the Basque Country was the assassination in Madrid in 1973 of Admiral Carrero Blanco, Franco's prime minister and designated successor.

Franco fell ill in 1974 and died on 20 November 1975.

## The Transition to Democracy

After the death of Franco, Spaniards began to reclaim their country and Madrid took centre stage.

King Juan Carlos I, of the Bourbon family that had left the Spanish political stage with the flight of Alfonso XIII in 1931, had been groomed as head of state by Franco. But the king confounded the sceptics by entrusting Adolfo Suárez, a former moderate Francoist with whom he had long been in secret contact, with government in July 1976. With the king's approval Suárez quickly rammed a raft of changes through parliament while Franco loyalists and generals, suddenly rudderless without their leader, struggled to regroup.

Suárez and his centre-right coalition won elections in 1977 and set about writing a new constitution in collaboration with the now-legal opposition. It provided for a parliamentary monarchy with no state religion, and guaranteed a large degree of devolution to the 17 regions (including the Comunidad de Madrid) into which the country was now divided.

Spaniards got the fright of their lives in February 1981 when a pistol-brandishing, low-ranking Guardia Civil (Civil Guard) officer, Antonio Tejero Molina, marched into the Cortes in Madrid with an armed detachment and held parliament captive for 24 hours. Throughout a day of high drama the country held its breath as Spaniards waited to see whether Spain would be thrust back into the dark days of dictatorship or if the fledgling democracy would prevail. With the nation glued to their TV sets, King Juan Carlos I made a live broadcast denouncing Tejero and calling on the soldiers to return to their barracks. The coup fizzled out.

A year later Felipe González' PSOE won national elections. Spain's economic problems were legion – incomes were on a par with those of Iraq, ETA terrorism was claiming dozens of lives every year and unemployment was above 20%. But one thing Spaniards had in abundance was optimism and when, in 1986, Spain joined the European Community (EC), as it was then called, the country had well and truly returned to the fold of modern European nations.

The grandiose folly of Franco's Valle de los Caídos monument northwest of Madrid was largely constructed through the forced labour of republican prisoners of war.

HISTORY THE TRANSITION TO DEMOCRACY

| 1980s | 1981 | 1986 | 1991 |
|---|---|---|---|
| *La movida madrileña* (the Madrid scene) takes over the city, and becomes a byword for hedonism. The era produces such talents as Pedro Almodóvar, Agatha Ruiz de la Prada and Alaska. | On 23 February a group of armed Guardia Civil led by Antonio Tejero Molina attempt a coup; the king denounces them and the coup collapses. | Spain joins the European Community (EC), later the European Union (EU). EU subsidies and other assistance will later be credited with building the foundations of the modern Spanish economy. | Madrid elects a conservative mayor, José María Álvarez del Manzano of the Partido Popular (PP; Popular Party), for the first time, bringing an end to *la movida*. |

## La Movida Madrileña

Madrid's spirits could not be dampened and, with grand events taking place on the national stage, the city had become one of the most exciting places on earth. What London was to the swinging '60s and Paris to 1968, Madrid was to the 1980s. After the long, dark years of dictatorship and conservative Catholicism, Spaniards, especially *madrileños,* emerged onto the streets with all the zeal of ex-convent schoolgirls. Nothing was taboo in a phenomenon known as *la movida madrileña* (the Madrid scene), as young *madrileños* discovered the '60s, '70s and early '80s all at once. Drinking, drugs and sex were suddenly OK. All-night partying was the norm, drug taking in public was not a criminal offence (that changed in 1992), and the city howled. All across Madrid, summer terraces roared to the drinking, carousing crowds and young people from all over Europe flocked here to take part in the revelry.

What was remarkable about *la movida* is that it was presided over by Enrique Tierno Galván, an ageing former university professor who had been a leading opposition figure under Franco and was affectionately known throughout Spain as 'the old teacher'. A Socialist, he became mayor in 1979 and, for many, launched *la movida* by telling a public gathering *'a colocarse y ponerse al loro',* which loosely translates as 'get stoned and do what's cool'. Unsurprisingly, he was Madrid's most popular mayor ever and when he died in 1986 a million *madrileños* turned out for his funeral.

But *la movida* was not just about rediscovering the Spanish art of *salir de copas* (going out for a drink). It was also accompanied by an explosion of creativity among the country's musicians, designers and filmmakers keen to shake off the shackles of the repressive Franco years. The most famous of these was film director Pedro Almodóvar. Still one of Europe's most creative directors, his riotously colourful films captured the spirit of *la movida,* featuring larger-than-life characters who pushed the limits of sex and drugs. Although his later films became internationally renowned, his first films, *Pepi, Luci, Bom y otras chicas del montón* (Pepi, Luci, Bom and the Other Girls; 1980) and *Laberinto de pasiones* (Labyrinth of Passion; 1982), are where the spirit of the movement really comes alive. When he wasn't making films, Almodóvar immersed himself in the spirit of *la movida,* doing drag acts in smoky bars that people-in-the-know would frequent.

Madrid's first democratically elected conservative mayor, José María Álvarez del Manzano of the PP, ruled from 1991 until 2003 and became known as 'The Tunnelator' for beginning the ongoing mania of Madrid governments for semipermanent roadworks and large-scale infrastructure projects.

| 1992 | 11 March 2004 | 2007 | 2011 |
|---|---|---|---|
| In the same year that Barcelona hosts the Summer Olympics, Madrid is designated a European Capital of Culture. Drug taking in public is finally outlawed in the capital. | Terrorist bombings on Madrid commuter trains kill 191 people and injure 1755. The next day three million take to the streets in protest. The PSOE wins national elections on 14 March. | Twenty-one people are convicted of involvement in the March 2004 terrorist attacks, although the trial uncovers no evidence of Al-Qaeda involvement in the planning or execution of the bombings. | Protesters known as *indignados* (those who are indignant) occupy the Plaza de la Puerta del Sol, a forerunner to the worldwide Occupy protests. |

So what happened to *la movida*? Many say that it died in 1991 with the election of the conservative Popular Party's José María Álvarez del Manzano as mayor. In the following years rolling spliffs in public became increasingly dangerous and creeping clamps (ie closing hours) were imposed on the almost-lawless bars. Things have indeed quietened down a little, but you'll only notice if you were here during the 1980s.

## Madrid Sobers Up

After 12 years of Socialist rule, the conservative Partido Popular (PP; Popular Party) won mayoral elections in 1991 (they would hold the town hall until 2015) and from 1996 until 2004, the three levels of government in Madrid (local, regional and national) remained the preserve of the PP. Throughout this period, observers from other regions claimed that the PP overtly favoured development of the capital at the expense of Spain's other regions. Whatever the truth of such accusations, the city moved ahead in leaps and bounds, and as the national economy took off in the late 1990s, Madrid reaped the benefits. Extraordinary expansion programs for the metro, highways, airport and outer suburbs, and for inner-city renewal are unmistakable signs of confidence. By one reckoning, up to 75% of inward foreign investment in Spain was directed at the capital.

On 11 March 2004, just three days before the country was due to vote in national elections, Madrid was rocked by 10 bombs on four rush-hour commuter trains heading into the capital's Atocha station. When the dust cleared, 191 people had died and 1755 were wounded, many of them seriously. It was the biggest such terror attack in the nation's history.

If this attack united the city, political division lay ahead. On 15 May 2011, at the height of the economic crisis and with dissatisfaction with Spain's political class at an all-time high, *indignados* (those who are indignant) took over the Plaza de la Puerta del Sol in the centre of Madrid in a peaceful sit-in protest. Their popularity maintained by social media networks, they stayed for months, and were the forerunners to numerous such movements around the world, including Occupy Wall Street and its offshoots. It was the start of a movement that would transform Spanish politics.

The Popular Party's Esperanza Aguirre became the country's first-ever woman regional president in close-run elections for the Comunidad de Madrid in 2003, a position she held until 2012. In 2015, the leftist coalition Ahora Madrid, backed by the nationwide Podemos, won municipal elections, and retired judge Manuela Carmena became Madrid's first female mayor.

| 2014 | 2015 | 2016 | 2017 |
|---|---|---|---|
| Real Madrid football team wins a record 10th European Champions League, defeating cross-city rivals Atlético de Madrid 4-1 in Lisbon. | Despite finishing second in municipal elections, Manuela Carmena of the leftist Ahora Madrid becomes mayor, a post held by the conservative Popular Party since 1991. | Madrid records annual GDP growth of 3.7% (compared with 3.2% in Spain overall). | Real Madrid wins the second of two consecutive Champions League titles, taking their tally to a record 11. |

# City of Painters

**Spanish kings through the centuries were a pretty vain and decadent lot, and they loved to pose for portraits or compete with other European royals for the prestige that came from lavishing money on the great artists of the day. This marriage of royal money and personal patronage transformed Madrid into one of the world's richest producers and storehouses of paintings. Since the early 20th century, Spain's finest artistic academies have drawn Spain's most creative talents.**

## The Early Days

With royal patronage of the arts kicking off in the 16th century, it was difficult for local artists to get a look in. Felipe II – the monarch who made Madrid the permanent seat of the royal court – preferred the work of Italian artists such as Titian (Tiziano in Spanish) ahead of home-grown talent. Even some foreign artists who would later become masters were given short shrift. One of these was the Cretan-born Domenikos Theotokopoulos (1541–1614), known as El Greco (the Greek), who was perhaps the most extraordinary and temperamental 'Spanish' artist of the 16th century, but whom Felipe II rejected as a court artist. The Museo del Prado is the place to see works by Titian and El Greco.

## Velázquez & the Golden Age

As Spain's monarchs sought refuge from the creeping national malaise of the 17th century by promoting the arts, they fostered an artist who would rise above all others: Diego Rodríguez de Silva Velázquez (1599–1660). Born in Seville, Velázquez later moved to Madrid as court painter and stayed to make the city his own. He composed scenes (landscapes, royal portraits, religious subjects, snapshots of everyday life) that owe their vitality not only to his photographic eye for light and contrast but also to a compulsive interest in the humanity of his subjects, who seem to breathe on the canvas. His masterpieces include *Las meninas* (The Maids of Honour) and *La rendición de Breda* (The Surrender of Breda), both on view in the Museo del Prado.

Francisco de Zurbarán (1598–1664), a friend and contemporary of Velázquez, ended his life in poverty in Madrid; it was only after his death that he received the acclaim that his masterpieces deserved. He is best remembered for the startling clarity and light in his portraits of monks, a series of which hangs in the Real Academia de Bellas Artes de San Fernando. Several of his works also appear in the Museo del Prado.

Other masters of the era whose works hang in the Prado, though their connection to Madrid was limited, include José (Jusepe) de Ribera (1591–1652), who was influenced by Caravaggio and produced fine chiaroscuro works, and Bartolomé Esteban Murillo (1617–82).

# The 20th Century & Beyond

The 17th century may have been Spain's golden age, but the 20th century was easily its rival.

## Sorolla & Solana

Valencian native Joaquín Sorolla (1863–1923) flew in the face of the French Impressionist style, preferring the blinding sunlight of the Mediterranean coast to the muted tones favoured in Paris. He lived and worked in Madrid and his work can be studied in Madrid's Museo Sorolla, where he once lived.

Leading the way into the 20th century was Madrid-born José Gutiérrez Solana (1886–1945), whose disturbing, avant-garde approach to painting revels in low lighting, sombre colours and deathly pale figures. His work is emblematic of what historians now refer to as *España negra* (black Spain). A selection of his work is on display in the Centro de Arte Reina Sofía.

## Picasso, Dalí & Juan Gris

Málaga-born Pablo Ruiz Picasso (1881–1973) is one of the greatest and most original Spanish painters of all time. Although he spent much of his working life in Paris, he arrived in Madrid from Barcelona in 1897 at the behest of his father for a year's study at the Escuela de Bellas Artes de San Fernando. Never one to allow himself to be confined within formal structures, the precocious Picasso instead took himself to the Prado to learn from the masters, and to the streets to depict life as he saw it. Picasso went on to become the master of cubism, which was inspired by his fascination with primitivism, primarily African masks and early Iberian sculpture. This highly complex form reached its high point in *Guernica,* which hangs in the Centro de Arte Reina Sofía.

Picasso was not the only artist who found the Escuela de Bellas Artes de San Fernando too traditional for his liking. In 1922 Salvador Dalí (1904–89) arrived in Madrid from Catalonia, but decided that the eminent professors of the renowned fine-arts school were not fit to judge him. He spent four years living in the 'Resi', the renowned students' residence (which still functions today), where he met poet Federico García Lorca and future film director Luis Buñuel. The three self-styled anarchists and bohemians romped through the cafes and music halls of 1920s Madrid, frequenting brothels, engaging in pranks, immersing themselves in jazz and taking part in endless *tertulias* (literary discussions). Dalí, a true original and master of the surrealist form, was finally expelled from art school and left Madrid, never to return. The only remaining link with Madrid is a handful of his hallucinatory works in the Centro de Arte Reina Sofía.

In the same gallery is a fine selection of the cubist creations of Madrid's Juan Gris (1887–1927), who was turning out his best work in Paris while Dalí and his cohorts were up to no good in Madrid. Along with Picasso and Georges Braque, he was a principal exponent of the cubist style and his paintings can also be seen in the Museo Thyssen-Bornemisza and Real Academia de Bellas Artes de San Fernando.

## Contemporary Art

The death of Franco in 1975 unleashed a frenzy of activity and artistic creativity that was central to *la movida madrileña* (the Madrid scene). The now-closed Galería Moriarty became a focal point of exuberantly artistic reference. A parade of artists marched through the gallery, including leading *movida* lights such as Ceesepe (b 1958; real name

For paintings whose subject matter is Madrid (although she also paints other cities), Málaga-born Paula Varona (www.paulavarona.com) has few peers. Her website (which also lists upcoming exhibitions) has a stunning overview of her work.

## GOYA – A CLASS OF HIS OWN

Francisco José de Goya y Lucientes (1746–1828), who was born in the village of Fuen-detodos in Aragón, started his career as a cartoonist in the Real Fábrica de Tapices in Madrid. In 1776 Goya began designing for the tapestry factory, but in 1792 illness left him deaf; many critics speculate that his condition was largely responsible for his wild, often merciless style that would become increasingly unshackled from convention. By 1799 Goya was appointed Carlos IV's court painter.

Several distinct series and individual paintings mark his progress. In the last years of the 18th century he painted enigmatic masterpieces, such as *La maja vestida* (The Young Lady Dressed) and *La maja desnuda* (The Young Lady Undressed), identical portraits but for the lack of clothes in the latter. The rumour mill suggests the subject was none other than the Duchess of Alba, with whom he allegedly had an affair. What-ever the truth of Goya's sex life, the Inquisition was not amused by the artworks, and covered them up. Nowadays, all is bared in the Museo del Prado.

At about the same time as his enigmatic *Majas*, the prolific Goya executed the play-ful frescoes in Madrid's Ermita de San Antonio de la Florida, which have recently been restored to stunning effect. He also produced *Los Caprichos* (The Caprices), a biting series of 80 etchings lambasting the follies of court life and ignorant clergy.

The arrival of the French and war in 1808 had a profound impact on Goya and in-spired his unforgiving portrayals of the brutality of war: *El dos de mayo* (The Second of May) and, more dramatically, *El tres de mayo* (The Third of May). The latter depicts the execution of Madrid rebels by French troops.

After he retired to the Quinta del Sordo (Deaf Man's House) west of the Río Man-zanares in Madrid, he created his nightmarish *Pinturas negras* (Black Paintings). Ex-ecuted on the walls of the house, they were later removed and now hang in the Prado.

Goya spent the last years of his life in voluntary exile in France, where he continued to paint until his death.

---

Carlos Sánchez Pérez), who captures the spirit of 1980s Madrid with his eight short films and busy paintings full of people and activity (but recently veering towards surrealism). Another Moriarty protégé was Ouka Leele (b 1957, whose real name is Bárbara Allende), a self-taught photographer whose sometimes weird works stand out for her tangy treatment of colour. Her photos can be seen at the Centro de Arte Reina Sofía, Museo de Historia and the Museo Municipal de Arte Contem-poráneo. Another *movida* photographer who still exhibits around town is Alberto García-Alix (b 1956).

The rebellious, effervescent activity in the 1980s tends to cloud the fact that the visual arts in the Franco years were far from dead, although many artists spent years in exile. The art of Eduardo Arroyo (b 1937), in particular, is steeped in the radical spirit that kept him in exile for 15 years from 1962. His paintings tend in part towards pop art, brimming with ironic sociopolitical comment. Of the other exiles, one of Spain's greatest 20th-century sculptors, Toledo-born Alberto Sánchez (1895–1962), whose works can be seen at the open-air Museo al Aire Libre, lived his last years in Moscow. The work of Benjamín Palencia (1894–1980) shows striking similarities with some of Sánchez' sculptures.

Antonio López García (b 1936) takes a photographer's eye to his hyper-realistic paintings. Settings as simple as *Lavabo y espejo* (Wash Basin and Mirror, 1967) convert the most banal everyday objects into scenes of extraordinary depth, and the same applies to his Madrid street scenes, which are equally loaded with detail, light play and subtle colour, especially *La Gran Vía* (1981) and *Vallecas* (1980). He won the coveted Premio Príncipe de Asturias for art in 1985 and a couple of his works are in the Centro de Arte Reina Sofía.

# Architecture

Madrid's architecture spans the centuries and tells the broad sweep of Spain's history: the grandeur of Spain's imperial past sits alongside *barroco madrileño* (Madrid baroque), belle époque buildings and innovative contemporary architecture. It all comes together in the grand historical buildings that have been transformed by stunning modern projects of regeneration. It may lack the signature buildings of Paris or Barcelona, but the overall package is one of grace and elegance.

## Madrid up to the 16th Century

Madrid's origins as a Muslim garrison town yielded few architectural treasures, or at least few that remain. The only reminder of the Muslim presence is a modest stretch of the town wall, known as the Muralla Árabe, below the Catedral de Nuestra Señora de la Almudena. The bell towers of the Iglesia de San Pedro El Viejo and Iglesia de San Nicolás de los Servitas are the only modest representatives of the rich Mudéjar style (developed by the Moors who remained behind in reconquered Christian territory) that once adorned Madrid.

## Madrid Baroque & Beyond

Architect Juan de Herrera (1530–97) was perhaps the greatest figure of the Spanish Renaissance and he bequeathed to the city an architectural style all of its own. Herrera's trademark was to fuse the sternness of the Renaissance style with a timid approach to its successor, the more voluptuous, ornamental baroque. The result was an architectural style known as *barroco madrileño* (Madrid baroque). Herrera's austere masterpiece was the palace-monastery complex of San Lorenzo de El Escorial, but the nine-arched Puente de Segovia, down the southern end of Calle de Segovia, is also his.

The most successful proponent of the *barroco madrileño* style was Juan Gómez de Mora (1586–1648), who was responsible for laying out the Plaza Mayor, as well as the Convento de la Encarnación and the Palacio de Santa Cruz. Gómez de Mora's uncle, Francisco de Mora (1553–1610), added to an impressive family portfolio with the Palacio del Duque de Uceda on Calle Mayor. Other exceptional examples of the style are the Real Casa de la Panadería on Plaza Mayor and the main entrance of what is now the Museo de Historia.

Ventura Rodríguez (1717–85) dominated the architectural scene in 18th-century Madrid. He redesigned the interior of the Convento de la Encarnación. He also sidelined in spectacular fountains, and it is Rodríguez whom we have to thank for the goddess Cybele in the Plaza de la Cibeles and the Fuente de las Conchas in the Campo del Moro.

Where Ventura Rodríguez leaned towards a neoclassical style, Juan de Villanueva (1739–1811) embraced it wholeheartedly, most notably in the Palacio de Villanueva that would eventually house the Museo del Prado. Villanueva also oversaw the rebuilding of the Plaza Mayor after it was destroyed by fire in 1790 and designed numerous outbuildings of the royal residences, such as San Lorenzo de El Escorial.

**Notable New or Fusion Buildings**

.........................
*Centro de Arte Reina Sofía*
.........................
*Caixa Forum*
.........................
*Museo del Prado*
.........................
*Antigua Estación de Atocha*
.........................
*Terminal 4, Aeropuerto de Barajas*

# Belle Époque

As Madrid emerged from the chaos of the first half of the 19th century, a building boom began. The use of iron and glass, a revolution in building aesthetics that symbolised the embracing of modernity, became all the rage. The gorgeous Palacio de Cristal in the Parque del Buen Retiro was built at this time.

By the dawn of the 20th century, known to many as the belle époque, Madrid was abuzz with construction. Headed by the prolific Antonio Palacios (1874–1945), architects from all over Spain began to transform Madrid into the airy city you see today. Many looked to the past for their inspiration. Neo-Mudéjar was especially favoured for bullrings. The ring at Las Ventas, finished in 1934, is a classic example of the neo-Mudéjar style. A more bombastic (and perhaps the most spectacular) interpretation of the belle époque style is Palacios' Palacio de Comunicaciones, with its plethora of pinnacles and prancing ornaments, which was finished in 1917.

**Notable Old Buildings**

Palacio Real

Plaza de la Villa

Palacio de Comunicaciones

Sociedad General de Autores y Editores

Plaza de Toros Monumental de Las Ventas

Edificio Metrópolis

# Contemporary Architecture

Madrid's contribution to the revolution taking place in Spanish architecture circles has been muted, although there are some stand-out buildings.

Designed by Richard Rogers, Terminal Four (T4) of the Adolfo Suarez Madrid Barajas International Airport is a stunning, curvaceous work of art, which deservedly won Rogers the prestigious Stirling Prize in October 2006.

Another significant transformation on a grand scale has been Madrid's once-low-rise skyline, with four skyscrapers rising up above the Paseo de la Castellana in northern Madrid. Of these, the Torre Caja Madrid (250m, designed by Sir Norman Foster) is Spain's tallest building, just surpassing its neighbour, the Torre de Cristal (249.5m, designed by César Pelli). The Torre Espacio (236m, designed by Henry Cobb) has also won plaudits for its abundant use of glass.

Among the architectural innovations that travellers to Madrid are more likely to experience up close and at greater depth, the most exciting is perhaps the extension of the Museo del Prado, which opened in October 2007. The work of one of Spain's premier architects, the Pritzker Architecture Prize–winning Rafael Moneo, the extension links the main gallery with what remains of the cloisters of the Iglesia de San Jerónimo el Real. He won plaudits for his use of traditional building materials such as granite, red brick and oak. Moneo met two other major Madrid challenges with his acclaimed remodelling of the Antigua Estación de Atocha and his conversion of the Palacio de Villahermosa into the Museo Thyssen-Bornemisza, both in the mid-1990s.

International Architecture Day, which usually falls in early October, offers a chance to visit otherwise-closed architectural landmarks, including the Sociedad General de Autores y Editores.

Another landmark project in recent years has been the extension of the Centro de Arte Reina Sofía by the French architect Jean Nouvel. It's a stunning red glass-and-steel complement to the old-world Antigua Estación de Atocha across the Plaza del Emperador Carlos V and to the austerity of the remainder of the museum's 18th-century structure.

Between the Reina Sofía and the Prado and opposite the Real Jardín Botánico, the Caixa Forum, completed in 2008, is one of Madrid's most striking buildings. Designed by Swiss architects Jacques Herzog and Pierre de Meuron, its aesthetic seems to owe more to the world of sculpture than of architecture with its unusual iron-and-brick form. It's a worthy yet surprising addition to the Paseo del Prado's grandeur.

And one final thing for those who love architecture: while in Madrid you really must stay at the Hotel Silken Puerta América, where each floor has been custom designed by a world-renowned architect.

# Madrid's Film Scene

**Madrid is the uncontested capital of the Spanish film industry, which is defined by some exceptional individual talents (such as Pedro Almodóvar, Penélope Cruz, Antonio Banderas and Javier Bardem), and a local film-making industry that turns out work of real quality but struggles for both funding and international success. Hollywood and the home-grown industry come together for the annual Goya Awards (Spain's Oscars) in Madrid in February.**

## Directors

The still-young Alejandro Amenábar (b 1973) is already one of Spain's most respected directors. He was born in Chile but his family moved to Madrid when he was a child. He announced his arrival with *Tesis* (1996), but it was with *Abre los ojos* (Open Your Eyes; 1997), which was later adapted for Hollywood as *Vanilla Sky,* that his name became known internationally. His first English-language film was *The Others* (2001), which received plaudits from critics, but nothing like the clamour that surrounded *Mar adentro* (The Sea Inside; 2004), his stunning portrayal of a Galician fisherman's desire to die with dignity, which starred Javier Bardem. His 2009 *Ágora* was a stunning follow-up and, with a budget of US$50 million, is the most expensive Spanish film ever made. His film *Regression* (2015) starred Ethan Hawke and Emma Watson. Not content with directing, Amenábar also writes his own films.

Madrid-born Fernando Trueba (b 1955) has created some fine Spanish films, the best of which was his 1992 release *Belle Époque*. It portrays gentle romps and bed-hopping on a country estate in Spain in 1931 as four sisters pursue an ingenuous young chap against a background of growing political turbulence. *Belle Époque* took an Oscar for Best Foreign Language Film in 1993. His more recent works include *El baile de la victoria* (2009), *El artista y la modelo* (2012) and *La Reina de España* (2016). Trueba is equally well known for his documentary *Calle 54* (2000), which did for Latin jazz what the *Buena Vista Social Club* did for ageing Cuban musicians. Trueba was a leading personality in the craziness that was *la movida madrileña* in the 1980s.

**Almodóvar's Madrid Locations**

........................

Plaza Mayor – *La Flor de mi secreto*

El Rastro – *Laberinto de pasiones*

........................

Villa Rosa – *Tacones lejanos*

Café del Circulo de Bellas Artes – *Kika*

........................

Viaducto de Segovia – *Matador*

........................

Museo del Jamón (Calle Mayor) – *Carne Trémula*

## Actors

Of Spain's best-loved actors, few have enjoyed international popularity in recent times quite like the Oscar-winning heart-throb Javier Bardem, one of the best-known faces in Spanish cinema. Having made his name alongside Penélope Cruz in *Jamón Jamón* (1992), his popular roles include those in *Before Night Falls* (2000), *Mar adentro* (The Sea Inside; 2004), *Love in the Time of Cholera* (2007) and *No Country for Old Men* (2007); remarkably his Oscar for Best Supporting Actor in 2008 was a first for Spanish actors. Like so many of Spain's best actors, Bardem has passed through the finishing school that is Pedro Almodóvar's movies, appearing in *Carne trémula* (Live Flesh; 1997). Javier Bardem

## PEDRO ALMODÓVAR

Born in 1951 in a small, impoverished village in Castilla-La Mancha, Almodóvar moved to Madrid in 1969 where he found his spiritual home and began his career making underground Super 8 movies and by selling secondhand goods at El Rastro flea market. He soon became a symbol of Madrid's counterculture, but it was after Franco's death in 1975 that Almodóvar became a nationally renowned cult figure. His early films *Pepi, Luci, Bom y otras chicas del montón* (Pepi, Luci, Bom and the Other Girls; 1980) and *Laberinto de pasiones* (Labyrinth of Passion; 1982) – the film that brought a young Antonio Banderas to the country's attention – announced him as the icon of *la movida madrileña,* the explosion of hedonism and creativity in the early years of post-Franco Spain. Almodóvar had both in bucketloads; he peppered his films with candy-bright colours and characters leading lives where sex and drugs were the norm. By night Almodóvar performed in Madrid's most famous *movida* bars as part of a drag act called 'Almodóvar & McNamara'. He even appears in this role in *Laberinto de pasione*s.

He went on to broaden his fan base with quirkily comic looks at modern Spain, generally set in the capital, such as *Mujeres al borde de un ataque de nervios* (Women on the Verge of a Nervous Breakdown; 1988) and *¡Átame!* (Tie Me Up! Tie Me Down!; 1990). Oscar-winning *Todo sobre mi madre* (All About My Mother; 1999) is also notable for the coming of age of Madrid-born actress Penélope Cruz, who'd starred in a number of Almodóvar films and was considered part of a select group of the director's leading ladies long before she became a Hollywood star. Other outstanding movies in a formidable portfolio include *Hable con ella* (Talk to Her; 2002), for which he won a Best Original Screenplay Oscar; and *Volver* (2006), which reunited Almodóvar with Penélope Cruz to popular and critical acclaim. His most recent work, *Julieta* (2016), his 20th feature film, was screened at the Cannes Film Festival.

also comes from one of Spain's most distinguished film-making families: his uncle, Juan Antonio Bardem (1922–2002), is often considered Madrid's senior cinematic bard.

Penélope Cruz is another Hollywood actress with roots in Madrid (where she was born in 1974). In the late 1990s Penélope Cruz took a leap of faith and headed for Hollywood where she has had success in such films as *Captain Corelli's Mandolin* (2001) and *Vanilla Sky* (2001), but recognition of her acting abilities has come most powerfully for her roles in the Almodóvar classics *Carne trémula* (Live Flesh; 1997), *Todo sobre mi madre* (All About My Mother; 1999) and *Volver* (2006). The last was described by one critic as 'a raging love letter' to Cruz and earned her a Best Actress Oscar nomination, a remarkable achievement for a foreign-language film. She finally won an Oscar for Best Supporting Actress in 2009 for her role in Woody Allen's *Vicky Cristina Barcelona.*

Although not born in Madrid, Málaga-born Antonio Banderas moved to Madrid in 1981, at the age of 19, to launch his career and soon became caught up in the maelstrom of *la movida madrileña,* where he made the acquaintance of Almodóvar. After an early role in *Laberinto de pasiones* (Labyrinth of Passion; 1982), Banderas would return to the Almodóvar stable with *Mujeres al borde de un ataque de nervios* (Women on the Verge of a Nervous Breakdown; 1988), as his Hollywood career was taking off.

# Flamenco

**Flamenco seems to capture in musical form all the passion of this most passionate of countries. The power of flamenco is clear to anyone who has heard its melancholy strains in the background of a crowded Spanish bar, and taking in a live performance can be a highlight of any visit to Madrid.**

## Flamenco's Roots

Flamenco's origins have been lost to time. While some experts have suggested that flamenco derives from Byzantine chants used in Visigothic churches, most musical historians speculate that it probably dates back to a fusion of songs brought to Spain by the Roma people, with music and verses from North Africa crossing into medieval Muslim Andalucía. Flamenco as we now know it first took recognisable form in the 18th and early 19th centuries among the Roma in the lower Guadalquivir valley in western Andalucía.

## Flamenco in Madrid

At first the Roma and Andalucians were concentrated in the area around Calle de Toledo. The novelist Benito Pérez Galdós found no fewer than 88 Andalucian taverns along that street towards the end of the 19th century. The scene shifted in the early 20th century to the streets around Plaza de Santa Ana. As flamenco's appeal widened and became a tourist attraction, more *tablaos* (flamenco venues) sprang up throughout Madrid.

Now, Madrid claims to be Spain's capital of flamenco, which is true, but only to an extent. The Cádiz–Jerez–Seville axis in Andalucía remains the genre's spiritual home and it's still the area with the most authentic flamenco venues. But Madrid is undoubtedly flamenco's biggest stage, the place where the best performers of flamenco always turn up at one time or another. And therein lies the essence of Madrid's contribution to the development of flamenco: it has always been a stage, often a prestigious one, that has brought flamenco to a wider audience. Most Madrid venues may lack the intimate atmosphere and gritty authenticity that is an essential element of the flamenco experience, but the quality is usually excellent.

One of Spain's most prestigious flamenco festivals, **Suma Flamenca** (www.madrid.org/sumaflamenca), happens in Madrid every June.

### Madrid Flamenco Venues
Casa Patas
Café Ziryab
Teatro Flamenco Madrid
Villa Rosa
Las Tablas
Corral de la Morería
Las Carboneras

## Flamenco Stars

Two names loom large over the world of flamenco – Paco de Lucía and El Camarón de la Isla – who were responsible for flamenco's revival in the second half of the 20th century. Theirs is the standard by which all other flamenco artists are measured.

Paco de Lucía (1947–2014) was the doyen of flamenco guitarists with a virtuosity few could match. For many in the flamenco world, he was the personification of *duende,* that indefinable capacity to transmit the

## FLAMENCO – THE ESSENTIAL ELEMENTS

A flamenco singer is known as a *cantaor* (male) or *cantaora* (female); a dancer is a *bailaor* or *bailaora*. Most of the songs and dances are performed to a blood-rush of guitar from the *tocaor* or *tocaora* (male or female flamenco guitarist). Percussion is provided by tapping feet, clapping hands and sometimes castanets. Flamenco *coplas* (songs) come in many different types, from the anguished *soleá* or the intensely despairing *siguiriya* to the livelier *alegría* or the upbeat *bulería*. The first flamenco was *cante jondo* (deep song), an anguished instrument of expression for a group on the margins of society. *Jondura* (depth) is still the essence of pure flamenco.

power and passion of flamenco. Other guitar maestros include members of the Montoya family (some of whom are better known by the sobriquet of Los Habichuela), especially Juan (b 1933) and Pepe (b 1944).

In 1968 Paco de Lucía began flamenco's most exciting partnership with his friend El Camarón de la Isla (1950–92); together they recorded nine classic albums. Until his premature death, El Camarón was the leading light of contemporary *cante jondo* and it's impossible to overstate his influence on the art; his introduction of electric bass into his songs, for example, paved the way for a generation of artists to take flamenco in hitherto unimagined directions. Although born in San Fernando in Andalucía's far south, El Camarón was the artist in residence at Madrid's Torres Bermejas (p65) for 12 years, and it was during this period that his collaboration with Paco de Lucía was at its best. In his later years El Camarón teamed up with Tomatito, one of Paco de Lucía's protégés, and the results were similarly ground-breaking. When El Camarón died in 1992 an estimated 100,000 people attended his funeral.

Another artist who reached the level of cult figure was Enrique Morente (1942–2010). Referred to by one Madrid newspaper as 'the last bohemian', Morente was careful not to alienate flamenco purists but through his numerous collaborations across genres he helped lay the foundations for Nuevo Flamenco and Fusion. His daughter, *cantaora* Estrella Morente (b 1980), is considered one of the genre's most exciting talents.

One of the most venerable *cantaoras* is Carmen Linares (b 1951), who has spent much of her working life in Madrid. Leading contemporary figures include the flighty, adventurous Joaquín Cortés (b 1969), and Antonio Canales (b 1962), who is more of a flamenco purist.

### Top Flamenco Albums

Paco de Lucía
*Antología* (1995)

*Una Leyenda Flamenca* (1993)

*Blues de la Frontera* (1986)

*Cositas Buenas* (2004)

*Lágrimas Negras* (2003)

*Sueña la Alhambra* (2005)

## Nuevo Flamenco & Fusion

Two of the earliest groups to fuse flamenco with rock back in the 1980s were Ketama and Pata Negra, whose music is labelled by some as gypsy rock. In the early 1990s, Radio Tarifa emerged with a mesmerising mix of flamenco, North African and medieval sounds. A more traditional flamenco performer, Juan Peña Lebrijano, better known as El Lebrijano, has created some equally appealing combinations with classical Moroccan music. Diego el Cigala, one of modern flamenco's finest voices, relaunched his career with an exceptional collaboration with Cuban virtuoso Bebo Valdés (*Lágrimas Negras;* 2003) and has released critically acclaimed albums in the years since.

Chambao is the most popular of the Nuevo Flamenco bands doing the rounds at the moment, while Barcelona group Ojos de Brujo has won acclaim for its gritty sound. Also popular is Diego Amador (b 1973), a self-taught pianist. All of these artists perform in Madrid from time to time.

### Flamenco Resources

A good website for all things flamenco is www.deflamenco.com.

El Flamenco Vive, a store near Plaza Mayor, has a wide range of flamenco books and CDs.

# Survival Guide

# Transport

## ARRIVING IN MADRID

Madrid's Barajas Airport is one of Europe's busiest and is served by almost 100 airlines. Direct flights – whether with low-cost carriers or other airlines – connect the city with destinations across Europe. A smaller but nonetheless significant number of airlines also fly into Madrid direct from the Americas, Asia and Africa, and there are plenty of domestic flights to Madrid from other Spanish cities. Flight times include less than one hour to Lisbon and around two hours to London, Paris and some Moroccan cities.

Within Spain, Madrid is the hub of the country's outstanding bus and train network. Bus routes radiate into and out from the Spanish capital to all four corners of the country, and long-haul cross-border services fanning out across Europe, with some also going to Morocco. The ongoing expansion of Spain's high-speed rail network has dramatically cut travel times between Madrid and the rest of the country. The rail link to Barcelona in particular has also brought Madrid that much closer to the rest of Europe and there are plans for a direct high-speed rail link between Paris and Madrid.

Flights, cars and tours can be booked online at lonelyplanet.com.

## Aeropuerto de Barajas

Madrid's **Adolfo Suárez Madrid-Barajas airport** (📞902 404 704; www.aena. es; Ⓜ Aeropuerto T1, T2 & T3, Aeropuerto T4) lies 15km northeast of the city, and it's Europe's sixth-busiest hub, with almost 50 million passengers passing through here every year.

Barajas has four terminals. Terminal 4 (T4) deals mainly with flights of Iberia and its partners, while the remainder leave from the conjoined T1, T2 and (rarely) T3. To match your airline with a terminal,

visit the Adolfo Suárez Madrid-Barajas section of www.aena.es and click on 'Airlines'.

Although all airlines conduct check-in *(facturación)* at the airport's departure areas, some also allow check-in at the Nuevos Ministerios metro stop and transport interchange in Madrid itself – ask your airline.

There are car rental services, ATMs, money-exchange bureaus, pharmacies, tourist offices, left luggage offices and parking services at T1, T2 and T4.

### Metro

One of the easiest ways into town from the airport is line 8 of the metro to the Nuevos Ministerios transport interchange, which connects with lines 10 and 6 and the local overground *cercanías* (local trains serving suburbs and nearby towns). It operates from 6.05am to 1.30am. A single ticket costs €4.50 including the €3 airport supplement. If you're charging your public transport card

## CLIMATE CHANGE & TRAVEL

Every form of transport that relies on carbon-based fuel generates $CO_2$, the main cause of human-induced climate change. Modern travel is dependent on aeroplanes, which might use less fuel per kilometre per person than most cars but travel much greater distances. The altitude at which aircraft emit gases (including $CO_2$) and particles also contributes to their climate change impact. Many websites offer 'carbon calculators' that allow people to estimate the carbon emissions generated by their journey and, for those who wish to do so, to offset the impact of the greenhouse gases emitted with contributions to portfolios of climate-friendly initiatives throughout the world. Lonely Planet offsets the carbon footprint of all staff and author travel.

with a 10-ride Metrobús ticket (€12.20), you'll need to top it up with the €3 supplement if you're travelling to/from the airport. The journey to Nuevos Ministerios takes around 15 minutes, around 25 minutes from T4.

## Taxi

A taxi to the centre (around 30 minutes, depending on traffic; 35 to 40 minutes from T4) costs a fixed €30 for anywhere inside the M30 motorway (which includes all of downtown Madrid). There's a minimum €20, even if you're only going to an airport hotel.

## Minibus

**AeroCITY** (☑91 747 75 70, 902 151654; www.aerocity.com; ⊘24hr) is a private minibus service that takes you door-to-door between central Madrid and the airport (T1 in front of Arrivals Gate 2, T2 between gates 5 and 6, and T4 arrivals hall). You can reserve a seat or the entire minibus; the latter operates like a taxi. Book by phone or online.

## Bus

The **Exprés Aeropuerto** (Airport Express; www.emt madrid.es; per person €5; ⊘24hr; 🛜) runs between Puerta de Atocha train station and the airport. From 11.30pm until 6am, departures are from the Plaza de Cibeles, not the train station. Departures take place every 13 to 20 minutes from the station or at night-time every 35 minutes from Plaza de Cibeles.

Alternatively, from T1, T2 and T3 take bus 200 to/from the **Intercambiador de Avenida de América** (Ⓜ Av de América), the transport interchange on Avenida de América. A single ticket costs €4.50 including the €3 airport supplement. The first departures from the airport are at 5.10am (T1, T2 and T3). The last scheduled service from the airport is 11.30pm; buses leave every 12 to 20 minutes.

A free bus service connects all four airport terminals.

## Estación de Atocha

### Bus

Not as easy to decipher as the metro, numerous bus routes (one-way/10-trip ticket €1.50/12.20) pass close to the station. For route maps check the website of the **Empresa Municipal de Transportes de Madrid** (EMT; ☑902 507 850; www.emtmadrid.es).

### Metro

The Atocha Renfe metro station (line 1; one-way/10-trip ticket €1.50/12.20), not to be confused with the nearby Atocha station, is inside the Renfe train station. From Atocha Renfe it's 10 to 15 minutes to Sol station, with connections elsewhere via lines 2 and 3. Buy tickets from machines at the station.

While the *cercanías* suburban rail network mostly services outlying suburbs, it does operate a useful service that connects Atocha Renfe with Sol, Nuevos Ministerios and Estación de Chamartín. If you have a connecting Renfe ticket, travel on the *cercanías* network is free. Buy your ticket by scanning your Renfe ticket bar code at one of the Renfe *cercanías* machines close to the platform exit.

### Taxi

Taxis leave from the top floor of the station. A taxi to the centre (five to 10 minutes, depending on traffic) costs from €5 to €8, plus a €3 train station surcharge.

## Estación de Chamartín

North of the city centre, **Estación de Chamartín** (☑902 432343; Paseo de la Castellana; Ⓜ Chamartín) has numerous long-distance rail services, especially those to/from northern Spain. This is also where long-haul international trains arrive from Paris and Lisbon.

### Bus

Numerous bus routes (one-way/10-trip ticket €1.50/12.20) pass close to the station. Check www.emt madrid.es for route maps.

### Metro

Chamartín station has its own metro station (lines 1 and 10; one-way/10-trip ticket €1.50/12.20). From Chamartín station to Sol takes from 15 to 20 minutes with connections elsewhere via lines 2 and 3. Buy tickets from machines at the station.

There's also the Chamartín–Nuevos Ministerios–Sol–Atocha *cercanías* service that's free if you have a connecting Renfe ticket. Again, there are dedicated machines for this service.

### Taxi

A taxi to the centre (around 15 minutes, depending on traffic) costs around €10 plus a €3 train station surcharge.

## Estación Sur de Autobuses

**Estación Sur de Autobuses** (☑91 468 42 00; Calle de Méndez Álvaro 83; Ⓜ Méndez Álvaro), just south of the M-30 ring road, is the city's principal bus station. It serves most destinations to the south and many in other parts of the country. Most bus companies have a ticket office here, even if their buses depart from elsewhere.

**Avanzabus** (☑902 020052; www.avanzabus.com) has services to Extremadura (eg Cáceres), Castilla y León (eg Salamanca and Zamora) and Valencia via Cuenca, as well as Lisbon, Portugal. All leave from Estación Sur.

### Metro

The bus station's metro stop is Méndez Álvaro (line 6; one-way/10-trip ticket €1.50/12.20). To get to the central Sol station, take line 6 to Legazpi station and change to line 3. Buy tickets from machines at the station.

### Taxi

A taxi to the centre (around 20 to 30 minutes, depending on traffic) costs around €10 to €15 plus a €3 bus station surcharge.

# GETTING AROUND

Madrid has an excellent public transport network. The most convenient way of getting around is via the metro, whose 11 lines criss-cross the city; no matter where you find yourself you're never far from a metro station. The bus network is equally extensive and operates under the same ticketing system, although the sheer number of routes (around 200!) makes it more difficult for first-time visitors to master. Taxis in Madrid are plentiful and relatively cheap by European standards.

## Bicycle

Lots of people zip around town on *motos* (mopeds) and bike lanes are increasingly a part of the inner city's thoroughfares. Be aware, however, that the latter are relatively new and few drivers are accustomed to keeping an eye out for cyclists.

You can transport your bicycle on the metro all day on Saturday and Sunday, and at any time from Monday to Friday except 7.30am to 9.30am, 2pm to 4pm and 6pm to 8pm. You can also take your bike aboard *cercanías* at any time.

### Hire

**Bike Spain** (Map p232; ☑91 559 06 53; www.bikespain. info; Calle del Codo; bike rental half/full day from €12/18, tours from €30; ☺10am-2pm & 4-7pm Mon-Fri Mar-Oct, 10am-2pm & 3-6pm Mon-Fri Nov-Feb; MÓpera) Bicycle hire plus English-language guided city tours by bicycle, by day or (Friday) night, as well as longer expeditions.

**Trixi.com** (Map p238; ☑915 231 547; www.trixi.com; Calle

---

---

de los Jardines 12; 1/2/8/24hr incl helmet €4/6/12/15, tour €25; ☺10am-2pm & 4-8pm Mon-Fri, 10am-8pm Sat & Sun, tour 11am daily; MGran Vía) Bicycle hire and cycling tours of central Madrid.

**Bike & Roll** (☑91 142 77 93; www.bikeandroll.es; Calle de Áncora 36; per hr/day from €4/20; ☺10am-2pm & 5-8pm Mon-Fri, 10am-2pm Sat; 🚲; MPalos de la Frontera) Rents out bikes close to the Estación de Atocha.

**DiverBikes** (☑91 431 34 24; www.diverbikes.es; Ave Menendez Pelayo 9; per hr from €4; ☺10am-9pm; MPríncipe de Vergara) Rentals just across the road from the northeastern corner of El Retiro.

**Mi Bike Río** (Map p255; ☑91 139 46 52; www.mibikerio. com; Calle de Aniceto Marinas 26; bike per hr/day €5/30; ☺10.30am-2.30pm & 4-8pm Mon-Fri, 10am-8pm Sat & Sun; MPríncipe Pío) Good choice for riding along the river; it's a short walk down the hill from the royal palace or Plaza de España.

## Bus

Buses operated by **Empresa Municipal de Transportes de Madrid** (EMT; ☑902 507 850; www.emtmadrid.es) travel along most city routes regularly between about 6.30am and 11.30pm. Twenty-six night-bus *búhos* (owls) routes operate from 11.45pm to

5.30am, with all routes originating in Plaza de la Cibeles.

The **Intercambiador de Autobuses de Moncloa** (Plaza de la Moncloa; MMoncloa) has buses to many villages around the Comunidad de Madrid.

## Car & Motorcycle

However you got *to* the city, avoid driving once you're in Madrid if you can. The morning and evening rush hours frequently involve snarling traffic jams. They're even possible in the wee hours of the morning, especially on weekends when the whole city seems to either be behind the wheel or in a bar. The streets are dead between about 2pm and 4pm, when people are either eating or snoozing.

### Hire

**Avis** (☑902 180 854; www. avis.es; Gran Vía 60; MSanto Domingo)

**Enterprise/Atesa** (☑915 42 50 15, 902 100 101; www.atesa. es; Plaza de España, underground parking area; MPlaza de España)

**Europcar** (☑902 105 030; www.europcar.es; Calle de San Leonardo de Dios 8; MPlaza de España)

**Hertz** (☑915 42 58 05, 902 402 405; www.hertz.es; Edificio de España, Calle de la Princesa 14; MPlaza de España)

## Parking

If you've parked in a street parking spot and return to find that an inspector has left you a ticket, don't despair. If you arrive back within a reasonable time after the ticket was issued (what constitutes a reasonable time varies from place to place, but it is rarely more than a couple of hours), don't go looking for the inspector, but instead head for the nearest parking machine. Most machines in most cities allow you to pay a small penalty (usually around €5) to cancel the fine (keep both pieces of paper just in case). If you're unable to work out what to do, ask a local for help.

It's also worth noting that metered street-parking zones (*zonas azules*, indicated by blue lines on the road or roadside) are generally free of charge at the following times, although always check the signs: from about 2pm to 4pm or 5pm through the night from about 8pm to 9am or 10am on Saturday afternoons/evenings all day Sunday and public holidays.

## Metro

Madrid's modern metro (www.metromadrid.es), Europe's second largest, is a fast, efficient and safe way to navigate Madrid, and generally easier than getting to grips with bus routes. There are 11 colour-coded lines in central Madrid, in addition to the modern southern suburban MetroSur system, as well as lines heading east to the population centres of Pozuelo and Boadilla del Monte. Colour maps showing the metro system are available from any metro station or online. The metro operates from 6.05am to 1.30am.

## Taxi

Daytime flagfall is, for example, €2.40 in Madrid, and up to €2.90 from 9pm to 7am, and on weekends and holidays. You then pay €1.05 to €1.20 per kilometre depending on the time of day. Several supplementary charges, usually posted inside the taxi, apply. These include: €5.50 to/from the airport (if you're not paying the fixed rate); €3 from taxi ranks at train and bus stations; €3 to/from the Parque Ferial Juan Carlos I; and €6.70 on New Year's Eve and Christmas Eve from 10pm to 6am. There's no charge for luggage.

Among the 24-hour taxi services are **Tele-Taxi** (☑91 371 21 31; www.tele-taxi.es; ⏲24hr) and **Radio-Teléfono Taxi** (☑91 547 82 00; www.radiotelefono-taxi.com; ⏲24hr).

A green light on the roof means the taxi is *libre* (available). Usually a sign to this effect is also placed in the lower passenger side of the windscreen.

Tipping taxi drivers is not common practice, though rounding fares up to the nearest euro or two doesn't hurt.

## Train

The short-range *cercanías* regional trains operated by Renfe are handy for making a quick, north–south hop between Chamartín and Atocha train stations (with stops at Nuevos Ministerios and Sol), or for the trip out to San Lorenzo de El Escorial.

# TOURS

**Insider's Madrid** (☑91 447 38 66; www.insidersmadrid. com; tours from €70) An impressive range of tailor-made tours, including walking, shopping, fashion, fine arts, tapas, flamenco and bullfighting tours. 'The Botín Experience' (€75) covers the history of the world's oldest restaurant, Restaurante Sobrino de Botín. Tours run for 45 minutes at 12.15pm and 7pm, and includes a six-course lunch or dinner and a small ceramic gift.

**Madrid Original** (☑91 521 04 49; www.madridoriginal. com; tours €100-150) Privately run tours (for up to six people) in English, Spanish or French by professional guides. Tours include the major museums, Gran Vía, the Parque del Buen Retiro and tailor-made itineraries.

**Adventurous Appetites** (☑639 331 073; www. adventurousappetites.com; 4hr tours €50; ⏲8pm-midnight Mon-Sat) English-language tapas tours through central Madrid. Prices include the first drink but exclude food.

**Devour Madrid Food Tour** (☑69 511 18 32; www. madridfoodtour.com; tours €50-130) With five tours for different tastes and budgets, Devour Madrid shows you the best of Spanish food and wine in the centre of Madrid. Tours are themed: wine and tapas, flamenco, authentic local markets, history or (for the most serious foodies) the Ultimate Spanish Cuisine tour, which takes you to eight tasting stops in four hours.

**Wellington Society** (☑609 143203; www.wellsoc.org; tours from €95) A handful of quirky historical tours laced with anecdotes and led by the inimitable Stephen Drake-Jones.

**Madrid City Tour** (☑902 024 758; www.madridcitytour. es; 1-/2-day ticket adult €19/22.50, child/free €9/11.70; ⏲9am-10pm Mar-Oct, 10am-6pm Nov-Feb) Hop-on, hop-off open-topped buses that run every 10 to 20 minutes along two routes: one that takes in the main highlights downtown, the other heads north along Paseo de la Castellana and returns via Salamanca. You can buy tickets online or on the bus. There are also nocturnal departures from mid-June to mid-September.

**Spanish Tapas Madrid** (☑672 301231; www.spanish tapasmadrid.com; per person from €70) Local boy Luis Ortega takes you through some iconic Madrid tapas bars, as well as offering tours that take in old Madrid, flamenco and the Prado.

**Madrid Segway Tours** (☑659 824499; www. madsegs.com; Paseo del Virgen del Puerto 45; 2/3hr tour per person €45/65, plus refundable deposit €15) Segway tours of downtown Madrid.

# Directory A–Z

## Customs Regulations

People entering Spain from outside the EU are allowed to bring in duty-free:

→ one bottle of spirits

→ one bottle of wine

→ 50mL of perfume

→ 200 cigarettes

There are no duty-free allowances for travel between EU countries. For duty-paid items bought at normal shops in one EU country and taken into another, the allowances are 90L of wine, 10L of spirits, unlimited quantities of perfume and 800 cigarettes.

## Discount Cards

→ The International Student Identity Card (ISIC; www.isic.org), the Euro<26 card (www.euro26.org) and (sometimes) university student cards entitle students to discounts of up to 50% at many sights.

→ If you're over 65, you may be eligible for an admission discount to some attractions. Some attractions limit discounts to those with a Seniors Card issued by an EU country

### TAP WATER

Tap water is safe to drink in Madrid.

or other country with which Spanish citizens enjoy reciprocal rights.

→ If you plan to visit the Museo del Prado, Museo Thyssen-Bornemisza and Centro de Arte Reina Sofía, the Paseo del Arte ticket covers them all in a combined ticket (€29.60) and is valid for one visit to each gallery during a 12-month period; buying separate tickets costs €36.

## Electricity

The electric current in Madrid is 220/230V, 50Hz, as in the rest of continental Europe. European-style, two-pin plugs are used.

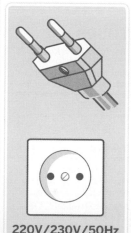

**220V/230V/50Hz**

## Emergency

| Ambulance | ☎061 |
|---|---|
| EU Standard Emergency Number | ☎112 |
| Fire Brigade (Bomberos) | ☎080 |
| Local Police (Policía Municipal) | ☎092 |
| Military Police (Guardia Civil) For traffic accidents. | ☎062 |
| Policía Nacional | ☎091 |
| Teléfono de la Víctima, hotline for victims of racial or sexual violence. | ☎902 180995 |

## LGBTQI Travellers

Homosexuality is legal in Spain and the age of consent is 16, as it is for heterosexuals. Same-sex marriages were legalised in Spain in 2005.

Long before that, Madrid had always been one of Europe's most gay-friendly cities. The city's gay community is credited with reinvigorating the once down-at-heel inner-city *barrio* (district) of Chueca, where Madrid didn't just come out of the closet, it ripped the doors off in the process. Today the *barrio* is one of Madrid's most vibrant and it's very much the heart and soul of gay Madrid, with cafes, bars, hotels, shops and nightclubs clearly oriented to a gay clientele. But there's nothing ghetto-like about Chueca. Its extravagantly gay-and-lesbian personality is anything but exclusive and the crowd is almost always mixed gay-straight. As gay and lesbian residents like to say, Chueca isn't gay-friendly, it's hetero-friendly.

The best time of all to be in town is around the last Saturday in June for Madrid's gay and lesbian pride march, **Día del Orgullo de Gays, Lesbianas y Transexuales** (www.orgullo lgtb.org).

Madrid also hosts the annual **Les Gai Cine Mad festival** (☑915 930 540; www.lesgaicinemad.com; ☻late Oct/early Nov), a celebration of lesbian, gay and trans-sexual films.

## Websites

**LGBT Madrid** (www.esmadrid. com/en/madrid-lgbt) Madrid's tourist office has useful information.

**Chueca.com** (www.chueca. com) Useful gay portal with extensive links.

**Gay Iberia** (www.gayiberia. com) Gay guide to Madrid.

**Gay Madrid 4 U** (www.gay madrid4u.com) A good over-view of Madrid's gay bars and nightclubs.

**NightTours.com** (www.night tours.com) A reasonably good guide to gay nightlife and other attractions in Madrid.

**Shangay** (www.shangay.com) For news, upcoming events, reviews and contacts. It also publishes *Shanguide*, a Madrid-centric biweekly magazine jammed with listings (including saunas and hardcore clubs) and contact ads. Its companion publication *Shangay Express* is better for articles with a hand-ful of listings and ads. They're available in gay bookshops and in gay and gay-friendly bars.

## Organisations

**Colectivo de Gais y Lesbianas de Madrid** (Cogam; ☑91 523 00 70, 91 522 45 17; www. cogam.es; Calle de la Puebla 9; ☻5-9pm Mon-Fri, 6-8pm Sat; Ⓜ Callao, Gran Vía) Offers activities and has an informa-tion office and social centre.

**Federación Estatal de Les-bianas, Gays, Transexuales & Bisexuales** (☑91 360 46 05; www.felgtb.org; 4th fl, Calle de las Infantas 40; ☻8am-8pm Mon-Thu, 8am-3.30pm Fri; Ⓜ Gran Vía) A national advo-cacy group, based in Madrid; it played a leading role in lobby-ing for the legalisation of gay marriages.

**Fundación Triángulo** (Map p255; ☑91 593 05 40; www. fundaciontriangulo.org; 1st fl, Calle de Meléndez Valdés 52; ☻10am-2pm & 4-8pm Mon-Fri; Ⓜ Argüelles) One of several sources of information on gay issues in Madrid.

## Insurance

We strongly recommend that you don't leave home without travel insurance. Find out in advance if your insurance plan will make payments directly to provid-ers or reimburse you later for overseas health expenditures (many Spanish hospitals and doctors expect payment up front). It's also worth making sure that your travel insur-ance will cover repatriation home or to better medical facilities elsewhere. Your insurance company may be able to locate the nearest source of medical help, or you can ask at your hotel.

In an emergency, contact your embassy or consulate. Your travel insurance will not usually cover you for any-thing other than emergency dental treatment. Not all insurance covers emergency aeromedical evacuation home, which may be the only way to get medical attention for a serious emergency.

## Internet Access

Most midrange and top-end hotels, as well as some cafes and restaurants, have wi-fi. Otherwise, check out www. madridmemata.es/madrid-wifi for a reasonable list of wi-fi hot spots.

Most of Madrid's internet cafes have fallen by the wayside. You'll find plenty of small *locutorios* (small shops selling phonecards and cheap phone calls) all over the city and many have a few computers out the back.

## Medical Services

All foreigners have the same right as Spaniards to emergency medical treat-ment in a public hospital. EU citizens are entitled to the full range of health-care services in public hospitals free of charge, but you'll need to present your Euro-pean Health Insurance Card (EHIC); enquire at your na-tional health service before leaving home. Even if you have no insurance, you'll be treated in an emergency, with costs in the public system ranging from free to €150 for a basic consulta-tion. Non-EU citizens have to pay for anything other than emergency treatment – one good reason among many to have a travel-insurance policy. If you have a specific health complaint, obtain the necessary information and referrals for treatment be-fore leaving home.

**Unidad Medica** (Anglo Ameri-can; ☑91 435 18 23, 24hr 916 56 90 57; www.unidadmedica. com; Calle del Conde de Aranda 1; ☻9am-8pm Mon-Fri, 10am-1pm Sat Sep-Jul, 10am-5pm Mon-Fri, 10am-1pm Sat Aug; Ⓜ Retiro) A private clinic with a wide range of specialisations and where all doctors speak Spanish and English, with some also speaking French and Ger-man. Each consultation costs around €125.

**Hospital General Gregorio Marañón** (☎91 586 80 00; Calle del Doctor Esquerdo 46; MSáinz de Baranda, O'Donnell, Ibiza) One of the city's main (and more central) hospitals.

## Money

The easiest way to travel is to take a small amount of cash and withdraw money from ATMs as you go.

### Changing Money

You can change cash or travellers cheques without problems at virtually any bank or bureau de change (usually indicated by the word *cambio*). Central Madrid also abounds with banks – most have ATMs.

Exchange offices are open for longer hours than banks but generally offer poorer rates. Also, keep a sharp eye open for commissions at bureaus de change.

### Credit Cards & ATMs

Major cards, such as Visa, MasterCard, Maestro, Cirrus and, to a lesser extent, Amex, are accepted throughout Spain. They can be used in many hotels, restaurants and shops; in doing so you'll need to show some form of photo ID (eg passport) or, increasingly, you'll be asked to key in your PIN. Credit cards can also be used in ATMs displaying the appropriate sign (if there's no sign, don't risk it), or, if you have no PIN, you can obtain cash advances over the counter in many banks. Check charges with your bank.

### Tipping

Tipping is not common in Madrid.

**Taxis** Locals usually round up fares to the nearest euro.

**Restaurants** Locals leave a few coins; in better restaurants, 5% is considered ample.

## Opening Hours

**Banks** 8.30am–2pm Monday–Friday; some also open 4–7pm Thursday and 9am–1pm Saturday

**Central Post Offices** 8.30am–9.30pm Monday–Friday, 8.30am–2pm Saturday (most other branches 8.30am–2.30pm Monday–Friday, 9.30am–1pm Saturday)

**Nightclubs** midnight or 1am–5am or 6am

**Restaurants** Lunch 1–4pm, dinner 8.30–11pm or midnight

**Shops** 10am–2pm and 4.30–7.30pm or 5–8pm Monday–Saturday; some bigger shops don't close for lunch and many shops open on some Sundays, usually from 10am or 11am–7pm or 8pm

**Supermarkets** Big supermarkets and department stores generally open 10am–10pm Monday–Saturday

## Post

Correos, the national postal service, is generally reliable, if a little slow at times. It has its **main post office** (Map p242; ☎91 523 06 94; www. correos.es; Paseo del Prado 1; ◷8.30am-9.30pm Mon-Fri, to 2pm Sat; MBanco de España) in the ornate Palacio de Comunicaciones on Plaza de la Cibeles.

*Sellos* (stamps) are sold at most *estancos* (tobacconists' shops, with *Tabacos* in yellow letters on a maroon background), as well as post offices.

A postcard or letter weighing up to 20g costs €1.25 from Spain to other European countries, and €1.35 to the rest of the world. For a full list of prices for *certificado* (certified) and *urgente* (express post), go to www.correos.es and click on 'Tarifas'.

Delivery times are erratic but ordinary mail to other Western European countries can take up to a week; to North America up to 10 days; and to Australia or New Zealand anywhere between one and three weeks.

## Public Holidays

Madrid's 14 public holidays are as follows:

**Año Nuevo** (New Year's Day) 1 January

**Reyes** (Epiphany or Three Kings' Day) 6 January

**Jueves Santo** (Holy Thursday) March/April

---

### GOVERNMENT TRAVEL ADVICE

The following government websites offer travel advisory services and information for travellers:

**Australian Department of Foreign Affairs & Trade** (www.smartraveller.gov.au)

**Canadian Department of Foreign Affairs & International Trade** (www.voyage.gc.ca)

**French Ministère des Affaires et Étrangères Européennes** (www.diplomatie.gouv.fr/fr/conseils-aux-voyageurs)

**Italian Ministero degli Affari Esteri** (www.viaggia resicuri.mae.aci.it)

**New Zealand Ministry of Foreign Affairs & Trade** (www.safetravel.govt.nz)

**UK Foreign & Commonwealth Office** (www.gov.uk/foreign-travel-advice)

**US Department of State** (www.travel.state.gov)

**Viernes Santo** (Good Friday) March/April

**Labour Day** (Fiesta del Trabajo) 1 May

**Fiesta de la Comunidad de Madrid** 2 May

**Fiestas de San Isidro Labrador** 15 May

**La Asunción** (Feast of the Assumption) 15 August

**Día de la Hispanidad** (Spanish National Day) 12 October

**Todos los Santos** (All Saints' Day) 1 November

**Día de la Virgen de la Almudena** 9 November

**Día de la Constitución** (Constitution Day) 6 December

**La Inmaculada Concepción** (Feast of the Immaculate Conception) 8 December

**Navidad** (Christmas) 25 December

## Safe Travel

Madrid is generally safe, but as in any large European city, keep an eye on your belongings and exercise common sense.

➡ El Rastro, around the Museo del Prado and the metro are favourite pickpocketing haunts, as are any areas where tourists congregate in large numbers.

➡ Avoid park areas (such as the Parque del Buen Retiro) after dark.

➡ Keep a close eye on your taxi's meter and try to keep track of the route to make sure you're not being taken for a ride.

### Pickpocketing

Madrid is generally a safe city, although you should, as in most European cities, be wary of pickpockets on transport and around major tourist sights. Although you should be careful, don't be paranoid; remember that the overwhelming majority of travellers to Madrid rarely encounter any problems.

You're most likely to fall foul of pickpockets in the most heavily touristed parts of town, notably the Plaza Mayor and surrounding streets, the Puerta del Sol, El Rastro and around the Museo del Prado. Tricks abound. They usually involve a team of two or more (sometimes one of them an attractive woman to distract male victims). While one attracts your attention, the other empties your pockets. Be wary of jostling on crowded buses and the metro and, as a general rule, dark, empty streets are to be avoided; luckily, Madrid's most lively nocturnal areas are generally busy with crowds having a good time.

### Police Stations

To report thefts or other crime-related matters, your best bet is the **Servicio de Atención al Turista Extranjero** (Foreign Tourist Assistance Service; ☑91 548 85 37, 91 548 80 08; www.esmadrid.com/informacion-turistica/sate; Calle de Leganitos 19; ⊙9am-midnight; Ⓜ Plaza de España, Santo Domingo), which is housed in the central *comisaría* (police station) of the National Police. Here you'll find specially trained officers working

alongside representatives from the Tourism Ministry. They can also assist in cancelling credit cards, as well as contacting your embassy or your family.

There's also a general number (☑902 102 112; 24-hour English and Spanish, 8am to midnight other languages) for reporting crimes.

There's a **comisaría** (☑913 22 10 21; Calle de las Huertas 76; Ⓜ Antón Martín) down the bottom end of Huertas, near the Paseo del Prado.

## Taxes & Refunds

➡ In Spain, value-added tax (VAT) is known as IVA (ee-ba; *impuesto sobre el valor añadido*).

➡ Hotel rooms and restaurant meals attract an additional 10% (usually included in the quoted price but always ask); most other items have 21% added.

➡ Visitors are entitled to a refund of the 21% IVA on purchases costing more than €90.16 from any shop, if they are taking them out of the EU within three months. Ask the shop for a cash-back (or similar) refund form showing the price and IVA paid for each item, and identifying the vendor and purchaser.

➤ Present your IVA refund form to the customs booth for refunds at the airport, port or border when you leave the EU.

## Telephone

Mobile (cell) phone numbers start with ✆6. Numbers starting with ✆900 are national toll-free numbers, while those starting ✆901 to ✆905 come with varying conditions. A common one is ✆902, which is a national standard rate number, but which can only be dialled from within Spain. In a similar category are numbers starting with ✆800, ✆803, ✆806 and ✆807.

### Mobile Phone

➤ Spain uses GSM 900/1800, which is compatible with the rest of Europe and Australia but not with the North American system unless you have a GSM/GPRS-compatible phone (some AT&T and T-Mobile cell phones may work), or the system used in Japan. From those countries, you will need to travel with a tri-band or quadric-band phone.

➤ You can buy SIM cards and prepaid time in Spain for your mobile phone, provided you own a GSM, dual- or tri-band cellular phone. This only works if your national phone hasn't been code-blocked; check before leaving home.

➤ All the Spanish mobile-phone companies (Telefónica's MoviStar, Orange and Vodafone) offer *prepagado* (prepaid) accounts for mobiles. The SIM card costs from €10, to which you add some prepaid phone time. Phone outlets are scattered across the country. You can then top up in their shops or by buying cards in outlets, such as *estancos* (tobacconists) and newspaper kiosks. Pepephone (www.pepephone.com) is another option.

➤ If you're from the EU, there is now EU-wide roaming so that call and data plans for mobile phones from any EU country should be valid throughout in Spain without any extra roaming charges. If you're from elsewhere, check with your mobile provider for information on roaming charges.

### Phonecards

Cut-rate prepaid phonecards can be good value for international calls. They can be bought from *estancos*, small grocery stores, *locutorios* (private call centres) and newspaper kiosks in the main cities and tourist resorts.

Many of the private operators offer better deals than those offered by Telefónica. *Locutorios* that specialise in cut-rate overseas calls have popped up all over the place in bigger cities.

The once-widespread but now almost-disappeared blue payphones are easy to use for international and domestic calls. They accept coins, *tarjetas telefónicas* (phonecards) issued by the national phone company Telefónica and, in some cases, various credit cards.

## Time

Like most of Western Europe, Madrid is one hour ahead of Greenwich Mean Time/Coordinated Universal Time (GMT/UTC) during winter, two hours during the daylight-saving period from the last Sunday in March to the last Sunday in October. Spaniards use the 24-hour clock for official business (timetables etc), but often in daily conversation switch to the 12-hour version.

## Toilets

Public toilets are almost nonexistent in Madrid and it's not really the done thing to go into a bar or cafe solely to use the toilet; ordering a quick coffee is a small

price to pay for relieving the problem. Otherwise you can usually get away with it in a larger, crowded place where they can't really keep track of who's coming and going. Another option is the department stores of El Corte Inglés that are dotted around the city.

## Tourist Information

**Centro de Turismo de Madrid** (Map p232;✆010, 91 578 78 10; www.esmadrid.com; Plaza Mayor 27; ⏰9.30am-8.30pm; Ⓜ️Sol) The Madrid government's Centro de Turismo is terrific.

**Centro de Turismo Colón** (Map p252; www.esmadrid.com; Plaza de Colón 1; ⏰9.30am-8.30pm; Ⓜ️Colón)

**Punto de Información Turística Plaza de Callao** (Map p232; www.esmadrid.com; Plaza de Callao; ⏰9.30am-8.30pm; Ⓜ️Callao)

**Punto de Información Turística CentroCentro** (Map p242;✆91 578 78 10; www.esmadrid.com; Plaza de la Cibeles 1; ⏰10am-8pm Tue-Sun; Ⓜ️Banco de España)

**Punto de Información Turística del Paseo del Prade** (Map p242;✆91 578 78 10; www.esmadrid.com; Plaza de Neptuno; ⏰9.30am-8.30pm; Ⓜ️Atocha)

**Punto de Información Turística Adolfo Suárez Madrid-Barajas T2** (www.esmadrid.com; between Salas 5 & 6; ⏰9am-8pm)

**Punto de Información Turística Adolfo Suárez Madrid-Barajas T4** (www.esmadrid.com; Salas 10 & 11; ⏰9am-8pm)

The regional Comunidad de Madrid government chips in with a helpful website (www.turismomadrid.es) covering the city and surrounding region.

# Travellers with Disabilities

Although things are slowly changing, Madrid remains something of an obstacle course for travellers with a disability. Audio loops for the hearing impaired in cinemas are almost nonexistent, although most Spanish TV channels allow you to turn on subtitles.

## Accessible Madrid

Your first stop for more information on accessibility for travellers should be the Madrid tourist office website section known as **Accessible Madrid** (www.esmadrid.com/en/madrid-accesible), where you can download a PDF of their excellent *Guia de Turismo Accesible* in English or Spanish. It has an exhaustive list of the city's attractions and transport and a detailed assessment of their accessibility, as well as a list of accessible restaurants.

For hotels and *hostales*, go to 'Alojamientos Accesibles' to download their similarly excellent *Guia de Alojamiento Accesible*.

One attraction specifically for visually impaired travellers and Spaniards is the **Museo Tifológico** (Museum for the Blind; ☑91 589 42 19; www.museo.once.es; Calle de la Coruña 18; ☺10am-2pm & 5-8pm Tue-Fri, 10am-2pm Sat, closed Aug; ⓂEstrecho) **FREE**. Run by the National Organisation for the Blind (ONCE), its exhibits (all of which may be touched) include paintings, sculptures and tapestries, as well as more than 40 scale models of world monuments, including Madrid's Palacio Real and Cibeles fountain, as well as La Alhambra in Granada and the aqueduct in Segovia. It also provides leaflets in Braille and audioguides to the museum.

## Transport

When it comes to transport, metro lines built (or upgraded) since the late 1990s generally have elevators for wheelchair access, but the older lines can be ill equipped; the updated metro maps available from any metro station (or at www.metromadrid.es) show stations with wheelchair access. Remember, however, that not all platforms will necessarily have functioning escalators or elevators, even in supposedly wheelchair-accessible stations. On board the metro the name of the next station is usually announced (if the broadcast system is working...).

The single-deck *piso bajo* (low floor) buses have no steps inside and in some cases have ramps that can be used by people in wheelchairs. In the long term, there are plans to make at least 50 of the buses on all routes accessible to people with a disability.

**Radio-Teléfono Taxi** (☑91 547 82 00; www.radiotelefono-taxi.com; ☺24hr) runs taxis for people with a disability in addition to standard taxis. Generally, if you call any taxi company and ask for a 'euro-taxi', you should be sent one adapted for wheelchair users.

## Further Information

**ONCE** (Organización Nacional de Ciegos Españoles; Map p250; ☑91 532 50 00, 91 577 37 56; www.once.es; Calle de Prim 3; ⓂChueca, Colón) The Spanish association for the blind. You may be able to get hold of guides in Braille to Madrid, although they're not published every year.

**Fesorcam** (Federación de Personas Sordas de la Comunidad de Madrid; ☑91 725 37 57; www.fesorcam.org; Calle de Florestan Aguilar, 11 Bajo D; ⓂManuel Becerra, Ventas) Hearing-impaired travellers can contact the Comunidad de Madrid's Federation for the Deaf, Fesorcam. It also runs guided tours of Madrid for the hearing impaired.

**Plena Inclusión Madrid** (Federación de Organizaciones en favor de Personas con Discapacidad Intelectual; ☑91 501 83 35; www.plenainclusionmadrid.org; Av de la Ciudad de Barcelona 108; ⓂMenéndez Pelayo) Travellers with an intellectual disability may wish to contact this organisation, although it has limited appeal for tourists.

**Accessible Travel & Leisure** (www.accessibletravel.co.uk) Claims to be the biggest UK travel agent dealing with travel for people with a disability, and encourages independent travel. Spain is one of the countries it covers in detail.

**Society for Accessible Travel & Hospitality** (www.sath.org) A good resource, with advice on how to travel with a wheelchair, kidney disease, sight impairment or deafness.

# Visas

Spain is one of 26 member countries of the Schengen Convention, under which EU member countries (except the UK and Ireland) plus Switzerland, Iceland and Norway have abolished checks at common borders. Legal residents of one Schengen country do not require a visa for another Schengen country. Citizens of the UK and Ireland are also exempt, although the future remains uncertain at the time of writing due to Brexit negotiations. Nationals of many other countries, including Australia, Canada, Israel, Japan, New Zealand and the US, do not require visas for tourist visits of up to 90 days every six calendar months. All non-EU nationals entering Spain for any reason other than tourism (such as study or work) should contact a Spanish consulate, as they may need a specific visa.

If you're a citizen of a non-Schengen country, check with a Spanish consulate about whether you need a visa.

# Language

Spanish (*español*) – or Castilian (*castellano*), as it's also called – belongs to the Romance language family, with Portuguese, Italian and French as its close relatives. It has more than 390 million speakers worldwide.

Most Spanish sounds are pronounced the same as their English counterparts. If you read our coloured pronunciation guides as if they were English, you won't have problems being understood. Note that the kh is a guttural sound (like the 'ch' in the Scottish *loch*), r is strongly rolled, ly is pronounced as the 'lli' in 'million' and ny as the 'ni' in 'onion'. In our pronunciation guides, the stressed syllables are in italics.

Where necessary in this chapter, masculine and feminine forms are marked as 'm/f', while polite and informal options are indicated by the abbreviations 'pol' and 'inf'.

## BASICS

| Hello. | Hola. | o·la |
| Goodbye. | Adiós. | a·dyos |
| How are you? | ¿Qué tal? | ke tal |
| Fine, thanks. | Bien, gracias. | byen gra·thyas |
| Excuse me. | Perdón. | per·don |
| Sorry. | Lo siento. | lo syen·to |
| Yes./No. | Sí./No. | see/no |
| Please. | Por favor. | por fa·vor |
| Thank you. | Gracias. | gra·thyas |
| You're welcome. | De nada. | de na·da |

### WANT MORE?

For in-depth language information and handy phrases, check out Lonely Planet's *Spanish phrasebook*. You'll find it at **shop. lonelyplanet.com**, or you can buy Lonely Planet's iPhone phrasebooks at the Apple App Store.

**My name is ...**
| Me llamo ... | me *lya*·mo ... |

**What's your name?**
| ¿Cómo se llama Usted? | *ko*·mo se *lya*·ma oo·ste (pol) |
| ¿Cómo te llamas? | *ko*·mo te *lya*·mas (inf) |

**Do you speak English?**
| ¿Habla inglés? | a·bla een·*gles* (pol) |
| ¿Hablas inglés? | a·blas een·*gles* (inf) |

**I don't understand.**
| No entiendo. | no en·*tyen*·do |

## ACCOMMODATION

| guesthouse | pensión | pen·*syon* |
| hotel | hotel | o·*tel* |
| youth hostel | albergue juvenil | al·*ber*·ge khoo·ve·*neel* |

| I'd like a ... room. | Quisiera una habitación ... | kee·*sye*·ra oo·na a·bee·ta·*thyon* ... |
| double | doble | *do*·ble |
| single | individual | een·dee·vee·*dwal* |

| air-con | aire acondicionado | ai·re a·kon·dee·thyo·*na*·do |
| bathroom | baño | *ba*·nyo |
| bed | cama | *ka*·ma |
| window | ventana | ven·*ta*·na |

**How much is it per night/person?**
| ¿Cuánto cuesta por noche/persona? | kwan·to kwes·ta por no·che/per·so·na |

**Does it include breakfast?**
| ¿Incluye el desayuno? | een·*kloo*·ye el de·sa·*yoo*·no |

## DIRECTIONS

**Where's ...?**
| ¿Dónde está ...? | don·de es·ta ... |

**What's the address?**
| ¿Cuál es la dirección? | kwal es la dee·rek·*thyon* |

**Can you please write it down?**
*¿Puede escribirlo,*    pwe·de es·kree·*beer*·lo
*por favor?*    por fa·*vor*

**Can you show me (on the map)?**
*¿Me lo puede indicar*    me lo pwe·de een·dee·*kar*
*(en el mapa)?*    (en el *ma*·pa)

| | | |
|---|---|---|
| **at the corner** | *en la esquina* | en la es·*kee*·na |
| **at the traffic lights** | *en el semáforo* | en el se·*ma*·fo·ro |
| **behind ...** | *detrás de ...* | de·*tras* de ... |
| **far away** | *lejos* | *le*·khos |
| **in front of ...** | *enfrente de ...* | en·*fren*·te de ... |
| **left** | *izquierda* | eeth·*kyer*·da |
| **near** | *cerca* | *ther*·ka |
| **next to ...** | *al lado de ...* | al *la*·do de ... |
| **opposite ...** | *frente a ...* | *fren*·te a ... |
| **right** | *derecha* | de·*re*·cha |
| **straight ahead** | *todo recto* | to·do rek·to |

## EATING & DRINKING

**What would you recommend?**
*¿Qué recomienda?*    ke re·ko·*myen*·da

**What's in that dish?**
*¿Que lleva ese plato?*    ke *lye*·va e·se *pla*·to

**I don't eat ...**
*No como ...*    no *ko*·mo ...

**Cheers!**
*¡Salud!*    sa·*loo*

**That was delicious!**
*¡Estaba buenísimo!*    es·*ta*·ba bwe·*nee*·see·mo

**Please bring us the bill.**
*Por favor, nos trae*    por fa·*vor* nos *tra*·e
*la cuenta.*    la *kwen*·ta

| | | |
|---|---|---|
| **I'd like to book a table for ...** | *Quisiera reservar una mesa para ...* | kee·*sye*·ra re·ser·*var* oo·na me·sa pa·ra ... |
| **(eight) o'clock** | *las (ocho)* | las (o·cho) |
| **(two) people** | *(dos) personas* | (dos) per·*so*·nas |

## Key Words

| | | |
|---|---|---|
| **appetisers** | *aperitivos* | a·pe·ree·*tee*·vos |
| **bar** | *bar* | bar |
| **bottle** | *botella* | bo·*te*·lya |
| **bowl** | *bol* | bol |
| **breakfast** | *desayuno* | de·sa·*yoo*·no |
| **cafe** | *café* | ka·*fe* |
| **(too) cold** | *(muy) frío* | (mooy) *free*·o |
| **dinner** | *cena* | *the*·na |

### KEY PATTERNS

To get by in Spanish, mix and match these simple patterns with words of your choice:

**When's (the next flight)?**
*¿Cuándo sale*    *kwan*·do sa·le
*(el próximo vuelo)?*    (el *prok*·see·mo *vwe*·lo)

**Where's (the station)?**
*¿Dónde está*    don·de es·*ta*
*(la estación)?*    (la es·ta·*thyon*)

**Where can I (buy a ticket)?**
*¿Dónde puedo*    don·de pwe·do
*(comprar*    (kom·*prar*
*un billete)?*    oon bee·*lye*·te)

**Do you have (a map)?**
*¿Tiene (un mapa)?*    tye·ne (oon *ma*·pa)

**Is there (a toilet)?**
*¿Hay (servicios)?*    ai (ser·*vee*·thyos)

**I'd like (a coffee).**
*Quisiera (un café).*    kee·*sye*·ra (oon ka·fe)

**I'd like (to hire a car).**
*Quisiera (alquilar*    kee·*sye*·ra (al·kee·*lar*
*un coche).*    oon ko·che)

**Can I (enter)?**
*¿Se puede (entrar)?*    se pwe·de (en·trar)

**Can you please (help me)?**
*¿Puede (ayudarme),*    pwe·de (a·yoo·*dar*·me)
*por favor?*    por fa·*vor*

**Do I have to (get a visa)?**
*¿Necesito*    ne·the·*see*·to
*(obtener*    (ob·te·*ner*
*un visado)?*    oon vee·*sa*·do)

| | | |
|---|---|---|
| **food** | *comida* | ko·*mee*·da |
| **fork** | *tenedor* | te·ne·*dor* |
| **glass** | *vaso* | *va*·so |
| **highchair** | *trona* | *tro*·na |
| **hot (warm)** | *caliente* | ka·*lyen*·te |
| **knife** | *cuchillo* | koo·*chee*·lyo |
| **lunch** | *comida* | ko·*mee*·da |
| **main course** | *segundo plato* | se·*goon*·do *pla*·to |
| **market** | *mercado* | mer·*ka*·do |
| **(children's) menu** | *menú (infantil)* | me·*noo* (een·fan·*teel*) |
| **plate** | *plato* | *pla*·to |
| **restaurant** | *restaurante* | res·tow·*ran*·te |
| **spoon** | *cuchara* | koo·*cha*·ra |
| **supermarket** | *supermercado* | soo·per·mer·*ka*·do |
| **vegetarian food** | *comida vegetariana* | ko·*mee*·da ve·khe·ta·*rya*·na |
| **with/without** | *con/sin* | kon/sin |

## Meat & Fish

| | | |
|---|---|---|
| beef | *carne de vaca* | *kar*·ne de *va*·ka |
| chicken | *pollo* | *po*·lyo |
| cod | *bacalao* | ba·ka·*la*·o |
| duck | *pato* | *pa*·to |
| lamb | *cordero* | kor·*de*·ro |
| lobster | *langosta* | lan·*gos*·ta |
| pork | *cerdo* | *ther*·do |
| prawns | *camarones* | ka·ma·*ro*·nes |
| salmon | *salmón* | sal·*mon* |
| tuna | *atún* | a·*toon* |
| turkey | *pavo* | *pa*·vo |
| veal | *ternera* | ter·*ne*·ra |

## Fruit & Vegetables

| | | |
|---|---|---|
| apple | *manzana* | man·*tha*·na |
| apricot | *albaricoque* | al·ba·ree·*ko*·ke |
| artichoke | *alcachofa* | al·ka·*cho*·fa |
| asparagus | *espárragos* | es·*pa*·ra·gos |
| banana | *plátano* | *pla*·ta·no |
| beans | *judías* | khoo·*dee*·as |
| beetroot | *remolacha* | re·mo·*la*·cha |
| cabbage | *col* | kol |
| (red/green) capsicum | *pimiento (rojo/verde)* | pee·*myen*·to (*ro*·kho/ver·de) |
| carrot | *zanahoria* | tha·na·o·rya |
| celery | *apio* | *a*·pyo |
| cherry | *cereza* | the·*re*·tha |
| corn | *maíz* | ma·*eeth* |
| cucumber | *pepino* | pe·*pee*·no |
| fruit | *fruta* | *froo*·ta |
| grape | *uvas* | *oo*·vas |
| lemon | *limón* | lee·*mon* |
| lentils | *lentejas* | len·*te*·khas |
| lettuce | *lechuga* | le·*choo*·ga |
| mushroom | *champiñón* | cham·pee·*nyon* |
| nuts | *nueces* | *nwe*·thes |
| onion | *cebolla* | the·*bo*·lya |
| orange | *naranja* | na·*ran*·kha |
| peach | *melocotón* | me·lo·ko·*ton* |
| peas | *guisantes* | gee·*san*·tes |
| pineapple | *piña* | *pee*·nya |
| plum | *ciruela* | theer·*we*·la |
| potato | *patata* | pa·*ta*·ta |
| pumpkin | *calabaza* | ka·la·*ba*·sa |
| spinach | *espinacas* | es·pee·*na*·kas |

| | | |
|---|---|---|
| strawberry | *fresa* | *fre*·sa |
| tomato | *tomate* | to·*ma*·te |
| vegetable | *verdura* | ver·*doo*·ra |
| watermelon | *sandía* | san·*dee*·a |

## Other

| | | |
|---|---|---|
| bread | *pan* | pan |
| butter | *mantequilla* | man·te·*kee*·lya |
| cheese | *queso* | *ke*·so |
| egg | *huevo* | *we*·vo |
| honey | *miel* | myel |
| jam | *mermelada* | mer·me·*la*·da |
| oil | *aceite* | a·*they*·te |
| pepper | *pimienta* | pee·*myen*·ta |
| rice | *arroz* | a·*roth* |
| salt | *sal* | sal |
| sugar | *azúcar* | a·*thoo*·kar |
| vinegar | *vinagre* | vee·*na*·gre |

## Drinks

| | | |
|---|---|---|
| beer | *cerveza* | ther·*ve*·tha |
| coffee | *café* | ka·*fe* |
| (orange) juice | *zumo (de naranja)* | *thoo*·mo (de na·*ran*·kha) |
| milk | *leche* | *le*·che |
| red wine | *vino tinto* | vee·no *teen*·to |
| sparkling wine | *vino espumoso* | *vee*·no es·poo·*mo*·so |
| tea | *té* | te |
| (mineral) water | *agua (mineral)* | *a*·gwa (mee·ne·*ral*) |
| white wine | *vino blanco* | *vee*·no *blan*·ko |

## EMERGENCIES

| | | |
|---|---|---|
| Help! | *¡Socorro!* | so·*ko*·ro |
| Go away! | *¡Vete!* | *ve*·te |

### Signs

| | |
|---|---|
| **Abierto** | Open |
| **Cerrado** | Closed |
| **Entrada** | Entrance |
| **Hombres** | Men |
| **Mujeres** | Women |
| **Prohibido** | Prohibited |
| **Salida** | Exit |
| **Servicios/Aseos** | Toilets |

| **Call ...!** | ¡Llame a ...! | lya·me a ... |
| a doctor | un médico | oon me·dee·ko |
| the police | la policía | la po·lee·thee·a |

**I'm lost.**
*Estoy perdido/a.*   es·toy per·dee·do/a (m/f)

**I'm ill.**
*Estoy enfermo/a.*   es·toy en·fer·mo/a (m/f)

**It hurts here.**
*Me duele aquí.*   me dwe·le a·kee

**I'm allergic to (antibiotics).**
*Soy alérgico/a a*   soy a·ler·khee·ko/a a
*(los antibióticos).*   (los an·tee·byo·tee·kos) (m/f)

**Where are the toilets?**
*¿Dónde están los*   don·de es·tan los
*servicios?*   ser·vee·thyos

## SHOPPING & SERVICES

**I'd like to buy ...**
*Quisiera comprar ...*   kee·sye·ra kom·prar ...

**I'm just looking.**
*Sólo estoy mirando.*   so·lo es·toy mee·ran·do

**Can I look at it?**
*¿Puedo verlo?*   pwe·do ver·lo

**I don't like it.**
*No me gusta.*   no me goos·ta

**How much is it?**
*¿Cuánto cuesta?*   kwan·to kwes·ta

**That's too expensive.**
*Es muy caro.*   es mooy ka·ro

**Can you lower the price?**
*¿Podría bajar un*   po·dree·a ba·khar oon
*poco el precio?*   po·ko el pre·thyo

**There's a mistake in the bill.**
*Hay un error en*   ai oon e·ror en
*la cuenta.*   la kwen·ta

| **ATM** | cajero | ka·khe·ro |
| | automático | ow·to·ma·tee·ko |
| **credit card** | tarjeta de | tar·khe·ta de |
| | crédito | kre·dee·to |
| **internet cafe** | cibercafé | thee·ber·ka·fe |
| **post office** | correos | ko·re·os |
| **tourist office** | oficina | o·fee·thee·na |
| | de turismo | de too·rees·mo |

| **Question Words** | | |
|---|---|---|
| **How?** | ¿Cómo? | ko·mo |
| **What?** | ¿Qué? | ke |
| **When?** | ¿Cuándo? | kwan·do |
| **Where?** | ¿Dónde? | don·de |
| **Who?** | ¿Quién? | kyen |
| **Why?** | ¿Por qué? | por ke |

## TIME & DATES

**What time is it?**
*¿Qué hora es?*   ke o·ra es

**It's (10) o'clock.**
*Son (las diez).*   son (las dyeth)

**Half past (one).**
*Es (la una) y media.*   es (la oo·na) ee me·dya

**At what time?**
*¿A qué hora?*   a ke o·ra

**At (five) o'clock.**
*A las (cinco).*   a las (theen·ko)

| **morning** | mañana | ma·nya·na |
| **afternoon** | tarde | tar·de |
| **evening** | noche | no·che |

| **yesterday** | ayer | a·yer |
| **today** | hoy | oy |
| **tomorrow** | mañana | ma·nya·na |

| **Monday** | lunes | loo·nes |
| **Tuesday** | martes | mar·tes |
| **Wednesday** | miércoles | myer·ko·les |
| **Thursday** | jueves | khwe·bes |
| **Friday** | viernes | vyer·nes |
| **Saturday** | sábado | sa·ba·do |
| **Sunday** | domingo | do·meen·go |

| **January** | enero | e·ne·ro |
| **February** | febrero | fe·bre·ro |
| **March** | marzo | mar·tho |
| **April** | abril | a·breel |
| **May** | mayo | ma·yo |
| **June** | junio | khoo·nyo |
| **July** | julio | khoo·lyo |
| **August** | agosto | a·gos·to |
| **September** | septiembre | sep·tyem·bre |
| **October** | octubre | ok·too·bre |
| **November** | noviembre | no·vyem·bre |
| **December** | diciembre | dee·thyem·bre |

## TRANSPORT

### Public Transport

| **boat** | barco | bar·ko |
| **bus** | autobús | ow·to·boos |
| **plane** | avión | a·vyon |
| **train** | tren | tren |
| **tram** | tranvía | tran·vee·a |

## Numbers

| 1 | uno | oo·no |
|---|---|---|
| 2 | dos | dos |
| 3 | tres | tres |
| 4 | cuatro | kwa·tro |
| 5 | cinco | theen·ko |
| 6 | seis | seys |
| 7 | siete | sye·te |
| 8 | ocho | o·cho |
| 9 | nueve | nwe·ve |
| 10 | diez | dyeth |
| 20 | veinte | veyn·te |
| 30 | treinta | treyn·ta |
| 40 | cuarenta | kwa·ren·ta |
| 50 | cincuenta | theen·kwen·ta |
| 60 | sesenta | se·sen·ta |
| 70 | setenta | se·ten·ta |
| 80 | ochenta | o·chen·ta |
| 90 | noventa | no·ven·ta |
| 100 | cien | thyen |
| 1000 | mil | meel |

| **first** | primer | pree·mer |
|---|---|---|
| **last** | último | ool·tee·mo |
| **next** | próximo | prok·see·mo |

**I want to go to ...**
*Quisiera ir a ...*　　　kee·sye·ra eer a ...

**At what time does it arrive/leave?**
*¿A qué hora llega/sale?*　a ke o·ra lye·ga/sa·le

**Is it a direct route?**
*¿Es un viaje directo?*　　es oon vya·khe dee·rek·to

**Does it stop at ...?**
*¿Para en ...?*　　pa·ra en ...

**Which stop is this?**
*¿Cuál es esta parada?*　kwal es es·ta pa·ra·da

**Please tell me when we get to ...**
*¿Puede avisarme*　　pwe·de a·vee·sar·me
*cuando lleguemos a ...?*　kwan·do lye·ge·mos a ...

**I want to get off here.**
*Quiero bajarme aquí.*　kye·ro ba·khar·me a·kee

| **a ... ticket** | un billete de ... | oon bee·lye·te de ... |
|---|---|---|
| **1st-class** | primera clase | pree·me·ra kla·se |
| **2nd-class** | segunda clase | se·goon·da kla·se |
| **one-way** | ida | ee·da |
| **return** | ida y vuelta | ee·da ee vwel·ta |

| **aisle/window seat** | asiento de pasillo/ventana | a·syen·to de pa·see·lyo/ven·ta·na |
|---|---|---|
| **bus/train station** | estación de autobuses/trenes | es·ta·thyon de ow·to·boo·ses/tre·nes |
| **cancelled** | cancelado | kan·the·la·do |
| **delayed** | retrasado | re·tra·sa·do |
| **platform** | plataforma | pla·ta·for·ma |
| **ticket office** | taquilla | ta·kee·lya |
| **timetable** | horario | o·ra·ryo |

# Driving & Cycling

| **I'd like to hire a ...** | Quisiera alquilar ... | kee·sye·ra al·kee·lar ... |
|---|---|---|
| **4WD** | un todo-terreno | oon to·do·te·re·no |
| **bicycle** | una bicicleta | oo·na bee·thee·kle·ta |
| **car** | un coche | oon ko·che |
| **motorcycle** | una moto | oo·na mo·to |

| **child seat** | asiento de seguridad para niños | a·syen·to de se·goo·ree·da pa·ra nee·nyos |
|---|---|---|
| **diesel** | gasóleo | ga·so·le·o |
| **helmet** | casco | kas·ko |
| **mechanic** | mecánico | me·ka·nee·ko |
| **petrol** | gasolina | ga·so·lee·na |
| **service station** | gasolinera | ga·so·lee·ne·ra |

**How much is it per day/hour?**
*¿Cuánto cuesta por*　　kwan·to kwes·ta por
*día/hora?*　　dee·a/o·ra

**Is this the road to ...?**
*¿Se va a ... por esta*　　se va a ... por es·ta
*carretera?*　　ka·re·te·ra

**(How long) Can I park here?**
*¿(Por cuánto tiempo)*　　(por kwan·to tyem·po)
*Puedo aparcar aquí?*　　pwe·do a·par·kar a·kee

**The car has broken down (at ...).**
*El coche se ha averiado*　el ko·che se a a·ve·rya·do
*(en ...).*　　(en ...)

**I have a flat tyre.**
*Tengo un pinchazo.*　ten·go oon peen·cha·tho

**I've run out of petrol.**
*Me he quedado sin*　　me e ke·da·do seen
*gasolina.*　　ga·so·lee·na

**Are there cycling paths?**
*¿Hay carril bicicleta?*　ai ka·reel bee·thee·kle·ta

**Is there bicycle parking?**
*¿Hay aparcamiento*　　ai a·par·ka·myen·to
*de bicicletas?*　　de bee·thee·kle·tas

# GLOSSARY

**abono** – season pass

**albergue juvenil** – youth hostel; not to be confused with *hostal*

**alcázar** – Muslim-era fortress

**Almoravid** – Islamic Berbers who founded an empire in North Africa that spread over much of Spain in the 11th century and laid siege to Madrid in 1110

**Ayuntamiento** – city or town hall; city or town council

**asador** – restaurant specialising in roasted meats

**baño completo** – full bathroom, with a toilet, shower and/or bath and washbasin

**barrio** – district, quarter (of a town or city)

**biblioteca** – library

**bodega** – literally, 'cellar' (especially a wine cellar); also means a winery or a traditional wine bar likely to serve wine from the barrel

**bomberos** – fire brigade

**calle** – street

**callejón** – lane

**cama** – bed

**cantaor/cantaora** – flamenco singer (male/female)

**capilla** – chapel

**Carnaval** – carnival; a period of fancy-dress parades and merrymaking, usually ending on the Tuesday 47 days before Easter Sunday

**carnet** – identity card or driving licence

**carretera** – highway

**castizo** – literally 'pure'; refers to people and things distinctly from Madrid

**catedral** – cathedral

**centro de salud** – health centre

**cercanías** – local trains serving big cities, suburbs and nearby towns; local train network

**cerrado** – closed

**cervecería** – bar where the focus is on beer

**chato** – glass

**churrigueresque** – ornate style of baroque architecture named after the brothers Alberto and José Churriguera

**comedor** – dining room

**Comunidad de Madrid** – Madrid province

**consejo** – council

**coro** – choir stall

**correos** – post office

**corrida (de toros)** – bullfight

**Cortes** – national parliament

**cuesta** – lane (usually on a hill)

**cutre** – basic or rough-and-ready

**discoteca** – nightclub

**ducha** – shower

**duende** – an indefinable word that captures the passionate essence of flamenco

**entrada** – entrance; ticket for a performance

**estanco** – tobacconist shop

**farmacia** – pharmacy

**feria** – fair; can refer to trade fairs as well as city, town or village fairs, bullfights or festivals lasting days or weeks

**ferrocarril** – railway

**fiesta** – festival, public holiday or party

**fin de semana** – weekend

**flamenco** – traditional Spanish musical form involving any or all of guitarist, singer and dancer and sometimes accompanying musicians

**gasolina** – petrol (a *gasolinera* is a petrol station)

**gatos** – literally 'cats'; colloquial name for *madrileños*

**gitanos** – the Roma people (formerly known as the Gypsies)

**glorieta** – big roundabout

**guiri** – foreigner

**habitación doble** – twin room

**hostal** – hostel; not to be confused with *albergue juvenil*

**iglesia** – church

**IVA** – impuesto sobre el valor añadido (value-added tax)

**judería** – Jewish quarter

**lavabo** – washbasin; a polite term for toilet

**lavandería** – laundrette

**librería** – bookshop

**locutorio** – telephone centre

**madrileño/a** – a person from Madrid (m/f)

**marcha** – action, life, 'the scene'

**marisquería** – seafood eatery

**media ración** – a serving of tapas, somewhere between the size of tapas and *raciones*

**menú del día** – fixed-price meal available at lunchtime, sometimes evening, too; often just called a *menú*

**mercado** – market

**meseta** – the high tableland of central Spain

**mezquita** – mosque

**monasterio** – monastery

**morería** – former Islamic quarter in town

**moro** – 'Moor' or Muslim, usually in medieval context

**moto** – moped or motorcycle

**movida madrileña** – the halcyon days of the post-Franco years when the city plunged into an excess of nightlife, drugs and cultural expression

**mozarab** – Christians who lived in Muslim-ruled Spain; also style of architecture

**Mudéjar** – Muslim living under Christian rule in medieval Spain, also refers to their style of architecture

**muralla** – city wall

**museo** – museum

**oficina de turismo** – tourist office

**panteón** – pantheon (monument to a famous dead person)

**parador** – state-owned hotel in a historic building

**pensión** – guesthouse

**pijo/pija** – yuppie, snob, beautiful people (male/female)

**plaza mayor** – main plaza or square

**puente** – bridge

**puerta** – door or gate

**ración** – meal-sized serve of tapas

**ronda** – ring road

**Semana Santa** – Holy Week; the week leading up to Easter Sunday

**servicio** – toilet

**sierra** – mountain range

**taberna** – tavern

**tapas** – bar snacks traditionally served on a saucer or lid ('tapa' literally means a lid)

**taquilla** – ticket window/office

**tasca** – tapas bar

**temporada alta/media/baja** – high, mid- or low season

**terraza** – terrace; usually means outdoor tables of a cafe, bar or restaurant; can also mean rooftop open-air place

**torero** – bullfighter or matador

**toro** – bull

**torreón** – tower

**turismo** – means both tourism and saloon car

**zarzuela** – form of Spanish dance and music, usually satirical

## MENU DECODER

**a la parrilla** – grilled

**aceite de oliva** – olive oil

**aceite de oliva virgen extra** – extra virgin olive oil

**aceitunas** – olives

**adobo** – marinade

**aguacate** –avocado

**ajo** – garlic

**albóndigas** – meat balls

**alcachofas** – artichokes

**al horno** – baked in the oven

**almejas** – clams

**anchoas** – anchovies

**arroz** – rice

**asado** – roasted

**bacalao** – dried and salted cod

**bebida** – drink

**berenjena** – aubergine, eggplant

**bistec** – steak

**bocadillo** – bread roll with filling

**bonito** – tuna

**boquerones** – anchovies marinated in wine vinegar

**boquerones en vinagre** – fresh anchovies marinated in white vinegar and garlic

**boquerones fritos** – fried fresh anchovies

**butifarra** – Catalan sausage

**cabrito** – kid, baby goat

**calamares** – calamari

**calamares a la Romana** – deep-fried calamari rings

**caldo** – broth, stock

**callos** – tripe

**camarón** – small prawn, shrimp

**caracol** – snail

**carne** – meat

**cebolla** – onion

**cerdo** – pork

**champiñones** – mushrooms

**chipirones** – baby squid

**chipirones en su tinta** – baby squid in their own ink

**chorizo** – cured pork sausage, sometimes spicy

**chuleta** – chop, cutlet

**churro** – long, deep-fried doughnut

**cochinillo** – suckling pig

**cocido a la madrileña** – meat, chickpea and broth stew

**codorniz** – quail

**coliflor** – cauliflower

**conejo** – rabbit

**confitura** – jam

**cordero** – lamb

**cordero asado de lechal** – roast spring lamb

**croquetas** – croquettes

**de lata** – from a can or tin

**dorada** – bream

**empanadillas** – small pie, either savoury or sweet

**ensalada** – salad

**ensalada rusa** – Russian salad

**ensalada mixta** – mixed salad

**escabeche** – pickle, marinade

**espárragos** – asparagus

**estofado** – stew

**frito** – fried

**galleta** – biscuit

**gambas** – prawns, either done *al ajillo*, with garlic, or *a la plancha*, grilled
**garbanzos** – chickpeas
**garbanzos con espinacas** – chickpeas and spinach
**gazpacho** – cold, tomato-based soup
**granada** – pomegranate
**guarnición** – side order
**helado** – ice cream
**jamón** – cured Spanish ham
**judias** – beans
**langosta** – lobster
**langostino** – king prawn
**leche** – milk
**lechuga** – lettuce
**lenguado** – sole
**lentejas** – lentils
**lomo** – loin (pork unless specified otherwise)
**maíz** – corn
**mantequilla** – butter
**manzana** – apple
**marisco** – seafood or shellfish
**mejillones** – mussels
**merluza** – hake
**miel** – honey
**morcilla** – black pudding, blood sausage
**naranja** – orange
**ostra** – oyster

**pan** – bread
**pastel** – cake
**patatas bravas** – roasted potato chunks bathed in spicy tomato sauce
**patatas con huevos fritos** – baked potatoes with eggs, also known as *huevos rotos*
**patatas fritas** – French fries
**pato** – duck
**pavo** – turkey
**pescado** – fish
**pescaíto frito** – fried fish
**pil pil** – garlic sauce spiked with chilli
**pimentón** –paprika
**pimiento** – pepper, capsicum
**pimientos de Padrón** – little green peppers from Galicia – some are hot and some not
**plátano** – banana
**plato combinado** – combination (or all-in-one) plate, usually with meat and vegetables on the same plate
**pollo** – chicken
**postre** – dessert
**pulpo a la gallega** – boiled octopus served with paprika, Galician style
**queso** – cheese
**queso azul** – blue cheese
**rabo de toro** – bull's tail

**raciones** – large tapas serving
**rebozado** – in bread crumbs
**relleno** – stuffing
**repollo** – cabbage
**revuelto** – scrambled eggs
**riñón** – kidney
**rodaballo** – turbot
**salchichón** – salami-like sausage
**salmorejo** – cold, tomato-based soup
**salsa** – sauce
**sandía** – watermelon
**sardinas** – sardines
**sepia** – squid
**sesos** – brains
**seta** – wild mushroom
**solomillo** – sirloin (usually of pork)
**sopa** – soup
**sopa de ajo** – garlic soup
**tarta** – cake
**ternasco** – lamb ribs
**ternera** – beef or veal
**tortilla de patatas** – potato and (sometimes) onion omelette
**tostada** – buttered toast
**trucha** – trout
**verduras a la plancha** – grilled vegetables
**vinagre** – vinegar

# Behind the Scenes

## SEND US YOUR FEEDBACK

We love to hear from travellers – your comments keep us on our toes and help make our books better. Our well-travelled team reads every word on what you loved or loathed about this book. Although we cannot reply individually to your submissions, we always guarantee that your feedback goes straight to the appropriate authors, in time for the next edition. Each person who sends us information is thanked in the next edition – the most useful submissions are rewarded with a selection of digital PDF chapters.

Visit **lonelyplanet.com/contact** to submit your updates and suggestions or to ask for help. Our award-winning website also features inspirational travel stories, news and discussions.

Note: We may edit, reproduce and incorporate your comments in Lonely Planet products such as guidebooks, websites and digital products, so let us know if you don't want your comments reproduced or your name acknowledged. For a copy of our privacy policy visit lonelyplanet.com/privacy.

## OUR READERS

Many thanks to the travellers who used the last edition and wrote to us with helpful hints, useful advice and interesting anecdotes: Catalina Fernandez del Castillo, Cristhiam Gonzalez, Cristina Aparicio, Dana Al Dahabi, David McCann, Erik A N Kon, Helena Lehtonen, John F. Moore, Jorge de Esteban, Judy Yebernetsky, Marcelí Valdés, Michael Smith, Mike Aleckson, Roeland Bertrams

## WRITER THANKS

### Anthony Ham

A life built in Spain encompasses so many relationships that extend far beyond one trip. Heartfelt thanks to Sandra, Javi, Dani, Lucia, Marina, Alberto, Jose, Bea and so many others. *Gracias* also to Eli Morales. At Lonely Planet, I am grateful to my editor Tom Stainer and numerous editors who brought focus and much wisdom to the book. To my family – Marina, Carlota and Valentina – who have always made Madrid a true place of the heart: *con todo mi amor.* And to Jan, we hope to see you in Madrid again soon.

## ACKNOWLEDGEMENTS

Cover photograph: View of Gran Vía with Edificio Metrópolis in the foreground and the Telefónica building in the background, Riccardo Spila/4Corners ©

Illustration on pp102-3 by Javier Zarracina

## THIS BOOK

This 9th edition of Lonely Planet's *Madrid* guidebook was curated, researched and written by Anthony Ham, with contributions by Josephine Quintero. The previous edition was also written by Anthony. This guidebook was produced by the following:

**Destination Editor** Tom Stainer
**Product Editors** Jenna Myers, Genna Patterson
**Senior Cartographer** Anthony Phelan
**Book Designer** Mazzy Prinsep

**Assisting Editors** Bruce Evans, Vic Harrison, Gabby Innes, Anne Mulvaney
**Assisting Cartographer** Julie Dodkins
**Cover Researcher** Naomi Parker
**Thanks to** Grace Dobell, Kate Kiely, Anne Mason

See also separate subindexes for:

**✕ EATING P226**

**● DRINKING & NIGHTLIFE P227**

**☆ ENTERTAINMENT P228**

**🛍 SHOPPING P228**

**🛏 SLEEPING P229**

**🏃 SPORTS & ACTIVITIES 229**

# Index

# Madrid Maps

## Sights
- Beach
- Bird Sanctuary
- Buddhist
- Castle/Palace
- Christian
- Confucian
- Hindu
- Islamic
- Jain
- Jewish
- Monument
- Museum/Gallery/Historic Building
- Ruin
- Shinto
- Sikh
- Taoist
- Winery/Vineyard
- Zoo/Wildlife Sanctuary
- Other Sight

## Activities, Courses & Tours
- Bodysurfing
- Diving
- Canoeing/Kayaking
- Course/Tour
- Sento Hot Baths/Onsen
- Skiing
- Snorkelling
- Surfing
- Swimming/Pool
- Walking
- Windsurfing
- Other Activity

## Sleeping
- Sleeping
- Camping
- Hut/Shelter

## Eating
- Eating

## Drinking & Nightlife
- Drinking & Nightlife
- Cafe

## Entertainment
- Entertainment

## Shopping
- Shopping

## Information
- Bank
- Embassy/Consulate
- Hospital/Medical
- Internet
- Police
- Post Office
- Telephone
- Toilet
- Tourist Information
- Other Information

## Geographic
- Beach
- Gate
- Hut/Shelter
- Lighthouse
- Lookout
- Mountain/Volcano
- Oasis
- Park
- Pass
- Picnic Area
- Waterfall

## Population
- Capital (National)
- Capital (State/Province)
- City/Large Town
- Town/Village

## Transport
- Airport
- Border crossing
- Bus
- Cable car/Funicular
- Cycling
- Ferry
- Metro station
- Monorail
- Parking
- Petrol station
- S-Bahn/Subway station
- Taxi
- T-bane/Tunnelbana station
- Train station/Railway
- Tram
- Tube station
- U-Bahn/Underground station
- Other Transport

## Routes
- Tollway
- Freeway
- Primary
- Secondary
- Tertiary
- Lane
- Unsealed road
- Road under construction
- Plaza/Mall
- Steps
- Tunnel
- Pedestrian overpass
- Walking Tour
- Walking Tour detour
- Path/Walking Trail

## Boundaries
- International
- State/Province
- Disputed
- Regional/Suburb
- Marine Park
- Cliff
- Wall

## Hydrography
- River, Creek
- Intermittent River
- Canal
- Water
- Dry/Salt/Intermittent Lake
- Reef

## Areas
- Airport/Runway
- Beach/Desert
- Cemetery (Christian)
- Cemetery (Other)
- Glacier
- Mudflat
- Park/Forest
- Sight (Building)
- Sportsground
- Swamp/Mangrove

*Note: Not all symbols displayed above appear on the maps in this book*

N 0 ——————— 0.9 km
0 ——————— 0.4 miles

Parque de
Santander

RÍOS
ROSAS

**9**

ARAPILES

Parque del
Oeste

CHAMBERÍ

TRAFALGAR

**ARGÜELLES**

SALAMANCA

ALMAGRO

La Rosaleda

**MALASAÑA**

Parque
de la
Montaña

CHUECA

**7**

JUSTICIA

Casa de
Campo

**10**

Campo
del Moro

**8**

**6**

**1**

CAMPO

SOL

RETIRO

LOS AUSTRIAS

Parque
del Buen
Retiro

JERÓNIMOS

Río Manzanares

HUERTAS

LA
LATINA

**4**

**3**

ATOCHA

EL RASTRO

LAVAPIÉS

**2**

**5**

# MAP INDEX

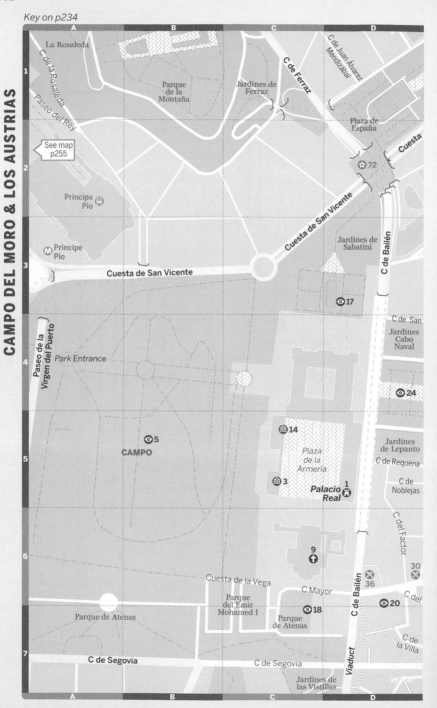

Key on p234

See map p255

See map p255

See map p238

See map p236

0    200 m
0    0.1 miles

**E**    **F**    **G**    **H**

103

22

Plaza de España

C de la Princesa

de San Vicente

C de los Reyes

C de Manzana

Noviciado

C de la Cruz Verde

C del General Mitre

C de Antonio Grillo

C de San Bernardo

C de Andrés Borrego

C de Pizarro

C del Pez

C de Jesús del Valle

C de la Madera

C de San Roque

C Beatas

C de García Molinas

C del Ricardo Leon

C Parada

C de la Estrella

C de la Luna

C de la Corredera Baja de San Pablo

31

C del Río

C de la Flor Baja

96

Gran Vía

C del Marqués de Leganés

C de los Libreros

Plaza de Santa María Soledad

C del Desengaño

C del Fomento

C de Leganitos

C de Isabel la Católica

Santo Domingo

C de la Flor Alta

C de los Mostenses

C de Silva

C del Reloj

C Guillermo Rolland

74

C de San Bernardo

78

C de Tudescos

C Miguel Moya

C del Arenal

Plaza de la Marina Española

C de Torija

49

Santo Domingo

C de Silva

69

13

Gran Vía

73

68

C de la Bola

C de la Encarnación

53

Santo Domingo

Plaza de Santo Domingo

C de Jacometrezo

Punto de Información Turística Plaza de Callao

Callao

39

Plaza del Callao

C de la Abada

10

100

106

111

51

C de Preciados

63

62

37

CENTRO

87

C del Carmen

Plaza de la Encarnación

Cuesta de Santo Domingo

C de Campomanes

67

C de Veneras

113

C Ternera

90

C de la Salud

Plaza de la Quintín

C Pavía

83

112

C de Caños del Peral

C Conchas

Travesía de Trujillos

Postigo de San Martín

C de Preciados

43    52

64

104

114

38

Plaza de San Martín

11

Callejón Preciados

C de Felipe V

44

C del la Priora Flora

C Donados

110

Plaza de las Descalzas

C de Galdo

27

28

Plaza de Isabel II

Opera

70

Plaza de San Martín

C del Maestro Victoria

Travesía de los Descalzas

105

60

C de las Hileras

77

92

94

C de Arrieta

59

42

29

54

C de las Fuentes

109

15

C del Arenal

Plaza de la Puerta del Sol

25

C de Vergara

57

55

93

65

21

Sol

C de la Amnistía

C de la Unión

C Lazo

47

108

C de San Nicolás

C Lepanto

Plaza Santiago

85

88

80

56

35

C Mayor

Sol

C del Conde de Lemos

C de Santiago

89

46

C de Postas

107

C del Correo

16

C de Biombo

C Señores de Luzón

32

26

C de San Cristóbal

107

C del Marqués Viudo de Ponteijos

91    76

C Juan de Herrera

102

66

2

Plaza Mayor

C de Zaragoza

C de Esparteros

C de la Paz

40

7    23

101

C de la Cava de San Miguel

95

Plaza de Santa Cruz

41

C de la Bolsa

Plaza de la Villa

8    81

84

48

6    86

12    71

98

C del Maestro Villa

97

Lechuga

19

C de Atocha

Sacramento

C del Cordón

82

LOS AUSTRIAS

58

79

115

C de San Tomós

Plaza del Cordón

4

C de San Justo

75

33

50

99

C Salvador

C de la Concepción Jerónima

C del Rollo

C Conde

C de Segovia

C de la Pasa

34

C de los Cuchilleros

90

C Toledo

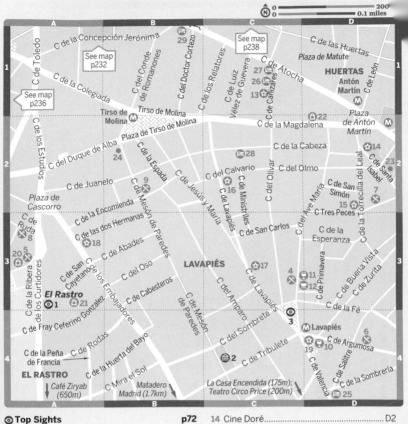

N

0    0.1 miles

Madrid Segway Tours (1.1km)

See map p232

See map p235

EL RASTRO

LA LATINA

Basílica de San Francisco El Grande

C de la Concepción Jerónima
C Salvador
C de la Colegiada
Plaza de Segovia Nueva
Plaza de Puerta Cerrada
C de San Justo
C Gral
Plaza del Duque de Alba
C del Duque de Alba
C de Juanelo
Plaza de Cascorro
C de los Embajadores
C de los Estudios
C de San Milán
M La Latina
C de las Maldonadas
C de Ruda
C de Segovia
C del Cordón
C del Nuncio
C de Toledo
Plaza de la Cebada
La Latina M
C de Toledo
C del Almendro
Cava Baja
Cava Alta
C del Príncipe Anglona
Costanilla de San Pedro
Costanilla de San Andrés
Plaza de la Paja
Plaza de San Andrés
Plaza de la Cebada
C de la Cebada
C de Humilladero
C de la Cebada
C de Alfonso VI
Costanilla de San Andrés
Plaza de la Puerta de Moros
C de Oriente
C de Luciente
C de las Aguas
Botería Julio Rodríguez (100m); Almacén de Vinos (230m)
Plaza del Alamillo
C de Segovia
C de Caños Viejos
Cuesta de la Vega
C de la Morería
Plaza de Granado
C de Granado
C de Redondilla
C de Mancebos
C de Don Pedro
Carrera de San Francisco
C de San Isidro Labrador
C de Bailén
C de Bailén
Viaduct
Costanilla de San Andrés
Cuesta de la Vega
C Beatriz Galindo
C de los Jardines de las Vistillas
C de Yeseros
Plaza de Gabriel Miró
C de la Morería
Plaza de San Francisco
C de San Buenaventura

# LA LATINA

# SOL, HUERTAS & THE CENTRE

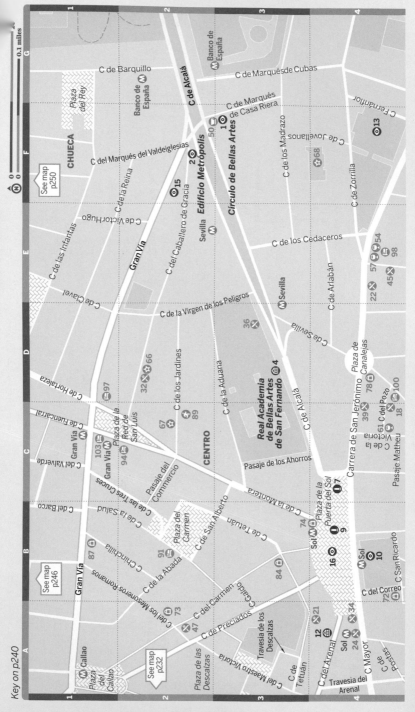

Key on p240

See map p250

See map p246

See map p232

**CHUECA**

**CENTRE**

Plaza del Rey

Banco de España

C de Barquillo

C de Alcalá

C de Marquésde Cubas

C de Marqués de Casa Riera

C del Marqués del Valdeiglesias

C de las Infantas

C de la Reina

C de VictorHugo

Gran Vía

C del Caballero de Gracia

**Edificio Metrópolis**

Sevilla

**Círculo de Bellas Artes**

C de los Madrazo

C de Jovellanos

C de Zorrilla

C de los Cedaceros

C de Arlabán

C de Sevilla

C de la Virgen de los Peligros

Sevilla

C del Clavel

C de Hortaleza

C de Fuencarral

C de las Tres Cruces

C de la Salud

Pasaje del Commercio

C del Barco

Plaza de la Red de San Luis

Gran Vía

Plaza del Carmen

C de San Alberto

C de la Abada

C de Tetuán

C de la Montera

C de los Jardines

C de la Aduana

Pasaje de los Ahorros

**Real Academia de Bellas Artes de San Fernando**

C de Alcalá

Carrera de San Jerónimo

Plaza de Canalejas

C del Pozo

C de la Victoria

Pasaje Matheu

Plaza de la Puerta del Sol

Sol

C de Chinchilla

Gran Vía

C del Valverde

C de los Mesoneros Romanos

C de la Abada

C de Preciados

C del Carmen

C Salud

Plaza de las Descalzas

Travesia de los Descalzas

C de Maestro Victoria

C de Tetuán

Sol

C del Arenal

C Mayor

Travesia del Arenal

C San Ricardo

C del Correo

C de Postas

Plaza del Callao

Callao

Banco de España

Gran Vía

C Fernánflor

50
1
13
68
2
15
36
57
54
98
22
45
66
32
97
67
94
103
89
39
78
18
100
74
7
9
16
10
21
12
24
34
84
91
73
47
87
72

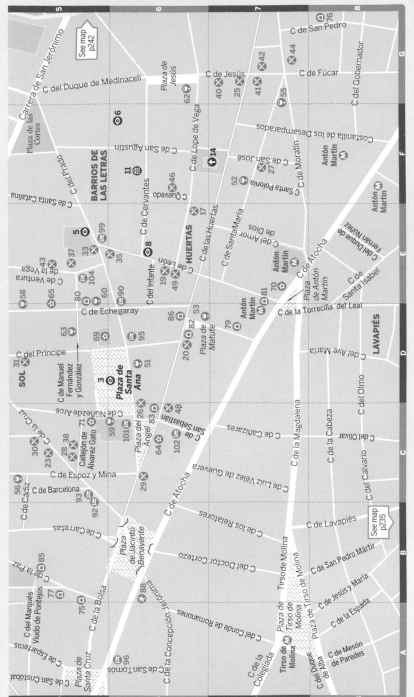

# SOL, HUERTAS & THE CENTRE

# SOL, HUERTAS & THE CENTRE

## SOL, HUERTAS & THE CENTRE Map on p238

PASEO DEL PRADO & EL RETIRO

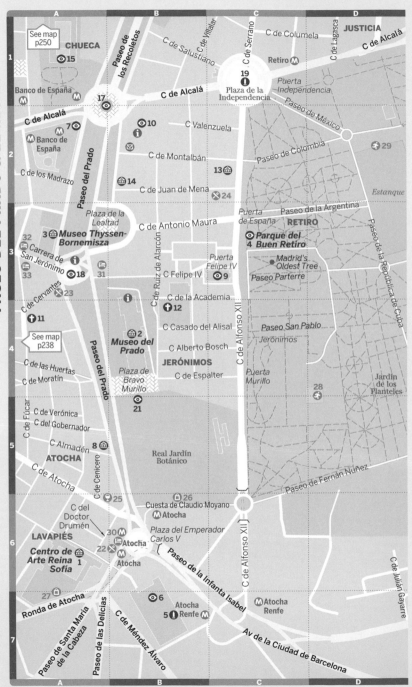

See map p250

CHUECA

15

Paseo de los Recoletos

C de Salustiano

C de Villalar

C de Serrano

C de Columela

C de Lagasca

JUSTICIA

C de Alcalá

Banco de España

17

C de Alcalá

Retiro

19

Plaza de la Independencia

Puerta Independencia

7

10

C de Alcalá

C Valenzuela

Paseo de México

Banco de España

C de Montalbán

Paseo de Colombia

29

C de los Madrazo

13

Estanque

14

C de Juan de Mena

24

Paseo del Prado

Plaza de la Lealtad

C de Antonio Maura

Puerta de España

Paseo de la Argentina

RETIRO

3 Museo Thyssen-Bornemisza

Parque del 4 Buen Retiro

Madrid's Oldest Tree

32

Carrera de San Jerónimo

C de Ruiz de Alarcón

Puerta Felipe IV

Paseo Parterre

33

18

31

9

C Felipe IV

Paseo de la República de Cuba

23

C de Cervantes

C de la Academia

11

12

C Casado del Alisal

Paseo San Pablo

Jerónimos

See map p238

Paseo del Prado

2

Museo del Prado

C Alberto Bosch

JERÓNIMOS

C de Espalter

Puerta Murillo

Jardín de los Planteles

C de las Huertas

Plaza de Bravo Murillo

C de Moratín

C de Fúcar

C de Verónica

C del Gobernador

21

28

C de Alfonso XII

C Almadén

8

ATOCHA

Real Jardín Botánico

C de Atocha

C de Cenicero

Paseo de Fernán Núñez

25

26

Cuesta de Claudio Moyano

Atocha

C del Doctor Drumén

Plaza del Emperador Carlos V

30

LAVAPIÉS

22

Atocha

Centro de Arte Reina Sofía

1

Atocha

Paseo de la Infanta Isabel

C de Alfonso XII

C de Julián Gayarre

27

6

Ronda de Atocha

Atocha Renfe

5

Atocha Renfe

Paseo de Santa María de la Cabeza

Paseo de las Delicias

C de Méndez Álvaro

Av de la Ciudad de Barcelona

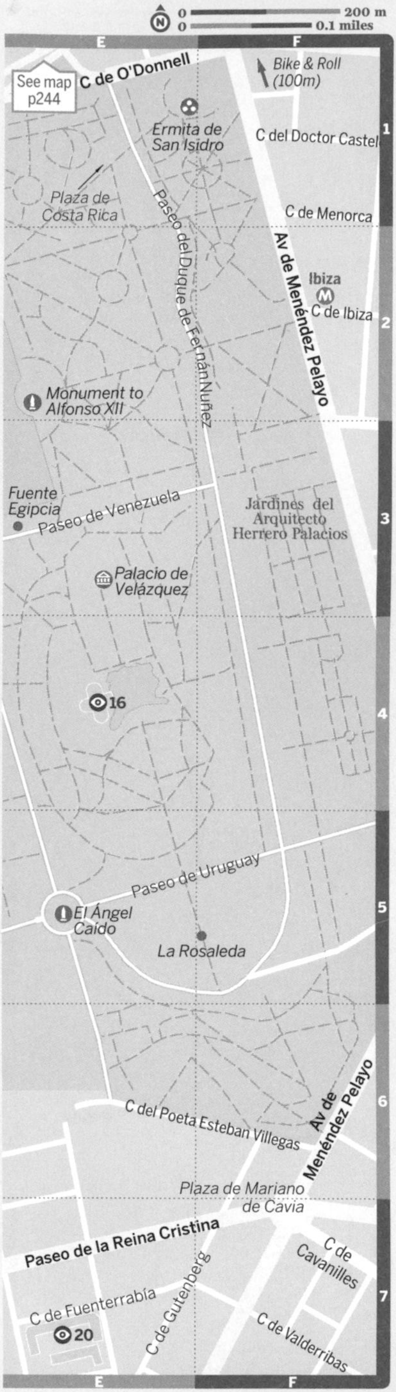

0 200 m
0 0.1 miles
E
F
See map p244
C de O'Donnell
Bike & Roll (100m)
Ermita de San Isidro
C del Doctor Castelo
Plaza de Costa Rica
Paseo del Duque de Fernán Nuñez
C de Menorca
Av de Menéndez Pelayo
Ibiza
C de Ibiza
Monument to Alfonso XII
Fuente Egipcia
Paseo de Venezuela
Jardines del Arquitecto Herrero Palacios
Palacio de Velázquez
16
Paseo de Uruguay
El Ángel Caído
La Rosaleda
C del Poeta Esteban Villegas
Av de Menéndez Pelayo
Plaza de Mariano de Cavia
Paseo de la Reina Cristina
C de Cavanilles
C de Fuenterrabía
C de Gutenberg
C de Valderribas
20
1
2
3
4
5
6
7

**Top Sights** p108

1 Centro de Arte Reina Sofía ... A6
2 Museo del Prado ... B4
3 Museo Thyssen-Bornemisza ... A3
4 Parque del Buen Retiro ... C3

**Sights** p112

5 11 March 2004 Memorial ... B7
6 Antigua Estación de Atocha ... B7
7 Banco de España ... A2
8 Caixa Forum ... A5
9 Casón del Buen Retiro ... C3
10 CentroCentro ... B2
11 Iglesia de Jesús de Medinaceli ... A4
12 Iglesia de San Jerónimo El Real ... B4
Mirador de Madrid ... (see 10)
13 Museo de Artes Decorativas ... C2
14 Museo Naval ... B2
15 Palacio Buenavista ... A1
16 Palacio de Cristal ... E4
17 Plaza de la Cibeles ... A2
18 Plaza de Neptuno ... A3
19 Puerta de Alcalá ... C1
20 Real Fábrica de Tapices ... E7
21 Real Jardín Botánico ... B5

**Eating** p114

22 El Brillante ... B6
23 Estado Puro ... A3
Palacio de Cibeles ... (see 10)
24 Viridiana ... C2

**Drinking & Nightlife** p115

25 Teatro Kapital ... A6

**Shopping** p115

26 Cuesta de Claudio Moyano Bookstalls ... B6
27 Librería la Central ... A7

**Sports & Activities** p115

28 Centro Deportivo La Chopera ... D4
29 Row Boats ... D2

**Sleeping** p176

30 60 Balconies Atocha ... B6
31 Hotel Ritz ... A3
32 Lapepa Chic B&B ... A3
33 Westin Palace ... A3

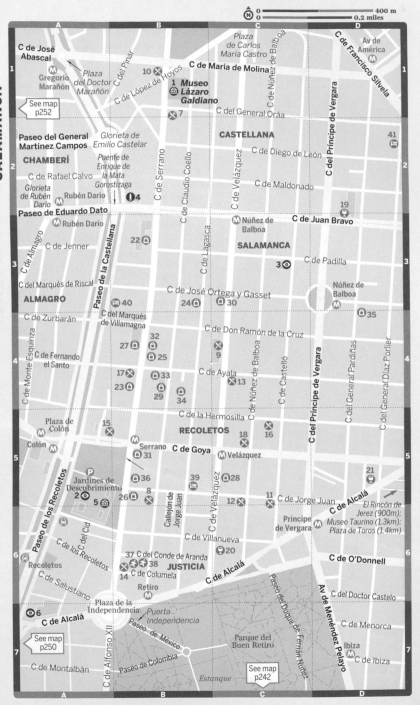

SALAMANCA

**0**            400 m
**0**            0.2 miles

C de José Abascal

Gregorio Marañón

Plaza del Doctor Marañón

Plaza de Carlos María Castro

C de María de Molina

Av de Francisco Silvela

Av de América

C del Pinar

C de López de Hoyos

10

1 **Museo Lázaro Galdiano**

C de Núñez de Balboa

C del General Oráa

See map p252

7

Paseo del General Martínez Campos

Glorieta de Emilio Castelar

**CASTELLANA**

C del Príncipe de Vergara

41

**CHAMBERÍ**

Puente de Enrique de la Mata Gorostizaga

C de Serrano

C de Claudio Coello

C de Velázquez

C de Diego de León

C de Rafael Calvo

C de Maldonado

Glorieta de Rubén Darío

Rubén Darío

4

Paseo de Eduardo Dato

Rubén Darío

Núñez de Balboa

C de Juan Bravo

19

C de Almagro

C de Jenner

C de Lagasca

**SALAMANCA**

22

C del Marqués de Riscal

Paseo de la Castellana

3

C de Padilla

Núñez de Balboa

**ALMAGRO**

C de Zurbarán

40

C de José Ortega y Gasset

24 30

35

C del Marqués de Villamagna

C de Don Ramón de la Cruz

C de Monte Esquinza

27

32

C de Fernando el Santo

25

C de Ayala

C de Núñez de Balboa

C de Castelló

C del General Pardiñas

C del General Díaz Porlier

9

17

33

23

29

34

13

C de la Hermosilla

Plaza de Colón

15

**RECOLETOS**

18

16

Colón

Serrano

C de Goya

Velázquez

31

Jardines de Descubrimiento

36

39

28

C del Príncipe de Vergara

21

8

26

2

5

12

11

C de Jorge Juan

C de Alcalá

El Rincón de Jerez (900m); Museo Taurino (1.3km); Plaza de Toros (1.4km)

Paseo de los Recoletos

Callejón de Jorge Juan

C de Velázquez

Príncipe de Vergara

C de Villanueva

20

C de O'Donnell

Recoletos

37 C del Conde de Aranda

14

38

C de Columela

**JUSTICIA**

C de Alcalá

C del Cid

C de los Recoletos

C de Salustiano

Retiro

C del Doctor Castelo

6

Plaza de la Independencia

Puerta Independencia

Paseo del Duque de Fernán Núñez

Av de Menéndez Pelayo

C de Menorca

C de Alcalá

Paseo de México

C de Alfonso XII

Parque del Buen Retiro

Ibiza

C de Ibiza

See map p250

C de Montalbán

Paseo de Colombia

Estanque

See map p242

# SALAMANCA

SALAMANCA

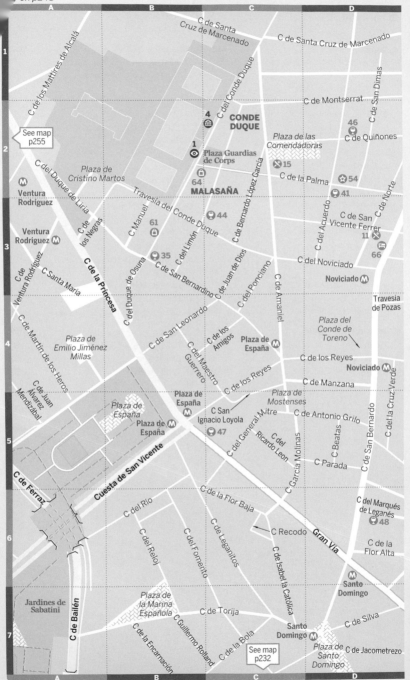

on p248

MALASAÑA

See map p255

C de Santa Cruz de Marcenado
C de Santa Cruz de Marcenado
C de los Mártires de Alcalá
C del Conde Duque
C de Montserrat
C de San Dimas
**4** CONDE DUQUE
**46** C de Quiñones
Plaza de las Comendadoras
Plaza de Cristino Martos
**1** Plaza Guardias de Corps
**15**
C de la Palma **54**
**64**
**41**
MALASAÑA
Ventura Rodríguez
Travesía del Conde Duque
C de San Vicente Ferrer
C del Acuerdo
C de Norte
C del Duque de Liria
C de los Negras
C Manuel
**44**
C de Bernardo López García
**11**
Ventura Rodríguez
**61**
**66**
C de la Princesa
**35**
C del Limón
C del Noviciado
C del Duque de Osuna
C de San Bernardino
C de Juan de Dios
Noviciado
C Santa María
C de Ventura Rodríguez
C de San Leonardo
C de Amaniel
C de Ponciano
Travesía de Pozas
C de Martín de los Heros
Plaza de Emilio Jiménez Millas
C del Maestro Guerrero
C de los Amigos
Plaza de España
Plaza del Conde de Toreno
C de los Reyes
Noviciado
C de Juan Álvarez Mendizábal
C de los Reyes
C de Manzana
Plaza de España
Plaza de Mostenses
C de Antonio Grilo
C de la Cruz Verde
Plaza de España
C San Ignacio Loyola
**47**
C del General Mitre
C del Ricardo Leon
C García Molinas
C Beatas
C de San Bernardo
Cuesta de San Vicente
C Parada
C de Ferraz
C del Marqués de Leganés
**48**
C de la Flor Baja
C del Río
C Recodo
Gran Vía
C de la Flor Alta
C del Reloj
C del Fomento
C de Leganitos
C de Isabela Católica
Santo Domingo
Jardines de Sabatini
C de Bailén
Plaza de la Marina Española
C de Torija
Santo Domingo
C de Silva
C de la Encarnación
C de Guillermo Rolland
C de la Bola
Santo Domingo
C de Jacometrezo
Plaza de Santo Domingo
See map p232

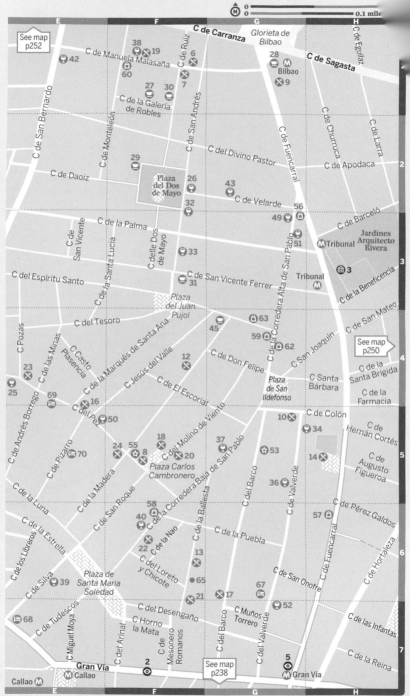

See map p252

C de Carranza

Glorieta de Bilbao

C de Sagasta

C de Eguilaz

42

C de Manuela Malasaña

38  19

C de Ruiz

6

60

28  Bilbao

9

C de Churruca

C de Larra

27  30

C de la Galería de Robles

7

C de San Andrés

C de Fuencarral

C de San Bernardo

29

C de Monteleón

C de Daoiz

Plaza del Dos de Mayo

26

C del Divino Pastor

C de Apodaca

43

C de Velarde

56

32

49

51

C de Barceló

C de la Palma

C de San Vicente

C de la Santa Lucía

C delle Dos de Mayo

33

C del Espíritu Santo

31

C de San Vicente Ferrer

C de la Corredera Alta de San Pablo

Tribunal  Jardines Arquitecto Rivera

Tribunal

3

C de la Beneficencia

C del Tesoro

Plaza del Juan Pujol

45

63

59

62

C de San Mateo

See map p250

C Pozas

C de las Minas

C de la Marqués de Santa Ana

C de Don Felipe

C San Joaquín

23

C Casto Plasencia

12

Plaza de San Ildefonso

C Santa Bárbara

C de la Santa Brígida

25

C Jesús del Valle

C de El Escorial

C de la Farmacia

69

16

C del Pez

50

C de Andrés Borrego

C de Pizarro

70

10

C de Colón

34

C de Hernán Cortés

18

37

53

14

C de Augusto Figueroa

24  55

8

C del Molino de Viento

C de la Madera

20

Plaza Carlos Cambronero

C de la Corredera Baja de San Pablo

C del Barco

36

C de Valverde

C de San Roque

58

57

C de Pérez Galdos

40

C de la Nao

C de la Ballesta

C de la Puebla

C de Fuencarral

C de Hortaleza

C de la Luna

22

13

C de la Estrella

C del Loreto y Chicote

65

67

C de San Onofre

C de los Libreros

39

Plaza de Santa María Soledad

21

17

52

C de Silva

C Muñoz Torrero

68

C de Tudescos

C del Desengaño

C de las Infantas

C Miguel Moya

C Horno la Mata

C de Mesonero Romanos

C del Barco

C del Valverde

C de la Reina

Gran Vía

2

See map p238

5

Callao  Callao

Gran Vía

# CHUECA *Map on p250*

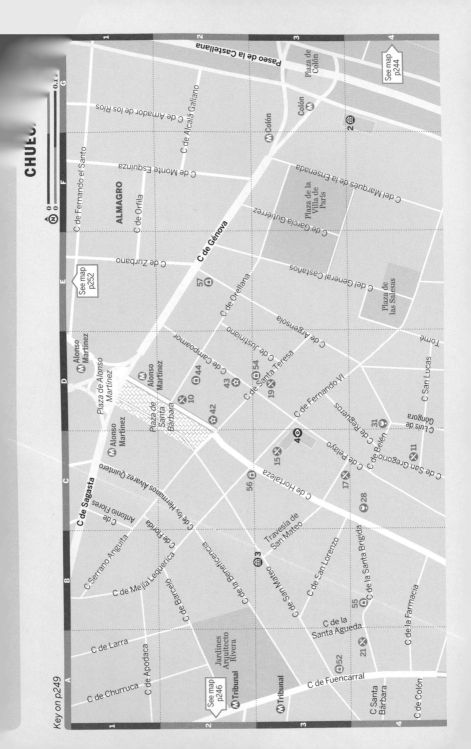

CHUECA

Key on p249

See map p252

See map p244

See map p246

Paseo de la Castellana

ALMAGRO

C de Génova

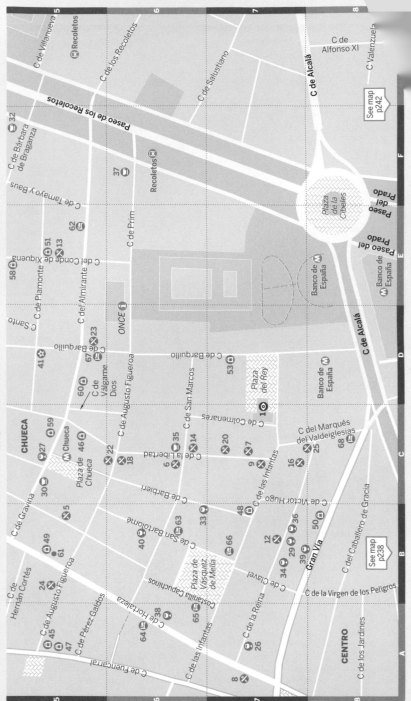

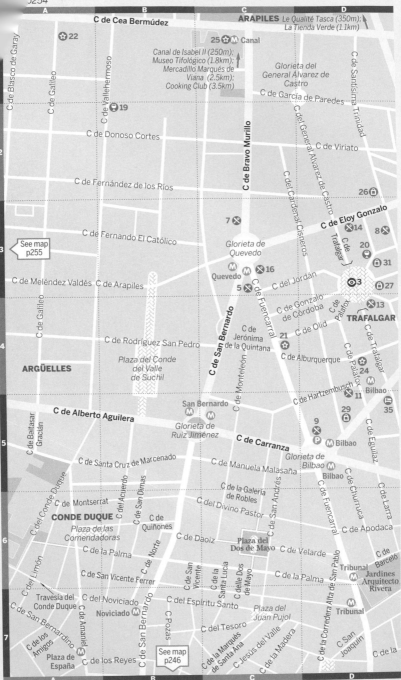

CHAMB...

**C de Cea Bermúdez**

**ARAPILES** Le Qualité Tasca (350m);
La Tienda Verde (1.1km)

C de Blasco de Garay

C de Galileo

⭐22

25 ⭐Ⓜ Canal

Canal de Isabel II (250m);
Museo Tifológico (1.8km);
Mercadillo Marqués de
Viana (2.5km);
Cooking Club (3.5km)

Glorieta del
General Álvarez de
Castro

C de Santísima Trinidad

C de Vallehermoso

🚇19

C de Donoso Cortes

C de García de Paredes

C de Bravo Murillo

C del General Álvarez de Castro

C de Viriato

C de Fernández de los Ríos

See map
p255

C de Fernando El Católico

Glorieta de
Quevedo

7 ❌

C del Cardenal Cisneros

26 🔒

C de Eloy Gonzalo

❌14

8 ❌

C de Trafalgar

20

🔒31

C de Meléndez Valdés   C de Arapiles

Ⓜ ❌16
Quevedo

5 ❌  C del Jórdan

◉3

🔒27

C de Galileo

C de Rodríguez San Pedro

C de Fuencarral

C de Gonzalo
de Córdoba

C de Olid

❌13

C de Palafox

TRAFALGAR

C de Trafalgar

**ARGÜELLES**

C de San Bernardo

C de
Jerónima
de la Quintana

21
🏛

C de Alburquerque

24

❌11 Bilbao

Plaza del Conde
del Valle
de Suchil

C de Monteleón

C de Hartzembusch

29
🔒

35

C de Baltasar Gracián

**C de Alberto Aguilera**

San Bernardo
Ⓜ   Ⓜ

Glorieta de
Ruiz Jiménez

**C de Carranza**

9
❌
🅿

Ⓜ Bilbao

C de Eguilaz

C de Santa Cruz de Marcenado

C de Manuela Malasaña

Glorieta de
Bilbao Ⓜ

Bilbao

C de Churruca

C de Fuencarral

C de Larra

C del Conde Duque

C del Acuerdo

C de San Dimas

C de Montserrat

**CONDE DUQUE**

C de
Quiñones

C de la Galería
de Robles

C del Divino Pastor

C de San Andrés

C de Apodaca

Plaza de las
Comendadoras

C de la Palma

C de Norte

C de Daoiz

Plaza del
Dos de Mayo

C de Velarde

C de Barceló

C del Limón

C de San Vicente Ferrer

C de San
Vicente

C de la
Santa Lucía

C delle Dos
de Mayo

C de la Palma

C de la Corredera Alta de San Pablo

Tribunal
Ⓜ

Jardines
Arquitecto
Rivera

Travesía del
Conde Duque

C del Noviciado

C de Amaniel

Noviciado Ⓜ

C de San Bernardo

C. Pozas

C del Espíritu Santo

C del Tesoro

Plaza del
Juan Pujol

Tribunal
Ⓜ

C de San Bernardino

C de los
Amigos

Plaza de
España

C de los Reyes

See map
p246

C de la Marqués
de Santa Ana

C de Jesús del Valle

C de la Madera

C San
Joaquín

C de la

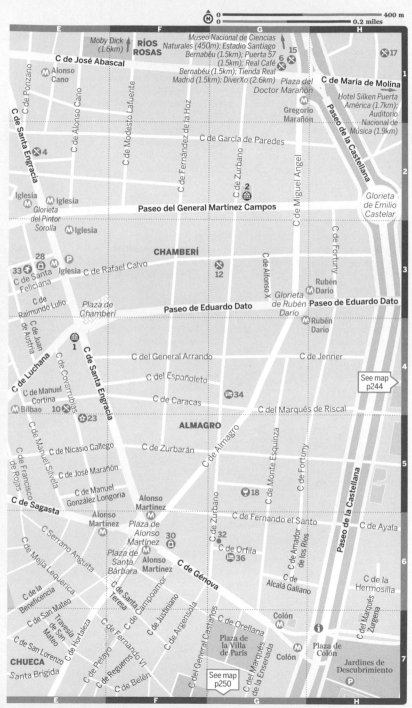

0          400 m
0          0.2 miles

Moby Dick
(1.6km)
RÍOS ROSAS
Museo Nacional de Ciencias
Naturales (450m); Estadio Santiago
Bernabéu (1.5km); Puerta 57
(1.5km); Real Café
Bernabéu (1.5km); Tienda Real
Madrid (1.5km); DiverXo (2.6km)
⊗15
⊗17
6 ⊗

C de José Abascal
Ⓜ Alonso
Cano
Plaza del
Doctor Marañón
C de María de Molina

Hotel Silken Puerta
América (1.7km);
Auditorio
Nacional de
Música (1.9km)

Gregorio
Marañón

C de García de Paredes

⊗4

Paseo del General Martínez Campos

Glorieta
de Emilio
Castelar

Iglesia Ⓜ
Ⓜ Iglesia
Glorieta
del Pintor
Sorolla
Ⓜ Iglesia

CHAMBERÍ

28
33 ⊖ Ⓜ Ⓟ
Ⓜ Iglesia C de Rafael Calvo
C de Santa
Feliciana
C de
Raimundo Lulio
Plaza de
Chamberí
⊗12

Paseo de Eduardo Dato
Glorieta
de Rubén
Darío
Rubén
Darío
Paseo de Eduardo Dato

Ⓜ Rubén
Darío

1
C de General Arrando
C del Españoleto
C de Caracas
C de Jenner

See map
p244

Ⓜ Bilbao 10
⊗23
🍴34

C del Marqués de Riscal

ALMAGRO

C de Nicasio Gallego
C de Zurbarán
C de José Marañón

C de Manuel
González Longoria
Alonso
Martínez
🍴18

C de Sagasta
Alonso
Martínez
Ⓜ
Plaza de
Alonso
Martínez
30
🔒
C de Fernando el Santo
C de Ayala

32
C de Orfila
36

Plaza de
Santa
Bárbara
Alonso
Martínez
Ⓜ
C de Génova
Alcalá Galiano
C de la
Hermosilla

CHUECA
Santa Brígida
Colón
Plaza de
la Villa
de París
Colón
Plaza de
Colón
Ⓘ
Jardines de
Descubrimiento

See map
p250
Ⓟ

## CHAMBERÍ *Key on p252*

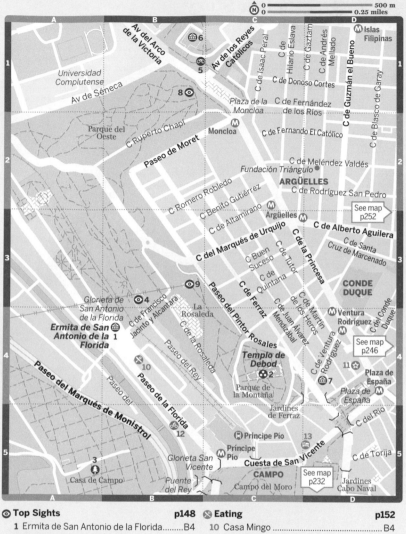

PARQUE DEL OESTE

# Our Story

A beat-up old car, a few dollars in the pocket and a sense of adventure. In 1972 that's all Tony and Maureen Wheeler needed for the trip of a lifetime – across Europe and Asia overland to Australia. It took several months, and at the end – broke but inspired – they sat at their kitchen table writing and stapling together their first travel guide, *Across Asia on the Cheap*. Within a week they'd sold 1500 copies. Lonely Planet was born.

Today, Lonely Planet has offices in Franklin, London, Melbourne, Oakland, Dublin, Beijing and Delhi, with more than 600 staff and writers. We share Tony's belief that 'a great guidebook should do three things: inform, educate and amuse'.

# Our Writer

### Anthony Ham

Anthony is a freelance writer and photographer who specialises in Spain, East and Southern Africa, the Arctic and the Middle East. When he's not writing for Lonely Planet, Anthony writes about and photographs Spain, Africa and the Middle East for newspapers and magazines in Australia, the UK and US.

In 2001, after years of wandering the world, Anthony finally found his spiritual home when he fell irretrievably in love with Madrid on his first visit to the city. Less than a year later, he arrived there on a one-way ticket, with not a word of Spanish and not knowing a single person in the city. When he finally left Madrid ten years later, Anthony spoke Spanish with a Madrid accent, was married to a local and Madrid had become his second home. Now back in Australia, Anthony continues to travel the world in search of stories.

**Contributing writer:** Josephine Quintero (Toledo)

**Published by Lonely Planet Global Limited**
CRN 554153
9th edition – Jan 2019
ISBN 978 1 78657 276 9
© Lonely Planet 2019   Photographs © as indicated 2019
10 9 8 7 6 5 4 3 2 1
Printed in China

# Sweetness and Lies

## Karen McCombie

with illustrations by
Jessica Secheret

For Ellie Gilmore –
happy reading!

First published in 2013 in Great Britain by
Barrington Stoke Ltd
18 Walker Street, Edinburgh, EH3 7LP

www.barringtonstoke.co.uk

Copyright © 2013 Karen McCombie
Illustrations © Jessica Secheret

ISBN: 978-1-78112-199-3

Printed in China by Leo